COOKING AND DINING IN MEDIEVAL ENGLAND

Frontispiece. The kitchen, Gainsborough Old Hall, Lincolnshire, *c.* 1480.

Cooking and Dining

in

Medieval England

Peter Brears

PROSPECT BOOKS

2012

First published in paperback in Great Britain in 2012 by Prospect Books, 26 Parke Road, London, SW13 9NG (www.prospectbooks.co.uk)

Reprinted in 2020.

The book was first published by Prospect Books in 2008.

BRITISH LIBRARY CATALOGUING IN PUBLICATION DATA:
A catalogue entry of this book is available from the British Library.

Typeset and designed by Tom Jaine.

ISBN 978-1-903018-87-3

Printed and bound in Malta by the Gutenberg Press Ltd.

Table of Contents

Acknowledgements

One of the most revealing and interesting aspects of the research undertaken for this book has been the opportunity to visit many medieval kitchens, especially those parts not generally open to the public. For this, particular thanks are due to John Goodall of English Heritage, and the late Richard Avent of Cadw, his colleagues Rick Turner, Peter Humphries and Diane Williams, along with John R. Kenyon, Librarian of the National Museums and Galleries of Wales, whose collective knowledge and perceptive observations were invaluable. I would similarly like to thank Mr Robert Falkingham for allowing me to visit Wressle Castle, Dr Richard Brickstock for conducting me round Durham Castle, Terry Suthers for access to Harewood Castle, and Lord Bolton to Bolton Castle. The staff at Gainsborough Old Hall have also allowed me to enter every part of their remarkably intact property.

Research of this type is impossible without the use of good libraries, and my thanks are due to Robert L. Frost and Janet Senior, Senior Librarian and Archivist and Librarian respectively of the Yorkshire Archaeological Society, and Gordon Foster of the Leeds Library, for their professional services. Dr Charles Kightley of York provided invaluable help in translating various Latin verses and texts.

My most sincere and grateful thanks must go to Mr Tom Jaine, for his perceptive and meticulous editing, typesetting and design. However, any remaining errors are entirely my own. My greatest debt of gratitude is to Susan Houghton and Catherine Allen, for their immense assistance in enabling me to bring this book to its final completion.

To all of these, I am most grateful.

Peter Brears,
Leeds,
2008.

Introduction

Over the last twenty years there has been a growing interest in medieval food, both as an academic subject and as a practical activity for those involved in cookery and historical re-enactment. The purpose of this book is to further this interest by exploring late medieval English domestic food in its broadest context, including all its more practical aspects. To do this, it has drawn on a variety of sources, ranging from historical records, recipes and illustrations, archaeological material and architectural studies, and the benefit of extensive experience of cooking and serving food in accurate historical contexts. In addition, it makes use of facts drawn from traditional English material culture and cookery, which can greatly inform the interpretation of a more distant past.

In pre-war England, good manners and breeding ensured that food, along with politics and religion, was carefully excluded from the dinner-table conversation of all polite households. This was not because this topic was without interest but, quite the contrary, that it was of such great importance that to enter into it could open up the most destructive of social minefields. In reality, the tiniest details of the dinner had been planned and re-planned to ensure perfection. Everything from the brilliance of the silver and the writing on the menu cards to the status of the guests and the order in which they were seated, had been subject to the closest scrutiny. On such minutiae reputations were either made or destroyed.

Since the 1930s, this thousand year-old tradition has experienced a massive decline. Table-servants are rarely found outside noble households, while starched tablecloths of heraldic damask, along with all the panoply of tableware, manners and dress have virtually disappeared from common use. In modern society the ready availability of pre-prepared foods, combined with simplification of our manners and eating habits, has allowed us to forget how important a part food played in everyday lives.

Late-medieval England provides an excellent context in which to explore the full potential of food history studies. From this period we have a wealth of documents, archaeological finds, and architectural survivals with which to work, and it represents a long, well-established and relatively stable culture. From their evidence comes understanding of the growing role of administrative and financial management in households, and the way in which food was used as a means of maintaining and enforcing hierarchies.

From the same evidence, we may discover how medieval buildings were the physical embodiment of pre-conceived human and resource-management concepts. Thus, the sequence of rooms from larders to dining-chambers was as close as possible to a smooth-running production line, an arrangement that subject none the less to frequent and subtle sophistication, as architects and builders introduced security barriers and surveillance systems, and administrators deliberately designed forms of practical inefficiency to obtain management benefits. Some of these had origins back in the late thirteenth century, when the lord stopped dining in the great hall, and retired into his chamber close to the kitchen. Realizing that no one could now see his fine food, he removed his chamber to the opposite end of the hall so that everyone should stand up and show each dish the respect it deserved as it was paraded under their noses. His food might lose a few degrees in temperature, but the prestige made this so worthwhile that the custom continued for a further three hundred years. This shows how the understanding of architectural change cannot be complete without knowledge of food history.

Even in the last twenty years the lack of such knowledge has seen leading architectural historians publishing unreasoned nonsense, whereby servants dined in unlit cellars, and great nobles scuttled down underground passages to make spectacular appearances in halls which, in reality, they had vacated centuries earlier. Archaeologists, too, should know a boiler is not an oven, and food historians should know that meat is roasted in front of, not over, a fire. These and other basic misunderstandings are still commonplace.

Only domestic food, its preparation and service will be discussed here: that carried out, in other words, in cottages, manor houses and castles. This means that we will largely ignore the great body of information regarding colleges, monasteries and other religious institutions, even though they led the field in many aspects of culinary activity – not least their water supply and drainage systems and their state-of-the-art kitchens. We will make reference, however, to the domestic arrangements of those clergy who maintained private kitchens and dining areas.

We can gain much insight into how domestic buildings were planned from Victorian household manuals such as Robert Kerr's *The Gentleman's House* of 1864, since they embody information based on centuries of continuity. We can recognize how the steward's table set on the dais of the medieval hall became the Victorian steward's room; how the body of the hall became the servants' hall; and how the counting house or chequer became the steward's or estate office at the back gate. Armed with such knowledge, it is surprising how the plans of medieval dwellings become much more transparent. They were designed by skilled administrators who knew how to shape a building so that every aspect of life fell under their tight control. Like all administrators, too, they also looked after their own comfort.

Modern evidence is also plentiful for the organization of royal and noble accommodation into separate suites of state and private or family rooms. However, the appearance of such suites in thirteenth-century castles and great manor houses has caused architectural historians considerable problems, even though they have apparently been used in the same way for some seven hundred years.

Another reason for this book is to dispel any remaining doubts of the exemplary standards of medieval food and table manners. Popular historical films from the 1930s to the present day show the Middle Ages at table in terms of dirt, squalor, belching and throwing food around. This myth has even infected 'educational' publications. In fact, most medieval households were kept exceptionally clean. A medieval peasant would have been shocked by the manners on display today in fast-food restaurants.

I have taken every opportunity to present visual as well as written evidence. Many drawings derive from illuminated manuscripts, woodcarvings and excavated artefacts, but others are based on archaeological and architectural reports. These have been redrawn, often to common scales, to show what the artefacts looked like, or how they were used, rather than following established conventions of archaeological illustration. A list of the sources used for each illustration is provided. Other drawings are the result of practical fieldwork.

Illustration has been used to solve another knotty problem. Anyone who has read medieval manners-books realizes that their authors, vastly experienced in their profession, while giving exact instruction, omitted significant details which they assumed were common knowledge. Only by reading a number of versions can the gaps be slowly filled, but true enlightenment might have ever been denied me, had I not arranged for a previous Archbishop of York to be served a feast according to the ceremonial observed for his medieval predecessor. Supervising this meal in the fourteenth-century hall of the York Merchant Adventurers, with fully-costumed guests and the Rosa Mundi re-enactment group as table-servants, was an impressive learning experience. Only when sound scholarship had been converted into rows of liveried servants bearing shining chargers of colourful food, into precise cuts executed with gilt-tipped carving sets, and a figure in jewelled mitre and glowing *opus Anglicanum* cope washing hands with ewer, basin and ten yards of pristine linen towel, did the true majesty of medieval formal dining become apparent. Even the most erudite would find it difficult to follow the seventy different procedures required to serve such a great lord in his hall, particularly when the use of which hand, which fingers and the location of numerous artefacts was specified to the smallest detail.

To present this information graphically, I have devised a strip-cartoon format (on pages 458–462 and 474–482). Here, observation of the drawings conveys as much, if not more detail than the captions, so that their full narrative may be comprehended, and perhaps re-enacted.

Finally, there comes the food itself. To experience this it must be cooked and tasted, for only in this way can its range of colours, flavours, textures and aromas be fully appreciated. By any standard, it is excellent, and we are fortunate that many manuscript recipes recording its preparation survive today. Anyone who wishes to study them in greater detail should obtain copies of C.B. Hieatt and S. Butler's *Curye on Inglysch* and Hieatt's *An Ordinance of Pottage*, which transcribe over six hundred fourteenth- and fifteenth-century recipes. However, since medieval cooks were so well trained and experienced, they hardly ever recorded the quantities of their ingredients, and probably judged temperatures in the same manner as our grandmothers, by simply thrusting a hand into the oven. The medieval recipes given within this book have therefore been rewritten in modern form, so that they may be cooked in the kitchen, or on an open fire. It should be remembered, however, that recipes are only written down when they are likely to be forgotten. This means that virtually all the surviving medieval recipes are for dishes which were not cooked every day. For this reason, a number of additional examples have been included, which are for everyday use, these being for those traditional English foods known to have been made before 1500 but which survived to recent times. This will go a little way to redress the unavoidable social imbalance which any book on this subject must accept – for the bulk of the surviving evidence we have to work on comes from the upper levels of society.

It is appreciated that the approach taken by this book, drawing together the widest body of available evidence from historical, archae-ological, ethnographic, culinary and re-enactment sources, will fall short of the academic standards expected by most university-based scholars. However, it should bring a completely new appreciation of the practical and human factors which late-medieval society sought to control through record-keeping and building design. Just as important, it should provide readers with a detailed introduction to late-medieval household life, enabling them to make more of their visits to historic sites, to make their medieval events and re-enactments more interesting and accurate, and to try authentic medieval dishes in their own kitchens and dining-rooms. This is not mere flimsy argument, but a potent way in which people can gain a real knowledge of England's social and culinary heritage. Despite its bad press in the late twentieth century, England has one of the world's longest, finest and best-documented cuisines, one well worth further study and appreciation.

A Note on the Recipes

Since the cooking, serving and eating of food are essentially practical matters, no study of their history can be complete without the provision of workable recipes. A full understanding of this subject is only possible if the range of raw materials, their individual properties, and the range of textures, consistencies, flavours and colours they can produce, is actually experienced both in the kitchen and at the table. It is similarly important that all those who wish to re-create period food for demonstrations, the stage, educational activities, or purely for their own interest and enjoyment, should be able to do so as readily and accurately as possible.

We are very fortunate that a number of excellent scholars, such as Samuel Pegge and Richard Warner in the eighteenth century, Thomas Austin and Mrs Robina Napier in the nineteenth and Constance Hieatt and Sharon Butler in the late twentieth, have skilfully transcribed, edited and published many of the most important medieval English culinary texts. These provide the modern researcher with unparalleled access to some 1500 late-fourteenth- and fifteenth-century recipes. When reading through them, it soon becomes apparent that most lack much essential information, including the required weight or measure of each ingredient, and the cooking times and temperatures. This is because they were essentially *aides-mémoire* for skilled cooks who could already judge such matters purely on the basis of their accumulated experience.

For precisely the same reason, the recipes which were written down were largely those for which the memory had to be refreshed, as they were not in everyday use. Most basic processes, from plain boiling and roasting, frying bacon and eggs, making gruels and oatcakes, or even boiling boars' heads, are therefore absent from early recipe collections, even though recorded in other manuscript sources. In this book, recipes for these dishes have been taken from the English cooking tradition, which appears to have continued making many of the same foods in virtually identical ways through to the recent past. In addition, instructions for unusual technical processes, such as skinning a peacock, are provided here, these being based on practical experience in the modern kitchen.

Even where quantities or proportions of ingredients are recorded in the late-fourteenth- and fifteenth-century recipes, they do not reflect the quantities we should use today to obtain similar results. This is particularly the case when dealing with spices. There is a vast difference in the potency of the individual spices as imported up to around the late nineteenth century, and those which we use today. The former were stored and shipped in poor conditions for several months at the least, usually being adulterated on the way, while the latter now arrive pure and at full strength. Anyone who has had their face totally anaesthetized by a single slice of 'Georgian gingerbread' baked with the original quantity of cloves fully appreciates this fact. As a further complication, not all spices lose their essential oils at the same rate, or were subject to the same degree of adulteration. Medieval cooks clearly understood these problems, for many recipes include basic spicing when commencing to cook a dish, but then add more just before serving, so that the flavours could be fine-tuned to produce a consistent taste.

Considering the above factors, it is glaringly obvious that it is unsustainable for anyone to claim that their modernized versions of medieval recipes are truly authentic, or that others' are not. All that can be said of those published here is that they have all been cooked a number of times, having considered all available published sources, by someone with over thirty years' experience of recreating historic recipes. It will be apparent from the texts of the recipes in the chapters which follow that I have kept as closely as possible to the original instructions, interpolating comments, precise temperatures and quantities as and when necessary. The actual source of each recipe is noted in the references.

In selecting the recipes, the decision was taken to exclude any which could not be cooked to modern standards of hygiene, or included ingredients rarely available or generally found unpalatable today, such as fish heads, fish offal, birds' feet, lampreys and the like. For similar reasons, modern food colouring has been specified where it does not affect the flavour, red standing in for ground red sandalwood, for example, or blue for indigo.

When choosing raw materials, every attempt should be made to source the best organic or home-grown produce. This is particularly important with poultry, for the original recipes expect it to contribute a substantial amount of its own flavour. A modern battery hen is decidedly bland when compared to a barnyard fowl, and appears sickly sweet or otherwise unsatisfactory when simmered with the original selection of ingredients. The only solution is to add sufficient chicken stock cubes to make up for its deficiencies. Organic free-range eggs have been used throughout, all being of the standard 'medium' size. If larger or smaller ones are used, their number should be decreased or increased accordingly.

With regard to cereals, wholemeal wheat flour should only be used where specified for, contrary to popular belief, medieval millers and bakers were highly skilled in extracting every grade of flour, from the coarsest to the finest. Unbleached white flour is best for general purposes, but ordinary white also gives good results. Similarly brown rice and brown rice flour are usually preferable to the usual white processed varieties. However, since pearled wheat is now virtually unobtainable, and troublesome to prepare at home, pearl barley makes an effective substitute. The sugars used may be either refined granulated or 'golden' granulated, both reflecting medieval standards of refining, but refined cane sugar rather than beet sugar is best for sugar-boiling recipes.

From the contexts in which they are used, it is clear that the culinary wines of the period were rather heavy and sweet, often being the only sweet ingredient in syrups. Where its colour has been stated in an early recipe, this has been followed in the modern version, but in all other cases the colour [in brackets] has been chosen to reflect the colour of the food judged either from its name, or from its other ingredients. A number of recipes call for the use of verjuice, either sour grape-juice or, more commonly in England, the juice of crab-apples. As neither of these is now readily available, either lemon juice or white wine vinegar has been substituted, as appeared most appropriate for each dish.

The original cooking methods have been followed as closely as possible, but modern labour-saving devices can eliminate an enormous amount of time and energy, with no deterioration in quality. Where the word 'mince' appears (i.e. to chop finely), a food-processor provides an excellent alternative, so long as it leaves the particles about one-eighth of an inch (2–3mm) in diameter. If instructed to 'grind', continue processing until they have been reduced to a smooth paste, perhaps finishing in a marble or ceramic mortar and rubbing through a sieve to obtain the best results.

For filtering, pieces of freshly-washed linen cloths of varying mesh-sizes were used, these traditionally being first rinsed with water and squeezed damp-dry before being filled with the cloudy paste or liquid, and hung up over a vessel in which to collect each clear drop as it ran through. While this is still an effective method, modern coffee filter papers in their funnels provide a good, disposable alternative.

Instead of using the animal stomachs and large guts usually specified for boiling puddings, the linen cloths used for these purposes in other medieval recipes have been recommended, since these are just as efficient, do not split, and are much more available today.

Finally, for measuring dry ingredients by the teaspoon or tablespoon, level, not heaped quantities should be used. Combining these notes with the individual recipes, it should now be possible for anyone with basic cooking skills to re-create either individual dishes or entire meals with a good degree of accuracy. It should always be remembered, however, that they come from a distant culinary culture, and therefore need to be approached with an open mind, rather than judged as versions of other foods with which we are familiar today.

CHAPTER ONE

The Counting House

Throughout history, the provision of sufficient food has always been one of the major challenges facing every household, whatever its place in society. For poorer families, especially in years of bad harvest, the overwhelming need was to gather together sufficient food to ward off starvation. In contrast, great households had to assemble enough provisions to supply tens of thousands of individual meals each year, some of them of the highest culinary standard. To meet these requirements, the manorial system, which governed the everyday lives of most inhabitants of medieval England, was predominately designed to produce food and to control its distribution. In return for gaining access to land on which to grow crops, flocks and herds for their own consumption, most manorial tenants had to provide an agreed amount of labour in their lord's fields, and often pay boon rents too. These were rents in kind, perhaps hens, geese or other produce paid at Christmas, when large quantities of food were required for the lord's kitchens. Rents were also paid in money, much of which was used to purchase food for the maintenance of the larger households.

The office of the receiver or cofferer responsible for collecting these rents was usually placed in the outer gatehouses of castles and great houses. Not only were these buildings constantly manned, even when the residential quarters were unoccupied, but they were secure and in positions which assured that those who came to pay their rent could do so without penetrating further into the premises. The receivers' or cofferers' offices built in the late fourteenth century were designed to provide their occupants with comfortable accommodation, a good light-source for writing, and secure and well-concealed vaults for the safekeeping of cash and records. Some of the best of these were designed by the architect

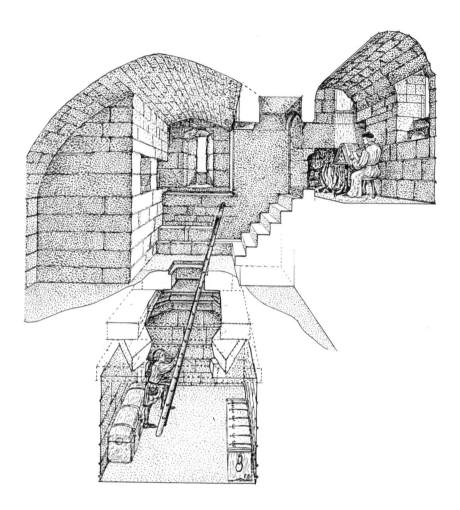

Figure 1. The cofferer/receiver's office, Warkworth Castle, Northumb.,
c. 1377–90. Light for the cofferer's desk comes from a purposely-designed
diagonal window-shaft; a wall-cupboard to his right holds his records and
writing equipment; a fire in front of him keeps his fingers supple; while a
window-sill wash-hand basin and latrine behind him ensure he is always
clean and comfortable. From his desk he can keep permanent watch on
the book-cupboards and the trapdoor to the basement strongroom, with
its coffers of records and cash.

John Lewyn in the outer gatehouse at Carlisle Castle, and probably for the Earl of Northumberland's new great tower at Warkworth Castle. Set just within the entrance passage, the latter has an inner office where the cofferer sat in front of a fire which would keep his fingers supple on the coldest days, a shaft projecting daylight onto his desk, and a wall-cupboard at his right hand holding his writing equipment and records. Behind him, he had his own latrine and a hand-washing sink, while from his chair he could constantly observe two record-cupboards in his outer office, as well as the trapdoor, probably usually concealed beneath a mat or rushes, which led down to his hidden, under-floor strongroom. Measuring some three yards square and deep, it was built of large ashlar blocks, these overhanging each other in ever-smaller octagonal, hexagonal and square courses at the top to reduce the size of the final trapdoor, and to ensure that no-one could enter or leave it without the use of a ladder (Fig. 1).

John Lewyn provided a similar cofferer's office at Lord Scrope's Bolton Castle in Wensleydale in c.1380. Entered by a spiral staircase up from the gate passage, it has an adjacent strongroom and a trapdoor in its base leading to a concealed strongroom beneath. The gatehouses at Dunstanburgh and Alnwick Castles also have these square strongrooms set into their foundations, while that at Kidwelly Castle was circular in plan, its walls corbelled in to produce a bottle-like section terminating as a round trapdoor.[1] The antiquarian tradition, which owes to more Gothick horror romanticism than to either practicality or scholarship, has invented the names of bottle-dungeon or oubliette for these strongrooms. Scott, Hood and Tennyson revelled in their gloom, depicting them as places into which prisoners were thrown and left to rot: 'In the dark oubliette/ Let your merchant forget/ That he e'er had a bank richly laden....'[2] The stench emanating from such a practice would alone have forced everyone to flee from its containing building. In contrast, there is a continuing tradition of using these strongrooms for their true purpose. At Wollaton Hall near Nottingham, for example, the Lords Middleton were still raising the trapdoor in their inner chamber in the south tower, to descend into their secure, concealed and fireproof muniment room all the way through to 1925.

From the receiver's or cofferer's office, the records of the receipts were transferred at regular intervals to the auditor's office for checking, and the money passed to the officers of the household in the exchequer or counting house to be used in the purchase of food and materials required.[3]

The efficient management of a major household was a matter of importance. Economic factors, ensuring that the best values were obtained when buying-in food and reducing waste to a minimum, were obvious aims, while the quality, quantity and regularity of the meals governed the level of satisfaction or disgruntlement of the entire establishment. Just as important, the administrative structure of the domestic management provided the household with its necessary cohesive hierarchy. In an earl's house, for example, knights might act as chief officers, even standing in the larders each morning to supervise the butchery of the carcasses, while gentlemen might serve as clerks or table-servants, yeomen as the heads of the practical departments, with numbers of grooms and children to assist them. By providing each ascending rank with better food, sometimes with additional meals too and with places at the table ever nearer to that of the lord, the established order of society was clearly demonstrated on each and every day.

Fully realizing the value of promoting this form of domestic hierarchy, the medieval English royal household fostered its formulation into an extensive series of written regulations or ordinances. To justify its precedence, the ordinances of King Edward IV claimed that their authority originated in the reign of King Solomon, progressing through the reigns of the legendary kings Lud and Cassibellan, on to Hardicanute, Henry I, Edward I, Edward III and Henry VI. The royal council revised its regulations in 1455 since it was then 'full, expedient, behoveful and necessary to advise, ordain and establish a steadfast and substantial rule to the King's household, by which it should grow to his Highness, not only great honour and worship to his realm, and comfort to his people, but it should be to his singular renown fame and laud in other lands and countries.'[4] In the 1460s, Edward IV's officers, in order 'to build upon a more perfect new house[hold]' completed a major revision and extension of these regulations.[5] The result was a masterpiece of medieval administrative practice, one which detailed the staff structure, job descriptions, rewards and perquisites of every member of his household, developed an amazingly comprehensive series of financial regulations designed to eliminate theft and waste, and even established closely detailed standards for food hygiene. No matter was too small to receive attention; the sergeant of the bakehouse was now to report on how much flour had been eaten by birds, lost in floods, or during transport, and how much bread had been eaten by rats.[6] It proved to be so successful that no further revision was required for more than sixty years.

This excellent exemplar was closely followed, albeit on a reduced scale, in great households throughout the country. Today it is difficult for us to comprehend the size, functions and influence of a great household. Most of its major roles have been taken over by the state. In modern terms, it was a combination of political power-base, company headquarters, barracks and regional administrative centre; it usually controlled local mills, markets and industries, financed religious establishments and relieved the poor, provided a liberal education for young nobles and gentry, maintained extensive libraries, and provided sponsorship for the arts. Primarily, however, it remained a family firm, designed to fulfil the personal needs of its hereditary lord.

Unlike today, when most people commute to their offices and factories, returning home each night, the staff of a great household was mainly residential, either attending full-time, half-yearly, or for some other specified period. This meant that around 100 to 150 people had to be provided with their food, heating, light and accommodation, along with clothing, transport facilities and other practical requirements. These households were rarely stationary, for although they usually had one major seat, they moved to others for particular seasons, for hunting and similar activities, or to attend the court in London or elsewhere. To meet these practical demands and to ensure the financial viability of the household, the lord was served by an effective team of administrators based in the counting house, chequer or exchequer.

Ideally, this office was situated at the lower service end of the great hall, close to the doorway leading in from the courtyard. Here it could be attended by the heads of the culinary departments without them having to enter the residential rooms. From here too the senior management could go out to supervise the preparation and service of all meals without leaving the building. By both working and sleeping here, the chief household officers could ensure the security of the records, money, food, drink and tableware stored in the adjacent rooms, and effectively supervise the doors through which everyone entered or left the residential and service rooms, either by day or by night.

There are good examples of exchequers/counting houses built over the buttery and pantry at the lower end of the hall at numerous castles such as Kidwelly, Dyfed (1270s), Warkworth, Northumberland (1380s?) and Kenilworth, Warwickshire (late fourteenth century) as well as at houses such as Dartington Hall, Devon (1390s) and South Wingfield, Derbyshire (c. 1439–56). At Dartington, a stair in the north porch gives access to two 30 by 20-foot rooms and two 10-foot-square rooms, arranged on two floors, all with fireplaces, the major ones with large windows and probably latrines too. Presumably, the lower suite was used as the counting house, with access to a gallery overlooking the interior of the adjacent kitchen, and the upper suite served as the chief officer's chamber.[7] At South Wingfield, meanwhile, a seated area in the north porch appears to have provided a waiting room for those attending the counting house offices on the first floor.[8] One of these has windows overlooking the kitchen and the service courts and a corridor leading to a gallery overlooking the kitchen, thus enabling the resident senior staff to enjoy visual oversight of the main service areas.

In residential towers where the sequence of rooms proceeded vertically rather than horizontally, the counting house might occupy a similar situation between the kitchen and the dining areas. This was certainly the case at Lord Hastings' Tower at Ashby de la Zouch, where it lay just outside the kitchen door, close to the portcullis winch which controlled access to the entire building (as at Warkworth too). It was provided with cupboards for records and so forth around its walls, and trapdoor access to a secure, concealed strongroom beneath.[9] At Kenilworth, the strongroom by the buttery appears to have been in a similar position, but had a spiral staircase descending into it.

At a number of castles, there are rooms which may have served either as receiver/cofferer's offices or as exchequers/counting houses, or perhaps combined these functions. At Caernarfon Castle, for example, a large room in the Treasury or Record Tower (now called the Well Tower) of *c*.1300 is comfortably appointed with a fireplace and latrine. A deep, well-lit window recess with seats down both sides would have been ideal for writing purposes and provided a commanding view over both the intended dock where supplies were to have been unloaded and over the back or service gate directly below. At the side of this window a small winch room controlled its portcullis, so that goods could be carried into a dark, cool basement store below and up to intended larders and storage space adjacent to the boiling house and kitchens. The upper storeys would have provided appropriate accommodation for a chief officer and his clerks, their presence here adding to the security of the back gate.[10]

The centrepiece of the counting house, chequer or exchequer was the chequerboard or table on which accounts were calculated and which gave its name to this office. In his *Dialogue Concerning the Exchequer* of 1178, Richard, Bishop of London and Treasurer to the royal household, described the King's chequer as a rectangular table covered with black cloth marked with white lines a foot or a palm apart, on which *calculi* (stones) were arranged to represent sums. The colour of the cloth soon changed to green, thus giving the title of the Board of the Greencloth to the department which still administers the royal household (Fig. 2). In 1299 the receiver of Chepstow Castle paid 4½*d*. for 3 yards of cloth for the Earl of Norfolk's exchequer board, and the dye required to stain it, while in 1493–4, 8 yards of narrow green cloth for the chequer board at Kidwelly cost 10*d*. a yard.[11] Similarly the bursar of New College, Oxford, bought 3 yards of green kersey, a coarse woollen cloth just over 38 inches wide, for his exchequer and counting house table, these references providing useful clues to the dimensions of these tables.[12] As to the *calculi*, these were soon replaced by metal counters. In the royal exchequer, for example, Venetian silver coins paid in by Rogero Ardyngelli, a Florentine merchant, were 'laid in rows upon several Distinctions of the chequered Cloth, viz. one row or place for pounds, another for shillings' and so on. Lesser households used jetons or counters of negligible value, these often being found in urban excavations. Alexander Barclay has presented us with an informative picture of 'The kitchen clarke…jingling his counters, chatting himselfe alone' as he cast his accounts.[13] In smaller establishments the role of the greencloth table was taken by the counter or reckoning board.

Figure 2. The Board of the Greencloth, 1472. Around the table, which has a number of counters, a standish with pen and ink, and rolls of records spread across its green baize-covered surface, the Lord Steward and Treasurer, with their white sticks of office, supervise the work of the Controller and the Clerks of the Greencloth.

Today, there is little evidence to suggest its appearance, but inventories confirm it as being a piece of wooden furniture, presumably with a flat top, often found in the chambers of prosperous merchants and the like.[14]

For their numerous daily meetings, the chief officers and clerks usually sat on long benches down each side of their greencloth table. In order of precedence, the first chief officer was the chamberlain, since he was responsible for the management of the lord's private quarters, including the dining chamber and the great chamber.[15] To help, he might employ his own chaplain, clerk, yeoman and horsekeeper. Next came the steward, in charge of all domestic matters including such practical departments as the slaughterhouse, woodyard, kitchen and chandlery. Working with the clerk of the kitchen, the controller, the cook and the surveyor of the dresser, he decided the lord's daily menu, buying-in any delicacy he would particularly enjoy. At meal times he sat on the dais in the hall, and in the counting house supervised the entry and totalling of the various accounts. Some of the junior officers brought theirs in the form of notes scratched with a stylus on panels of hard green wax set into wooden boards to act as a notebook, while others brought tallies in the form of split sticks, notched across to record quantities of bread, ale and similar commodities.

The treasurer took charge of the income gathered from the estates and elsewhere by the receiver or cofferer, and used it to provide the clerk of the kitchen with the silver coinage required to buy the household's provisions. These included those acquired by the caterer (or purchasing officer), the poultry, the bakehouse and the buttery. The controller's main duty was to record the food and materials consumed and those remaining in the household at the close of every day, checking the accounts of the clerk of the kitchen, and reporting back to the steward. The surveyor, meanwhile, ensured that everything went smoothly, and checked the food as it was delivered from the kitchens.

These chief officers replicated those probably established in the royal household from the time of the Conquest.[16] Like their royal counterparts, their duties were part ceremonial and honorary, and part practical, but they always conferred a high degree of social status on their bearers. Since they had their own estates to manage and households to maintain, they often served in rotation for specific periods of each year, receiving higher levels of payment and full accommodation for themselves and their own servants when in attendance on their lord.

The remainder of the clerks and culinary staff were usually full-time employees, the most senior being the cofferer, the finance officer. Doing much of the treasurer's work, he was responsible for gathering the household's income from its various estates; securely storing and issuing the lord's cash, silver, gold plate and jewels; drawing up the overall accounts; and keeping the lord constantly abreast of his financial position. He was assisted by a number of clerks. The clerk of foreign expenses controlled the purchase of inedible goods, while the clerk of the kitchen organized the bulk purchase of foodstuffs, especially those such as salt, salt meat, salt fish, grain, dried fruit and spices which could be stored for some time before use. These, the 'gross emptions', were bought by contract at a predetermined price, as agreed with the cofferer at Michaelmas (29

September), the start of the new financial year. Some indication of their quantities and prices can be obtained from those which the Earl of Northumberland and his council instructed Richard Gourge, controller, and Thomas Percy, clerk of the kitchen, to obtain for a single year:[17]

Quantity	Unit price	Total
Wheat 2116 qtrs (c.450 tons)	6s. 8d./qtr	£78
Malt 209 qtrs	4s./qtr	£49 16s. 6d.
Beefs 123	8s. to 14s. 4d.	£86 5s. 4d.
Muttons 667	1s. 8d.	£68 12s. 2d.
Porkers 25	2s.	£2 10s. 0d.
Veals 28	1s. 8d.	£2 6s. 8d.
Lambs 60	10d. to 11d.	£2 11s. 8d.
Stockfish 160	2½d.	£1 13s. 4d.
Salt fish 742	4d.	£17 14s. 0d.
White herring 9 barrels	10s.	£4 10s. 0d.
Red herring 10 cade (c.7,200)	6s. 8d.	£3 3s. 4d.
Sprats 5 cade (c.3,600)	2s.	10s. 0d.
Salt salmon 2080	6d.	£5 0s. 0d.
Salt sturgeon 3 firkins	10s.	£1 10s. 0d.
Salt eels 5 caggs (kegs)	4s.	£1 0s. 0d.
Figs 4 coppetts	1s. 8d.	6s. 8d.
Raisins 4 coppetts	1s. 8d.	6s. 8d.
Hops 556lb		£3 13s. 4d.
Honey 1½ barrels	12s.	£1 13s. 0d.
Oil 1 barrel (24 gallons)	11½d. gallon	£1 18s. 3d.
Bay salt 10 qtrs	4s.	£2 0s. 0d.
White salt 6½ qtrs	4s.	£1 6s. 0d.
Vinegar 4 gallons	4d.	13s. 4d.
Verjuice 90 gallons	3d.	£1 2s. 6d.
Mustard 160 gallons	2¼d.	£1 14s. 4d.

The clerk of the kitchen also supervised the operation of the kitchens, and maintained the chequer-roll, a daily record of how many members of the household and how many visitors had been present for meals. A further purchasing officer, the caterer, was responsible for buying fresh foods as and when required from the local markets and elsewhere. He travelled out on horseback with an advance of cash, perhaps £2 a week, and returned with his foods and lists of his expenditure, any payments over the agreed prices being closely scrutinized, and perhaps even rejected.[18]

The heaviest workload probably fell on the clerk controller, for he effectively ran the counting house, or general finance office, throughout a sixteen-hour day, constantly supervising numerous staff, issuing and collecting keys and other manifold duties. His main assistants were the clerks of brevement, who kept most of the records, and the clerk of the spicery, who administered the distribution of the spices, wax and linen which had been bought by the clerk of the kitchen. The household of the Earl of Northumberland in the first quarter of the sixteenth century listed such purchases for the year as follows: [19]

Spices

Pepper	51lb 4½oz	Currants	208lb
Ginger	21lb 8oz	Prunes	31½lb
Mace	6lb	Dates	30lb
Cloves	3lb 8oz	Almonds	132lb
Cinnamon	17lb 12½oz		
Nutmeg	1lb 4oz		
Grains of Paradise	74lb		
Turnsole	10lb 8oz	Sugar	2080lb 4oz
Saunders	10lb	Rice	19lb
Ground Aniseed	3lb 4oz		
Galingale	4oz		
Long pepper	8oz		
Blanch powder	2lb		
Saffron	3lb		

Total £25 19s. 7d.

Wax for the Chandlery

Wax light	4087lb	£12 5s. 7d.
Rosin (for wicks)	39lb	4s. 10½d.

Wicks	51lb	8s. 6d.
Paris candles	214lb	£4 11s. 2d.

Linen for the Ewery etc.
70 ells (87.5 yards)   £2 6s. 8d.

Below the officers in the counting house, there came the staffs of various practical departments which processed the raw materials issued to them in an efficient and logical sequence:

The Woodyard	Clerk of the Woodyard, with grooms etc.
The Poultry	?
The Slaughterhouse	1 slaughterman
The Butchery	1 yeoman or groom, 1 child
The Larder	1 groom
The Brewhouse	1 yeoman
The Cellar	1 yeoman, 1 groom
The Buttery	1 yeoman, 1 groom
The Corn Mill	1 miller
The Bakehouse	1 yeoman, 1 child
The Pantry	1 yeoman, 1 groom
The Kitchen	1 yeoman cook for the mouth, to serve at the dresser, 1 groom for the mouth, to serve in the kitchen, 1 child of the kitchen for the broches (spits)
The Scullery	1 child
The Ewery	1 yeoman, 1 groom
The Chandlery	1 chandler

Including the higher officers' servants, this household required some forty people, about a quarter of its total number, just to prepare its everyday meals, a quite separate and additional staff being employed for waiting and serving in the dining chamber and the hall.[20] By following their progress through a single day, we can begin to appreciate why such a large number of managers was required.

4 a.m. The clerk controller set the clerks to work in the counting house: the second clerk of the kitchen made up his rating book of meals, costing the meals served the previous day, the clerk of brevement calculated its totals, and the clerk of the spicery entered the gross emptions received.[21]

The clerk controller summoned the cooks, and presumably gave them access to their kitchens, so that fires could be lit, and other preparations made.

5 a.m. Accompanied by the head officer, the clerk of the kitchen, the yeoman cook and the groom of the larder, the clerk controller took the key of the larder and opened it up, revealing the carcasses which he had previously inspected in the slaughterhouse. Each had already been drawn, its head, 'sticking piece' of neck and, if an ox, its tail by the first joint removed as the slaughterman's 'vail' or perquisite. Their hides had also been stripped and sent off to the tanner, and their fat and suet weighed and stored ready for transfer to the chandlery for making candles. The officers now saw each carcass divided up into equally-sized 'messes', each sufficient to provide one dish when served in the chamber or hall. Since four people usually shared one mess, the clerks had merely to divide the number of meals recorded in the rating book by four to estimate how many joints were now required:

    1 beef carcass produced 64 messes for 256 people;
    1 mutton carcass produced 12 messes for 48 people;
    1 veal carcass produced 16 messes for 64 people;
    1 pig carcass produced 20 messes for 80 people.

If it was a fish-day, the salt fish would be similarly divided at this time:

    1 ling produced 6 messes, 3 each side, for 24 people;
    1 haberdine (cod) produced 4 messes, 2 each side, for 16 people;
    1 salt salmon produced 12 messes, 3 each quarter, for 48 people;
    1 stockfish produced 4 messes, 2 each side, for 8 people.

These portions were then carried to the kitchens where the cooks could start to prepare them ready for breakfast or dinner.

7 a.m. On returning to the counting house, the head officer, clerk controller and clerk of the kitchen found a queue of grooms waiting for them in predetermined order, the first being the groom of the hall, then those of the pantry, cellar, buttery, ewery and woodyard, and also an usher of the chamber. The clerk of the brevement carefully noted everyone's surname, in case of any future disputes.[22] In turn, each presented their 'brief', a list of what they had used on the previous day, and another of what remained in their offices, these details being entered in the breving book by the clerk of brevement or the clerk of the spicery. By 7.30 a.m. this process had been completed and the grooms went about their business.

7.30 a.m. The caterer now presented himself to the clerk controller, bringing with him his cater-parcels, these being his lists of the fresh foods he had bought with moneys advanced to him previously, their details being entered in the journal, or day-book, by the clerk of the brevement. They also noted here the number of loaves delivered from the bakehouse, where their weight had already been checked by the clerk controller. A split stick called a tally had the daily total recorded on it by cutting notches across both parts, one half being given to the baker, who delivered the bread, and the other to the pantler who had received it. This unforgeable device ensured that neither officer could dispute or change the totals, which were easily checked by re-uniting the split surfaces of each part, when any additional and unauthorized notches would become immediately apparent. The delivery of beer from the brewhouse to the buttery was then recorded in precisely the same way.

8 a.m. The clerk controller now issued the keys to those offices such as the cellars, butteries and pantries, and the dining areas which had been kept locked overnight to safeguard their contents, and to prevent staff from loitering there after their meals rather than returning to their duties.

8–9 a.m. Breakfast was issued from the dresser outside the kitchen. This was supervised by the head officer, the clerk controller, assisted by the clerk of the brevement, who ensured that it was only issued to those listed in the bill of breakfast.

9 a.m. After breakfast, the keys of the relevant offices were returned to the clerk controller in the counting house.

10 a.m. The keys were reissued in preparation for dinner.

10–11 a.m. (11–noon on fish-days) Dinner was served from the dresser, supervised as for breakfast.

11 a.m. (or 12 noon on fish-days) The keys were returned to the counting house.

12 noon. On feast days a further briefing was held, as at 7 a.m., to record the additional numbers of diners and the amounts of food and drink issued.

1 p.m. On ordinary days the head officer supervised the briefing as for breakfast and dinner.

The caterer, butcher, baker and brewer all reported to the counting house to enter their accounts into the journal, in the presence of witnesses and supervised by the clerk of the kitchen. The meat, fish, milk and eggs purchased by the caterer had also to be inspected by the clerk of the brevement to ensure that they were of good quality and value, and to question why there may have been any increase in their prices. Only if they passed this inspection were they taken down to the kitchens and locked away until next morning.

During the course of the day the clerk of the kitchens had to ensure that all the household regulations were being observed, and complete the chequer-roll. Meanwhile the clerk of the brevement had to check all the offices to discover if any unauthorized persons were present, record the names of all visitors, and receive the usher of the chambers' reports of any shortcomings regarding the supply of food and services to the lord's chamber. These might, for example, include beer pots being delivered part-empty, suggesting that someone was helping themselves on the way from the buttery.

2?–3 p.m. The keys were issued and returned; while 'drinkings' were served for those working in the porter's lodge and the stable.

4 p.m. The keys were reissued for supper.

4–5 p.m. Supper served, supervised as at breakfast.

5 p.m. The keys were returned to the counting house. The head officer now received the briefs of the food and drink served at the 'drinkings' and

supper, and those of the liveries of fuel and horsefeed which had been delivered that day. He then supervised the work of the various clerks, to ensure that all the day's records were completely up to date.

8 p.m. The counting house closed, having been in continuous operation for a full sixteen-hour day.

The information carefully recorded each day was next subjected to a weekly consolidation. This commenced before 7 a.m. every Saturday, when the clerk of foreign expenses attended the lord, accompanied by the lord's chosen witness. First he explained his accounts, obtaining permission to settle the bills just received, then detailed the moneys advanced to servants for purchases and so on, any loans which had been made to individuals for specific purposes, and finally the total sums of expenditure incurred: how much had been paid off, and how much was still owing. Lastly he requested the lord to nominate someone to witness the forthcoming issue of cash imprests to various purchasing officers, to avoid the risk of any future disputes. The cofferer similarly reported to the lord, informing him of how much money had been collected during that week, how much had been received in total since Michaelmas, and how much remained in his hands.

A further round of monthly reports required a head officer to present a priced list of the gross emptions which had been bought, while the clerk of the kitchens had to provide an account of the kitchen's total expenditure. This included details of the value of its unused stock and a list of everyone on the chequer-roll so that the cost of their meals could be efficiently estimated. Similarly the total of the caterer's costs had to be submitted, so that this figure could be compared to the monthly projections to ensure there was no major overspending. Internally-generated produce was also taken into account, the clerk of brevement recording the deliveries of hides, skins and tallow from slaughterhouse to tanner, glover and chandler, for example, or the amount of flour passed from the bakehouse to the kitchen for making pastries and other baked goods. By these means, along with further quarterly, half-yearly and, finally, yearly reviews, it was possible to control and predict the expenses of even the largest households with a high degree of accuracy.

Before leaving the counting house, we should take the opportunity to gain some impression of the calibre of the staff who worked here. This is provided by a reference in which John Paston recommended a prospective clerk of the kitchen to Lord Hastings: 'Thys man is meane of stature, yong I-nough, well wittyd, well manerd, goodly yong man on horse and foote. He is well spokyn in Inglyshe, mete well in Frenshe, and verry parfite in Flemyshe. He can wright and reed… .'[23] We do not know if he obtained this post, but with these qualities, he would have made an ideal administrator for the kitchens at Ashby de la Zouch and Kirby Muxloe castles.

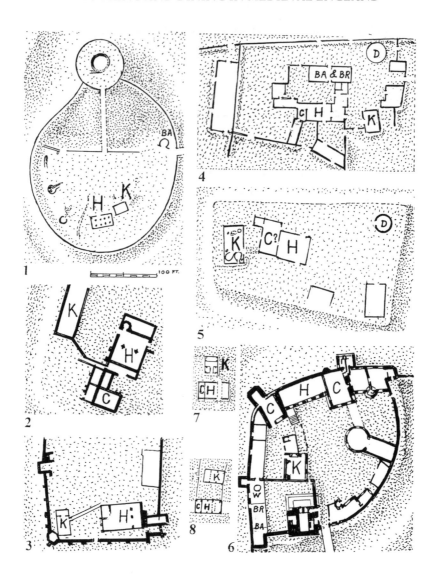

Figure 3. Detached kitchens:

(1) Sandal Castle, Yorks., early 12c.; (2) Prestbury Moat, Glos., c.1200;
(3) Weoley Castle, Birmingham, 13c.; (4) Wharram Percy, Yorks., early
14c.; (5) Wintringham, Hunts. late 13c.; (6) Ludlow Castle, Salop., 14c.;
(7) Comphurst, Wartling, Sussex, c.1500; (8) 12/13 High Street, Battle, 15c.
BA - Bakehouse; BR - Brewhouse; C - Chamber; D - Dovecote; H - Hall;
K - Kitchen; W - Well.

CHAPTER TWO

Planning for Cooking

Although many medieval castles and houses are impressive in terms of their architecture, defensive strength and sheer physical mass, their primary purpose always remained emphatically domestic. Unless they could provide the basic shelter, warmth and constant supplies of food and drink required by all inhabitants, they were virtually useless. The creation of workable and efficient service rooms was therefore a matter of considerable importance, and one which required both ingenuity and a thorough knowledge of domestic management. Medieval buildings are usually attributed either to those who commissioned them or to individual architects, since theirs are the documented names. However, observation of the design of the service rooms strongly suggests that a further group was perhaps equally influential – the professional household managers of the counting house. Their meticulous records and operational manuals reveal the existence of sophisticated organizational systems, carefully designed to exert the closest controls over staff and materials, and also to maintain strict hierarchies. Whenever a property was either newly built or remodelled, these were the people who actually collected and dispensed the funds, including those paid to the architect and builders. This placed them in an ideal position to influence the design of the new work, ensuring that it would incorporate every feature which would ease their future workload.

When planning domestic offices, one of the main priorities was the security of all food, fuel and utensils, for unauthorized consumption and pilfering could prove very expensive and troublesome. The imposition of secure perimeters around the various working departments, with close supervision of their doors and locks, was therefore essential, this having to be balanced by the need to process the food as efficiently as possible.

In addition, each room had to have the best environmental conditions to suit its particular purpose.

Since malt houses, brewhouses for ale and bakehouses for bread all required fuel, grain, water, long working hours and an ambient warmth to promote the growth of yeasts, it was best if they could be placed close to each other. In this way the staff could carry out the various tasks just as their processes required, malting, brewing or setting yeasts as necessary. Slaughterhouses for oxen, sheep, pigs and other animals, along with scalding houses for preparing poultry and game might be nearby, perhaps in an outer court, since their noise and smells, their blood, skins and foul offal had no place in any decent house, only clean meat being allowed to enter the larders. Wood and coal houses were also ideally placed in an outer court, where their supplies could be delivered without having to bring the woodmen and carters, and their dirt, anywhere near the residential areas.

On entering the service rooms of the building, goods such as grain, cereals and spices had to be secured in dry, well-ventilated stores, the meat and fish in cool, fresh larders ideally with a through draught, and ale and wine in cold cellars, perhaps a little damp. Each of these stores would be supervised by a particular officer, and usually kept locked unless opened in the presence of one of his superiors. Approaching the kitchens, there might be a number of specialized cooking areas, such as a boiling house for the bulk cookery of joints of meat, and pastries where pies and pasties were made and baked. The siting of the kitchen was a matter of first importance. Not only must it have good access to the woodhouse, the well, the larders, boiling house and pastry, but it had to be close to the bottom end of the hall so the food could be served hot.

All food leaving the kitchen had to be recorded as it was passed out through the hatches – which were bolted close except at meal times. Ideally, this area would have a room to accommodate the officers and clerks who supervised this operation. Next came a surveying-place where the waiting staff were marshalled into their correct order before processing into the hall where the domestic staff dined, and on to the chambers beyond, the dining area for the lord, his family, head officers and guests. Ale and wine for these rooms would already have been brought up from the cellars into the buttery, ready for distribution with the cups, while the bread, table linen and tableware would have been brought out of the pantry and set in place.

The size and number of these service rooms varied much from one building to another, depending on its age and status (Fig. 3). At the bottom of the scale the smallest urban houses might be totally devoid of service rooms, their residents apparently subsisting on cook-shop take-away food. Next, in most small urban and rural peasant houses all the cooking and dining facilities were gathered into single kitchen/living rooms. In many other properties there was a long-established tradition of having the kitchen located in a completely detached building. This kept the unavoidable smoke, smells, noise and vermin at bay and reduced the fire risk to the main house , but also meant that the hot food had to be carried across an open yard. At the late twelfth- and early thirteenth-century kitchens at Sandal and Weoley castles and the manor houses at Wharram Percy and Wintringham, the kitchens lay some 25 feet away from the hall door, but the distance could be much greater.[1] At the Bishop of Hereford's Prestbury Moat it was a full 75 feet, a pentice roof having to be built across to it in 1289 to protect the waiters.[2]

Most early kitchens, such as those built for Henry III at Clipstone in 1244, for Edward I at Woolmer in 1285, or at Weoley Castle before 1210, were timber-framed.[3] This meant that they could be quickly erected and even removed from one site to another, as at Ludgershall in 1254.[4] But their tendency to burst into flame meant that they were always kept at some distance from the hall and chambers. In the vernacular tradition, detached kitchens remained in use well into the post-medieval period.[5] Wherever funds allowed, they were usually replaced in fireproof stone close to the bottom end of the hall, although that at Ludlow was simply rebuilt on its original site, continuing to work as a detached kitchen until 1689.[6]

Even when the kitchens had taken up this new attached position, usually from the later thirteenth century, some households still thought it best to leave a substantial gap between them and their halls. At the Bishop's Palace in Lincoln a 12-foot bridge linked the kitchen to the spinal corridor passing between the buttery and pantry and on into the hall, but elsewhere completely unroofed servery courts occupied this space.

In 1320, for example, a small triangular court separated the new hall and its kitchen wing at Clevedon Court, Somerset. Rectangular servery courts were similarly created at the Bishop's Palace at Sonning, Caerphilly Castle, Ashby de la Zouch c.1350, Haddon Hall c.1370, Howden Manor 1390s, South Wingfield Manor c.1439–50 and Gainsborough Old Hall c.1480.[7] These courts not only separated off the unpleasant aspects of the kitchens, but also provided well-lit areas where the sewers and waiters could organize themselves before going into the hall (Fig. 4).

In smaller buildings such servery courts would have been inconvenient, unduly extending the perimeter of the domestic quarters. In such circumstances the kitchen might form part of the main structure of the house, but yet have no means of internal communication. Many examples of this type are fifteenth-century additions to earlier buildings, as at the Treasurer's House at Martock in Somerset, Markenfield Hall, Yorkshire and Stokesay Castle, Salop.[8] Others were purpose-built at this same period, such as that at Bowhill, Exeter which extended from one end of a chamber block, while the hall extended from the other. Their respective doors faced each other, but with 30 feet of open air between.[9] In contrast, the kitchen and hall doors at the Deanery in Wells are adjacent in one corner of its central courtyard and sheltered by a pentice. Even so, they still leave an unenclosed area between them.[10] It may seem that such precautions are excessive, but anyone who has cooked in country-house kitchens, where doors are left open for public access, knows only too well how rapidly and effectively smells and sounds can engulf an entire building. To many households, however, concerns regarding the saving of space, the exclusion of draughts, the temperature of the food and sheer convenience overrode those of noise and odour. For them, fully integrated kitchens were the only option.

In their simplest and most direct form, integrated kitchens took a linear arrangement, perhaps with larders, bakehouses and brewhouses preceding the kitchen itself, and then the usual sequence of servery/surveying-place, buttery and pantry, the hall and finally the chambers. Many of the castles rebuilt in stone during the early thirteenth to fourteenth centuries were of this type as seen in the keeps or inner baileys at Skipton and Alnwick, or in the outer baileys at Sandal and Chepstow. When such blocks traversed

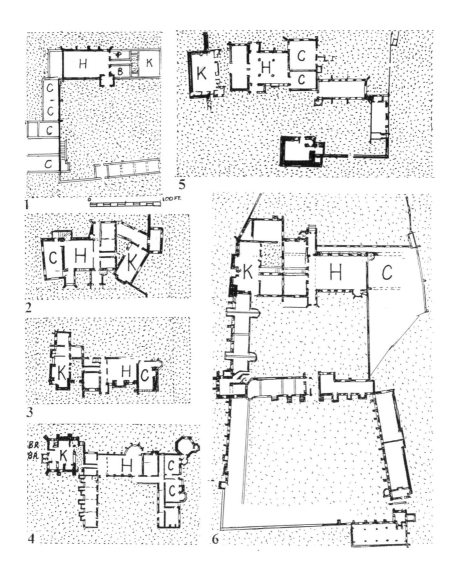

Figure 4. Unroofed servery-court kitchens:
(1) Howden Manor, Yorks., c.1388–1405; (2) Clevedon Court, Somerset, c.1320; (3) Haddon Hall, Derbys., 1325–50; (4) Gainsborough Old Hall, Lincs., c.1480; (5) Ashby de la Zouch Castle, Leics., c.1483; (6) South Wingfield, Derbys., 1439–56.
BA - Bakehouse; BR - Brewhouse; C - Chambers; H - Hall; K - Kitchen.

the total width of the defences, the kitchen, with its usual square plan and high roof, could be constructed as a major fortification in its own right. At Cockermouth its great bulk overlooking the course of the river Derwent makes it resemble a keep, while at Raby its towering 50-foot-square mass forms one of the major defences of the inner ward. In order to complete the kitchen-hall-chamber sequence at both Ashby de la Zouch and Amberley, meanwhile, the kitchen was actually thrust out beyond the curtain wall to form an effective flanking tower covering any attacks on the defences.[11] On a smaller scale, some houses comprised no more than a sequence of kitchen-hall-chamber as at Powderham Castle, Devon, and Yanwath Hall, Cumbria, a thirteenth-century tower house extended in the fifteenth century (Fig. 5).[12]

One of the major problems of such linear arrangements was that they could make houses inconveniently long and narrow. One solution to this was to elongate the kitchen wing, and turn it at right-angles to the hall, providing an L-shaped plan ideal for being enclosed within a rectangular courtyard. At Aydon Castle a small kitchen built at the bottom end of the first-floor hall in 1296–1305 was rapidly replaced by a long flanking wing in 1305–15, but new houses were already being designed to this plan by the early fourteenth century. The 1322–35 manor house at Meare, for example, had its kitchen in the ground floor of one wing, with a stair leading up to a first-floor hall in the

Figure 5, opposite.

External access kitchens:

(1) Martock Treasurer's House, Somerset, 15c.; (2) Stokesay Castle, Salop., 1240-1305; (3) Bowhill, Exeter, Devon, early 15c.; (4) The Deanery, Wells, Somerset, 1470s–90s; (5) Markenfield Hall, Yorks., in 15c.

Linear kitchens:

(6) Skipton Castle, Yorks., c.1230; (7) Alnwick Castle, Northumbria, 1309-15; (8) Sandal Castle, Yorks., 14c.; (9) Chepstow Castle, Gwent, 1270-1306; (10) Yanwath Hall, Cumbria, in early 15c.; (11) Powderham Castle, Devon, 1392–1406.

BA - Bakehouse; BR - Brewhouse; C - Chamber; H - Hall; K - Kitchen; L - Larder; W - Well.

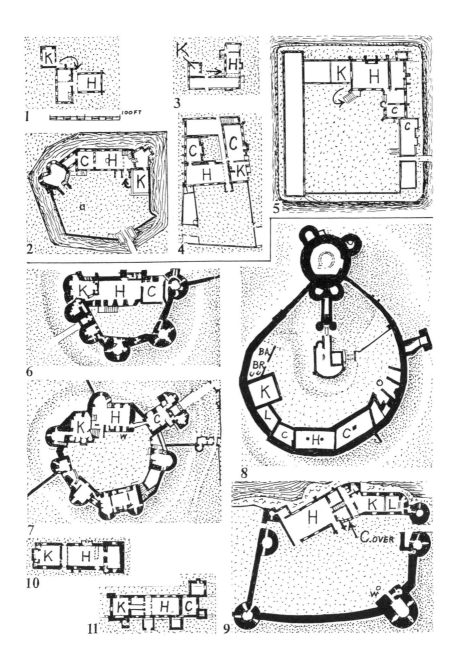

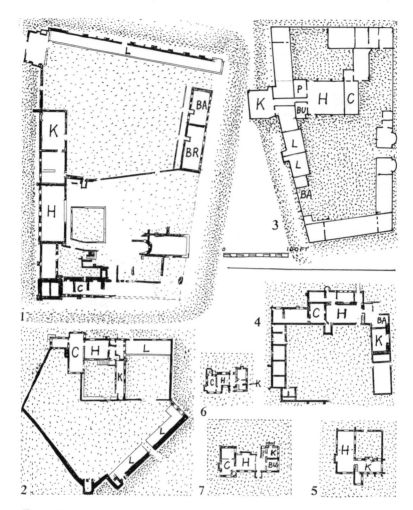

Figure 6.

Kitchen wings: (1) Bishop's Waltham Palace, Hants, 1367–1404; (2) Aydon Castle, Northumbria, 1296–1305; (3) Amberley Castle, Sussex, 1377–c.1383; (4) Minster Lovell Hall, Oxon., early 15c.; (5) Meare Manor House, Somerset, 1322–35.

Kitchens in service end: (6) Kingston Seymour, Somerset, 1470–80; (7) Nappa Hall, Yorks., 1459.

BA - Bakehouse; BR - Brewhouse; BU - Buttery; C - Chambers; H - Hall; K - Kitchen; L - Larder.

other.[13] In smaller houses, a similar result was produced by placing the kitchen in one of the areas normally occupied by the buttery or pantry at the lower end of the hall. Fifteenth-century examples still survive at Nappa Hall in Wensleydale of 1459, and at Kingston Seymour Manor House, c.1470–80, predecessors of an arrangement which was to become much more popular in the post-medieval period (Fig. 6).[14]

For similar reasons, square-planned kitchens were also placed to one side of the bottom end of the hall, with an open court, a screens passage, or a surveying-place linking the two. Bishop Beck's kitchen at Durham Castle was an early example of this plan, being built c.1153–95, and it can be found sporadically in the thirteenth century, as at Clarendon Palace, and the fourteenth century, as at Hull Manor and Dartington Hall.[15] In 1475 Edward IV adopted it when rebuilding Eltham Palace, as did Henry VII at Richmond in the 1490s, and Cardinal Wolsey at Hampton Court from 1514.[16]

Most of the first generation of Norman castles were essentially asymmetrical in plan, either because they wished to exploit the defensive potential of landscape features, or because they adopted the popular motte and bailey plan, with a crescent-shaped, defended domestic courtyard beside a great keep tower set on a high artificial mound. During the later thirteenth century new castles began to adopt a much more regular, rectangular plan, as exemplified by the great concentric Welsh castles built by Gilbert de Clare at Caerphilly from 1268, and by Master James of St George for Edward I at Harlech in 1283 and Beaumaris in 1295. Harlech has retained evidence of its original suite of domestic offices completed by 1289, a simple linear sequence of kitchen, surveying-room, buttery and pantry, screens passage and great hall, all lining the west wall of the inner ward, with a granary and a brewhouse/bakehouse in the south-east and north-east corners respectively.[17] Many rectangular castles built during the next two hundred years lined their curtain walls with similar suites of offices, from Goodrich c.1296, to Bodiam c.1385–90, Caistor c.1432 and Oxburgh and Kirby Muxloe of the early 1480s.[18]

The serious threat of invasion from Scotland and France in the late fourteenth century provoked the construction of a remarkable group of rectangular castles. In northern England, Bolton, c.1379, Wressle c.1380–

90, Sheriff Hutton c.1382–1400, Lumley c.1389–92 and Penrith c.1397, were all either designed or strongly influenced by John Lewyn, probably the finest domestic architect in medieval Britain.[19] The best preserved of these is Bolton Castle in Wensleydale which remains substantially complete except for its collapsed kitchen tower.[20] The gateway, lined with benches for those having business in the castle, and its porter's lodge to control them, lie beside the south-west tower, the centre of the castle's administration. Here the counting house would be located, complete with an under-floor strongroom for the storage of coin, records and valuables. The household officers and clerks were accommodated here too, with a separate staff kitchen for their own use, particularly when the rest of the castle was unoccupied. As in other castles, such as Alnwick and Ashby de la Zouch, the winch controlling the portcullis was also here. Below, at basement level, the south wing housed a sequence of horse mill, malt kiln with malthouse above, bakehouse and brewhouse. The eastern basements and kitchen undercroft were probably used as larders and fuel stores, while those to the north comprised the well, ale cellars with stairs up to the buttery and hall screen, and wine cellars with stairs up to the chambers. The principal first-floor sequence proceeds anticlockwise from the north-east tower-kitchen through a surveying-place, buttery and pantry, with offices above, the great hall, and then two levels of very impressive chambers along the west wing. The whole is ingeniously planned to serve every conceivable need of the domestic managers.

Because defence was a primary requirement of castles such as these, their perimeters were kept as small as conveniently possible, their living and service rooms being piled vertically rather than spreading horizontally (Fig. 7). Where houses were not intended to withstand major attacks, there was no need for this restraint, leaving them free to expand, often around two or more courts. Late fourteenth-century examples such as Farleigh Hungerford of 1370–83, Dartington c.1390s, and perhaps the great de la Pole mansion in Hull, had forecourts lined with lodgings extending from their gatehouses to their halls, their kitchens and service rooms then forming part of a further, private court beyond.[21] Mid-fifteenth-century great houses such as Herstmonceux of 1441 and Knole of 1460 elaborated this arrangement even further, the former having a

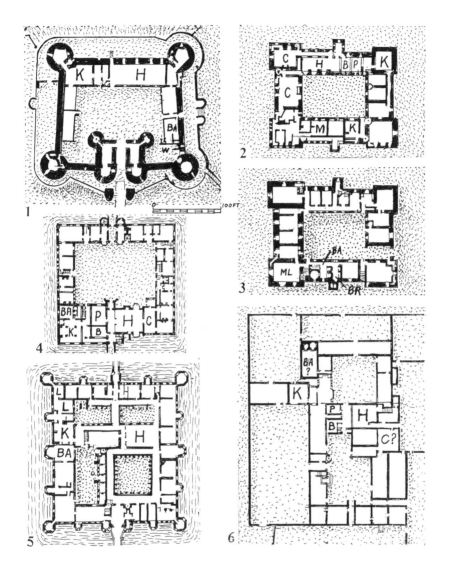

Figure 7.
Kitchens in rectangular castles: (1) Harlech Castle, Gwynedd, 1283–9; (2)
Bolton Castle, Yorks., c.1379 (1st floor); (3) Bolton Castle (ground floor);
(4) Oxburgh Hall, Norfolk, c.1482; (5) Herstmonceux Castle, Sussex,
c.1440; (6) Hull Manor, Yorks., 14c.
BA - Bakehouse; BR - Brewhouse; C - Chamber; H - Hall; K - Kitchen;
L - Larder; M - Malthouse; ML - Mill; P - Pantry; W - Well.

cloistered entrance court, besides pump, poultry and pantry courts to house its services.[22] These enabled a greater number of better-lit and better-ventilated offices to be incorporated within the overall plan.

In contrast to the buildings just described, tower houses incorporated most of the facilities required to feed a complete household, but all in one tall, vertical block. Most were built by gentry families, especially in Northumberland and Cumbria where feuding with the Scots and rival rievers continued well into the seventeenth century, but there were further examples in other northern counties and down the Welsh borders.[23] Three to five storeys high, battlemented and turreted, they usually had a narrow ground-floor doorway leading into stone-vaulted basement stores, ideally provided with a well. The kitchen might be at this level, or on the first floor, with the hall and chambers in the upper storeys. Although the smaller examples provided ideal facilities for a compact, highly defensive style of living, a number of the larger towers also displayed great sophistication. Among these is an impressive mid-fourteenth-century Northumbrian group including Chipchase and Belsay of c.1340, Edlingham c.1350, Houghton c.1373 and Langley, and fine individual examples ranging from Harewood in West Yorkshire c.1367, to Nunney in Somerset c.1373. In these a full suite of domestic offices was included, frequently with kitchens and halls designed to the highest standards, the latter sometimes having screens, dais, dais windows, and even built-in furniture of great quality.

The tower houses described above were chiefly intended to serve as one of their owner's principal residences, but a further group performed a rather different function. Since royal and major noble households comprised several hundred people, it soon proved impractical to move them all *en bloc* from one residence to another – the logistics became completely unmanageable. The solution was to leave the main household at a principal seat, and extract from it only those who were essential to attend their lord. The Earl of Northumberland's ordinances illustrate this particularly well.[24] His main household numbered 166, but his removing household, to accompany him on longer visits to his various castles, numbered 87, while his riding household, for shorter visits or for longer journeys, was only 32. In addition, he had a 'secret household' of 42 which served him during those brief periods when he moved out of his principal residences and disbanded his main household.[24] This was to allow the clerks to put their accounts in order and take stock of the Earl's financial position. It would also provide an opportunity for a major programme of cleaning and repairs to be carried out while most of the rooms were empty (Fig. 8).

To have housed such small households in castles designed to serve several hundred would have been both uncomfortable and expensive. Opening up their great kitchens or heating their vast halls for perhaps only twenty or thirty people to dine was clearly impractical. It was better to house the removing/riding/secret households in a single, compact tower or lodge specifically designed for that purpose. This arrangement gave further advantages too. It greatly reduced the length of the defences which had to be manned to ensure the lord's safety, it enabled visiting households to be provided with separate accommodation, and it provided an opportunity for building tall towers symbolic of great power, their lords appropriately housed in their top storeys, overlooking all beneath them. In effect these towers mark a further degree of separation between the lord and his chamber from the rest of the household, a process which had started around the opening of the fourteenth century.

Some of the keeps of earlier medieval castles may have performed the same function, but specially-built tower houses to house the lord's chamber/removing/riding/secret households appear around the mid-fourteenth century. They are remarkable for the ingenuity and elegance of their design, none more so than the donjon of Warkworth Castle on the Northumbrian coast.[25] Probably built by John Lewyn for Henry Percy, shortly before his elevation to the earldom of Northumberland in 1377, it is one of the finest concepts of efficient, sequential food preparation and management theory ever to be realized in stone, all sheathed in a building of great elegance.[25] The compact three-storey plan may at first appear confusing, but on analysis its excellence becomes remarkably clear, and can be expressed schematically as in the chart on page 50 (and see Fig. 9).

Every commodity arriving at the entrance could be recorded and locked in its appropriate store. Thence it could be carried up its dedicated staircase to the precise office where it was required for further preparation, recording and service into the hall and chamber on the first floor. At other times, when only the administrative staff was present, it

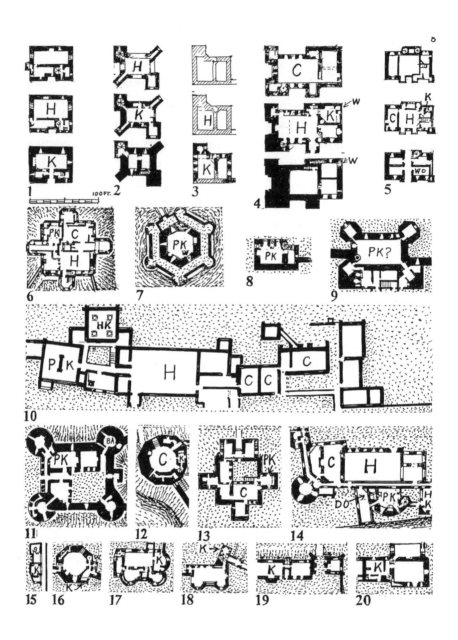

was equally efficient. The porter could admit and supervise those who came to transact business with the cofferer in his office, the records then being carried up to the counting house/clerk's chambers on the second floor for checking and recording, all the staff's food being cooked in their own kitchen, which normally acted as the pastry and boiling house when the household was present.

Probably as a result of observing French castles, Henry V began to build a great tower at his palace of Sheen, now Richmond on Thames, this being largely completed by his son Henry VI in 1429–35. Lying within its own moated enclosure, it had, judging from later sources, privy kitchens on the ground floor, with the Queen's chambers on the first floor, and the King's on the second.[26] From this period other magnates began to build great towers to house their chamber households, these only being sufficiently large to hold the select number of personal servants and clerks. Sir William ap Thomas' great hexagonal tower of 1435–45 at Raglan Castle was particularly majestic, but also intended to be self-contained.[27] Its vaulted basement storey had a 35-foot diameter kitchen complete with a fireplace and its own well. In the event, however it appears to have

Figure 8 (opposite). Specialized kitchens.

Tower house kitchens:

(1) Belsay Castle, Northumbria, 14c.; (2) Dacre Castle, Cumbria, early 14c.; (3) Arnside Tower, Cumbria, 15c.; (4) Harewood Castle, Yorks., 1366; (5) Hylton Castle, Tyne and Wear, early 15c.

Privy kitchens:

(6) Warkworth Castle, Northumbria, c.1377–90; (7) Raglan Castle, Gwent, 1435–45; (8) Ashby de la Zouch Castle, Warws., 1474; (9) Warwick Castle, c.1377–90; (10) Clarendon Palace, Wilts., 1245–6; (11) Conwy Castle, Gwynedd, 1283–7; (12) Caernarfon Castle, Gwynedd, post 1300; (13) Rushen Castle, Isle of Man, 14c.; (14) Caerphilly Castle, c.1277–90; (15) Lincoln Bishop's Palace, 1430s.

Staff kitchens:

(16) Caernarfon Castle, c.1283–92; (17) Kidwelly Castle, Dyfed, c.1390–1402; (18) Caerphilly Castle, c.1277–90; (19) Middleham Castle, Yorks., 1400–1483; (20) Bolton Castle, Yorks., c.1379.

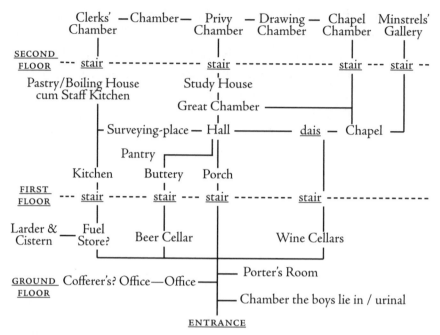

Chart. A schematic analysis of the arrangement of rooms and offices at Warkworth Castle, Northumbria.

Figure 9 opposite. The Donjon, Warkworth Castle, John Lewyn? *c.*1377–90.

Ground Floor: (1) entrance passage; (2) porter; (3) room, foot of stairs; (4) officer's chamber; (5) cofferer's? office; (6) beer cellar; (7) fuel store?; (8) wet larder & cistern; (9) wine cellar; (10) wine cellar; (11) boys' chamber; (12) chamber & urinal.

First Floor: (13) vestibule to hall; (14) buttery & pantry; (15) kitchen; (16) pastry/boiling house; (17) study house; (18) great chamber; (19) chapel; (20) hall.

Second Floor: (21) counting house?; (22) clerk's chamber & portcullis winch; (23) chamber; (24) upper part of kitchen; (25) privy chamber; (26) drawing chamber; (27) chapel chamber; (28) upper part of hall.

50

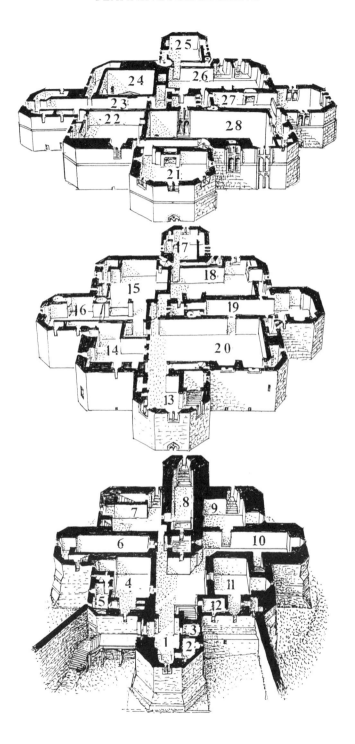

been rarely, if ever, used, there being little evidence for burning in the hearth, or of wear on the stairs. Probably like Treasurer Cromwell's great tower of *c.*1445 at Tattershall Castle, or Bishop Rotherham's tower of *c.*1480 at Buckden, it relied on the main household kitchen for its food.[28]

Lord Chamberlain Hastings' tower, built at Ashby de la Zouch Castle in 1474–83, is an exceptionally fine example of a residence designed for a chamber/removing/riding/secret household.[29] Its succeeding storeys housed a storage basement, an impressive vaulted privy kitchen, and two fine chambers. Flanking its stairs, a series of mezzanine offices, including a counting house with a concealed under-floor strongroom opposite the kitchen door, provided ample accommodation for the administrative staff. In 1483, the year Hastings was beheaded by Richard III, that monarch began to build a similarly conceived but larger tower at Warwick Castle. Here there was a kitchen at the lower level, apparently designed to serve a suite of chambers rising above. Unfortunately work ceased after Richard's death at Bosworth, but its plan was recorded by Robert Smythson in 1605.[30] Now only the bases of its turrets survive, incorporated into a later gateway.

In the intervening years, the Earls of Northumberland built further lodges to house their lesser households. One at Topcliffe was used by their heirs to entertain James I, and there was another called the New Lodge at Leconfield. This has now disappeared, but it is known to have had a great hall, a great chamber, four other chambers, a chapel and a garret.[31]

When monarchs and the high aristocracy dined and lived in their great halls, it was very difficult to change the meal times should they wish to accommodate affairs of state or hunting expeditions, to hold private conversations, or to ensure total security for their food. For all of these reasons, and to introduce a plainly visible hierarchy between the upper and lower divisions of the household, separate living rooms called *cameras* or chambers began to be introduced by the early twelfth century. A royal chamber of *c.*1100 still survives in the Tower of London.[32] Some time later, probably in the early thirteenth century, a similar separation took place in the domestic offices, when household kitchens began to be supplemented by privy (i.e. private) kitchens, staffed by separate cooks to the mouth. Here higher quality foods could be cooked in more elaborate ways, in smaller quantities, and served directly to those dining in the chamber, with little opportunity for tampering en route.

In 1245–6 a new household kitchen was built alongside the service rooms at the lower end of the hall at Clarendon Palace in Wiltshire, thus enabling the former household kitchen to be converted into a privy kitchen for Henry III.[33] Measuring 42 feet square, with 13-foot fireplaces and two ovens, each large enough to cook two whole oxen, it was clearly designed to cater for the entire body of occupants and staff of the chamber, rather than just the King himself. Queen Eleanor's chambers, lying beyond the King's chamber at the upper end of the hall, were provided with a pentice leading to her own privy kitchen of 1267, thus completing the suite of three kitchens now demanded in every major palace.

In royal castles where defence took priority over ceremony, it appears that a single privy kitchen might serve both the King and the Queen's chambers. This was the case at Edward I's Conwy of the 1280s.[34] This was a large room, over 30 feet long, similar in size to Earl Gilbert de Clare's contemporary privy kitchen at Caerphilly Castle.[35] Most other late thirteenth/early fourteenth-century privy kitchens, such as those in the Eagle Tower at Caernarfon,[36] the keep at Rushen Castle, Isle of Man, and a couple of yards outside the hall door at Kidwelly, were much smaller, and designed for smaller chambers.[37] Those which have been recognized in fifteenth-century castles were again quite large, Sir John Fastolf's at Caistor Castle having a 13-foot wide fireplace, while that in Lord Hastings' Tower at Ashby de la Zouch measured some 30 by 25 feet, large enough to cater for a large chamber staff.[38] In each case they were placed as close as possible to the chambers they were to serve, always with a discreet means of provisioning them with food and fuel without having to rely on the service rooms provided for the lower servants and lesser mortals who dined in the great hall.

Many of the large properties owned by both lay and clerical lords remained unoccupied for substantial parts of the year, or perhaps for much longer. They were still in use as administrative centres however, being manned by receivers, clerks, and perhaps a constable or other officer who ran the local estate and manorial affairs. To use the household kitchen would have been far too inconvenient and expensive, so they retreated to more manageable hearths. In small manor houses they might cook within their own living-rooms, as at Tretower Court.[39] Here the room over the late fifteenth-century gatehouse has an oven embedded into the side of its fireplace, presumably so that the official who administered the house and its manorial courts in his master's absence could bake his own bread and pies.

Staff kitchens were built on a more substantial scale in castles. At Caerphilly the main outer east gatehouse of the 1280s has a kitchen with a separate oven and fireplace on its first floor, while at Caernarfon the officers' chamber in the Well or Treasury Tower has its own kitchen just by its door. Middleham Castle's auditors' chamber lies next to its main gatehouse and has its own auditors' kitchen alongside.[40] Another example, at Carlisle Castle, was built by John Lewyn in 1378.[41] According to the contract, the gate tower was to include a 32 by 20-foot kitchen with two fireplaces, and a similarly-sized hall, presumably enabling it to serve the garrison too. Lewyn's Bolton Castle also features a staff kitchen in its first-floor administrative area, next to a large chamber where officers must have dined.[42] Warkworth Castle, almost certainly by Lewyn, was designed to enable staff to cook their meals in the pastry and boiling house, just a short flight of stairs below their chamber.[43]

Having set the scene by examining the principles behind the planning of medieval domestic quarters, we can now explore the form and function of the individual offices. We commence with the fuel and water supplies, and then continue through to the surveying-place, whence food was despatched for service into the halls and chambers.

CHAPTER THREE

Wood, Coals, Turves and Fires

In large households, the provision of fuel was the responsibility of the office of the woodyard. If the family's estates included extensive woodland, firewood might be cut either by in-house staff or by hiring the labour required to fell, trim and chop the trees for fuel.[1] From an administrative point of view, it was often far more convenient for the controller and clerk of the kitchen to enter into contracts with independent suppliers at previously agreed rates. This enabled the coming year's expenses to be predicted with accuracy and left the problems of acquisition, extraction and delivery in the hands of others.[2]

The work of the woodyard tended to be seasonal, since most of the fuel was used for room-heating between All Hallows on 1 November through to Lady Day on 25 March. Only members of the immediate family would be allowed fires in their rooms during the summer months. By contrast, the fuel requirements of the bakehouse, brewhouse, pastry and kitchens tended to be consistent throughout the entire year. Every day, fuel would be delivered to each office according to its predetermined allocation, the quantity being recorded by a member of the clerical staff. The clerk avenor (in charge of the stables) might undertake this, since he was regularly in the outer court area where the woodyard was usually located.

Unfortunately, there is hardly any visual or archaeological evidence to suggest how a woodyard was constructed and used. We know that they were enclosed to prevent pilfering, the woodhouse door at Abingdon being repaired at a cost of 5s. 8d. in 1356–7.[3] Presumably they had separate divisions or areas in which to store their great woods or logs, their faggots, turves, coal and charcoal. The latter at least would probably be kept under cover, since soaking rain would make it hard to ignite and then give off vast clouds of foul smoke.

In urban areas, where there was little readily available timber, professional woodmongers might bring in the necessary supplies. In London they had become an organized body by the fourteenth century, adopting arms emblazoned with some of the faggots they offered for sale. Most of their timber appears to have been either barged down the Thames into London (they had rights of the toll on Boveney Lock near Eton), or shipped in bulk from the Weald of Kent and Sussex, around the coast and up to the Thames wharfs.[4] Eighty-eight tons arrived in this way in 1400.[5] Further evidence of river-borne firewood delivery is provided by the 1423 funeral accounts of Henry Bowet, Archbishop of York. To furnish fuel for the feasts a ship was hired to carry 2,000 faggots and two hundredweight of split logs nine miles up the Ouse into York, where a cart awaited to carry them to the Minster precinct, all at a cost of £2 18s. 4d.[6]

Many people in both towns and villages were fortunate enough to have fuel-collecting privileges associated with their properties. Closely controlled by their local manor, burgesses and cottagers were permitted to gather underwood or dead wood from their lord's woods, parks and forests, but the valuable growing timber was always carefully protected. Practical experience made some of these supplies more desirable than others. Ash, beech, hornbeam and willow were excellent, but elm and poplar burned badly, while chestnut crackled and sent out showers of sparks.

For the commercial trade, it was important that the wood was marketable in standard sizes at standard prices. The best, sometimes called great wood, was usually cut into uniform pieces called billets. An Essex billet, for example, was 3 feet 6 inches long by 15 inches circumference in the middle. When these round timbers were split in two they became shides, those used in the Northumberland household being 3 feet long by 9 inches across. To regulate their sizes, the City of London introduced a numbered size system, each 'talshide' being 4 feet long and split to produce numbered cross-sections of uniform area, and therefore of uniform fuel and monetary value. For example:[7]

Talshide number	Round log	Half-split	Quarter-split
1	16" girth	19" girth	18½" girth
2	23" girth	27" girth	26" girth
3	28" girth	33" girth	32" girth
4	33" girth	39" girth	39" girth

These were ideal for sustaining good fires for roasting and general cookery, and for the steady heat required in boiler furnaces.

Timbers of less than 16-inch girth were presumably split into smaller sections to form astelwood, *hostella* being the Latin for a thin stick.

The smallest branches and longer twigs were next cut into convenient lengths and tied with two wooden bands to form faggots or kids. Smaller versions with just one band were called bavins, these, with faggots and kids, being ideal for producing shorter bursts of heat. They were the main fuel for ovens, for example, especially when made from hot, fast-burning wood such as thorn. Short bundles of the very smallest twigs bound into bundles about 3 inches diameter by 9 inches long, have been used from at least the eighteenth century for firelighting. Called pimps, they are not recorded in medieval sources, but may represent an early form of kindling.[8]

For a number of cooking operations, wood produced too much smoke, not enough heat, and burned at an unpredictable rate. To remedy these problems, it could be heated in a low-oxygen environment in order to drive off all its volatile material, and leave an almost pure carbon called charcoal. This was made in virtually every wooded area of England using a number of different woods, as they were locally available. At Sandal Castle in Yorkshire, for example, oak and birch predominated, along with hazel, poplar, sweet-chestnut, mountain ash and holly in the fifteenth century.[9] It was usually measured and sold in skeps, baskets of a certain but currently unknown volume. They may have held a quarter of a chaldron (i.e. 10.25 cubic feet), since the quarter was a standard measure for charcoal, costing a shilling in the early sixteenth century.[10] Those who only required a small quantity would buy directly from the colliers who brought their supplies into the local markets. Great households might also buy in their supplies, or have them made on their own estates, the Howards paying their 'colyer for makyng of coleys 2s.'[11] As well as being used for room-heating, charcoal was ideal in stoves for distilling or in chafing dishes for light cooking or re-heating food.

In areas where there were carboniferous outcrops, the use of coal probably started in the early thirteenth century when 'sea-coal' was apparently first dug out of Northumbrian sea-cliffs. Underground workings are recorded in the opening years of the fourteenth century when Robert Hood, the putative Robin Hood of legend, was an early coal miner in Wakefield.[12] The local court rolls describe coal as *lapis ardens* 'hot stone', *petram ad ardendam* 'stone with heat', or *carbones maritimos* 'sea-charcoal', this last name recording the seaside location from which it was first extracted, and differentiating it from wood-charcoal. By the mid-fourteenth century the Newcastle-London seaborne coal trade was already well established, keelboats carrying 50 tons or more regularly leaving the Tyne to supply all the coastal and inland ports down the east coast and beyond.[13] It was sold in bulk by the chaldron or chalder, a measure representing 53 hundredweight, and by the quarter or quarter chaldron of around 13 hundredweight. Smaller quantities were distributed in mets, two-bushel measures of some 3 hundredweight. The Northumberland household consumed 80 (Newcastle?) chaldrons of sea-coal, some 212 tons, each year. Although almost 8 hundredweight went to the kitchen daily, much of this must have been for room-heating, the principal rooms presumably having the best quality at 5s. the quarter, and others the second-best at 4s. 2d. the quarter. As might be expected, two thirds were used between the end of September and the end of March.[14] Archaeological evidence for the use of coal-fires for room-heating in the late fifteenth century is provided by the open hearths in the great hall in the bailey of Warkworth Castle. Square in plan and pitched with stone, their central areas take the form of a deep square ashpit designed to receive an iron grate. This arrangement is totally unsuitable for wood fires, which require a flat hearth, but is ideal for coal, since it provides the necessary under-draught, and allows the ashes and embers to fall away from the fire, rather than choking it to extinction. The creation of a coal-burning fireplace in the donjon hall at Warkworth is probably a mid-1520s introduction, since the 1512 household regulations stipulate that charcoal was to replace coal in the best rooms at Christmas each year 'bicause the Smook of the Seecolys wold hurt myne Arras (tapestry) when it ys hunge'.[15]

In kitchens, the problems of soot and smoke must have been just as great, although the great masonry fireplaces of the larger kitchens would have been perfectly suited for burning coal, given a new iron grate. For roasting, coal provided an excellent radiant heat, but its tarry soot made boiling over the fire a much dirtier process. If coal smoke swirls into the top of a boiling pot, it can give the contents a sulphurous taste, while the black deposits on the outside of the pot are much more difficult to remove than fine wood ash or the by-products of other fuels and soil any hands or cloths which come into contact with them. For the same reasons, it was totally unsuitable for heating bread and pastry ovens, where cleanliness and a lack of strong-smelling fumes were absolutely essential. Even so, there is sound documentation for the culinary use of coal in the fifteenth century, when John Carter of York's inventory of 1485 records a chalder of sea-coals in his kitchen.[16] Coal has also been found in quantity in the fifteenth-century levels of houses at the village of Wharram Percy, many miles away from the nearest outcrops.

In low-lying wetlands and on high, bleak moorlands, the mossy vegetation slowly decomposed and carbonized to form a compact, if soggy mass called peat. This could be made into a very useful fuel, plentiful in quantity, but requiring several months of preparation. Many cottagers and small households enjoyed rights of turbary (peat-cutting) within their manor, which took overall control of its harvesting. These rights and controls are still being exercised in some rural areas today. Cutting began in April, after the moss had begun to dry out, and might continue through to July. In some areas turves or fleights were pared off the surface. These dried quickly, did not shrink, burnt well, but devastated the land, which took a long time to regrow its vegetation. In contrast, when peat was cut from the underlying mass, the moor soon recovered if the turves were replaced afterwards. Turf spades, such as that purchased for Durham Priory for 8d. in 1477–8, traditionally had a flat triangular iron blade with a vertical section at one side, all mounted on a T-shaped wooden handle, so that it could be used like a breast-plough to pare off the top few inches of vegetation in long, broad strips.[17] Peat spades usually had an L-shaped cutting edge mounted on a wooden shaft, its size and proportion varying from one region to another. This was used either vertically or horizontally to cut out long blocks, perhaps three or four inches square, which had to be tossed into neat lines on the adjacent ground. After a few weeks they had half-dried, and were firm enough to be propped or stacked into small piles for further drying, after which they might be re-arranged in large stacks to dry out completely. Having lost perhaps two-thirds of their length and thickness, they were ready for carrying back to the house in late summer, between the hay and corn harvests. If kept dry by storing in a dense stack or an outhouse, the peats were now ready for use over the coming year. They tended to smoulder on the hearth, rather than to blaze, and gave off a pungent smoke, which could only be avoided by squatting, if burnt on an open hearth. As a fuel, peat was ideal for boiling, frying and baking on a bakestone, but was of little use for roasting or heating a large masonry oven. A good impression of the quantity of peat burned in medieval households is provided by the remains of the flooded peat-pits which now form the Norfolk Broads. In 1347–8 the household of Sir Hamon le Strange of Hunstanton, listed as a mere thirteen people, bought in over 24,000 'turves' at either a shilling or sixpence the thousand, in addition to 'two hundred of rushes used in the bakehouse.'[18]

In areas where other fuels were in short supply, cow shards or cassons, casings or casard, otherwise cow-pats, were used. In summer they could be simply gathered from the fields as convenient discs and stored until dry, while in winter they were taken up in their soft state, the womenfolk then 'clapping-cassons' into balls, and hurling them against the walls of their cottages, where they remained until dry, when they could be eased off for use. This practice, probably millennia old, continued up to quite recent times. In 1792 the vicar of Naseby in Northamptonshire complained that the local people spread dung all over the walls of their cottages once a year, before removing it, while Victorian visitors to the Isle of Purbeck found the cottages there 'passing strange with dung stuck on them to dry.'[19] In the East Riding of Yorkshire the dry cassons or 'blakes' were broken up and burnt with chalk stones, the resulting fire reputedly burning well and long, giving off great heat, little smoke, a pleasant perfume, and a very fine ash.[20] Having used it both for under-pan baking on an open hearth and in a chafing dish I can confirm its excellence. Its only problem is that its use deprives agricultural land of important fertilizer.

Although these fuels were the most commonly used, they were by no means the only ones. When William Harrison thought that London's wood supply was about to run out in the 1570s he considered that 'Jenny bote, broom, turf, gall, heath, furze, brakes (bracken), ling, dies, hassocks, flags, straw, sedge, reed, rush and also seascale' would have to be used instead.[21] These would certainly have been employed in periods of general fuel shortage, as well as kindling to get the fires going. We can learn much on this subject from dialect sources. On the Yorkshire Moors, for example, these record how cowls, tough heather stalks left after the vegetation had been burnt off areas of moorland, were gathered into 'boddins' for kindling.[22] In Cumbria 'bullens', 'bunnels' or 'spoots', the dried stems of cow parsley, were used for this purpose, along with dried butter-bur, while in Leicestershire straw was used as an emergency fuel.[23] In Devon a 'blast o' vuzz', a brand of dried gorse, or 'cricks', dry hedge trimmings, were the usual kindling, other regions having their own particular preference.[24]

To ignite a fire, the usual method was to strike sparks from a piece of flint or firestone (iron pyrites) held in one hand with a steel or fire-iron, a flat-edged implement which hooked over the knuckles of the other.[25] Once caught on a piece of tinder placed underneath, the sparks were gently blown to produce a flame, which lit the kindling, which in turn lit the wood or other fuel, which would then light coal or charcoal, if these were being burned. Tow, the bone-dry unworked fibres of flax, provided an excellent tinder. 'Of a lytill sparkyll in a hepe of towe or of tyndyr cometh sodaynly a grete fyre' wrote Trevisa, while in *Piers Plowman* we learn:[26]

> Ac hew fyre at a flynte fowre hundreth wyntre
> But thow have towe to take it with tondre or broches
> Al thi laboure is loste.

Although not recorded in the medieval period, other materials such as spunk, the dried fungus of the *polyporus* variety, or fungus-rotted wood called touchwood may have been used as tinder. Among the list of equipment taken to France by Henry 'the Magnificent' Earl of Northumberland when serving as Henry VIII's Grand Captain at the Battle of the Spurs in 1513 were 'fyre yrens flynte stones, Tinder, and Brimstone in tyme of nede'.[27] This suggests that short strips of wood tipped with brimstone (sulphur) were already being used as efficient firelighters. Once the sulphur touched the glowing tinder, it instantly sprang into flame and ignited its 'match', making fire and candle-lighting a much easier process. Due to its expense, this would have been a method restricted to the wealthier elements of society.

An even easier method of fire-lighting would be to carry glowing embers or coals from an existing fire onto another hearth. One of the small iron, bronze or earthenware chafing dishes would be ideal for this, but purposely-made fire-pans were also available. It is possible that earthenware cooking pots found with sooted interiors may have been used as firepans.[28] Some fuels, especially peat, rarely needed re-lighting however, since they could easily smoulder overnight and be revived each morning.[29]

There is little evidence to suggest how fires were laid ready for lighting, but traditional practice indicates that small bundles of kindling would be topped by successively larger twigs, only then moving on to talshides and billets. To get the fire started, bellows of the traditional pear shape might be used, as seen in one of the fifteenth-century misericords at Boston, Lincolnshire. These are found in the kitchen inventories of craftsmen and the like, but presumably most of the poor had to squat down and use the power of their lungs to blow life into their fires.[30]

From excavations, we know that kitchen hearths were usually flat, without any form of fender but sometimes a low kerb to help retain embers and ashes. They may be mere burnt areas on beaten earth floors, patches of rough-paved tile or stone, or neatly pitched panels of roofing tiles or flagstones set on edge to withstand the heat. One built in Nottingham in 1486, had 'Baceford ston for to mak the chimney harth with' and 'Breke [brick] for to make the reredose of the same chymney with'.[31] The reredos was the fire-back. The earliest of these appear to have been built freestanding at the back of fires set in the middle of their kitchens. Since they posed such a considerable fire-risk in highly combustible buildings, the City of London banned their use where meat, bread or ale were being heated near partition-walls of laths or boards, at the same time ordering the replacement of wooden chimneys with those of stone, tile or plaster.[32] In rural areas they continued to be used in half-timbered kitchen buildings, protecting the walls from conflagration. A 1567 description of Great Worge, Brightling, Sussex, states that its kitchen is made of timber, with a tile roof and has a 'reredashe' oven, this being a large reredos to cover much of the wall behind the hearth, and incorporating a baking oven.[33] When fires moved into arched fireplaces set into the walls, their firebacks were of stone, if sufficiently fire-resistant, brick, or roofing-tiles set on edge. There is not much evidence for the use of cast-iron plates to protect the masonry from burning logs and coals, these apparently being introduced during the sixteenth century. However, the payment for making a reredos, recorded just after a payment for iron racks in the Earl of Derby's accounts for 1392, suggests that they may have much earlier origins.[34]

Wood fires were relatively simple to manage, most being virtual bonfires, their size and number varying according to the needs of the cook. Andirons were infrequently used, but a furgon or fire fork, all iron or just an iron fork on a wooden shaft, and a pair of tongs, were useful for adjusting the logs.[35] Peat fires were similarly easy to manage, but coal and charcoal were quite different, since they needed a good under-draught in order to make them burn efficiently. The arrival of coal into the medieval kitchen brought with it a whole series of new implements. These included pack-saddles for coal-panniers, wheelbarrows and baskets to carry it, iron coal rakes to gather it together, shovels to scoop it up and put it on the fire, and chimneys in which to burn it.[36] Today we recognize chimneys as masonry ducts to carry away smoke, but in the fifteenth century the word also signified iron firebaskets or grates.[37] Unfortunately there is little, if any, archaeological or pictorial evidence to show how they were constructed, while documentary evidence is similarly scant. However, a 1421 reference to andirons for two chimneys for the chamber and one of 1423 to a pair of andirons for a chimney in the chamber suggest that they were firebaskets supported on tall fire dogs.[38] They were presumably used for charcoal, but coal-burning kitchen chimneys were probably of the same design.

Another fifteenth-century 'chimney' was called a chover, a word un-recorded in dictionaries of standard or dialect English, even though used up to the twentieth century. In 1900, J.H. Dixon collected a portable iron firebasket with a flaring body and a projecting handle, and close-set fire-bars set on three tall legs, from Top Withens, Haworth, the traditional location of *Wuthering Heights*.[39] He was told that it was a chaumindish, the alternative local name being a chover, these presumably being derived from the Latin *chaminus* 'fireplace' and medieval French *chauffer*, to heat. They had been used as the sole cooking devices in houses without any other fire-grates up to at least the 1850s, peats being set within them, ignited using flint and steel, and pans, frying-pans or bakestones placed on top, so as to cook complete meals.[40] Historians have presumed that me-dieval townsfolk living in small houses with neither kitchens nor fireplaces were unable to cook for themselves, but with a chaminus or chauffer, a few sticks, peats, cassons or lumps of charcoal, they could certainly cater for a family's needs, as this unbroken tradition clearly proves.

Before proceeding any further, it is important to discuss chafers, since they are a source of considerable confusion. They comprise utensils for six different functions, and may be described as:

1. chafers to hold fire in the kitchen, including the *chaminus* and *chaufers* described above, or the 'chauffer for the fire 6s' in William Gale's kitchen inventory of 1472;[41]
2. chafers to heat food in the kitchen, these being shallow bronze or earthenware cooking pots used for broths, frying, dripping-pans, etc.;
3. chafers to hold fire in the chamber, for room-heating;
4. chafers to hold hand-washing water, these being vessels in which perfumed water was warmed before being poured into ewers for the top table's hand-washing;
5. chafers on which hand-washing water chafers were heated, these presumably being higher quality versions of 2 above, for use in the buttery/pantry or chamber;
6. chafers to heat food at the table during the service of meals. These would be the very highest quality versions of 1 above.

It can be difficult to assign all excavated chafers to particular uses, but it is immediately obvious that some were for kitchen use and some for the table, just by their size, materials and quality. Many of the chafers to hold fire in the kitchen were made of earthenware from the thirteenth century onwards. They usually have a shallow bowl about 8 inches in diameter, with three projections rising from the rim to support either a dish, a chafer for holding food in the kitchen, or a frying-pan an inch or two above the smouldering charcoal, peat or cassons. Holes pierced in the bottom provided the necessary draught from a hollow base section, which also caught the fine ashes, and insulated the hot chafer from the tabletop. Made at potteries in most parts of England, they must have been in widespread use, even though their negligible price meant that they never appeared in inventories and documents of that sort (Fig. 10).

In well-equipped sixteenth-century kitchens iron chafers to hold fire were being mounted in table-height masonry benches, these being known as stoves. They were being used in mid-fourteenth-century England, when the distillation apparatus used on them for medicinal purposes – stills, stillatories, and alembics or limbecks – entered our vocabulary. Although this apparatus has been excavated from both lay and monastic sites, remains of the stoves on which it was mounted are singularly elusive.[42] It is possible that archaeological evidence of medieval kitchen stoves is extant, but still to be recognized. Currently, the most significant discovery was made at Newton St Loe Castle in Somerset around 1980.[43] Here the back wall of a fireplace at least 10 feet wide was lined with a low masonry bench incorporating three open-fronted, stone-lined furnaces about 1 foot 6 inches in diameter, their bases heavily burned and still containing charcoal. Although not a fully developed stove, it is half-way to being one. Having many of the stove's advantages, it permitted individual pots to be cooked at their own particular temperatures, enabled the cooks to enjoy much better access to the pots than they had on the virtual bonfire of the open fire, and brought considerable economies of fuel. It is interesting to note that there were extensive remains of charcoal on this hearth, confirming that this cleanest and most controllable of fuels had been burned here when it was last used in the early fifteenth century.

One of the benefits of burning wood, charcoal and brackens was that

Figure 10. Chafers for charcoal.

1. Chaumindish or *chaminus*, Calderdale, Yorks., mid-19c.

2. As shown on a 15c. Nottingham alabaster from the St William Altarpiece, York.

3. From Sandal Castle, Yorks., early 15c.

4. Furnaces or stoves for heating pots over charcoal fires, at Newton St Loe Castle, Somerset, 15c.

they produced ashes. When soaked in water, these produced a strong alkaline solution which, when it came in contact with grease or fat, combined with it to form soap, very useful for washing both kitchen utensils and textiles. In the royal household two yeomen of the laundry used a cloth to collect all the ashes from everyone's chambers and the kitchens at court in order to make the lye solutions for their wash-days. Ashes were so useful for this purpose that they were sometimes bought or sold, the executors of Thomas Vicars of Strensall in Yorkshire paying a penny for 'ashes for washing' in 1451.[44]

Kitchen Lighting

The amount of daylight entering a medieval kitchen was quite variable. Preparing food in the open air would make a pleasant change in good weather, particularly in small rural houses, but the actual cooking was usually carried out indoors. In the smallest houses, unglazed windows, perhaps covered with fenestrals of oiled linen stretched on wooden frames, along with open doors, would usually provide enough light for most purposes during daylight hours. If their locations allowed, major kitchens were very well lit, with long unglazed, shuttered or partially glazed windows, those at Cockermouth Castle being 24 feet high, for example. Top-light was often provided by an ornate louvre, while areas where the more complicated preparations were carried out, such as the pastry-making tables, might have conveniently placed windows close to their worktops, as at Gainsborough Old Hall.

Since window light provided the only really effective and safe level of illumination for cooking, meal-times had to be arranged to take the best advantage of what was available. For this reason, dinner, the main meal of the day, was taken around ten in the morning, and supper about four in the afternoon, thus providing the maximum daylight for preparation, cooking, and clearing away. Even so, there was generally insufficient light in the kitchen during the dark winter months. At these times, firelight from hearths at ground level left table-tops in deep gloom, so that various forms of artificial light had to be introduced.

In small houses, rushlights would be home-made in summer by carefully peeling the long, cylindrical pith of the juncus rush, and dragging it through molten animal fat. These burned quite rapidly and would make 'darkness visible' for a few minutes for brief spells of work, but were virtually useless for all practical purposes. Candles were quite an expensive alternative, but they and their candlesticks are not particularly common in kitchen inventories. To anyone who has tried to work by candle-light in a large medieval kitchen, this is hardly surprising, for their light barely penetrates the all-pervading gloom. Cressets were far more effective, these being carved stone columns or slabs with one or more hollows about 3 inches deep by up to 4 inches diameter cut into their flat top surfaces. These were filled either with oil or animal fats, particularly tallow saved from the boiling pots and dripping-pans, into which a wick was inserted. At night the dormitory of Durham Priory was lit by 'A four square stone, wherin was a dozen cressets wrought being ever filled and supplied with the cooks as they need to give light to the monks'.[45] Those found on excavations are usually much smaller, many having just a single wick.[46]

Many of the cressets which appear in kitchen inventories were quite different in construction and use, taking the form of iron firebaskets in which pitched rope, wood or coal were burned. It has been assumed that these were primarily for providing light, but it is significant that like chovers, to which they were probably identical, they were used for other purposes. They are often listed in association with frying-pans, and would certainly have provided an excellent source of gentle heat for frying.[47] One in a York kitchen in 1402 lay alongside a pair of woolcombs, confirming that they were also used to pre-heat the iron combs used to separate the tops from the noils of long-stapled wool ready for spinning it into worsted yarn.[48]

CHAPTER FOUR

Water Supplies

Water is an essential element in any kitchen, being indispensible as a means of sustaining life, as a cooking medium, and as a cleaning agent. An adequate water supply was therefore a major factor when choosing any location for human habitation. Medieval stomachs were more robust than those of today, however, and so a greater variety of sources could be used, especially since individual communities soon built up a resistance to particular biological contaminants unless of a particularly deadly strain. Our best description of early-Tudor opinion on water and its usage comes from Andrew Boorde:[1]

> Water is not holsome sole by it selfe, for an Englysshe man… Water is colde, slowe, and slacke of dygestyon. The best water is rayne-water, so be it that it be clene and purely taken. Nexte to it is ronnyng water, the whiche doth swyftly ronne from East in to the west upon stones or pybles. The thyrde water to be praysed, is ryver or broke water, the which is clene, ronning on pibles and graval. Standynge waters, the whiche be refresshed with a fresshe spryng is commendable; but standyng waters, and well-waters to the whiche the sonne hath no reflyxyon, althoughe they be lyghtern than other ronnyng waters be, yet they be not so commendable…
>
> The water the which every man ought to dresse his meate with all, or shall use bakynge or bruyng, let it be ronnyng, and put it in vessels that it may stande there 2 or 3 houres [before it is used]; then strayne the upper parte thorough a thycke lynnyn cloth, and cast the inferior parte away. If any man do use to drynk water with wyne, let it be purely strayned, and then seth [boil] it, and after it be cold, let hym put it to his wyne.

Few of us would wish to drink river water today, but as Boorde states, it was then considered perfectly satisfactory. In London, for example, the waters of the Thames, Fleet, Walbrook, Langbourn and Old Bourne (Holborn) provided much of the city's potable water supply, other towns and villages relying on similar sources. It is probable that large buildings built by rivers and streams would have developed efficient methods of accessing their waters. At Caerphilly Castle, for example, water for the kitchen and brewhouse was probably drawn from its stream-fed moat, while at Chepstow a winch drew water from a riverside spring at the base of its sheer cliff-face.

Where river water was not conveniently available, means were devised to deliver it through gravity-fed pipes. In the early thirteenth century Gilbert Sandford conveyed water from the Tyburn at Marylebone along 6-inch diameter lead pipes to the Great Conduit at Cheapside, from where it could be collected from stone basins. In 1345 London introduced new regulations to prevent the brewers from monopolizing the conduit's supplies, since they were depriving the rich and middling sorts of water needed for food preparation, and the poor of their drink.[2]

Most other communities relied on wells, this term being used to describe springs, shallow pits and deep shafts. If the water level was close to the surface, as in a spring, some form of kerb or paving was usually provided in order to prevent pollution and the ingress of plants, in addition to providing a firm foot-hold to all those who came to draw water. London's St Clement's Well was of this type, being 'fair curbed square, with hard stone, kept clean for common use… and always full'.[3] A good thirteenth- and fourteenth-century example excavated at St John Street, Bedford, has seven stone-slabbed steps descending between walls to the timbered brink of its 5 by 10-foot pool.[4]

Spring water began to be piped into English monastic sites from at least the early twelfth century, a number of major towns then being enabled to draw on these supplies. Around 1310, for example, the Franciscan friars allowed the town of Southampton to pipe water from its hand-washing sink by its refectory door to a cistern outside their precinct wall, provided that all unused water was returned to their cloister. In Bristol, the Carmelites provided St John's conduit; in Wells, Bishop Beckington provided one in the market place; in Gloucester, the Cathedral granted three-quarters of its supply to the citizens; while in Exeter the Cathedral granted one-third of its water in a similar way.[5] Spring-water conduits were also erected by private donors and civic authorities. In the fifteenth century both Hull and Exeter corporations, along with many others, went to considerable expense to provide supplies of freshwater which were entirely under their own control, with which their citizens could readily fill their buckets from stone or lead-lined cisterns.[6]

Open channels called leats were also dug from springs into urban centres, where they flowed along deep gutters in the main streets, providing dipping-places near each door. From the mid-thirteenth century, Tiverton's leat system was bringing in water from the Norwood Common springs over five miles away, other west-country towns such as Bere, Helston, Honiton, Salisbury and Wells having similar arrangements about the same time.[7]

Medieval workmen were skilled in the art of well-sinking, producing anything from timber or barrel-lined pits sunk a few metres into soft soil, to shafts over 400 feet deep cut through solid rock, perhaps 'steened' or masonry-lined where they passed through unsound levels. Most were fairly narrow, that at Dover Castle being just over a yard in diameter for its first 172 feet, but others could be much larger, that at Bristol Castle being 10 feet in diameter.[8] In order to keep their supplies as clean as possible, wells were usually protected from the elements by being enclosed within domestic buildings, detached well-houses, or beneath pitched roofs, walls around their perimeters preventing the accidental intrusion of humans, animals and any foreign matter blowing around the adjacent floor surface. For maximum convenience, some medieval kitchens had wells set against one of their internal walls. Bolton Castle and Harewood Castle each had one in the corner between their two fireplaces, while those in the great tower at Raglan and the great hall and Hastings Tower at Ashby de la Zouch Castle are in recesses in their side walls. The preceptory of the Knights Templar at South Witham even had one by the side of its great hall's central hearth. Only a couple of feet deep, it immediately half-filled itself with clear water when excavated on this incredibly damp site in the 1960s.[9]

If the water level was within some 10 feet of the surface, the quickest and most effective means of raising it was to use a bucket hung at the end of a long lever, a heavy weight counterbalancing not only the bucket, but also much of the water. These are shown in manuscript illuminations from the thirteenth century through to the sixteenth, one at Scarborough Castle's Well of Our Lady having a counterweight like a millstone to neutralize the weight of the bucket and its heavy chain (Fig. 11).[10]

In England, the preferred method of raising water from deep wells was the bucket and horizontal winch or windlass. *Jacob's Well* of c.1440 describes how 'When your well is made, you must have a windlass & a rope & a bucket to draw up water to drink, because your well is so deep'.[11] There are also numerous archival references such as 'For the well, a bucket with a chain of iron', or 'For a well bucket to Harry Williamson's well, and for the binding of the same 3s. 2d.'[12] Since the weight of a well-bucket and its rope or chain added considerably to the labour of winding up the water, some wells appear to have had two buckets on the same windlass, each counterbalancing the other as they simultaneously rose and descended. 'The well with 2 boketts a lytyll fro Seynt Elens' mentioned in London's Bishopgate in 1472 was probably of this type, as was 'the two bokettys heng by one corde renayng thurgh one pelley' in Caxton's *History of Reynard the Fox*.[13]

At Caernarfon Castle, the masonry of the late-thirteenth-century Well Tower provides evidence for a more sophisticated well with two buckets. Above the shaft there are sockets for three cross-beams which would support a pulley for each bucket, two beams at right-angles below them, to prevent the buckets being over-wound, and the bearing-blocks for the windlass roller, the rear wall being hacked back to accommodate a large pulley at its left side. As the drawing shows (Fig. 12.2), this suggests a counter-balanced two-bucket system, a continuous loop of rope around the large pulley allowing each bucket to be raised in turn, first pulling from the top of the large pulley to raise one, then pulling it from the bottom to raise the other. If, as the dimensions suggest, the pulley was some 6 feet in diameter, and the windlass roller 1 foot in diameter, this would allow 120lb of water to be raised using only 20lb of effort, an extremely efficient arrangement. The probable use of the continuous loop of rope on the pulley would have the advantages of permitting the windlass roller to be rotated both clockwise and anti-clockwise, and also of reducing the 340

Figure 11. Water supplies.

Manuscript illustrations show both wells and water-carriers, such as:

1–2. Counterweighted lever wells, 13 & 14c.

3. Our Lady's Well, Scarborough Castle, Yorks., early 16c.

4. Winch mechanism, with continuous haulage loops to each side of the actual well-rope, 13c.

5. A jug on the head, *c.*1340.

6. A yolk with buckets, 14c.

7–8. Soes or cowls, 15c.

9. Tankards in London, mid-16c.

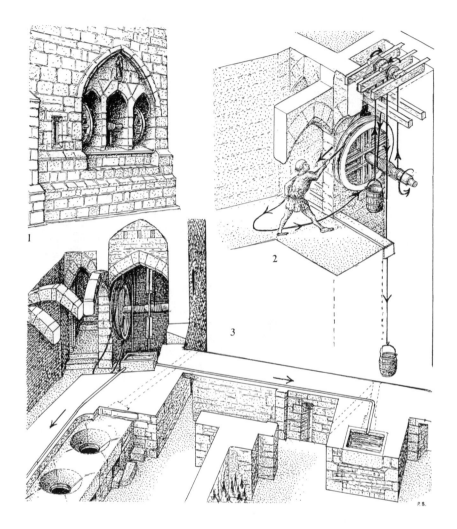

Figure 12. Deep wells.

1. With two pulley wheels flanking the well rope, Alnwick Castle, Northumb., 14c.

2. Reconstruction of pulley winding system at Caernarfon Castle Well Tower, 1283–92.

3. Lead pipes carrying water from the well-house cistern to supply cisterns in the boiling house (?) and kitchen at Caernarfon Castle, 1283–92.

feet of unruly rope required for a single lift to a single loop extending only a few yards into the well-house. A similar method may have been used at the fourteenth-century well built by Henry Percy in the central courtyard of Alnwick Castle, where the windlass is housed in an impressive triple-arched recess (Fig. 12).

As for the buckets used in the wells, we are fortunate that a number of examples tumbled down the shaft, were never recovered and so were preserved in the wet conditions.[14] Almost without exception they were stave-built in oak and usually kept together with iron bands. Holes bored through a couple of staves which rose above their rims, or sometimes a pair of iron staples, provided strong mounting for bow handles of iron or rope. Three staves similarly extending from the base might act as feet, raising the buckets off the ground to keep them clean and perhaps reduce the development of rot. Their capacities varied considerably, smaller ones holding under a gallon (8lb) of water, while others might hold perhaps 5 gallons or almost half a hundredweight of water. When combined with the weight of the perpetually soaked bucket, they were extremely heavy, demonstrating the need for efficient winches.

Caxton advised that fortresses should be supplied with fresh water, and cisterns 'where men may receive inne the rayne water that fallen doune a-long the thatches of thappentyzes and houses.' The simplest method was to place water-butts beneath the fall-pipes. In 1375 Robert Man, cooper, was employed to mend the water casks which received the rainwater coming down the lead pipes from the roofs of Queenborough Castle. Alternatively, permanent masonry collection pits might be constructed as at the Tower of London, where one beside the Lieutenants' kitchen, 'for the receiving of all the water falling there', was provided in 1386. Wolsey's Cardinal College, Oxford, had a similar system: 'For all the water which shall at rains issue into my Lord's Grace College is by a goodly vault conveyed into the sink of the kitchen; and that sink is in every place so large that any stopping should chance, a man may go in to purge the stoppage.'[15]

There is little archaeological evidence for rainwater collection in smaller households, but effective systems exist in a number of castles. One of the simplest, two stone-lined tanks at ground level, stands just within the gatehouse at Carreg Cennan in Dyfed, for example. One turret on the magnificent late twelfth-century century keep at Conisbrough also retains its cistern. It is not particularly large, but its significance is enhanced when its average delivery is calculated. Since each square foot of a roof collects half a gallon per inch of rainfall, modern annual rainfall records suggest that it collected some 650 gallons a year, or about 14 pints a day on average, a useful quantity in time of siege, and probably enough for baking and washing purposes when the keep was in everyday use. It was certainly more convenient than the 90-foot well in the courtyard below.

It is difficult to establish the intended collection area for the 10-foot diameter hexagonal cistern in the Cistern Tower at Caernarfon Castle. Built in the late thirteenth century, it was designed to hold several hundred gallons of clean rainwater, roofed over to prevent pollution, all the surplus being carried along an overflow channel to flush a garderobe shaft in the adjacent Queen's Gate. The most impressive surviving rainwater system is that probably designed by John Lewyn at Warkworth Castle in the late fourteenth century. Here all the water from the huge flat lead roof of the donjon tower was channelled into a pipe which descended a combined light-well, drain and perhaps latrine shaft before discharging into a collection tank and a separate cistern in the vaulted basement, or to a flushing system for the main drain. With a roof area of some 6,800 square feet and 25.5 inches of rainfall, this provided over 3,500 gallons a year, or 10 gallons a day on average. Given that the castle's well-house lay 250 feet away, down in the outer bailey, that running rainwater was, in medieval opinion, the finest water, and that Warkworth is one of the best-planned buildings of its period, it is obvious that this was a major source of water for both drinking, cooking and cleaning.[16]

Whatever its origin – river, spring, well, conduit or cistern – consider-able effort was necessary to carry water into the kitchens. Buckets, jugs or water-pots might be used for small quantities. Grisilde in Chaucer's *Clerk's Tale* fetched her water home in a water-pot, which she set down in an ox's stall beside her threshold.[17] Clearly such vessels would be insufficient for larger households. One alternative was the water-bouget, a pair of leather bags fastened together near their necks, so that they could be carried on a stick over the shoulder, or slung over a pack horse. These were ideal for use on campaign, or when a household was in transit between houses, since they were relatively strong, light and flexible. Another was the tankard, a tall, conical coopered vessel, its narrow neck fitted with an iron spout and a vertical loop handle. Once filled, it was hoisted over the right shoulder, a staff over the left shoulder holding up its heavy bottom end, and helping to control the flow of the water. Larger quantities were carried in a coopered tub called either a soe or a cowl. This had holes pierced through the two staves extending above its rim, allowing it to be hung from a stout cowl-staff and carried on the shoulders of two men. Only fictional strongmen such as Havelok the Dane could carry such heavy vessels single-handed. When working for the cook at Lincoln Castle:

> He cam to the welle, water up-draw.
> And filde ther a michel so.
> Bad he non agein him go,
> Bitwen his handes he bar it in
> Al him one[ly] to the kichin.

These vessels were potentially dangerous around the home, since children trying to scoop up a drink could easily overbalance head-first into them. A death from such an accident is recorded in the registers of York's parish church of St Michael le Belfrey.[18] Tankards and soes were the utensils of professional water-carriers such as the 'Cobs', those 'rough sturdy fellows hired to supply the houses of the rich merchants' in London, four thousand of whom formed the Company of Water Tankard Bearers by the end of the fifteenth century. Other towns had similar guilds, that in Chester being entitled 'The water-drawers and leaders of the Dee.'[19]

Within castles some of the better architects built piped water supplies into the fabric of their buildings. In the 1170s Maurice the Engineer arranged the well-chamber on the second floor of his keep at Newcastle upon Tyne. Once the buckets had been drawn up the 46 feet from water-level, they could be tipped into either of the two square sinks set in the walls to either side. From here, one lead pipe led down to an outlet in the central column of the main basement room, while the other filled a tank over the outer stairs, perhaps for kitchen use. Four years later he installed a similar system in the keep at Dover, where the well descends for at least 400 feet. As at Newcastle, the well-chamber is on the main upper floor, pipes from a recess in its eastern wall descending to another recess in a small chamber 20 feet below, and to a niche near the bottom of the south turret stairs. Such systems must have saved an anormous amount of time and energy, since carrying buckets of water up and down spiral staircases is extremely hazardous.[20]

At Caernarfon, Master James of St George's ground-floor well-room in the Well Tower still has a stone cistern, originally lead-lined, mounted on a tall plinth in one corner. This also has two outlets, one lead pipe-run going to a cistern in the proposed kitchen, and another passing behind the boiler furnaces, probably to serve further cisterns in the boiling house and the lower ward. There were probably similar systems in many other castles. At Warkworth, for example, the outer bailey kitchen has a paved wet area against its western wall. Here shallow wall-sockets suggest the presence of a cistern which, perhaps fed from the well-house, may have filled a nearby stone cistern sunk into the ground, its base being deeply worn by the countless buckets which have scooped up its water for kitchen use.

CHAPTER FIVE

The Dairy

The milk of cows, sheep and goats made an important contribution to the medieval diet, its processing into cream, butter and cheese taking place both in small peasant houses and in large manorial dairies. Their methods were virtually identical, only the scale varying to meet particular requirements. Both were subject to seasonal factors, for cows and sheep produced less milk, and that of a poorer quality, over the winter months. In spring, after the young had been born and a fresh crop of grass had sprung up, plentiful supplies of rich milk had to be converted into supplies of 'white meats' to serve the household through to the following year. No sheep was to be milked or suckled after Lady Day (8 September), nor any cow after Michaelmas (29 September), for this would weaken the animals, making it difficult for them to survive the winter.

Dairy work was essentially a female activity, as demonstrated by its name, *deie* being a female servant, and *-erie* the place where she worked. A late thirteenth-century text describes how, in a manorial dairy, she was solely responsible for its efficient management, controlling its staff, equipment, production and security, carefully recording how much and when butter and cheese was made, in addition to keeping hens and geese, and also helping with the winnowing and keeping the fire going over the winter months.[1] She must have developed a close relationship with all her cows, for each was known by its personal name. At milking time the fields would ring to the calls to 'Motherlyke', 'Galyan', 'Nutte', 'Cherry', 'New Yere', 'Lovely', 'Yoill', 'Lightfote', and even 'Goldelockes'.[2]

Although not mentioned in medieval texts, one essential tool was a cow-tie, a toggled loop of soft rope which hobbled the back legs, preventing the animal from kicking or running off. Then came a low three-legged milking stool and a skeel or kit, a coopered tub of around one-gallon capacity, with one stave projecting high above its rim. In addition to serving as a handle, this rested against the front of the stool, so that the milkmaid could hold the whole vessel firmly between her feet or shins while milking.

On returning to the dairy, it was first necessary to strain the milk to remove all traces of hair, bovine dandruff, grit and vegetable matter. This was carried out using a sile. Probably made in the same manner as its post-medieval successors, this would be a turned wooden bowl with a large hole pierced through its base. When turned rim-down, a piece of hair-cloth canvas or woollen cloth was tied across its foot-ring, so that when turned rim-up once more, the milk could be filtered into broad, shallow earthenware settling-pans.[3] Having been left overnight ('single cream') or for two nights ('double cream'), the cream rose to the surface, from where it could be either blown off or skimmed using a shallow saucer-shaped wooden fleeting-dish. If required for kitchen use, it was carried away in pots or tubs, but if for butter making, it was poured directly into a churn.

Various types of swinging churn may have continued in use in some parts of the country, but the early medieval period saw the widespread introduction of the plunge churn, a tall, narrow coopered vessel in which the milk was agitated by a piston-like wooden dasher or plunger.[4] After some time, depending on the temperature and the quality of the cream, small globules of butter began to separate from the buttermilk, this process continuing until the soft, wet mass could be lifted out. In this condition, the presence of so much buttermilk would cause it to rapidly turn sour, and so it had to be washed with clean water and then beaten to remove every trace of liquid. Traditionally this was done by 'clashing' it in a large wooden bowl held in the curve of the left arm, a few pounds at a time being repeatedly beaten until only pure butter remained.

In the West Country a completely different method of butter-making was used until the mid-twentieth century. The whole milk was poured into the milk pans and left overnight for the cream to rise as usual, but then the pans were set on embers until a head came to the top of the milk, with a ring rising in the centre, after which they were returned to the dairy for their second night. This produced a thick, semi-solid scald or clotted cream, delicious if mixed with an equal quantity of raw cream.[5]

To convert the clotted cream into butter, it was poured into a freshly scalded and rinsed shallow wooden tub and agitated by the flat hand of the dairymaid, which had similarly been washed in very hot water, and then in cold. After anything from half an hour to three hours, the butter came, and was washed with three or four waters before being beaten dry. This process gives a rather harder butter, with a superior flavour.[6]

Whether made from raw cream or clotted cream, salt was then beaten into the butter, to preserve it and to give it more taste. Accounts such as those of 1275/6 for the manor of Sevenhampton, Wiltshire: 'Two pots for putting butter in 2d.'; or Combe manor, Hampshire in 1307/8: 'one clay pot bought for butter 3d.', confirm that the salt butter was finally packed as tightly as possible into pottery jars for safe storage until required over the winter months.[7]

'Cheese is made of mylke; yet there is 4 sortes of chese, whiche is to say grene chese, softe chese, harde chese, and spermyse. Grene chese is not called grene by the reason of colour, but for newnes of it, for the whey is not halfe pressed out of it... Spermyse a chese the which is made with curdes and with the juice of herbes... Yet besyde these 4 natures of chese, there is a chese called rewene chese, the whyche yf it be well orderyd, doth passe all other cheses.'[8] This description, written in 1542 by Andrew Boorde, is probably the best available indicator of the cheeses made in England during the medieval period. Hard cheese appears to have been made with skim-milk, its low fat content giving it good keeping qualities, but resulting in considerable toughness. One dialect term for it was 'whangby', meaning as tough as leather bootlaces.[9] This was one of the main cheeses eaten by the poor. Soft cheese was made from either whole or semi-skimmed milk, closely resembling the Cheddar, Cheshire, or other regional varieties of cheese still made today. These are firm and rather waxy in texture, but distinctly soft in comparison to the former skim-milk hard cheeses. Green cheese was exactly what Boorde describes, a fresh cheese, most probably of whole or semi-skimmed milk, pressed enough to hold its shape, but still quite moist. Perhaps the best modern equivalent are the farmhouse creamy Lancashire or Caerphilly, ripe within a couple of weeks. The rowan, or eddish cheese took its name from the crop of grass which sprang up in

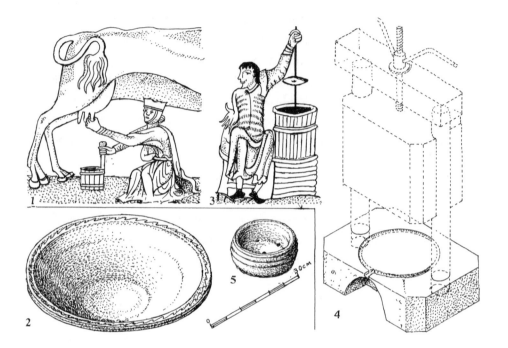

Figure 13. Dairy utensils in manuscript illustrations.

1. A skeel for milking.

2. A shallow pan in which milk was left for the cream to rise, from Norwich, mid-15–early 16c.

3. A churn for converting cream into butter, c.1150.

4. Cheese press at Blanchland, pre-16c.

5. A curd mould from Upper Heaton, West Yorks., late 13–early 14c.

the autumn meadows after their summer mowing. The milk it produced gave a curd which retained much of its moisture, and presumably a characteristic texture and flavour. Spermyse cheese was another soft cheese, its flavour and probably its colour varying considerably from one producer to another according to their personal selection of herbs and herb-juices. The only variety to survive through to the present day is traditional Sage Derby, with its bands of rich green-coloured sage cheese.

Probate inventories list the equipment used for cheesemaking. In 1485, Margaret Pigott's milkhouse at Ripon had a small kettle, a cheese press with six cheese vats, 26 stones of cheese and a scale with weights.[10] Once skimmed or strained, the milk was brought up to blood heat in the kettle, after which rennet was stirred in to convert it into a soft curded mass. Alternatively known as earning, cheese-lip, keslop, renning, rendles or runnet, this was a piece of salted and dried stomach of some suckling animal, usually a calf, dissolved in water, so that its enzymes would coagulate the milk. The juice of lady's bedstraw, *Galium verum*, worked in the same way, its dialect name being cheese-rennet.[11] Having been coarsely broken up and probably partly drained in a sieve, the curds were mixed with a little salt, and herb-juice in the case of spermyse, and transferred into a muslin-lined coopered tub called a cheese-vat. Once a piston-like sinker had been placed on top, this was put into a cheese press so that the whey would be expelled through small holes bored in the sides, resulting in a firm, hard or 'soft' cheese. Medieval cheese presses are extremely rare. Some may have been simple lever devices, like verjuice presses, but others would have relied on large stone weights. One bollard in the centre of the village of Blanchland in Northumberland is actually the base of an early cheese press, probably from the milkhouse of Blanchland Abbey. It has two round sockets to support an upper cross-bar, a circular groove to catch the whey, and a spout to carry it into a vessel placed in an arched recess below. After pressing, the cheeses were wrapped in cheese-cloth, and stood on cheese-boards mounted on a frame or rack called a flake or heck. Robert Crakhall's storeroom at York had a cheese 'fleck' and two shelves in 1395, and William Garton a cheese heck in his chamber in 1430.[12] Here they were regularly turned top-to-bottom to keep them in good condition until ready for use.

This scale of equipment was too expensive for most peasants, but small-scale production could be easily arranged by using milk warm from the cow or re-heated in a cooking pot, and pottery cheese-vats. From at least the tenth century to the fourteenth century or later a number of English potteries made vertical-sided dishes some 6 inches in diameter by 2 inches high, their centre and bases pierced with drainage holes. Once lined with muslin or cheesecloth, they were ideal for making either small cheeses or junkets.[13]

Instead of being pressed, the curds or 'cruds' could also be eaten fresh. Some were made by adding rennet to warm milk resulting in what we now call cottage cheese, while others were made by heating whey with either whole milk or buttermilk, the remaining thin, sharp-flavoured 'whig' making a refreshing drink. The curds could be used to make cheesecakes and various other dishes, eaten fresh with honey, cream, ale, wine or whey, or prepared as:[14]

VYAUNDE LECHE

2pt/1.2l full-cream milk	2tbs/30ml honey
1pt/600ml light ale	1lb/450g cottage cheese
a little red food colour	small pinch of salt

Mix the milk and food colour, heat to 40°C/100°F, pour in the ale, remove from the heat, and leave for 15 minutes.

Pour the curds and whey into a square of fine muslin, hang up, and leave to drain for 20 minutes.

Mix the cottage cheese, drained curds and honey together, with salt, if necessary, to taste, and pack into a small muslin-lined cylindrical vessel with holes pierced through its base and sides.

Leave to drain overnight, then turn out, unwrap, and serve in slices.

Another version was called junket, its name coming from the Latin *juncus* or rushes (especially the soft rush *Juncus communis*) on which its curd was drained. Since most modern milk has been pasteurized, and junket rennet is rarely available, the following recipe uses lemon juice to form the curd.[15]

CHINCHE (JUNKET)

bundle of field rushes
2pt/1·2l full-cream milk

6tbs/90ml lemon juice
ground ginger, sugar

Rinse the rushes, cut into 9-inch lengths, arrange half across the bottom of a dish, and the other half at right-angles on top.

Heat the milk to 40°C/100°F, remove from heat, stir, and continue stirring while slowly dribbling in the lemon juice, then leave to stand for 20 minutes.

Slowly pour the curds and whey over the rushes, without disturbing them, and leave to drain for 1 hour.

Pour off the whey, cover the dish with a serving dish, quickly turn over, remove the original dish and rushes, remove the surplus whey with a clean cloth, and sprinkle with ginger and sugar.

CHAPTER SIX

The Brewhouse

From at least the thirteenth century through to the late Victorian period, the brewing of ale and the baking of bread were virtually inseparable activities in major households, usually being carried out either in the same or adjacent rooms. The reasons for this were entirely practical. Both offices required ready access to grain, water and fuel, both required an ambient warmth to enable their yeasts to become active, and both were required to work outside the fixed routines of the rest of the household. In addition, they were unique in providing major every-day basic foods and drinks, a number of which only lasted for about a week, and so had to be in continuous production. Some

Figure 14, opposite. Bakehouses and brewhouses.

Top and 5. The bakehouse and brewhouse, Bolton Castle, Yorks., c.1379. From the first-floor malthouse, malt was passed on to the malt-kiln floor (right) for drying, ground by an adjacent horse-mill, and stirred into the mash-vat (far left), filled with water from the brewing copper. Flour was made into bread-loaves in the bakehouse (centre) and placed in the oven (dotted, front left) using peels.

1. Village bakehouse, Hangleton, Sussex, early 14c.

2. Bakehouse, White Castle, Gwent, 1350–70.

3. Bakehouse, Conwy Castle, Gwynedd, 1283–7.

4. Bakehouse and malthouse, White Castle, late medieval.

5. Brewhouse, bakehouse, malt kiln and horse-mill, Bolton Castle c.1379.

6. Bakehouse and brewhouse, Newton St Loe Castle, Somerset, 14–15c.

7. Bakehouse, Pontefract Castle, Yorks., 15c.

8. Bakehouse, Durham Castle, 1490s.

F - Furnace; K - Malt kiln; ML - Horse-mill; O - Oven.

establishments confirmed this close relationship by employing one person to act jointly as brewer and baker, someone who really understood the mysteries of fermentation, including the use of ale yeasts to raise bread and other baked goods. This was a great responsibility, for not only was he in charge of quantities of expensive materials and products which everyone wanted, but the domestic harmony of the entire enterprise depended heavily on his practical ability to produce good ale and bread.

When determining the site for a brewhouse and bakehouse, it was advisable to set them downwind of the residential areas so that their smoke and malty smells would cause minimal annoyance. Where there was a large service court, it provided an ideal location for these offices, but some more defensive structures found it convenient to have them placed in their basement rooms so that they could continue in use throughout sieges and other moments of constraint. Here the ground provided a firm foundation for building heavy masonry boiler furnaces and ovens, for moving large quantities of grain and water, and holding fully-laden vats and barrels. The thick walls and vaulted ceilings at this level also had a considerable insulating effect, important for preventing fermentations being spoiled by either excessive heat or cold. In contrast, the wives and maids responsible for all the brewing and baking in most small houses and cottages had to utilize the general working area around their hearths as best they could.

The first decision the brewer had to make was which type of malt to use. Today barley is virtually the only grain malted for brewing, but medieval ales were often made with blends of malt. Dame Alice de Bryene's ales comprised half wheat malt and half drage or dredge, a mixture of oats and barley which had been grown together, pure barley malt only being used in January and February.[1] A similar sequence was followed by Bishop Swinfield of Hereford, who used wheat malt and barley malts before Christmas and wheat and oat malts the following March.[2]

The manner in which grain was converted into malt was described in verse by Walter de Bibbesworth in the thirteenth century. Having risen early, you were to:[3]

In steep your barley in a vat, ['cuwe' or 'kive']
Large and broad, take care of that,
When you have steeped your grain,
And the water let out-drain,
Take it to an upper floor
If you've swept it clean before.
There couch, and let your barley dwell
Till it germinates full well.
Malt you now shall call the grain,
Corn it ne'er shall be again.
Stir the malt then with your hand
In heaps or rows now let it stand,
On a tray then you shall take it
To a kiln to dry and bake it,
The tray and eke a basket light
Will serve to spread the malt alright.
When your malt is ground in mill
And of hot water has drank its fill,
And skill has changed the malt to ale
Then to see you shall not fail.

Further details can be obtained by combining contemporary archival and archaeological evidence with practical manuals which record traditional methods of malting. First the grain was brought from the granary, measured, and tipped into a steep-vat, a vessel which could be made of lead, coopered in wood, or carved from stone.[4] The most complete archaeological examples are on monastic sites, which frequently retain the stone-built cases for their cylindrical vats, or even rectangular vats carved out of great stone blocks as at Kirkstall Abbey. Lay examples are much less common, but one built of mortared stone blocks and measuring some 5 feet square by just over 3 feet deep has been excavated at Montgomery Castle.[5] Once the grain had been covered, with some 6 inches of clear water above it, a quantity of light grains and other dross rose to the surface, and was skimmed off.[6] Over the next two days in summer, or three days in winter, the grain expanded by a fifth of its volume, and increased its weight by a half, so that each corn shed its flour when pressed between finger and thumb, rather than the milky fluid which indicated over-soaking. When this stage had been reached, the water was run off, and the grain left to drain for some 6 hours.

Having been scooped out of the steep-vat on to a stone floor, the grain was arranged in square or round heaps some 12 to 16 inches deep and left for a day. This caused it to sweat a little, rise in temperature by some 5°C, and send out three small 'fibrils' as germination commenced. Towards the end of the second day, the main shoot or aerospire began to develop, while from the end of the fourth day, as the temperature rose to some 16°C above the ambient, the heaps had to be turned and spread several times each day, the layer being gradually expanded until only 3 or 4 inches in depth. Two weeks after steeping, germination had completely converted the grain's starches into soluble sugars, and prepared them for sending out their main shoots. Now the layer was spread out even thinner and left for 6 hours to shoot, further turning and spreading encouraging this process should it proceed too slowly. After a further 6 hours all the healthy grains had sprouted, but still more thinning and turning was required until the root began to shrivel about the second or third week after steeping. The reason for this constant turning and thinning was to ensure that each grain retained the same degree of heat and moisture throughout the malting process, so that all would shoot simultaneously. Without it, some would have remained unripe while others would have developed into small plants, completely ruining the quality of the malt.

In order to stop the malt from growing any further, and to dry it for long-term storage, it had now to be heated in a malt kiln. This structure had a stoking area and combustion chamber at its base, a permeable grid or floor to support the malt, usually an accessible platform from which the maltster could turn the malt, and finally a roof which would keep out the elements, but still allow the fumes from the fire and the moisture from the malt to rapidly escape.

The simplest malt kilns, those most commonly found during excavations on medieval sites, were simply stoke-pits and circular combustion chambers dug into the surface of the ground, and perhaps lined with dry stone walls. Due to the impermanence of their wattle and daub or earthen superstructures, they rarely, if ever, survive above ground level, but ethnological evidence suggests cylindrical chambers with beams laid across the top, then a layer of laths or small sticks and finally three or four inches of straws lying parallel to each other to support the grain. A beehive-shaped thatched roof above kept out the rain, only a hole at the top being left for the escape of the steam. Such kilns were still in widespread use in late eighteenth-century Scotland, fuelled by peat or wood to dry corn as it was occasionally turned on its bed of straw.[7]

The main problem of this type of kiln was the fire risk, for if the fire was not carefully controlled, the straw and laths could easily burst into flame, damaging the kiln structure and ruining the grain. A more effective but more expensive technique was to build the kiln of stone and mortar, with a cloth of woven horse-hair replacing the bed of straw. William Plovell of York had one of these 'hairs for the kiln' in his domestic brewhouse in 1422. Many of these kilns were rectangular in plan, presumably reflecting the rectangular shape of the hair-cloth, a manorial example excavated at Appleton-le-Moors, North Yorkshire, operating c. 1200–1400.[8] From the stoking area a short, arched combustion passage led into the base of the kiln, so that the low fire could be more easily controlled, and its mix of cold draughts and hot fumes given the opportunity to mellow together before reaching the kiln-hair. In some kilns this passage terminated at the bottom of an inverted pyramidal flue, which dispersed the heat beneath the malting chamber, but others led directly into the side or corner of the kiln base. A separate doorway gave access to the malting chamber, and to a walk-way level with the kiln hair, supported on its wooden joists and laths some 2 or 3 feet above the fire. In most kilns, the superstructure has been destroyed, but those built at Caerphilly Castle c. 1277–90 and at Bolton Castle c. 1378 remain substantially intact, the former still standing some 40 feet high, up to its combined window and ventilation duct.

One of the greatest concentrations of urban malt kilns was in Nottingham.[9] Here, from the mid-thirteenth century, the soft nature of the underlying sandstone permitted maltings to be carved out as caves. Having cut a descending staircase or ramp, various rooms were created, including a porch, featuring a well for water, a rectangular steeping-vat for the grain, and areas presumably used to store dry fuel. Here bracken

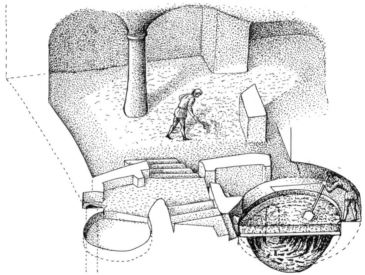

Figure 15. Malting.

Top: malting floor, malt kiln, and a boiling copper fired from a separate woodstore/stokehole, all beneath the kitchen of Laugharne Castle, Dyfed, late 13–early 14 c.

Bottom: underground maltings, with a well and steep-vat (bottom left), malting floor (top), and malt kiln (bottom right) at 8, Castle Gate, Nottingham, 13–14c?

was used to heat the kilns, its ashes presumably being sold off to soap-boilers and laundresses to make their strong alkaline lyes. The adjoining malting floors were large rectangular rooms, their roofs being carved in the form of vaults springing from central columns. In contrast the kilns were circular in plan, some 10 feet in diameter by 10–13 feet high, with a 2-foot wide firemouth at the base, a joisted floor for the hair-cloth some 2–4 feet above, and an access door, set at right-angles to the firemouth, just beneath the domed roof. It is interesting to note that the malting floors are four or five times the area of the kiln floors, this proportion helping us to identify malting floors in other medieval buildings. The great advantages of Nottingham's underground maltings were that they were completely fireproof, and could not endanger the town's numerous timber buildings, and that their temperature remained constant throughout the year. This meant that malting was a twelve-month activity here, instead of being seasonal as it was elsewhere. As a result, Nottingham's malt was carried by packhorse into the surrounding counties, loads of Cheshire salt and other goods being brought back on the return journeys.

In use, the new malt was spread 3–6 inches deep across the kiln hair with a basket or tray and a low fire of oven-dried oak, willow, ash or perhaps straw or bracken lit in the fireplace to maintain a temperature of 32–37°C.[10] Working from his walk-way, the maltster constantly turned the malt until most of the moisture had been driven off, then turning it every three or four hours until nearly dry, the temperature now being raised to some 62–66°C, depending on the colour required. It is probable that the pale to yellow stages were those required, Harrison advising that the malt was sufficiently kilned when it had acquired a yellow hue, and was hard enough to write with like a piece of chalk. After one or perhaps two days, when the kilning was complete, the fire was allowed to die, and the malt left to cool down. On removal from the kiln, a coarse sieve was used to separate the brittle roots and so forth which had broken off during the kilning. Now the malt was ready for either immediate use, or for storage in the malt-house, where bushel measures were kept to measure it in and out.

Before the malt could be used for brewing it had to be ground into a floury grist, many major establishments completing this process in-house, rather than carrying their malt to the local public mill. Where there was

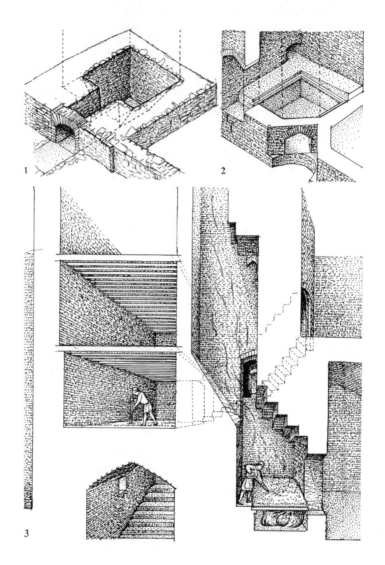

Figure 16. Malt kilns.

1. Montgomery Castle, Powys.

2 and 3. Grain barged across the moat was winched up into the malthouse (left, 1st floor), malted, carried up an internal staircase, and poured into the malt kiln (right) for drying, and delivery into the adjacent brewhouse, Caerphilly Castle, 1277–90.

a good flow and fall of water, substantial water mills were installed, as on the great dam at Castle Rushen on the Isle of Man and Caerphilly Castle. If there was no water, horse-mills provided an effective alternative, the brewhouse/bakehouse at Bolton Castle in Yorkshire retaining its circular cobbled horse-walk, while the stone from Pontefract's horse-mill still lies on its bakehouse floor. Sir John Fastolf's Caistor Castle horse-mill is listed in his 1448 inventory, while that in Robert Schylbotyll's Scarborough millhouse and brewhouse was valued at £2 in 1409.

There is little useful evidence to suggest how these medieval horse-mills were constructed, there being few archival sources, and architecturally nothing more than a few wall-sockets and the like in those few rooms known to have contained them. It is easy to imagine a pair of millstones set in the centre of a circular horse-walk, the power being transferred by means of a radial beam, but this would not work, for mills cannot operate at only two or three revolutions per minute. Illustrations of early post-medieval examples show the horses harnessed to arms which turned a central vertical shaft, at the top of which was mounted a large horizontal gear-wheel. This, meshing with a small spindle wheel on a vertical shaft, rotated the upper millstone at the correct speed for milling. Measurements of nineteenth-century horse-wheels show that the ideal diameter for a farm horse to work was about 24–26 feet, only slightly longer than that originally erected in the mill-house at Bolton Castle.

In the 1295 accounts for Dunstable Abbey, it is recorded that Brother John the Carpenter had designed a new type of horse-mill, promising that only one horse would be required to turn it. Once he had built it, it was discovered that even four strong horses could scarcely move it and so it was dismantled, and the old one re-installed. This provides useful confirmation that a horse-mill at this period was expected to work with two horses, each at the end of an opposing arm. The strains on these arms must have been considerable, especially when overcoming the inertia while proceeding from stationary to working speed. When those at the horse-mill at West Derby, Liverpool, broke in 1443, the carpenter charged 4s. for their replacement.[11]

Medieval household accounts frequently provide details of the staff and services required to operate these mills. At Wressle and Leconfield castles, for example, there was 'A Groom Mylner, Who attends hourly in the Mylne for Grynding of Corn for Backing and Brewing for my Lord's house.'[12] He may have periodically dressed or sharpened the stones himself or, since this was always a specialist craft, have employed a professional millwright. In 1419 one Hadley earned 4d. for sharpening and setting a pair of millstones in the bakehouse at Acton Hall, Suffolk.[13]

Lesser properties which could not afford such large mills had to rely on hand-turned mills. Presumably the larger of these had their stones mounted on tall rectangular frames enclosing wooden lantern-wheel gearing just like their post-medieval successors. The simplest handmills were called querns, small millstones turned by a handle or quernstaff thrust into a hole near the perimeter of their upper stones. Valued at anything between 1s. and 10s. the pair, the most basic were enclosed in wooden cases which caught the flour as it emerged from between the stones.[14] Others, traditionally called pot-querns, had the centres of their bottom stones recessed to enclose the base of the top stones so that they could contain the flour and discharge it from a single spout into a separate container.

Although the use of a quern or mill was an absolute necessity for every home, these implements were usually banned by the local manorial administration. By its right of soke, tenants were obliged to have all their corn ground at the manorial mill, this monopoly ensuring a large income for the lord. Anyone discovered using an unauthorized quern or mill would have it confiscated or destroyed and be punitively fined in the manorial courts. In some areas these restrictions remained in place up to remarkably recent times, those in Wakefield only being terminated in 1853.[15]

Whether the malt had been home-produced or bought from the local market, home-ground or ground at the manorial mill, it was now ready for brewing into ale. Except in the smallest town houses, and some great households which found it more convenient to buy in their ale, brewing was a regular year-round domestic chore since, although it would keep for weeks or months, the drink was in constant demand. Basic brewing was quite simple. First the water was boiled to sterilize it, then allowed to cool for a short while before mixing with the malt. The resulting mash was left for a few hours to allow its sugars to dissolve into the water to produce a sweet liquid called grout, which was then strained off, the remaining

Figure 17. Domestic milling for flour and malt.

1. A pot-quern, 14c.

2. and 3. Hand-mills, 14c.

4. Water mill, the wheel turning an internal pit-wheel which meshes with a stone-nut, which turns the millstones housed in the wooden hurst-frame above, the corn being fed in through the hopper, to emerge as flour from the spout, late 12c.

5. Arrangement of a late-medieval horse-mill.

malt being mixed with a second, or even a third batch of water to produce successively weaker grouts. These were poured into wooden tubs, mixed with yeast to form gyles or worts, which were left in a warm place for a few days while fermentation converted their sugars to alcohol. Only then were they baled into storage vessels ready for drinking over the next few days, weeks or months, by which time the next brew would be ready for use.

Since brewing was such an everyday process, its methods were never recorded in medieval recipe books. However, by combining brief archival and archaeological evidence with the methods recorded from later generations of farmhouse brewers, it is possible to re-create medieval ales with a reasonable degree of accuracy. In the smallest households, the water would be boiled in the largest available cooking pot, and any rising scum carefully skimmed off.[16] It was then left to cool to around 65°C/150°F when it was poured into either a large pottery jar or a wooden tub called a mash-vat, which had a spiggot or tap fitted into a round hole just above its base. This vessel had been prepared by first laying a branch of gorse or bundle of wheat straw around the inner end of the tap, to prevent it being blocked by the malt. Alternatively a basket-like frame of twigs was used for this purpose, its dialect name being a betony or betwan. This suggests that stalks of the native herb betony (*Stachys betonica*) were originally used for this purpose, Barbour recording around 1375 that it was then used to spice drink.[17] A measured volume of malt, two-thirds that of the water, was spread on top, the hot water poured on, stirred in, and the vessel covered with insulating layers of woollen cloth for the next 2 or 3 hours. Having probably cooled to around 54°C/130°F, the spiggot tap was gently opened, permitting the grout to run out without disturbing the malt sediment, through a sieve and into a gyle-vat. These processes were then repeated with two further batches of water, to fill two further gyle-vats. Next, the liquid yeast from the previous brew was stirred in and left to ferment at 18–23°C/65–75°F for a few days, its frothy head being skimmed off into a jar ready for the next brew and for baking. Once the fermentation had subsided, each of the three strengths of ale was poured into horizontal barrels or vertical coopered 'stands' fitted with wooden spiggot-taps, and left in a cool place ready for use within the next few weeks or months. In the mid-fifteenth century some Yorkshire households owned between four and twenty ale jars costing anything from 1*d*. to 3*d*. each, these probably being used to hold smaller quantities.[18]

Officially all ale was made of nothing more than malt and water fermented with yeast, but it is probable that traditionally-used herbs were well known in the medieval period. These included ale-hoof or ground ivy (*Nepeta gelchoma*) with which, as Cotgrave noted, 'the women of our northerne parts do tunne…into their ale', for it had a reputation for helping ale to ferment, to keep longer, and to purge the head of 'rheumatic humors flowing from the brain.'[19] Alecost (*Balsamita vulgaris* or *Chrysanthemum balsamita*) was similarly used to give ale a bitter taste. In south-western counties further additives apparently included flour, milk or eggs which produced a grey-white colour and a heavy sediment. Andrew Boorde famously described it as 'starke, nought, loking whyte & thycke, as pygges had wrasteled in it.'[20] In the early twentieth century it was 'so thick that the *habitués*…have a particular knack of placing the little finger of the left hand under the cup and giving it a rolling motion from the left to the right, as they raise it to their lips in order to prevent a settlement from taking place in the glass.'[21] Unfortunately, detailed instructions for making these white ales have not survived.

In large households, brewing required a far greater investment of time, materials and equipment, and so demanded particular attention from the administrative clerks. Some establishments found it more convenient to buy in their ale, their butlers arranging to purchase it from local brewers at prices agreed with the treasurer, controller and clerk of the kitchen in the counting house.[22] Others found that they could save money by brewing for themselves, being careful where they acquired their malt and where they brewed. When the Earl of Northumberland required 496 gallons of beer for his house at Topcliffe, some 40 miles up-river from his base at Wressle, his clerks calculated the various options:[23]

To buy beer from Ripon	96*s*.
To brew at Wressle and carry to Topcliffe	47*s*. 9*d*.
To buy malt at Topcliffe and brew there	42*s*. 5*d*.
To carry Wressle malt to Topcliffe and brew there	37*s*. 5*d*.
[brewing at Wressle, presumably using grain malted there, cost only 32*s*. 5*d*.]	

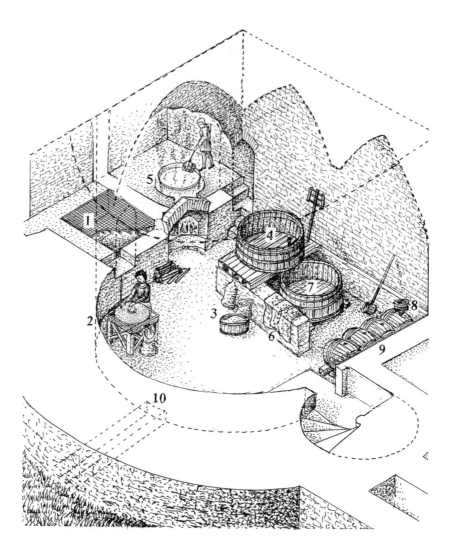

Figure 18. The brewhouse, Caerphilly Castle, c. 1277–90 reconstructed. From the malt kiln (1), the malt was ground in the hand-mill (2), and measured with bushel measures (3). The mash-vat (4), would be half-filled with boiling water from the brewing copper (5), have the malt stirred in, and then be covered with brewing blankets (6), for a time. The resulting wort would then be run off into the gyle-vat or underback (7), allowed to cool, fermented with yeast, and then poured through a tundish (8), into the barrels (9).

These figures show clearly why most major households carried out the bulk of their malting and brewing themselves.

The most important item in the brewhouse was the lead which, despite its name, was made from sheets of beaten copper, rivetted to a cylindrical form, with its base beaten to a sagging, domed shape, almost identical to those of boiling coppers used for meat in the kitchens. For maximum efficiency, these were set in either wattle and daub or masonry structures called furnaces or cases, these keeping the flames and hot fumes rising from the fireplace beneath close to the sides of the lead, ensuring the most efficient transfer of heat to its contents.

Where ale was brewed, only one lead was required. At Caerphilly Castle the furnace built c. 1277–90 was designed to receive a lead holding some 18 bushels of water, that being sufficient to mash some 12 bushels of malt, just one batch from the adjacent malt-kiln, if there had been a 5-inch layer on the kiln hair. This would have produced some three hogsheads or five barrels of first quality ale, the same of the second quality, and of the third quality too, called small ale, totalling some 430 gallons in all, perhaps sufficient to meet the weekly demands of the castle's garrison. Since the adjacent malting floor is large enough to process two batches of malt, each taking two weeks, this level of production is quite feasible.

To start brewing, the lead was filled with water, a fire of faggots lit beneath, and a wooden lid placed on top to reduce evaporation and help bring it rapidly to the boil.[24] After skimming and cooling, the water was poured into a large coopered mash-vat and stirred with a framed paddle, variously called a mash-comb, maschel, mash rother or mash roll, until all the malt had been thoroughly mixed in.[25] A brew-cloth was then placed on top to keep the mash warm until it was ready for being run off by pulling out a long plug called a tap-tree, and allowing it to pass through a sieve into the gyle-vat. As it fermented, lids made of woven willow or straw kept it clean and warm, skimmers probably made of metal or more commonly of wood being used to take off the yeast.[26] Once all the sugars had been converted to alcohol, a tap-trough of lead and a coopered funnel called a tundish were used to fill the barrels and hogsheads on their stillage frames and left in the cool to settle ready for use.

TO BREW 5 GALLONS OF ALE OF 3 STRENGTHS

1 boiling vessel of 20pt/12l capacity
1 brewing thermometer
4 tubs each of 30pt/15l capacity, with a corked hole at the base
1 sieve
1 large, thick blanket
6lb/2.7kg (12pt/7.2l) ground pale malt
6tsp/30g dried real-ale yeast

Allow some 8 hours to complete the mashing etc., and 6 days to completion.

Boil 16pt/9.5l water, allow to cool to 62–68°C/145–155°F, and pour into one of the tubs at the same time as pouring in most of the malt. Stir for 10 minutes, cover and wrap with the blanket, and leave to stand for two hours.

Gently withdraw the cork and allow a narrow stream of wort to drain out through the sieve into one of the other tubs.

When the wort stops running, re-cork the tub, and repeat the two stages above, running the wort into another tub.

Repeat this last stage, running the final wort into the final tub.

These mashings will produce some 10pt/6l strong ale wort of *c*.0.085 specific gravity; 14pt/8.4l second quality wort of *c*.0.025 sp.gr.; and 15pt/9l small ale wort of *c*.0.05 sp.gr.

Allow each wort to cool to 16°C/60°F, then stir in 2 teaspoonfuls of the dried yeast. Cover and leave in a temperature of 16°C/60°F to ferment for the next 5 days, skimming the top yeast off on the third day for further brews and breadmaking.

Remove to a cool place, allow to clear, and run off the ales without disturbing their sediment

Brewing in this manner produces firstly an excellent strong light ale of around 10% alcohol by volume, about the same strength as a good claret. It is dark straw-coloured, very smooth, with a rich light malt flavour and is perceptibly alcoholic. Its flavour, strength and quality bear a remarkable resemblance to the long-keeping strong pale ales brewed by Clarence Hellewell in Lord Halifax's Hickleton brewhouse in the 1980s, suggesting a long continuity in the country house tradition.[27] In practice, this ale is found to have a far longer life than the five days or so suggested by written sources, lasting a few months at least when barrelled in a cool cellar. The second ale is rather paler in colour, with a weaker and slightly drier flavour. With some 3% alcohol by volume it is essentially a fairly weak pale mild ale, suitable for accompanying food. The third or small ale is very pale and even weaker, having well under 1% of alcohol. It is refreshing and slightly sharp, however, with a slight malt and almost lemon-juice flavour. It would make a good thirst-quenching drink, and certainly be much safer than most unboiled water; but it does turn sour after a few days.

After clearing for three or four days, either the strong ale, or probably a mixture of the strong and middle ales too, could be transformed into braggot. This ancient celebratory drink took its name from the Old Celtic *bracata*, a kind of cereal grain. One recipe started by double-mashing the ale to make it especially strong, before boiling a quantity of it with honey, ground pepper and cloves, returning it to the remainder along with fresh yeast to ferment for a further three or four days, and finally spiking it with *aqua vitae* or brandy. The following recipe is for a simpler version.[28]

TO MAKE BRAGGOT

5 gallons/23l stale wort
5 pints/3l clear honey
2tbs/30g dried yeast
2tbs/30g ground cinnamon

2tbs/30g ground galingal
2tbs/30g ground pepper
2tbs/30g grains of paradise

Simmer the honey and spices in 2 gallons/9l of the wort for 20 minutes. Strain off the spices through a piece of fine muslin.

Mix the spiced wort with the remaining wort, allow to cool to 24°C/75°F, stir in the dried yeast. Cover and leave in a warm place for 2 weeks, during which time it will produce a particularly active fermentation, and then settle in a cool place to produce a clear amber liquid which has a clean, slightly sharp and spicy taste, and a particularly high alcoholic content.

In 1400 a consignment of beer was landed at the port of Winchelsea in Sussex, apparently to satisfy the needs of Continental traders temporarily staying in this country. Although brewed in the same basic manner as ale, beer was boiled with hops before being fermented, thus giving it much improved keeping properties and a pleasantly bitter taste, to which the English soon became very partial.[29] By 1418 beer was already being brewed in London, where, in 1424, the City and its ale-brewers protested against the new 'adulteration'. By 1436, Henry VI was commending this new drink 'called biere' as 'notable, healthy and temperate'. Its growing popularity caused it to become subject to assize in 1441.[30] Now it was to be sufficiently boiled, well hopped and not sweet before being offered for sale eight days after being brewed. From this time onwards, most households brewed both ale and beer, the latter soon becoming the main drink for all servants.

In the brewhouse, the conversion to the production of both ale and beer required the addition of a second boiling lead and furnace and new vats to hold the grout or wort between mashing and boiling with the hops. As an interim measure, some fifteenth-century households may have supplemented their existing lead with a cauldron, cooking pot or kettle, but by the 1440s second leads were already being installed to boil the wort with hops, these 'wort leads' usually being half the volume of the main lead.[31] This enabled the brewer to heat more water for the second and third mashes while the first worts were being boiled with their hops. Great care had to be taken at this stage, for the wort and hop mixture had a tendency to boil over, completely wasting the costly brew.

Compared to later recipes, which recommend 2lb 8oz of hops per 32-gallon barrel for drinking within a month, or 6lb for keeping a year, medieval ales were very lightly hopped. In the Earl of Northumberland's brewhouse, only a third of a pound of hops were used for each barrel, which can only have slightly extended its keeping qualities. From the quantities of malt and hops recorded for each of his brews, and the volume of beer they were known to produce, it has been possible to reproduce them accurately, albeit on a miniature scale.[32]

TO BREW 5 GALLONS OF THE NORTHUMBERLAND HOUSEHOLD BEER

12lb/5.4kg ground pale malt   *1tbs/15g ale yeast*
½oz/15g hops

Use the same equipment as for the ale recipe on p. 102, but with a 3 gallon/15l and a 5 gallon/25l tub. Allow 6 hours to complete the mashing and 6 days to completion.

Follow the first three stages of the ale recipe, using 28pt/16l water for each pair of mashings, then combining their worts to produce a wort of about 0·1040 specific gravity.

Bring the wort and hops up to the boil, continue boiling for 45 minutes, then tap off through a strainer back into the larger tub.

Leave to cool to 16°C/60°F, and follow the last two stages of the ale recipe.

The resulting beer is very similar to a modern pale-coloured but lightly hopped bitter, and has a similar alcoholic content. It is interesting to note that the required volume is obtained without a third mash. This suggests that a third mash of small beer was made to serve the general needs of the household, its absence from the accounts probably being due to its low value and its free availability to the servants and people of that sort.

All the strong ale, braggot and household beer prepared to the above recipes keep remarkably well, certainly for many months in casks in a cool cellar. This is far longer than suggested by most modern writers, explaining the great size of medieval cellars.

Cider pressed from apples and perry pressed from pears are recorded as beverages from the late thirteenth and early fourteenth centuries, but there is very little evidence to suggest how they were made.[33] Presumably they used methods later followed in English, particularly south-western English, farmhouses. Here, selected types of apple were picked in autumn, left to brown slightly, then crushed, sometimes using mallets in stone or wooden troughs, as shown in fourteenth-century manuscripts. The

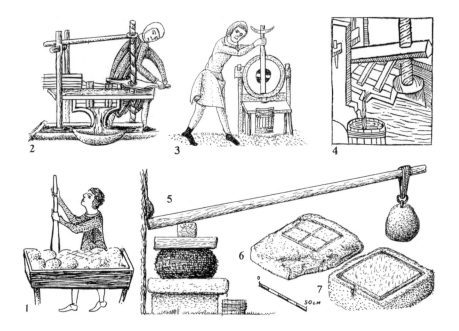

Figure 19. Cider and verjuice presses.
1. Pounding the apples, 14c.
2–4. Screw-presses of the late 13c., 14c., and 1495.
5. Reconstruction of a lever-press.
6–7. Lever-press base-stones from Ryedale and from Langley Hall,
Middleton, Manchester.

resulting pommace was prepared for pressing by being either built up in layers with straw between, as along the Welsh border, or wrapped in horse- or goat-hair mats, as in the West Country. All medieval illustrations of cider presses show the apples being squeezed between a square, spouted base, and boards pressed down by a screw-operated lever. The alternative mechanism, used probably into the nineteenth century in some rural areas, had a simple weighted lever or 'brake' mounted over a stone which had been grooved to collect the juice.[34] This type was particularly associated with the production of verjuice, the sharp-flavoured crab-apple juice which replaced the raw grape juice used on the Continent both in cookery and as a sauce.

In comparison to ale, beer and cider, mead or metheglin was consumed in relatively small quantities. Around midsummer, the bees were killed off or driven from their hives, so that the combs could be crushed and the honey wrung out into bowls. The residue was then put into a tub of water, which absorbed the honey, and left the wax ready for clarification ready for making candles or for modelling into various subtleties. The sweetened water was then fermented to produce a rather dry, honey-flavoured long drink called mead or metheglin, each hive producing around 3 gallons. This was quite different from the heavy, sweet liquor usually marketed as mead today.

Figure 20. Bakehouse ovens and bread in manuscript illustrations.

1–4. 13–14c. bread ovens, one (4) having a tile-covered dome to keep it dry.

5. Bread basket, *Dream of Pharoah* window, Great Malvern, Worcs., 1430–40.

6. Bread basket, *Acts of Corporal Mercy* window, All Saints, North Street, York, early 15c.

7–10. The farthing wheat (white?) loaf, horse loaf, wastel and halfpenny wheat loaf, *c.* 1450.

11–12. Baking on a bakestone and under a pot.

CHAPTER SEVEN

The Bakehouse

B read probably formed the most substantial part of the medieval diet, being served at every meal. Not only did it provide a high level of nutrition combined with comforting, stomach-filling bulk, but it was also essential for the mannerly use of spoons and knives at table. Its other great advantage was its year-round availability. When harvested, dried and stored indoors, bread-corn would last from one year to the next, ready to be sent to the mill as required. In large households, it was stored in a granary, its regular transfer to the bakehouse being recorded by the clerks as it was carried out in either sacks or bushel measures. The use of chests or arks for the storage of grain and meal appears to be a later practice, medieval arks being almost exclusively used for the storage of clothing, linens or books in well-furnished chambers.

In cottages and small farms where there was no separate bakehouse, the making of bread was a kitchen/living-room activity. From here, grain from home-grown crops, from gleaning after harvest, or perhaps even bought at market in times of scarcity, would be measured out, sent to the mill for grinding, and received back somewhat lighter, after the miller had extracted his percentage or multure by way of fee. Sieving to remove the coarser bran may have taken place, but wholemeals appear to have predominated. Once mixed and kneaded into dough, most peasant breads were not oven-baked, since this was relatively costly in terms of time and fuel. Instead, they were baked over the fire on flat stones or inside a cooking pot.

From prehistory through to the early twentieth century, baking on a flat stone remained a very efficient method of cookery.[1] Our earliest documentary evidence comes from place-names, *Bacestaingrave* being recorded in the North Riding *c.*1170 and *Bacstenbec* on Fountains Earth in the West Riding in 1198. These and similar names usually refer to places where flat, easily split and fireproof stones could be readily obtained, especially on exposed hilltops or on slopes where stream-cut gulleys laid bare suitable strata. The Baxtone area of a ridge just to the north of Helmsley on the North York Moors was probably the source of a substantially complete mid-twelfth-century example excavated 20 miles away in the village of Wharram Percy. Measuring some 14 inches in diameter by an inch in thickness, it had been skillfully carved to produce a slightly domed section, which enabled it to expand and contract over the heat, and a smooth top to receive the items to be baked. Wear-marks underneath show that this example had been supported over a low fire on a circular brandreth measuring some 8 inches in diameter, but bakestones could also be heated over a chafing dish or a chover. Because of their low value, bakestones rarely, if ever, appear in medieval inventories, and since they were essentially for everyday cookery, they are not mentioned in recipes. Since most archaeologists cannot differentiate between broken bakestones and roofing slates, few have been recognized during excavations. This combination of factors means that we have to look elsewhere for evidence of their use. Botanical remains from Wharram Percy show that wheat, barley, oats, peas and a little rye were grown there, the local seventeenth-century practice being to bake them as wheat and rye, barley, rye and pea, or pea and barley breads, all of which could have been baked on bakestones in the form of flat bannocks. William Howitt found Northumbrian farm labourers baking mixed barley and pea meal bannocks over their fires on iron plates in the 1830s, while in Lancashire, Derbyshire, Yorkshire and Cumbria the same were baked as 'girdle cakes', 8–10 inches in diameter by an inch in thickness.[2]

MEAL GIRDLE CAKES

1lb/450g mixed wheat and rye meal, or barley and pea meal
1tsp salt   *½pt/300ml water*

Mix the salt with the meal, make a well in the centre, mix in the water, and knead (with a little additional water if necessary) to form a stiff dough.

Roll out on a floured board to make an 8-inch/20cm disc.

Heat a bakestone or girdle until a little flour sprinkled on it slowly browns but does not smoulder, then brush it clean. Brush off the flour, slide the girdle cake on to the bakestone, bake for 10 minutes, then turn over and bake for a further 10 minutes. Every few minutes, move the cake a little to prevent it sticking to the bakestone.

Iron versions of the bakestone appear to have been used from around the thirteenth century. When excavating a cottage of this date at Beere, Devon, E.M. Jope found one lying where it had last been used on two patches of burnt clay adjacent to the paved central hearth.[3] Measuring about 7 or 8 inches in diameter, by ⅛ inch in thickness, it had probably been supported over a low fire by an iron brander in order to bake wheat flatbreads, this being the major grain crop here at this time. The 'grydel pro pane' listed in the Durham Priory accounts for 1352 was almost certainly used for the same purpose.[4]

WHEAT GIRDLE CAKES (YEAST RAISED)[5]

9oz/250g wholemeal flour	*½tsp dried yeast*
½ tsp salt	*¼pt/150ml warm water*

Sift the flour and salt together, dissolve the yeast in the water, and knead together to form a soft dough, adding a little more warm water if necessary.

Cover the dough, and leave to rise in a warm place for 2 hours.

Divide the dough into 3 pieces, and roll or pat each out into a round ¼-inch thick. Set on lightly floured boards in a warm place for a further 10 minutes.

Heat a bakestone or girdle until a sprinkling of flour slowly browns, but does not smoulder.

Slide each cake in turn on to the bakestone, and bake for 5 minutes on each side. When baked, remove from the bakestone, and prop up vertically to cool. [At this point, in our West Yorkshire village in the 1950s, almost identical flat cakes were torn open, buttered and eaten hot, being truly delicious but a sure source of heartburn.]

Bakestones were also used to make oatcakes, *Piers Plowman* mentioning both 'cakes of oats' and 'havercakes' being eaten with curds and cream in the mid-fourteenth century, 'haver' being the Norse word for oats, retained in Northern English usage through to modern times.[6] Having little gluten, oatmeal was best baked either as bannocks, or as thin, crisp oatcakes. There were many different oatcake-making traditions throughout upland Britain, but the following are probably the easiest for the unskilled to master today, while retaining methods most probably used in the medieval period.

THICK HAVERCAKE[7]

6oz/170g fine oatmeal   *4tbs/60ml water*
pinch of salt

Mix the salt and flour, mix in the water, knead to form a stiff dough, and roll out as a ¼-inch thick round. Use a thin layer of oatmeal as dusting on the worktop to guard against sticking.

Heat a bakestone as described in the recipe above.

Slide the havercake on to the bakestone, and leave to bake for 5–6 minutes until the edges begin to curl up. Turn over, using a thin board to give it support, and bake on the other side. Once cooked, it should still be very pale in colour on both sides.

Remove from the bakestone and prop in front of the fire to dry out and slightly toast.

THIN OATCAKE

3oz/85g fine oatmeal   *1tsp/5g lard or dripping*
3tbs/45ml warm water   *pinch of salt*

Melt the lard or dripping in the water and mix into the oatmeal and salt to form a dough. Knead quickly and roll or pat out on a thin layer of oatmeal to form a 10-inch diameter disc.

Follow the instructions given above for the havercake, baking each side for some 4–5 minutes.

The most basic method of baking bread in a heated, enclosed utensil, was to take a cooking pot, and turn it upside down on the bakestone or hearth. Fifteenth-century glossaries describe this technique as '*Subcinericius* – Bakyn under askys' or 'some brede is bake under ashen'.[8] Very efficient for small-scale baking, it was still being practised in rural areas in the late nineteenth century. In its simplest form, part of the fire was moved to one side, the exposed area of hearth (or a bakestone previously placed there) brushed clean, the leavened loaf set down upon it, covered with a cooking pot, and the glowing embers piled around and above to give a good all-round heat. I have used this method to produce good loaves with wood, peat, and dried cow-dung fires, their slow heat and deep ash and embers being ideal for this style of baking. In some areas, such as Caernarfonshire and the west of England, the bakestone was raised above the fire on a low iron brandreth to give a better bottom-heat for the loaf and its ember-covered pot.[9]

Another method was to support the cooking pot on a brandreth or pot-hook over the fire, and use it as an oven. Any leavened or unleavened breads could be baked in this way, but it was particularly associated with flead cakes or the crock cakes made in Dorset, Surrey and other places up to the early twentieth century. Flead is the internal fat from around the kidneys and ribs of pigs, but could also refer to the outer fat of pork.[10]

CROCK OR FLICK CAKES

8oz/225g wholemeal flour, with the coarse bran sifted out
1 pinch of salt   *¼pt/150ml milk*
4oz/120g raw pork fat

Grease the bottom of a cooking pot, and place it over a gentle heat to warm up.

Chop the fat into small pieces, ¼ inch or less, mix into the flour and salt, and then mix in just enough milk to produce a stiff dough, and form into an 8-inch diameter round cake, floured top and bottom.

Place in the bottom of the cooking pot, cover, and bake each side for 10 minutes then remove and allow to cool.

SURREY FLEAD CAKES

Make as above, but replace the pork fat with the same weight of pork scratchings (i.e. small pieces of crisp pork fat from which the lard has been rendered).

Although neither of these cakes is mentioned in medieval recipe collections, their ingredients and techniques certainly suggest medieval peasant origins.

In larger households, bread was made in greater bulk, to higher standards. As already described, the bakehouse was often either adjacent to the brewhouse, or integrated into it, being a large room capable of maintaining an internal temperature of 15–23°C/60–70°F to promote the growth of yeasts. Inventories provide informative lists of their movable contents, that of William Duffield at York in 1452 having:[11]

a tempse and a sieve	10d.	a kimnel	4d.
a bolting tun	8d.	3 water tubs	9d.
2 bolting cloths	4d.	a tine (tub)	6d.
a long [kneading] trough	1s.	a moulding board	1s. 4d.

There might also be a pot to heat the water for mixing the dough on cold mornings, and a variety of small hand-tools, too cheap to be worth valuation and listing.

Since its high gluten content enabled wheat to rise better and produce a lighter, spongier bread than other grains, it was the chosen bread-corn for those who could afford it, rye and barley reckoned decidedly inferior. Wheat did not produce just one kind of bread, however, but a number of different types, their quality and status depending on their degree of refinement.[12]

In its basic state, it was ideal for making trencher loaves, slices of which served as personal cutting-boards at most dinner and supper tables. Its first grading for making finer breads was a relatively easy process, since the coarser particles of bran readily separated from the remainder when shaken through a piece of open-weave canvas or horsehair cloth stretched across the base of a hoop made of wood or brass. This utensil was variously entitled a sieve, searce, crest, cribble or range. That which remained inside it was used to make bran- or treat-bread, while that which passed through could be baked as cheat, cribble or ranged loaves, rather similar to a modern brown bread.

The sieved, searced or ranged flour also formed the basis of the finer breads. Since shaking it through a finer seive was not an effective method, the usual alternative was to bolt or bunt it. For this, a quantity of sieved flour was loosely rolled within a piece of fine-meshed linen bolting cloth.[13] Grasping each end, the baker then vigorously jerked the flour up and down, so that only the almost dust-like particles could escape and drop into a wooden chest or tub placed below. Depending on the closeness of the weave, this produced either fine flour for making manchets, cockets, cracknels, simnels and similar good-quality breads, or the finest white flour for the superior wastel and paindemaine loaves served only at the most important of tables. Bolting flour in this way is a time-consuming and laborious process, one which gave real status to the whitest breads, and to those to whom they were served. Some impression of the perceived value of white flour may be gained from its being transported in locked sacks of good leather.[14] For general storage, however, flour was put into sacks made of twill rather than plain cloth, in order to contain its fine particles. Dame Alice de Bryene's appear to have been some 6 by 3 feet, large enough to hold four bushels of flour in her bakehouse.[15]

For mixing the dough, the wooden or pottery bowls probably used by the lowliest cottagers would have been far too small. Instead, coopered tubs called kimlins, and wooden kneading- or dough-troughs were employed. Some of these must have been quite large, since the miller in Chaucer's tale expected to survive a flood by using 'A knedying trogh or ellis a kymelyn' as his boat.[16] Kneading-troughs were found everywhere, from prosperous peasant cottages to major bakehouses, as were kimlins, utensils called dough-ribs enabling the trough to be scraped clean after use.[17]

Next came the weighing or measuring of the flour. A number of household accounts record that loaves were made at the rate of between 20 and 35 to the bushel of flour.[18] Given that flour weighs 56lb per bushel this suggests that each required some 2.8 to 1.6lb of flour. In the early fifteenth century, Dame Alice de Bryene of Acton Hall, Suffolk, had her baker produce 230 white loaves and 36 black loaves from each quarter (8 bushels) of wheat every five days. This suggests that the flour content of each white loaf may have weighed 1.5lb (about 2lb when baked), and of the black loaves 3lb (over 4lb when baked), assuming that the coarser weighed twice as much as the finer. The Northumberlands' household bakery certainly made this allowance. In the 1460s, Edward IV's sergeant of the bakehouse had to produce 27 loaves from each bushel of meal, half of them being cheat, and half of them round, each to weigh 1lb 9oz (i.e. just over 1lb of flour before mixing with water and baking) 'whyche breade shalle honestly enough serve this honourable household'.[19] As these examples show, the surviving evidence makes it very difficult to establish the sizes and qualities of the breads baked in individual households, since they were not subject to national regulations. Our first real evidence for the size of the manchet appears in *The Good Huswife's Handmaide for the Kitchen* of 1594, which states that each should weigh 1lb. This is far larger than the small dinner-bun size of manchets currently specified by some historians and used by re-enactors and in historic food displays. Given the above evidence, and allowing for the weight of water used to mix the dough, it may be reasonable to bake manchets at 1lb or 2lb, and coarser cheat loaves at 4lb out of the oven. Practical confirmation for this comes from experience when wrapping manchets in their ceremonial portpains or fine linen covers for service at table. Their recorded dimensions of 7 feet 6 inches by some 2 feet 3 inches, even when folded end to end, require eight substantial loaves to fill them out.[20]

Unfortunately, bread-making was such an everyday task that its recipes and techniques were hardly ever written down, but it is possible to combine descriptions of medieval breads with early post-medieval recipes to trace the most probable methods used in the fifteenth century, and perhaps even earlier. For trencher and coarse cheat breads, sourdough leavens were used. These were made by putting the meal into a dough trough which still had soured dough from previous batches adhering to it, making a well in the centre, and working in hot water and salt, before leaving it overnight to ferment. Next morning more flour was kneaded in to make a stiff dough, ready to be baked at a high temperature.

For the best cheat bread, using sieved flour, a piece of sour bread dough from a previous batch was beaten into small pieces in warm water, thoroughly mixed and poured through a sieve to leave a liquid leaven. This was then poured into a well in the flour in its trough or kimnel, and the hand used to mix in sufficient flour from the sides to form a smooth batter. Having been covered with a layer of dry flour, it was left to ferment overnight, a little warm water, yeast and salt added, and then kneaded to make a stiff dough. In order to make it smooth and elastic, it could be kneaded by hand where it lay, but it was easier to fold it in a cloth and knead it under-foot, or to work it on a brake. This device was a strong, low bench, above one side of which was hinged a long wooden lever. With the dough on the bench, the baker placed the lever across one end, and squashed it down, sitting on the lever to take full advantage of his body weight, repeatedly raising the lever until all the dough had been kneaded. Only then was it moulded into loaves, allowed to rise, and baked at 'an indifferent good heat'.[21]

Baking a 4lb cheat loaf purely by the sourdough method is a decidedly uncertain process for all but the most experienced. The following recipe therefore introduces modern dried yeast to help produce a more reliable fermentation.

A CHEAT LOAF

3lb/1.4kg strong, wholemeal flour, from which the coarse bran has been sieved out

1½pt/900ml water at 24°C/75°F   *2tsp/8g sugar*
4tsp/20g salt   *4½tsp/23g dried yeast*

Put the flour into a large bowl, make a well in the centre, pour in 1pt/600ml water, stir to form a batter, cover with some of the flour and leave in a warm place overnight.

Mix the yeast and sugar with the remaining half-pint of warm water, leave for 15 minutes until frothy, then stir into the batter in the flour.

Sprinkle on the salt, and knead all together to form a dough, then continue kneading for 10 minutes.

Form into a large ball, place on a large baking sheet, cover with a light cloth, and leave at 21°C/70°F until almost doubled in size.

Bake at 200°C/400°F/gas mark 6 for about 45 minutes. Remove and leave to cool.

Since the sourness produced by these methods was unsuitable for the finest white manchets and paindemain, they were replaced by a leaven of the frothy yeast carefully skimmed off the top of ale around the second day of its fermentation. This could be kept sweet and fresh for a week or more by being sealed in a jar, and buried in the ground, as practised in rural areas during the nineteenth century.[22] When required, a volume of it equal to one twentieth of the white flour was mixed with salt and warm water, mixed to a batter in the flour in the dough trough, and then processed just like the cheat dough. Having been left to rise, it was moulded into round, flat cakes, their edges cut all the way round, and their centres pricked through. This ensured that they rose vertically producing a lighter crumb, and occupying far less space in the oven. As fresh ale yeast is not readily available today, the following recipe is designed to use modern dried yeasts in an historical manner.

MANCHETS

1½lb/675g plain white flour
1tsp/5g salt
1tsp/5g dried yeast
1tsp/5g sugar
¾pt/450ml water at 24°C/75°F

Sift the flour and salt into a bowl, and make a well in the centre.

Beat the yeast and sugar into the water, pour into the flour, then stir in, and knead for 10 minutes to produce a soft dough.

Return the dough to the bowl, cover with a light cloth, and leave at 21°C/70°F for 1 to 1½ hours, until doubled in size.

Knead the dough for 2–3 minutes on a floured board, then divide into two or three pieces, form these into balls, and place them on a baking sheet, allowing room for expansion.

Make a cut all around the sides of each ball, and form a dimple down through the middle. Cover with a light cloth and return to the warm for a further 30–60 minutes until risen.

Bake in an oven pre-heated to 230°C/450°F/gas mark 8 for 20 minutes.

One of the few medieval English bread recipes comes from a manuscript of around 1420. Entitled rastons, it is for an egg-enriched white loaf which, when baked, has a hole cut into the top, the crumb scooped out, mixed with butter and replaced inside. Served hot, with its lid replaced, it would look like a normal loaf, but its succulent filling could then be spooned out. It is the direct ancestor of the buttered and filled loaves of the seventeenth century.[23]

RASTONS

2 whites and 1 yolk of egg	*1½lb/550g plain white flour*
1tbs/15g sugar	*½pt/300ml water at 75°F*
1tsp/5g salt	*1lb/450g clarified butter*
½oz/14g dried yeast	

Lightly beat the eggs, sugar, salt and yeast to form a smooth liquid, then mix in the water.

Sift the flour into a bowl, make a well in the centre, pour in the eggs etc. Stir continuously to draw flour in from the sides, until it forms a soft dough, then knead in the rest of the flour.

Knead the dough for 10 minutes, replace in the bowl, cover with a light cloth, and leave in a warm place for about an hour to rise.

Knead the dough again, divide into two, mould into two round loaves, place on a baking sheet, cover with a light cloth, and return to the warm for a further 20 minutes until risen once more.

Bake at 230°C/450°F/gas mark 8 for some 30 minutes, then remove from the oven and allow to cool beneath a thick cloth.

Using a sharp, pointed knife, cut around the top of each loaf in a bold zig-zag, pull the tops from the bottoms, and tear the crumb out of the bottom crusts in small pieces.

Melt the butter in a saucepan, mix with the crumbs, pack into the bottoms of the loaves, replace the tops, and re-heat at 180°C/350°F/gas mark 4 for about 5 minutes. Serve hot.

In major houses and castles, such loaves were baked in stone or brick-built ovens, their domed interiors being anything up to around 14 feet in diameter by perhaps 3 feet in height. Some were independent freestanding structures protected by some form of roof, some were built inside their bakehouses, and others embedded within the massive thickness of major walls. Since the bakers had to be able to look across the whole area of the oven when managing the internal fires and placing and drawing their loaves, the oven floors were usually 2 or 3 feet above that of the bakehouse. Most of those 'ovens' found with floors at ground level and stoke-pits before their doors are actually boiler furnaces, mis-identified by archaeologists. Where the surviving remains of excavated ovens are only a few inches high, they are sometimes recognizable by having their bases packed with rubble which supported their raised floors, or by rectangular pits into which embers were discharged after being raked out of the oven.

Where a masonry oven would have been either too expensive or inconvenient to construct, a clay and sand oven could provide an effective alternative. Although no English source provides instructions for building such ovens, the technique was apparently continued into the eighteenth century by those who had emigrated to Canada.[24] First a 6- or 7-foot square base of earth, stone or wood was built up to a height of 3 feet, and covered with a 6-inch layer of two parts clay mixed with one part sand and a little water. The circular plan of the oven was then set out on top and long, flexible laths, twigs or small branches inserted around the perimeter, these being bowed over and their loose ends stuck in the opposite side to form a domed frame with a space at one side to serve as a doorway. An inch-thick layer of the clay-sand mixture was then daubed over the frame and allowed to dry to leather hardness. Subsequent layers were added in the same way to produce an 8 or 9-inch thick dome, which was left to dry out completely. A fire of wood and coal was then lit inside and slowly built up to burn off the wooden frame and convert the interior to a soft brick, any cracks being filled with more of the mixture. Once protected by a roof, such ovens were virtually permanent, but when neglected, they would quickly weather away, leaving little but a scatter of frost-blown burnt clay with the imprint of wattle and daub to indicate their former presence.

Faggots formed by binding small diameter sticks and branches into bundles some 2 feet or more in length provided the usual fuel for both masonry and clay ovens. They were first spiked on the iron prongs of a long-handled oven-fork called a furgon or fruggin, and held over a fire until aflame, when they were thrust into the back of the oven.[25] To the medieval mind, this provided a potent image of the fate of those condemned to hell, 'suche folk...to bynde in fagottes and cast them with forkes into the fyre' threatened the 1413 *Pilgrimage of the Soule*.[26] For large bread ovens sixteen faggots might be used at a single baking, their flames licking the

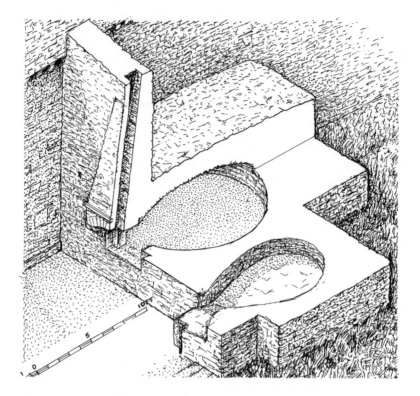

Figure 21. A pair of late medieval bread ovens in the bakehouse at Kidwelly Castle, Dyfed. Strong corbels projecting from each side of their doors supported the tall conical flues which conducted the smoke up into the open air.

domed roof of the oven before spouting from the oven door, and perhaps carried away by a smoke-hood and chimney directly above.[27] Once the oven was up to temperature, as judged by experience or, if following the traditional methods, by seeing if a stick struck sparks from the oven floor, if a scattering of new flour blackened without bursting into flame, or if a particular 'watch and tell' pebble glowed red, the embers were raked out.[28] All the fire ash which remained was then swept out with a wet mapple or mop mounted on a long handle, so that all was clean before the bread was placed inside.[29]

This operation was executed with a peel, a long-handled oven slice with a flat, square-ended blade usually of wood, but of iron in the more prosperous bakehouses.[30] To set each loaf in place so that it did not touch another, and yet utilize the space efficiently, was an especially skilful task, particularly as the interior of the oven was quite gloomy. When full, a door was placed in the doorway, sealed with mud, and the bread left to bake. The timing was a matter of skill, dependent on a deep knowledge of the unique characteristics of each individual oven.

After being withdrawn from the oven, the loaves would be packed into cylindrical bread baskets or bread-skeps, and carried up to the pantry, the baker and the pantler each keeping half of a split tally-stick which was notched across to record the numbers of loaves delivered.[31]

Particularly in urban areas, many great households, merchant families and the urban poor found it more convenient to buy their bread rather than bake it for themselves. In London, for example, baking had been an established trade from at least the eleventh century, its White Bakers' and Brown Bakers' guilds being incorporated about 1207. By the Assize of Bread of 1266, the weights of various types of loaf were fixed nationally. Halfpenny and penny cocket, the fine white bread, halfpenny and penny wheaten, and penny coarse household bread were baked in various sizes according to the current price of corn. However, a penny cocket loaf had always to weigh the same as two-thirds of a penny wheaten, and be half the size of a penny household loaf, thus reflecting the qualities of their ingredients.

As the price of a quarter of wheat rose and fell, the authorities revised the weights of the loaves to the above formula, making an allowance for the bakers' expenses and profits. In 1495, for example, when wheat was 12s. a quarter, a baker was to charge at 14s. a quarter, the 2s. difference being allocated as follows;

oven and firewood	6d.
millers' fees	4d.
2 journeymen's and 2 pages' wages	5d.
salt, yeast, candles and sack bands	2d.
the baker, his wife, house, horse, cat and dog	7d.
	24d.

Searchers regularly checked the weight and quality of the loaves offered for sale, so that anyone breaking the Assize could be punished in the pillory, or by being dragged through the streets on a hurdle with an offending loaf tied around their neck.[32]

The establishment of bakers' ovens was closely controlled by civic and manorial authorities, both the inhabitants and professional bakers in many towns and villages being obliged to bring all their bakery to their lord's oven and pay an appropriate fee for this service. In Wakefield, for example, a manorial bakehouse built in 1336 produced an annual income of 6s. 9d., its pre-1469 successor then continuing in active use through to the 1840s.

CHAPTER EIGHT

The Pastry

When reading medieval recipes for pastries, it soon becomes apparent that most were very different in character from anything we are familiar with today. Our pies and pasties are chiefly used to cook their raw fillings by a slow, enclosed simmering process, which involves keeping them in the oven for relatively long periods after their pastry has baked hard. As traditional pie-makers say, we don't bake pies, we boil them, stressing that the important factor is the complete cooking of their contents. Even so, the crust has always to be crisp and palatable, since it forms an integral part of the experience of eating any pastry. In contrast, medieval pastry was essentially a mouldable substance in which very quickly-cooked delicate foods could be enclosed while being briefly baked in the oven. This meant that it had to be capable of holding its shape when merely dried, and it might be little more than half-baked when its custard, fish or pre-boiled meat fillings were fully cooked. This explains why the contemporary manners books make no mention of pastry as a food to be eaten; it was essentially the disposable cookware of polite society, although it was probably consumed by the poorer patrons of the urban pie-maker.

In royal and noble households, pastry work came under the control of the main kitchen department, being prepared by the master, yeoman and groom cooks as part of their general duties. This explains the presence of pastry ovens within most medieval kitchens. Usually, they are virtually identical to bread ovens in their design and construction, but tend to be smaller. At Wressle Castle the bakehouse ovens required sixteen faggots at each baking, for example, while the kitchen's great pastry oven, perhaps some 10-feet diameter, required six faggots, and the little 4-foot oven just three.[1]

Figure 22. Pastries. Top: probably designed by John Lewyn at Warkworth Castle, Northumberland, c.1377–90. Bottom: the dry and well-lit area for the pastry table (left), the pastry office with store/pastry staff chamber (?) above (centre) and pastry ovens (right), Gainsborough Old Hall, Lincs., c.1480.

In the later medieval period, there is some evidence to suggest that the pastry had begun to gain a degree of independence from the kitchen. In 1390, for example, the Earl of Derby was employing Hankyn Edeyne, pasteler, to make the pastries for his household. In the fifteenth century separate pastry offices began to be constructed.[2] At Gainsborough Old Hall (c.1480), one occupies a small room in the south-west corner of the main kitchen. Just outside its door a pair of shallow-domed brick pastry ovens are set beneath a tall flue which carried away the smoke. Adjacent to its other side, the only ground-floor window in the main kitchen provides an ideal well-lit working area for making up pies and pasties.

Following the standard medieval practice, the pastry dough would have been mixed, kneaded and shaped as empty crusts on the work-table, and then briefly dried off or hardened in the ovens. For custards and the like, the fillings would be poured into the empty shells while still inside the oven, but for most other recipes they were returned to the work-table, filled, any lids set in place, then put back into to the oven for perhaps only 20–40 minutes. Baked in this way, pastries represented a very convenient method of cooking for dinners and feasts. Crusts and fillings could all be prepared in advance, then quickly baked immediately before they were required for the table.

Even though ovens were usually available, it was possible to bake pastry in an open fire. To do this, two identical earthenware pans or dishes were required. Having been pre-heated on the embers, one had its interior greased and a stiff flour-and-water batter poured in and around it to form a thick internal coating. When covered by the other pan, it was replaced on the embers, and more embers piled on top, thus forming a miniature oven which quickly baked the batter into a crisp pastry. Fillings could now be added and the baking continued beneath the top pan and its embers until all was cooked, the tart or flan removed from the pans, and served.[3]

One recipe using this method is entitled 'sew trap', meaning a pottage cooked in a 'trap' or earthenware baking dish. Although most pastries were baked in their own free-standing crusts, a number of fourteenth-century and later recipes show that traps were used both to support pastry crusts, and also as our earliest oven-to-table ware. From a functional point of view, we should expect them to be broad, round and shallow, their walls only an inch or two in height. Looking at the ceramic record, such vessels have been made in England from the late ninth century onwards, those of the thirteenth to early sixteenth centuries being around 7 to 19 inches in diameter.[4] Some were probably used as dishes, but the fact that a number had their rims pinched in the same manner as pastry suggests that they were traps for baking. When using traps of unglazed or poorly glazed earthenware, they had to be coated with a thin layer of butter or lard to prevent their contents sticking to the pottery. Dishes cooked in this way include erbolat, a mixture of whole eggs and ground herbs, and also malaches made of eggs and breadcrumbs, pork and cheese, or of pig's blood, diced lard and flour.[5] Almost identical black puddings were still being baked in dishes in the North East in the twentieth century. The following tart was baked on Ember Days, these being the fasts held on the Wednesday, Friday and Saturday following the first Sunday in Lent, Whitsunday, Holy Cross Day on 14 September and St Lucia's Day on 13 December, when dairy produce, but not meat, was allowed.[6]

TART ON EMBER DAY

1lb/450g onions	pinch of saffron
1tsp each, sage & thyme	½tsp salt
4oz/100g drained cottage cheese	1tbs/15g sugar
2 eggs, beaten	pinch cinnamon
1oz/25g butter	2tbs/30g currants

Peel the onions, simmer with the herbs for some 20 minutes until just tender, allow to cool, drain, and chop finely.

Grind the cheese to a smooth paste, beat in the eggs to make a smooth batter, mix in the onions and other ingredients, pour into a greased 8-inch shallow dish, and bake at 180°C/350°F/gas mark 4 for some 40 minutes.

A number of other recipes specify that the trap should be lined with a thin layer of pastry rising an inch up the sides. Tarts were often made in this way, including meat, fish and cheese versions, as well as one for an elderflower cheesecake mixture.[7]

SAMBOCADE

8oz/225g curds or rinsed cottage cheese
3tbs/45g sugar   *4tbs elderflowers*
3 egg whites   *1tbs/15ml rose-water*
8oz/225g flour

Make a batch of pastry as in the following recipe and use to line an 8-inch diameter flan dish.

Lightly beat the egg white, mix with the remaining ingredients, and bake at 200°C/400°F/gas mark 6 for 30 minutes.

Most other pastry items were made with self-supporting crusts. Where the ingredients are mentioned, they are usually just flour and water, with no indication of any fats, such as we now use in shortcrust and hot-water crust pastries. Bolted white flour would certainly have been used for all good quality pastries, but sieved wholemeal may have been used for cheaper versions despite its inability to stay light and crisp.

As to how they were made into pastry dough, there appears to be no real evidence, but trials using either cold or boiling water suggest the latter was used, since it immediately softens the gluten and produces a dough which is easy to handle, and holds its shape well before and during baking.

PASTRY CASES FOR 8-INCH TARTS AND FLANS

8oz/225g plain white flour
¼pt/150ml boiling water

Place the flour in a bowl, make a well in the centre, pour in the boiling water, and use a knife or spatula to form into a firm dough. (A little more water or flour may be required, depending on the absorbency of the flour.)

Turn onto a floured board, knead, and pat out on a layer of dry flour to form a disc about 6 inches in diameter, with a thick rim. Pinch the rim up to form vertical walls just over one inch in height, then pat out the base and sides to form an 8-inch diameter case.

If necessary, the walls may be pressed against a vertical straight edge to give them a better shape, care being taken not to have a thick triangular section between the walls and the base. Finally, prick the base and pinch the rims to give a rope-like top.

Bake at 200°C/400°F/gas mark 6 for 20 minutes, then either fill with the contents, or remove and keep for use.

It is probable that such cases would have been made in quantity prior to any major meal, so that they could be filled and baked immediately when required for the table.

For finer work, paste royal was used, this being listed in Durham Priory account rolls in 1389–90 as '3 coffins of pasteroyal' and in the royal household ordinances of *c.*1440 as 'half a pound of paste royal' – apparently as an ingredient and also as a garnish like sugar plate.[8] Clearly the latter was a spiced icing-sugar and gum-tragacanth sugar plate, a recipe for which was published in W.I.'s *True Gentlewoman's Delight* of 1653, while the former was obviously a form of pastry crust. No recipes for making it appear to have survived, but it might have been the richer paste of fine flour, sugar, saffron and salt used for pies such as pety pernantes.[9] This too required a hot-water method.

SWEET SAFFRON PASTRY

10oz/275g plain white flour	*large pinch saffron*
3oz/75g caster sugar	*small pinch salt*

Sift the flour into a bowl and make a well in the centre.

Place the sugar, saffron, salt and ¼ pint/150ml water into a saucepan. Simmer for 5 minutes, stirring all the while, to produce a bright yellow syrup.

Pour most of the syrup into the flour, stir rapidly and vigorously, knead to form a stiff dough.

Follow the instructions for preparing pastry cases in the

preceding recipe but also prick the base with a fork and bake for 15 minutes in the oven set as before to produce a sweet saffron-flavoured yellow crust.

Two different methods were used to put the fillings into these crusts. Once they had hardened in the oven, they could be removed, and the fillings poured in from a hand-held dish. For more liquid mixtures, spillage could be avoided by using 'a pele with a dyssche on the ende' to fill the cases as they lay on the oven floor.[10]

It is difficult to establish the distinguishing features which separated tarts from flans and other similar designations. While most were open, some had lids like pies and all could enclose a variety of ingredients.[11] Tarts, for example, might contain pork, birds and rabbits, fish, cheese and fruits, as in the following recipes.

TART OF FLESH[12]

12oz/350g plain flour	1 tsp mixed ground cloves,
4 dried figs	mace, pepper, ginger &
¼pt/150ml wine or ale	saffron
2tbs/30g raisins	1tsp salt
2tbs/30g pine kernels	1tbs sugar or clear honey
1oz/25g lard	6 dates, finely chopped
4oz/100g white cheese	1tbs/15ml almond [or cow's]
10oz/275g minced pork	milk yellowed with saffron
1 egg, beaten	

Prepare the tart case with the flour and 6 fl.oz./200ml boiling water, to make an 8-inch case and its lid.

Simmer the figs in the wine or ale for 5 minutes, allow to cool, drain and chop.

Fry the raisins and pine kernels in lard until they start to brown, then cool in the pan.

Chop the cheese finely, combine with the pork and egg, then stir in the raisins and pine kernels, spices, salt, and sugar or honey.

Pack the filling into the case, top with the chopped dates, moisten the edges of the pastry, fit the lid and pinch the edges, and cut a hole in the centre.

Brush the tart with the saffron milk, and bake at 190°C/375°F/gas mark 5 for some 40 minutes.

LESE FRYES (CHEESE TART)[13]

1 pre-baked 8-inch tart case
1lb/450g white cheese, such as creamy Lancashire or Wensleydale
2 eggs, beaten   *1oz/25g butter*
1tbs/15g sugar   *a little salt if necessary*

Chop the cheese and grind to a smooth paste. Mix with the eggs, sugar, butter and salt until it is soft and smooth.

Fill the tart case, and bake at 180°C/350°F/gas mark 4 for about 30 minutes, until completely set.

APPLE TART[14]

1 pre-baked 8-inch tart case
4 dried figs   *pinch of saffron*
1lb/450g peeled and cored dessert apples
4oz/100g peeled pear   *¼tsp ground cinnamon and*
2tbs/30g raisins   *ginger*

Simmer the figs for 5 minutes, cool, drain and chop.

Mix all the ingredients, and grind to form a smooth paste.

Fill the tart case and bake at 190°C/375°F/gas mark 5 for about 40 minutes, until the fruit pulp is cooked.

Crustardes or custards were also baked in open-topped cases or coffins, but contained rich mixtures of meat, bone-marrow and dried fruits set in egg and milk batters. 'Gentle' or noble versions contained ground meat, others were for fish-days, while Lombard versions were sweeter, with cream instead of meat. The following demonstrate something of their range.

CRUSTARDE OF FLESH[15]

12oz/350g pigeon or chicken meat, cubed
½pt/300ml light stock   pinch of saffron
3tbs/45ml cider vinegar   ¼tsp ground cinnamon
1oz/25g butter or lard   2tbs/30g currants
1tbs/15g sugar   12oz/350g plain white flour
1tsp/5g salt   2 eggs, beaten & strained

Gently stew the meat in the stock, vinegar, fat, sugar, salt and spices for one hour, and allow to cool.

Prepare the tart case with the flour and 6 fl.oz./200ml boiling water to make an 8-inch case and its lid.

Drain the meat, reserving the stock, arrange in the crustarde and scatter with the currants.

Beat the eggs into the stock, pour over the meat, dampen the edges, put on the lid, pinch the edges, cut a hole in the centre, and bake at 200°C/400°F/gas mark 6 for 35 minutes.

CRUSTARDE OF HERBS ON FISH-DAYS[16]

3tbs chopped fresh herbs such as parsley, fennel, sage, mint etc.
4oz/100g walnut kernels   ¼tsp ground cinnamon
4tbs/60ml cider vinegar   8oz/225g plain white flour
pinch of saffron   12oz/250g white fish fillets
1tbs/15g sugar   1tbs/15ml olive oil

Grind the herbs with the walnuts, vinegar, saffron, sugar and cinnamon with 4tbs/60ml water to form a smooth paste. Simmer for 5 minutes, stirring continuously, and set aside to cool.

Mix ¼pt/150ml boiling water into the flour, knead to form a dough, and use to line a greased 8-inch pie dish.

Place the fish in the crustarde, drizzle with the oil, and bake at 180°C/350°F/gas mark 4 for 10 minutes. Spoon out any surplus liquid, cover with the walnut mixture, and continue baking for a further 10–15 minutes until all is hot and the fish is tender.

CUSTARD LOMBARD[17]

1 pre-baked 8-inch custard case	*¾pt/450ml whipping cream*
1oz/25g bone marrow (or butter)	*3 eggs*
8 prunes, soaked	*3tbs/45g sugar*
8 dates, cut in 2 or 3 strips	*pinch of salt*

Arrange the marrow or butter, prunes and dates on the bottom of the custard case, and bake at 180°C/350°F/gas mark 4 for 5 minutes.

Beat and strain the eggs, beat in the sugar, salt and cream, pour into the custard case, and continue baking for a further 25–30 minutes until the custard has set.

Similar custard mixtures were very popular, some including either whole eggs or just the yolks, some with almond milk, cow's milk, cream, stock or wine, some with white or brown sugar, some with honey, some with butter, some with salt, some with cinnamon, ginger, pepper and saffron, and some unspiced. Individual recipes might also include whole blanched almonds, sliced dates, figs, currants, raisins, and fat cheese. In terms of size, the smallest were darioles, which had coffins 2 inches deep by just over 2 inches in diameter, one recipe specifying a quart of cream and 40 yolks to fill 20 darioles, suggesting a capacity of around 3 fluid ounces.[18]

DARIOLES[19]

8oz/225g plain white flour
¼pt/150ml boiling water

Make into hot-water pastry (see p. 129) and form into four 2-inch high by 2½-inch diameter dariole cases. This is easiest done by raising the pastry around a floured cylindrical wooden block. Pinch the top edges and pre-bake at 200°C/400°F/gas mark 6 for 20 minutes.

These can be filled with the custard batter of the previous recipe or one of these two alternatives. Having selected your batter, prepare the fruit detailed below.

Batter A	*Batter B*
¼pt/150ml whipping cream	¾pt/450ml almond milk
¼pt/150ml sweet white wine	3 eggs, beaten
¼pt/150ml light stock	3tbs/45g sugar
4 egg yolks, beaten	pinch of saffron
1oz/25g bone marrow or butter	¼tsp salt
pinch of ground cloves, mace,	
ginger and saffron	

4 dates, chopped
4 strawberries, chopped

Arrange the dates and strawberries in the bottoms of the darioles, beat either of the batter ingredients together, almost fill the darioles, and bake at 180°C/350°F/gas mark 4 for 25–30 minutes, until the contents have just set.

'Doucets' were similar, but around 3 inches diameter by an inch high, while 'flathons', 'flawnes brode and flat' (flans) were much wider. Most had identical fillings to darioles, but a 'Flaun of Almayne' contained currants or raisins, ground apples or pears, cream, breadcrumbs, spices and ten whole eggs, suggesting a diameter of well over a foot. The existence of pottery traps of 19 inches diameter reflects the size which some flans might attain.[20] Flampoints, another form of open pastry, had fillings of ground boiled pork bound with eggs or cheese, surmounted by 'flame-points' of pastry, some being glazed with egg-yolks to give them an appropriate yellow colour.[21] Others topped their pork layer with one of spiced ground curds studded with alternate rows of pine kernels and cloves, while one described in Fabyan's *Chronicles* of 1494 was 'flourisshed with a Scocheoun [coat of arms] royall'. It is difficult to determine the sizes in which they were made, some recipes suggesting that their filling alone might weigh over 10lb, while others state that they should be only an inch in height.[22] This combination suggests a diameter approaching 2 feet. It is most probable that they were made in different sizes to suit the particular requirements of the household.

FLAMPOINTS[23]

12oz/350g pork	1tbs/15g lard
12oz/350g plain white flour	¼tsp black pepper
2oz/50g caster sugar	pinch saffron
6 eggs	½tsp salt
2 dried figs	¼pt/150ml ale

Put the pork in a pan, cover with water, simmer one hour, then drain and cool

Meanwhile sift the flour and sugar together, mix in 3 beaten eggs, and knead to form a stiff dough

Roll a piece of dough about ½-inch diameter by 12 inches long, cut in ¼-inch lengths, roll each into a ball, and gently fry in the lard until golden brown, then drain and leave to cool

Pinch two-thirds of the remaining dough to form a 7 to 8-inch diameter case, with walls just over an inch in height.

Simmer the figs in the ale, drain and chop.

Grind the pork, cheese, figs, pepper, salt, saffron and 2 beaten eggs, to form a soft paste

Fill the case with the paste, roll out the remaining pastry to form a lid, cover the paste, seal the edges using a little egg, and pinch the edges tightly together

Make 4 or 6 cuts (as if forming an asterisk or star) through the lid, almost to the edges, then fold each point back, and the tips forward again, to form petal-like 'flames' around the edge.

Brush the 'flames' with beaten egg yolk, arrange the fried balls of pastry on top of the paste, and bake at 180°C/350°F/gas mark 4 for 20 minutes. The resulting flampoint closely resembles the head of a sunflower.

Alternatively, the pastry balls and cut lid may be omitted, and individual flames cut from the pastry, fried in lard, and stuck into the paste just before placing in the oven.

Most impressive and flamboyant of all the open pastries was the castelette, a round 'keep' flanked by four round towers, all battlemented and served flambé at great feasts. A dish of this quality required good knowledge and skill in pastry-work. The water-based pastries dried very unevenly in the oven, usually remaining soft and damp within, and subject to extensive blistering. In contrast, the pastry made with whole eggs and sugar, as specified for flampoints, quickly hardens and rarely blisters.

CASTELETTES[24]

A. For the pastry

3lb/1·4kg plain white flour   12 eggs, beaten
6oz/150g caster sugar

Sift the flour and sugar together, and make a well in the centre. Pour in the eggs, stir in the flour from the sides, then mix and knead in sufficient flour to form a very stiff dough. Turn out on a floured board and knead thoroughly.

Roll a piece of pastry out on a baking sheet to form an 8-inch square base a quarter-inch in thickness

Roll out a 12 by 4 inch rectangle of pastry. Cut one long edge in the form of battlements or crenellations. Form into a round tower, joining the sides with a little beaten egg. Stick this to stand in the centre of the base in the same way. A roll of stiff paper placed inside will help it keep its shape.

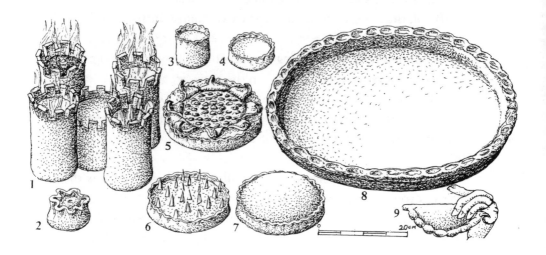

Figure 23. Fourteenth- and fifteenth-century pastries.

1. Castelettes, served *flambés*.
2. Chewets.
3. Darioles.
4. Doucets.
5–6. Flampoints.
7. Pie with blown-up lid.
8. Earthenware trap or flan-dish,
   Flitwick, Beds., 15c.
9. Pasty, 12c.

Roll out 4 rectangles of pastry, each 8 by 6 inches. Again, cut one long edge of each rectangle in the form of battlements, and bend each into a round tower, joining the edges and supporting them with a loose roll of paper as before.

Stick each tower onto the base and to the side of the central tower with a little beaten egg, one tower towards each corner as in the illustration above.

Trim the base tight to the bottoms of the towers, discarding the surplus.

Bake at 180°C/350°F/gas mark 4 for 10 minutes, then remove the paper rolls and allow to cool.

B. Filling for the central tower

12oz/350g pork   ½tsp salt
2 eggs, beaten   pinch of saffron

Put the pork in a pan, cover with water, simmer gently for 1 hour, drain, cool and grind or pound with the eggs, salt and saffron.

C. For the first tower or turret, an almond cream (white)

12oz/350g almonds   8tbs/120ml white wine or
3pt/1·8l water   rose-water
3tbs/45ml white wine vinegar   6tbs/90g sugar

Grind the almonds with half the water until very smooth, strain the liquid through muslin into a saucepan, then blend the residue with the remaining water, and strain into the pan once more.

Heat the almond milk to boiling, stirring continuously; stir in the vinegar, remove from the heat, allow to stand 10 minutes, then pour into a double layer of wet muslin placed across a bowl. Gather up each corner, and hang up to drain off the whey.

Turn the almond cream into a bowl, and stir in the white wine or rose-water, and the sugar.

D. For the second tower or turret, custard (red)

½pt/300ml whipping cream
red food colouring (for sanders)
2 eggs, beaten and strained

Mix the cream and eggs together, and stir in sufficient colouring to produce a dark pink.

E. For the third tower or turret – farse of fruit (brown)

1 dessert apple   3 dried figs
1 pear   2tbs raisins

Peel and core the fresh fruit, chop finely with the figs and raisins.

Put in a pan with 3tbs/45ml water, and stir over a gentle heat until soft and brown.

F. For the fourth tower or turret – fritter batter (green)
4tbs fresh green herbs, such as spinach, parsley, sorrel etc., chopped
4oz/100g ground almonds   1tbs/15g sugar
½tsp ground ginger   ½tsp salt

Grind the herbs to form a rich, green paste, then add the remaining ingredients, and grind together, adding water little by little to produce a smooth, soft paste.

Once all these mixtures have been prepared fill the castelette, and bake at 180°C/350°F/gas mark 4 for some 15 minutes, until the custards etc. have set. On removing from the oven, two tablespoons of brandy, the medieval 'ew ardaunt', may be poured into the tops of the towers, ignited and the whole served immediately with its towers aflame. In France, Taillevent made much plainer castelettes called Parmerian tarts for his master, Charles V. These were garnished with three or four banners of France and of the lords who were in the royal presence, each having a strip of gold, silver or tinfoil set on the piecrust before them.[25]

Moving on from open pastries to closed ones, it is noticeable that there are relatively few recipes for pies and pasties. This may indicate that the methods were so well known that they were not worth recording; menus include baked eels, partridges and teals for example, but there are no recipes for any of these.[26] In their simplest form, bakemeats had their main ingredients spiced and flavoured, and enclosed within a pastry crust or coffin. In order to give the lid a good domed appearance, and to prevent it from drooping into the contents and becoming soggy, it could be inflated. Having sealed on the lid, a 'lytel hole [was cut] in the middelle

& at that hoole, blow in the cofynne with thin mowthe a gode blast of wynde. And sodenly stoppe the hole, that the wynd a-byde with-ynne, to reyse uppe the coffyne, that he falle nowt y-dowan, & whon he is a lytel y-hardid in the oven, pryk the cofyn with a pynne y-stekyd on a roddys ende, for brekyng of the coffynne, & than let bake'.[27] This takes a little practice, but is certainly effective for making pies such as the following.

SALMON Y-BAKE[28]

1lb/450g salmon fillets	*¼tsp ground ginger*
12oz/350g plain white flour	*¼tsp black pepper*
½tsp salt	

Sift the flour into a bowl, make a well in the centre, pour in 8 fl.oz./225ml boiling water, stir in the flour from the sides, mix, and knead to form a firm pastry dough. Take two-thirds of this, and pinch out to form a coffin 7 inches in diameter with a raised border 1-inch high.

Sprinkle half the salt and spices in the coffin, lay in the skinned salmon, sprinkle on the remaining salt and spices, and use the rest of the pastry to form a lid, carefully dampening and pinching the edges together.

Insert a drinking straw between the lid and the wall of the pie, inflate the lid, and pinch the pastry while removing the straw.

Bake at 200°C/400°F/gas mark 6 for 15 minutes, until the pastry has set, then pierce the lid near the edge with a skewer, and continue baking for a further 15–20 minutes.

Herring was apparently cooked in a similar manner. In accordance with its charter, Yarmouth corporation had to send a hundred herrings to the sheriffs of Norwich each year, so that they could have them baked as twenty-four pies or pasties which were in turn given to the lord of the manor of East Carlton for delivery to the King.[29]

Whole chickens, rubbed with salt, coloured with saffron and flavoured with diced bacon fat, verjuice and spices, were baked in just the same way, but larger joints of meat tended to be parboiled, so that most of their cooking was completed before they were baked.[30] Venison pasties were also made in this way, the meat being parboiled in salted water, then drained and either left whole or cut into pieces. They were put in the pastry crust with pepper, ginger and salt.[31] Since fruit cooked quite quickly, it was usually baked from raw.[32]

WARDENS [PEARS] IN PASTE

4 cooking pears
1lb/450g plain flour
2tbs sugar or honey

large pinch ground ginger
large pinch black pepper

Mix the flour with ½pt/300ml boiling water to make pastry, as in the previous recipe, and use half to make a 5 or 6-inch pie case.

Peel the pears, remove the pips and core from the base or larger end of the fruit. Fill the hole with either sugar and ginger, or honey, ginger and pepper, and stop the hole with a small piece of pastry.

Place the pears in the pie case, cover with the remaining pastry, moistening the edges and pinching them together, and cut a hole in the top.

Bake at 200°C/400°F/gas mark 6 for 15 minutes. Try the pears with a skewer, and continue to bake until they are tender.

The smallest medieval pies were called chewets, their pinched rims seemingly resembling the leaves of a small *chou* or cabbage. They were either baked or deep-fried, and were filled with spiced mixtures of raw or pre-cooked meat or fish such as are demonstrated by the following receipes.[33]

CHEWETS OF BEEF

8oz/225g lean beef	*½tsp mixed ginger and cloves*
3oz/75g chicken	*pinch of saffron*
1 hard-boiled egg yolk	*1tsp salt*
8 grapes	*1tbs/15ml cider vinegar*
8oz/200g plain flour made into pastry as described on page 141	

Chop the beef, chicken and egg yolk, and mix with the remaining ingredients.

Use two-thirds of the pastry to make 4 pie cases some 2½ins/ 6cm diameter by 1½ inches/4cm high. Pack with the mixture. Use the remaining pastry to make the lids, moistening the edges and pinching them into place. Cut a hole in the centre of each lid.

Bake at 200°C/400°F/gas mark 6 for 1 hour.

CHEWETS ON FLESH DAYS

8oz/225g pork, chopped	*½tsp ground ginger*
4oz/100g chicken, chopped	*1tsp salt*
1 hard-boiled egg yolk	*1oz/25g butter or lard*

Gently fry the pork and chicken in the butter or lard for 5 minutes.

Mix in the remaining ingredients, make up as above, and bake for 20 minutes.

CHEWETS ON FISH-DAYS

10oz/275g haddock, cod, hake [or salmon] fillets	
6 dates	*large pinch ginger &*
1oz/25g raisins	*cinnamon*
1oz/25g pine kernels	*½tsp salt*

Poach the fish and dates for 10 minutes, drain, grind, and mix with the remaining ingredients.

Make and bake as above, for 20 minutes. Alternatively, deep-fry in olive oil, or stew in a wine and sugar syrup.

Chewets are best served hot.

Pies of Paris were apparently larger than chewets but, since no quantities were quoted, the following recipe, like those for the chewets, is based on what may have been suitable for a mess of four people. Like a number of baked recipes, the meats are pre-cooked, so the baking time is reduced considerably.[34]

PIES OF PARIS

12oz/325g pork, or pork and veal, chopped in small pieces
¼pt/150ml mixed sweet wine and meat stock

2oz/50g currants	½tsp salt
6 minced or chopped dates	3 egg yolks, beaten
¼tsp ground ginger	12oz/325g plain flour
1tsp sugar	8 fl.oz./225ml boiling water

Stew the meat in the wine and stock in a covered pan for some 45 minutes until tender, stir in all the remaining ingredients except the yolks, and leave until tepid.

Following the recipe on page 129, make the pastry with the flour and water, and use two-thirds to form a piecrust some 8ins/ 20cm diameter and 1½ inches/4cm high, reserving the remainder for the lid.

Mix the yolks into the meat mixture, pour into the pie case on a baking sheet, put the lid in place, pinch the edges together, and cut a hole in the centre of the lid.

Bake at 200°C/400°F/gas mark 6 for 30 minutes. It is best served hot.

Largest of all were the great pies. For these, a special minced beef forcemeat was used to provide an internal lining for a filling of parboiled poultry, game and dried fruit. This technique ensures that the piecrust will retain all the juices from the expensive filling, which might be lost if they softened the crust or if the crust were to leak. Such pies continued to be made up to the early twentieth century, under the title of Yorkshire Christmas Pies.[35]

GREAT PIES

3lb/1·35kg lean beef	*1tsp ground cinnamon*
4oz/100g suet	*large pinch saffron*
2tbs/30g salt	*6 hard-boiled egg yolks*
½tsp ground black pepper	*4oz/100g butter*
4½lb/2·1kg plain flour	*12 dates, sliced in two*
3lb/1·35kg poultry & game	*6oz/275g currants*
1tsp ground cloves	*6oz/275g prunes*
1tsp ground mace	

Mince the beef, suet, salt and pepper together to make a smooth forcemeat.

Put the flour into a bowl, make a well in the centre, pour in 2pt/1.2l boiling water. Mix in the flour from the sides; knead to form a firm dough once cool enough to handle.

Use two-thirds of the dough to form a pie case about 11 inches/27cm in diameter by 4 inches/10cm in height on a paper-lined baking sheet. Use a double-thickness band of paper of the same height to hold the walls in place, encircling the paper itself with string to give additional strength.

Line the pie case with two-thirds of the beef forcemeat.

Fill the centre with fillets of poultry and game, layered with the sprinkled spices, lumps of butter, halved egg yolks and dried fruit, until the pie is almost full, then top with the remaining beef forcemeat.

Make a lid from the remaining pastry, moisten the edges, set in place, pinch the edges, and cut a 1-inch/2·5cm hole in the centre of the lid.

Bake at 220°C/425°F/gas mark 7 for 45 minutes, then reduce to 180°C/350°F/gas mark 4 for a further 4 hours, until the contents are cooked. Traditionally, these pies were served cold, but they may be served hot.

The original recipe parboiled the poultry and game to reduce the baking time. This recipe has been adapted to use raw poultry and game, to avoid any risk to health involved in the parboiling, cooling and re-heating stages, hence the longer baking time.

CHAPTER NINE

The Boiling House

From the late thirteenth and early fourteenth centuries, boiling houses or seething-places were being built close to major kitchens. Their function was to boil meat, fish and simple pottages for the bulk of the household servants who dined in the hall. In 1455, for example, Henry VI's master-cook for the hall, William Hekeling, had a yeoman, a groom and a page to cook the basic boiled meats, fish and pottages in the palace seething-place.[1] As this was a very simple task, there was no need to write down any recipes, but fortunately a number of accounts and regulations, along with boiling pots and their furnaces, still survive and are available for study.

The most common raw ingredients cooked here would include beef, mutton and pork, as well as fish such as cod, hake, herring, mackerel and pollock which were relatively cheap and plentiful. Back in the larders, the meat and larger fish would have been cut up into pieces of perhaps 2lb weight, each sufficient to serve a mess of around four people.[2]

Much of the food cooked here would have been salted, this being the most usual form of preservation for meat and fish. Most salt was produced around the coast, where seawater was used to dissolve the salt which had accumulated in tide-washed sands, the resulting brine being initially evaporated by exposure to the sun and wind. The only major inland source were the brine springs of the Cheshire wiches. The concentrated brines from both were boiled to crystallization in shallow metal pans heated by peat, wood or coal fires, the solution being regularly stirred, topped up, and skimmed to remove most unwanted elements.[3] Finally, it was scooped into baskets and left to dry out completely, ready for the transport networks of saltersgates or salt-ways which allowed packhorses to carry their loads from either the coast or the Cheshire wiches to every market town. After the fourteenth century, salt was also imported from the Bay of Biscay, particularly around Bourgneuf near Nantes. Having large crystals, bay salt was ideal for dry-salting, dissolving much more slowly than most English salt.

In the house, salt was usually stored in coopered tubs in order to keep it clean and dry. Pipes, barrels of 106 gallons capacity, were used in the largest establishments, casks and tubs in lesser ones, and probably small pots and boxes in cottages.[4] A wall-hung wooden salt-box with a sloping lid, identical to later examples, appears in one of the misericord carvings of *c.*1500 in Manchester Cathedral, but this may not represent English practice as it was copied from a Continental woodcut.

Post-medieval salting employed salt, saltpetre and coarse sugar to produce preserved meats which were deeply penetrated, soft and well-coloured. They might also have been hung up in a chimney to dry out and obtain a piquant flavour. However, there appears to be no evidence for the use of saltpetre, sugar or smoking in medieval meat preservation, only salt. This could be used either dry, being rubbed into the meat every day, forming a strong brine with the extracted juices, or wet, being dissolved in water in which the meat could be soaked. In either case, the meat or other material for salting would be prepared in a coopered vat, kit or kimnel, its top left open for inspection and for turning and rubbing its contents.[5] In 1542 Andrew Boorde recommended that young ox-beef should be 'moderately powderyd, that the groose blode by salte may be exhaustyd' in order to 'make an Englysshe man stronge'.[6] This process of green salting is probably the best to use today for boiling small joints of meat, rather than for preserving them.

SALT BEEF, PORK OR MUTTON

2lb/900g joints of meat
4oz/100g bay salt (large-crystal sea salt) per joint

Place the joint in a ceramic bowl or dish, sprinkle with the salt, rub in for 10 minutes, and leave in a cold place overnight. Turn and rub the joint in its brine for 10 minutes for the next 4 days.

Rinse the joint, truss if necessary, place in a pan, cover with cold water, cover, bring to the boil very slowly, then skim, and simmer gently for about 75 minutes until tender.

Drain the joint, allow to stand for 10 minutes in a warm place to rest, then serve.

An alternative method is to dissolve the salt in 2 pints/1l of boiling water, then allow to go perfectly cold. Immerse the meat in this brine, leave in a cold place for 4 nights, and follow the last two stages above.

If beef was to be kept over the winter, after the autumn Martinmas slaughter, or if the pork and bacon was to be preserved as pigs were killed throughout the year, they would be more heavily salted, and for longer periods. The same was true for the carcasses of sheep which had died of murrain. Although butchers were forbidden to sell such meat, some careful people had the flesh put into water for a period between the hour of nine and vespers, and afterwards hung up so that the water drained off. It was then dried and salted to feed labourers and household servants, a practice which continued in some areas up to the nineteenth century.[7] Salted meats, all a uniform dull brown-grey, since they lacked the rosy-pink colour provided by saltpetre, were either stored in barrels to form the basic diet of households, armies and the crews of ships, or were hung up to dry in kitchens and halls. In 1430, for example, John Gadeby, a Beverley mason, had two flitches of bacon worth 3s. 4d., and three tilds or quarters of beef and a piece of bacon hanging in his hall.[8] Here they were well ventilated and dried, rather than smoked, and provided comforting visual evidence that the house was plentifully provisioned. It is interesting to find complete sides of pigs carved on the misericords of Ludlow parish church and Worcester Cathedral, these probably representing a subject of great interest to the craftsmen who created them.

Fish formed a very important part of the medieval diet, since it replaced meats every Friday, Saturday and, up to the early fifteenth century, Wednesdays too, as well as throughout Lent. Freshwater fish was netted or trapped from rivers and lakes, while almost every coastal port had a well-developed packhorse or water-borne transport system capable of delivering fresh sea-fish to markets many miles inland.[9] This fish tended to be rather expensive, however, and most peasants and household servants had to rely on salt fish for almost half the days of the year. A fifteenth-century schoolboy recorded the common experience of his contemporaries: 'Thou will not believe how weary I am of fish, and how much I desire that flesh were come in again, for I have ate none other but salt fish this Lent, and it hath engendered so much phlegm within me that it stoppeth my pipes that I can neither speak nor breathe.'[10]

Some expensive freshwater fish such as salmon or lamprey were salted for the luxury market, but most salt fish was either imported or salted at the ports using the methods described by Walter of Bibbesworth:[11]

> When [cod] is taken in the far seas and it is desired to keep it for ten or twelve years, it is gutted and its head removed and it is dried in the air and sun and in no wise a fire, or smoked; and when this is done it is called *stockfish*. And when it hath been kept a long time and it is desired to eat it, it behoves to beat it with a wooden hammer for a full hour, and then set it to soak in warm water for a full two hours or more, then cook and scour it well like beef, then eat it with mustard or soaked in butter.

In the fourteenth century Winchelsea had a reputation for its fresh plaice, Rye for marling, and Grimsby for cod. Scarborough inshore fishermen concentrated on cod in Lent, skate in summer, and plaice in winter. From the early fifteenth century, English mariners began to use salting as a means of exploiting the rich northern fishing-grounds. Setting sail in early February or March from the east-coast ports or from Bristol, they took large quantities of cod from around Ireland, Shetland and the Faroes, salting it and drying it before returning in time for the autumn markets. Some cod was simply barrelled in salt and left to cure in its own pickle, to form 'green fish', either sold in this form or dried off at the end of the voyage.[12] It is probable that they also brought back the fish caught and dried by the northern Scottish fishermen, although this was a predominantly Dutch fishing ground in the medieval period.[13] In household accounts salted and/or dried members of the cod family were usually described as stock-fish, or ling. Ling is a separate species, but often meant a superior variety of cod, being about double the price of ordinary stockfish. The importance of salt fish in the diet is clearly illustrated in the account of the Northumberland household, which paid 4d. each for 942 fish each year.[14]

The other major source of salt fish was the herring. The first shoals appeared off Shetland in early June, then progressed down both sides of Scotland and England. The best were caught from the east coast, especially off Yarmouth. This was the major English herring port, with a great autumn fair for the sale of pickled herrings to serve households over the coming winter and Lent. The west of England's herrings were caught off Ireland, and distributed from Bristol, while both Devon and Cornwall caught the rather smaller pilchards which appeared off their shores in the latter half of each year. Herrings were prepared by being gutted, brined for some 15 hours and packed into barrels between layers of salt. Each barrel traditionally held 900 fish, and was sealed to exclude the air.[15] Known as white herrings in the late fifteenth and early sixteenth centuries, they cost 10s. the barrel, and £6 the 'last' of twelve barrels, or a farthing each fish if sold retail.[16]

In the late thirteenth century herring began to be soaked in strong brine and hung up to smoke in special chimneys for several hours which gave them a reddish colour. These red herrings were sold by the 'cade', a barrel of 500, or by the 'last' of 20 cades. The Duke of Clarence's household used 12 cades, 6000 red herrings, each Lent, and the Northumberland household 10,500 red herrings, all at the cost of £1 for 3 cades.[17]

Other economical salt fish for household use included sprats, £1 buying 6 cades; all these contrasting to the more exclusive varieties reserved for lordly tables. Barrels of 30 salt salmon cost 30s., salt sturgeon £3 a barrel, salt eels £3 6s. 8d. and salt lamprey even more.[18]

Having considered the fresh and salt foods cooked in the boiling house, we can now move on to the boiling vessels. These had to be very large. A ducal household which cooked two oxen and twelve muttons each day, divided into 196 two-pound joints, that is some 7.25 cubic feet of solid meat with perhaps double that quantity of water, required 136 gallons of boiler capacity daily.[19] The largest surviving English medieval cauldron, that at Warwick Castle, measures just over 3 feet in diameter, and has a working capacity of around 56 gallons. In theory, this would be capable of boiling 80 two-pound joints at once. These would feed over 300 men with 8oz (raw weight) of meat and a pint of pottage apiece, using just one fire for about 2 to 3 hours, including heating-up time. This is a very efficient method of cookery, and demonstrates why the boiling house boiler, or boilers, formed a major element in any household kitchen.

The ideal boiling vessel had to be non-toxic, non-porous, heatproof, highly conductive, resistant to corrosion, tough enough to withstand rough usage, and capable of being suspended over a fire. For all of these reasons, those with sufficient means always invested in metal cooking pots, especially those of copper and of lead and tin alloys variously called bronze, pot-metal, latten or brass. The earliest method of making these involved beating blocks of copper-rich metal into sheets which could be raised and rivetted together, a practice continued from the Bronze Age through to modern times. In the royal household, huge hemispherical boilers of tin-lined copper appear to have been used both in its boiling houses and in the field through to the 1650s, each being supported on immensely strong circular wrought-iron frames called brandreths. Edward I's boiling house at Caernarfon Castle (1294–c.1301) still retains the stone furnaces designed to heat such vessels. Similar ones are also seen in the 1545 painting of the *Field of the Cloth of Gold*, and were probably the '6 very large copper pots, tinned' in the Hampton Court inventory of 1659.[20]

Since copper vessels were extremely expensive both to buy and to be regularly re-tinned, most other sheet-metal boiling vessels were made in an essentially lead-free, low-tin bronze, their rims usually being rolled around strong iron hoops to keep them in shape and provide a means of suspension. The largest examples of this type were called either cauldrons or kettles. Cauldrons must have been big enough to hold a whole human, since they were specified as the vessels required for boiling to death all those found guilty of poisoning.[21] In 1440 the *Gesta Romanorum* similarly presents us with an image of two devils who 'Caste hem into a Cawderon and helde hem there till the fleshe was sothyn fro the bone'.[22] The kettle, which took its name from the Old English, Saxon and Norse word for a beaten sheet-metal boiling vessel, probably had a distinctive shape, growing wider towards its rim, as described in Dr Johnson's great *Dictionary*.[23] Cheese kettles of this type were still in use in small English dairy farms in the nineteeth century.

By the thirteenth century a new kind of metal cooking vessel had begun to be made in England. Instead of being constructed from sheets, the leaded bronze of approximately two-thirds copper, one-third lead, and up to one-eighth tin, was being cast in clay moulds, in a similar method to bell-founding.[24] Their bodies were either globular or squatter and more bag-shaped, with narrow rims flaring outwards to provide both great structural strength and an efficient seating for lids. They were ideal for boiling, their walls rapidly conducting heat from the fire all around their contents, enhancing the convection currents within so that everything cooked efficiently and evenly.

If made freestanding on three stout integral legs, with a pair of hanger-loops at the rim, these cast vessels were called standards, since they stood unmoved, as virtual fixtures. Moving one of these was not an easy task, since the great weight of the larger examples would demand the skills and expertise of a bell-hanger or gunnery engineer. It stayed on the hearth while being filled, heated and emptied. The earliest surviving example is at Lacock Abbey, Wiltshire. A raised band around its girth bears a Latin inscription which informs us that it was cast in Mechelen (Malines) in Flanders by Peter Weghevens in 1500. A number of cooking pots were being imported from this source in the fifteenth century, the Prior's kitchen at Durham having 'one pot of Melan' in 1459/60.[25] The Earl of Huntingdon had nine standards in his kitchen at Dartington Hall in *c.*1400, while Earl John de Warenne probably had one heated over its own hearth at Sandal Castle in the 1330s–1340s.[26]

Other cast boiling vessels had neither legs nor hanging loops, but three or four horizontally projecting fins about half or three-quarters way up their bodies. One probable English early fourteenth-century example has a 27-gallon bag-shaped body, the Warwick boiler described above being rather more globular, and datable to around 1500.[27] These were both designed to fit within furnaces, cylindrical structures which supported their fins, so as to hold them over fires lit at ground level. This arrangement ensured that the fierce heat of the flames played around the

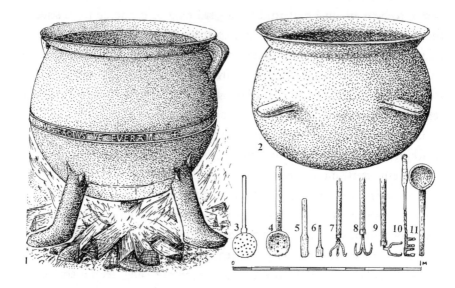

Figure 24. Boiling pots and utensils.

1. A standard, Lacock Abbey, cast by Peter Waghevens of Mechelen (Malines), 1500.

2. The Warwick Castle furnace pot, 'Guy of Warwick's Porridge Pot', English c. 1400.

3. William Coke's skimmer, St Mary Redcliffe, Bristol, 1479.

4. A wooden skimmer from St Nicholas' Hospital, Hambledown, Kent, 15–16c?

5–6. Potsticks of oak and yew from medieval London.

7–8. Iron flesh-hooks on wooden handles, late medieval York.

9. Iron flesh-hook on wooden handle, from Salisbury.

10. All-iron flesh-hook, from Potter Street, Norwich, c. 1507.

11. Wooden ladle from St Nicholas' Hospital, Hambledown, Kent, 15–16c.

pot for as long as possible, without being dispersed by draughts. It also made for cleaner and safer cooking too, making it easier to regulate the fire, containing sparks and burning logs, and protecting the cooks as they filled, stirred and emptied the boilers. There are numerous documentary references to furnaces of this type, the 'Sethyng-howse' at Durham having two great pots 'in furnis' in 1459/60, while at Down Ampney in Gloucestershire, 'a lead vat called fourneys' was valued at 13s. 4d. in 1400. In England the term 'lead' had actually referred to bronze vessels, rather than leaden ones, from at least the fourteenth century, when there are references to 'a lede of bras'.[28]

The simplest furnaces for large boilers were probably just low encircling kerbs of stone as in the twelfth-century keep at Middleham Castle, but soon were being replaced by more efficient versions with a thick wall of clay around a wattle frame, leaving an arched fireplace at one side. Those constructed c.1250–1340 at the moated house at Wintringham, Huntingdonshire, had their fireplaces designed to pierce the kitchen wall, so that they could be fired from outside, and thus keep the kitchen clean and tidy.[29] The furnaces of 1294–c.1301 in the Caernarfon Castle boiling house are set in a long masonry hob along one side of the room, all beneath a huge arched flue designed to carry off their smoke and steam. A window at one side provides good illumination, while at the other there was probably a cistern fed from the well-house, providing the necessary water. The actual furnaces have an almost hourglass section, the bottom half containing the burning logs and faggots in its combustion chamber. The flames were then constricted, to emerge as a strong, vertical blast directly under the convex base of the boiler mounted above, the bowl-shaped upper section of the furnace keeping the flames just a few inches from the boiler's sides, before they passed up the flue. The same highly efficient system was used to boil the brewing water and the wort in the Fountains Abbey brewhouse, where the bottom halves of their massive furnaces still remain intact.[30]

Where boilers were located within the main kitchen, they were often built into the sides of the fireplace recesses. At their simplest, as in the Dartington Hall kitchen of 1388–99, they take the form of tall 2-foot-square niches set into the side walls, each probably intended to take one of the four great standard pots of bronze, four great copper ladles, and four small bronze ladles listed there in 1400.[31] Even though each niche has a vent in its roof, by which steam and fumes could be drawn up and away into the upper part of the chimney, the actual form of their furnaces is unknown, as any internal masonry has been removed. The surviving furnaces at Warkworth, Ashby de la Zouch and a number of other castles all adopt a common form, having a cylindrical interior with a ledge some 30 inches from ground level, an arched fireplace facing into the side of the adjacent hearth, and an enclosed space above, with a vent leading either to the open air or to the upper part of the main chimney. Once a large pot had been suspended inside, and its rim sealed to the inner ledge with mortar and sheet lead, this type of furnace could be fired like a bread oven, burning faggots being thrust to the back of its firing chamber, so that the flames would pass beneath and around the pot, before emerging from the top of the fireplace arch and ascending the main chimney. This ensured that as much of their heat as possible was transferred to the pot, rather than being lost to the open air. In use, a large rectangular opening facing into the kitchen above the top of the pot gave the cooks ready access for tipping in water and meat, skimming, and removing the cooked joints and pottage in much greater safety and comfort. Now their toes and shins were completely protected from the fire, no ashes or embers rolled onto the kitchen floor, and no steam billowed out into the kitchen, this being drawn off by the vent above.

In a later development, the fireplace was still located in the side-wall of the hearth, but the flames were now conducted backwards under the bottom of the boiler, around a baffle, and then forwards around both the upper sides of the boiler to a chimney directly above the fireplace. This made for a much more efficient use of fuel, since the flames passed twice their former distance around the boiler. This system was later used for most great boiling houses, including those at Hampton Court Palace.

Unlike most other domestic utensils, boilers could bring their owners great benefits even after death, helping him or her to progress more easily through purgatory. In 1485 Dame Margaret Pigot left the great brass pot which stood in her furnace to the monks of Coverham Abbey, in return for which each was to give a requiem mass, placebo and

Figure 25. Boiler furnaces.
1. Boiling house, Caernarfon Castle, Gwynedd, 1294–c.1301.
2. Kitchen fireplaces, Dartington Hall, Devon, c.1388–99.
3. Boiling house/kitchen, Warkworth Castle, Northumb., c.1377–90.
4. Privy kitchen, Ashby de la Zouch Castle, Leics., 1474–83.

dirige for the benefit of her soul.[32] Similarly John Brown, the Yorkshire bronze-founder, left a great brass pot to St Anthony's Guild in return for prayers, while Isabell Wilton of Hull left her brass pot and two copper kettles 'to our Lady kirk' so that they could be melted down as a material contribution to the new bells which would ring out over her parish.[33]

Before starting to boil, it was first necessary to soak the salted ingredients. Fresh or green-salted beef had only to be rinsed or wiped, but long-salted beef had to be soaked for perhaps a day, depending on its hardness, changing the water from time to time. Good quality salt ling, like the best quality modern salt cod, might be ready for cooking after only 2 to 4 hours, but traditional stockfish was much harder. It was customary to soak it in water for 12 hours, leave it on a board for another 12 hours and soak it for 12 hours more in clean water before it was ready for use. Some medieval stockfish demanded even more desperate measures, having to be laid on a block and pounded with a heavy mallet to soften it before soaking. Durham Priory had two 'stokfisshammers' in its kitchen in 1480/81.[34]

Having prepared the ingredients, the boiling could now begin. For fresh meat, the boiler would be half to two-thirds filled with cold water, brought up to boiling point, the joints put in, brought back to the boil, and the foamy scum skimmed off the surface to keep the stock clear and bright. To medieval cooks this process was absolutely essential. Henry Watson confirms the fact by a remark in his 1509 translation of *Ship of Fools*: 'This foole settynge his pottes to the fire is so lunatyke that he taketh no hede to scumme them'.[35] Scummers, the utensils used both to take off the scum and to remove small items of food, were made of iron, bronze or wood. Each had a very shallow round bowl about 6 inches in diameter and pierced by concentric circles of small holes, all mounted on the end of a long handle.[36]

William Coke's 1479 gravestone in Bristol's church of St Mary Redcliffe bears the outline of an all-metal skimmer, while at St Nicholas' Hospital at Hambledown, Kent, the lepers were reputed to have used a completely wooden example as a begging bowl for collecting alms. A copy of this is now to be seen in the Science Museum in London.[37]

From time to time the boiler would have to be stirred, initially to prevent the joints sticking together and at a later stage once thickening had been added to the stock. One fifteenth-century recipe even instructs, 'But stir it well with 2 stirrers for setting too' [sticking].[38] Round sticks like the Cumbrian and Scottish spurtle, the medieval 'potstyks of tre', and 'thivels', the north-country version, would have proved satisfactory for the thinner gruels, but for thicker mixtures flat sticks were much more efficient. These were variously known as 'spatures', 'spatyles of tree', or 'sklyces', a slice still being a porridge stick in Victorian Lancashire.[39] A number of oak and yew examples have been excavated from the City of London. There is also documentary evidence for slices of iron but to date none has been recognized from excavations.

As simmering proceeded, the cook would check the flavour of the stock. If too salty, a dishful of oatmeal would be tied in a piece of linen cloth and suspended near the bottom of the boiler where it would absorb the salt and make the stock palatable. This simple but practical solution had very significant implications for English cookery. Having discovered that oatmeal cooked in this way was both easy to prepare and good to eat, Elizabethan cooks developed the technique to create the boiled pudding, one of our most characteristic national dishes.

Once the joints had cooked to tenderness, they were removed from the boiler with a flesh-hook. The earliest of these had two or three hooked iron tines projecting from the end of a long wooden handle, but from the fourteenth century the tines moved down to one side.[40] Those shown in a manuscript from the monastery of St Bartholomew, Smithfield, and on a misericord in Maidenhead parish church, have three tines driven through the handle. Others, from excavations at Northolt Manor, Middlesex, the City of London and other places, have heads completely forged in one piece driven into the end of the handle. This would make them easy to use, and to replace once the handle had worn out.[41] After being lifted out of the boiler, the joints, now half their original weight, were presumably left to rest for some 10 to 20 minutes so that they would be easier to carve when served.

Fish, meanwhile, would have been cooked in the boiling house each fish-day using the following recipes. A skimmer or an iron dish would be used to lift it from the boiler, due to its delicacy.[42]

HADDOCK OR CODLYNG[43]

Haddock or codling   *salt*

Draw the fish by slicing along the belly, removing all the internal organs, and rinsing it clean.

Put sufficient water in the boiler, add 1 tsp salt per pint, or 10g per litre, bring to the boil, put in the fish, skim, and poach gently for some 10–15 minutes per lb/450g weight of individual fish.

Drain the fish, retaining the stock, and serve with either garlic sauce, ginger sauce, mustard or verjuice and pepper.

STOCKFISH[44]

1lb/450g salt cod, soaked overnight and drained
½pt/300ml fish stock   *¼tsp ground ginger*
2tbs fresh parsley, chopped   *4tbs/60ml wine vinegar*

Place the fish in a pan with plenty of cold water, slowly bring to the simmer, skim, and poach gently for some 10–15 minutes until tender, then remove onto a dish.

Meanwhile, simmer the remaining ingredients for 10 minutes and pour over the fish in the dish, or serve with the following sauce.

SAUCE FOR STOCKFISH[45]

3oz/75g walnut kernels   *4tbs white soft breadcrumbs*
1 clove garlic   *½tsp salt*
large pinch ground black pepper

Grind all the ingredients together to form a smooth paste, moisten to a runny consistency with a little of the liquid the fish was cooked in, and serve in a saucer.

Now that the meat and the fish had been cooked and drained, attention turned to the remaining stocks, for these had to be converted into well-flavoured and slightly thickened pottages. Before proceeding any further, however, the cooks would diligently remove every scrap of fat which floated in a molten layer on top of the stock. This might have made the pottages more palatable but, more to the point, this fat or 'kitchen-fee' was one of the cooks' major perquisites, something they could sell off and pocket the proceeds. This was common practice from the earliest times through to at least the late nineteenth century, but the better organized households imposed regulations to prevent the privilege being abused. The Duke of Clarence's cook had to agree that 'no fees to be had of greace comynge of the lede, till my lords and his householde be sufficiently served, for fryinge, and for the uncture of the chariottes and cartes, as it shall be needful, by the oversight of the clerk of the averye; the remanent to be feeable.'[46] This fat was also used to fuel lamps, such as stone cressets, used for the cheaper forms of lighting.

Ladles were essential for this fat-removing process, *Piers Plowman* describing 'A ladel bugge with a longe stele [handle], That cast for to keppe a crokke to save the fatte abouven.' In Chaucer's *Knight's Tale* 'the coke yscalded [was], for al his longe ladel', but presumably it was worth the effort, Dame Alice de Bryene's steward selling 162lb of the household's 'floteys' or kitchen fee at a penny a pound in 1418–19.[47] In major kitchens, the ladles would be of copper, brass or iron, those used in smaller establishments being of wood, their bowls turned on a lathe, and the handles carved all from a single block, as seen in contemporary illustrations.

With the fat removed, the cook would now stir the pre-cooked and chopped pot-herbs and cereal thickening into the stock in the boiler. Since the resulting pottage had to be served before the boiled meats and fish, it was essential that these additions were pre-cooked and chopped beforehand, so that the whole boilerful of pottage was ready for serving within a matter of minutes. The principal pottage herbs were recorded in verse by one of the King's sergeant-cooks in the late fifteenth century:[48]

All maner of herbys for potage
Take the croppe of red brere [briar]
Rede nettyll croppe and avence also
Prymerose, Violet togeder most goo
Letyse, betys and borage gode
Towne cresse and cresse that groweth yn flode
Clare, savery, tyme gode wone
Parsle, warth other herbe many one.
All thes herbes thow not forsake
But best of prymerose thow schalt take,
Red cole halfe parte of potedge ys
Fro June to Saynte Jame tyde [25 July] I Wys,
Then Wynter his cowrse schall holde,
In lent seson porray [leeks] be bolde.

Other recipes include mallows, langue de boeuf, orach (mountain spinach), fennel and onions, but Piers Plowman confirmed that the main pottage herbs were his 'porettes [leeks] and percyl and moni Col-plantes'.[49] Coles included virtually every edible variety of brassica, such as sea-kale and other cabbage-like plants which did not form a solid head. Planted at different seasons, they were available for much of the year, along with onions. It is not surprising that their name became synonymous with pottage, the English cole, Irish *cál* and Scots *kail* all owing their origins, reflected in similar words in Norwegian, Swedish, German and French, to the early introduction of these plants from Latin-speaking countries further south.[50] The following recipes give a good impression of the type of pottage which would be cooked in the boiling house, all the greens being pre-cooked ready for stirring into the simmering stock so as to produce virtually instant results.[51]

LANGE WORTYS DE CHARE

Worts, the leaves cut in 2 or 3, saffron and salt, marrow bones, and grated white bread in beef stock.

JOUTS

Avens, beet leaves, borage, langue de boeuf, mallow, orach, parsley, violet leaves and young worts, finely chopped and ground with white bread and marrow bones in beef stock.

CABOGES

Cabbages, with marrow bones, saffron, salt and white breadcrumbs in either beef stock or beef stock thickened with fine oatmeal.

WHYTE WORTS

The same herbs as jouts, with rice flour, almond milk, saffron, salt and a little honey in beef stock.

BEEF Y-STEWYD

Minced onions, parsley and sage, with cinnamon, cloves, grains of paradise, cubebs and mace. Boil a white loaf in stock and vinegar, rub this through a sieve, and mix with the herbs, spices and remaining stock, then adjust the taste with saffron, vinegar and salt.

WORTIS

Kale leaves, avens, beet leaves, betony, borage, the white of leeks, nettles, mallow, parsley, primrose and violet leaves, all minced with fine oatmeal and salt, in fish stock. Boned stewed eels may be ground to a paste and stirred in, or the pottage made with the liquor of stewed mussels, and the mussels removed from their shells.

Figure 26. From pig to pork in manuscript illustrations.
(1) fattening on acorns; (2) stunning as it feeds; (3) cutting the jugular; (4) burning off the hair; (5) hanging on a cameral and drawing; (6) cleaning the gut for making chitterlings and cases for puddings; (7–9) the sides hung up; (10) the organ-meat and lights for immediate consumption; (11) a sucking pig trussed onto its spit for roasting.

LANGE WORTYS DE PESOUN

> Boiled green peas rubbed through a sieve, shredded onions and
> worts boiled whole before being cut into 3 or 4 pieces, with
> saffron and salt in fish stock.

Finally, the pottage could be ladled into large dishes, one for each mess
waiting in the hall, and passed through the dresser hatch to the assembled
waiters. Just a few minutes later, either the joints of meat or the fish
would follow the same route, hundreds of servants thus being served
with two courses of hot nourishing food in the most efficient manner.

The role of the boiling house often extended to other parts of the
kitchen, especially in the making of more delicate pottages. As the meat
simmered, chickens might be inserted alongside it to pre-cook and have
their flavour enriched before making berandyles, a dish of spiced ground
chicken.[52] The boiler also acted as the kitchen's stock-pot, its beefy liquor
being ladled out into smaller pots with pre-soaked wheat to make frumenty, with rice to make rice pottage, or with beans, cabbages, leeks, onions
or turnips to give them a richer taste.[53] Its great boilers might also have
been used for preparing two of the most prestigious of all medieval dishes,
brawn and boar's head. The wild boar, the fiercest native game in England,
was intelligent, strong, bulky, swift and armed with razor-sharp tusks
designed to disembowel men, horses and hounds. To take one required
horses, mastiffs, bows and arrows, swords, boar spears and nerves of steel.
Sir Gawain and the Green Knight vividly describes the whole adventure. It
is not surprising that boar meat formed the centrepiece of any great feast.
It was particularly associated with Christmas, and was ideally obtained in
late November so that the cooks could start its long period of preparation.
On 23 November, 1502, Sir Gilbert Talbot presented Queen Elizabeth
of York, wife of Henry VII, with a wild boar, ready for her Christmas
feasts.[54] The muscular shoulders of the boar were called brawn: excellent,
well-flavoured solid meat, rather than the jellied head-meat known by that
name in later centuries.

The brawn was prepared by sousing, a method of preserving or
pickling in ale, wine, cider or vinegar and salt. This method was known

in the fourteenth century, but no contemporary recipe appears to have been recorded.[55] Seventeenth-century versions probably follow well-established medieval precedents by boning the meat and trussing it with either bulrushes, osier, or linen tape. Then it was plainly boiled until it was so soft that its fat could be pierced by a straw. After being drained and allowed to cool, it was plunged into barrels filled with sousing pickle, and left until required for use at Christmas. Only then was it drained, sliced, and the slices built up in a deep layer on a large charger ready for elaborate garnishing. Stems of yew or gorse were dipped in beaten egg-white and strewn with flour to resemble hoar-frost before being stuck into the centre of the slices, or perhaps even gilded rosemary used instead. Small pieces of gold and silver leaf were then dotted onto the brawn, three concentric rings of bayleaves stuck in vertically around the edge, and the perimeter decorated with red and yellow jelly, carved lemons and oranges, barberries, gilded bayleaves and more. This treatment ensured that the brawn would make a spectacular appearance when carried through the hall at Christmas.[56]

The boar's head made an even more impressive dish, so much so that in 1170 Henry II was proud to serve his son as sewer, bringing up a boar's head with trumpets in an already old-established tradition.[57] By the fifteenth century, if not earlier, it was being brought in at Christmas to its own robust, almost martial carol.[58]

> The bores hed in hondis I brynge
> with garlondis gay & byrdis syngynge;
> I pray you all will helpe me to synge
> Qui estis in conivio
>
> *Chorus*   *Caput Apri Refero*
> *Resonen laudes domino*

> The boris hede, I understand
> Ys cheffe servyce in all this londe;
> Wher-so-ever it may be fonde
> Servitur cum sinapio

The boris hede I dare well say,
Anon after the XIIth day
He taketh his leve & goth away
Exivit tune de patria

Today we see television chefs baking pig's heads in the oven without any preparation, thus producing an unhygenic, inedible and wasteful mess, totally alien to the magnificent medieval dish. Since there are no early recipes for its preparation, we have to fall back on later versions, which apparently continued medieval practice through to the twentieth century. These record how it should be boned, cured, stuffed and boiled to emerge as a fine, sliceable pork terrine. Since wild boar's heads are not generally available today, the following uses the head of a modern bacon pig.[59]

THE BOAR'S HEAD

Stage 1. Boning and pickling, 2 to 3 weeks before required

1 pig's head, about 12–14lb/5.5–6.5kg
3lb/1.5kg pork shoulder with skin   12oz/350g salt
8oz/225g large-crystal sea salt   1oz/25g saltpetre
12oz/350g dark brown/muscovado sugar

Boil a kettle of water, and pour a little boiling water over each part of the head in turn, scraping it with the edge of a knife to remove all dirt and hair. Do not immerse the head, for this will raise the temperature of the meat. Today, a disposable razor may effectively remove the bristles. Finally pour boiling water into the ears and nostrils, and use a stiff paintbrush to remove every trace of dirt.

Rinse the head in cold water, dry with a cloth, and lay face down on a board. Using a sharp knife, make a deep cut from beneath the tip of the chin back to the neck, then cut the gums from the lower jaw, to leave it completely exposed. Now remove the tongue.

Turn the head face upwards, probe for the top of the skull with the point of the knife, then gradually cut the flesh free from the forehead and cheek, linking up with the cuts made along the gums so that it may be peeled back. Be careful not to pierce the skin.

Continue working down to the snout, finally cutting through its tough inner sinews to remove the face completely.

Cut the rind from the pork shoulder and cut the meat into long strips some 1in/2.5cm square, along the grain of the meat. Place the rind, strips and face in a shallow ceramic container.

Mix the salts, sugar and spices, tip onto the meat, and rub them into all the pieces for a total of 10 minutes.

Place the container in a cool but frost-free place, and rub the meats in their own brine for 5–10 minutes each day, until required.

Stage 2. Boiling, the day before serving

Drain and rinse the meat, dry with a cloth, and, using a strong trussing needle and strong twine, sew up the eyes and mouth. Cut the cured rind to fit the open back of the head, and sew the bottom half in place.

Prepare a forcemeat by finely mincing and grinding the following:

3lb/1.5kg pork shoulder meat	2oz/50g salt
3lb/1.5kg rindless streaky bacon	2tsp mixed spice
meat of 4 rabbits	half a nutmeg, grated
8oz/225g English onions	2tsp ground black pepper

Cut a further 1lb/450g streaky bacon into long strips about ¾in/2cm square.

Line the bottom of the head with some of the forcemeat, lay on a few strips of the cured pork shoulder alternating with those of the streaky bacon, covering these with more forcemeat, continuing this process until the head is completely stuffed.

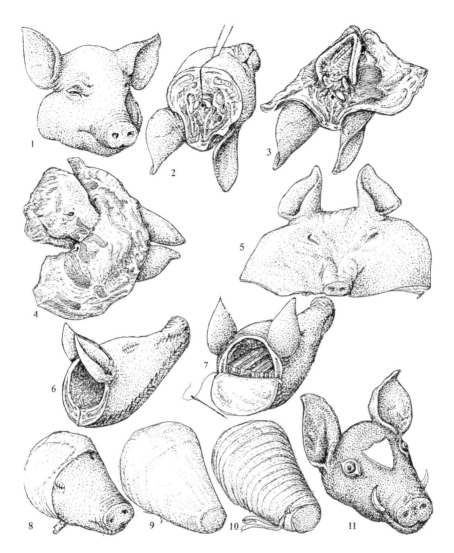

Figure 27. To cook a boar's head.

(1) scald and shave the head; (2) cut from the throat to chin; (3) expose the bottom jaw; (4) turn over and expose the skull; (5) remove the face, and cure it with salt etc.; (6) sew up the throat and other orifices; (7) pack with pork forcemeat and strips of cured pork, sewing up the neck with a piece of cured belly-pork; (8) bandage down the ears; (9) tie in a piece of linen cloth; (10) truss with bandage, boil, cool, and (11) rub with soot and lard, erect the ears, and garnish with the tusks and eyes, shield etc. in lard.

Sew up the loose flap of rind to completely enclose the stuffing. Lay the head face upwards on a board, fold the ears down across the forehead, and bind in place with a broad strip of muslin. This prevents the ears from dissolving during boiling.

Lay the head face down on a 2ft/60cm-square of muslin, and tie diagonal corners tightly together to cover the head.

Using some 20-foot by 3-inch (6m by 8cm) strips of muslin, tightly bind the head, to give it the required shape.

Place the head either on a trivet or on a bed of carrot, parsnip and onions in a large pan, cover with water, bring slowly to the boil, skim, and simmer gently with the lid on for 5 hours. (Victorian recipes boil the head in rich stocks with Madeira.)

Remove from the heat and allow to cool. When tepid, drain, turn onto a large dish, remove the binding, and carefully unfold the ears to their erect position, holding them in place with skewers stuck into the ear-holes. Leave in a cool place overnight to set.

Stage 3. Garnishing, the day of serving

8oz/225g lard
1 pair boar tusks (or celery curled to represent them)
black food-colouring paste (replacing chimney soot)
1 glacé cherry (formerly, artificial glass eyes were used)
sprays of fresh bayleaves and rosemary

Chill half the lard. The remainder is beaten or warmed a little until soft and beaten with the black food colouring to form a black paste. Rub this over the head to give it the colour of a black wild boar.

Set the head on a bed of bay and rosemary on its serving dish, and replace the skewers in the ears with sprigs of rosemary. (Those who put herbs in the ears and nostrils to prevent catching the Plague were said to resemble boar's heads.)

Cut open a little of each side of the mouth and insert the tusks.

Cut out a flat shield-shape from the chilled lard, decorate with an appropriate coat of arms or badge, and set in the centre of the forehead.

Cut eye shapes from thin slices of the chilled lard, place over the eyes, securing a half-round of glacé cherry over each one with a clove.

Having been brought in with the appropriate ceremonial, the head may be sliced across, working from the neck end, and trimming off the skin around the area to be sliced. It has a very good flavour, resembling that of a very superior pork pie.

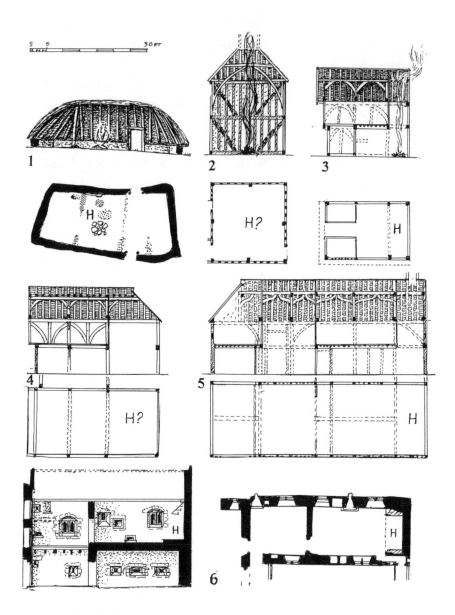

Figure 28. Smaller kitchens.

1. Peasant house, Beere, Devon 13c.
2. Little Braxted, Essex, 1398–1424.
3. Comphurst, Wartling, Sussex.
    H - Hearth.

4. Hever Brocas, Kent, early 15c.
5. Old Rectory, Northfleet, Kent 1488–9.
6. Aydon Castle, Northumb., 1300–15.

CHAPTER TEN

The Kitchen

The size, construction and facilities of medieval kitchens varied enormously from one household to another, depending on the number and status of those to be fed. At the most basic level, some families lacked any room which could be recognized as a kitchen. Their food preparation, if any, was carried out in the living-room without a fireplace. These were the town-dwellers who lived in houses such as Lady Row, Goodramgate, York, one-up and one-down cottages lining a major city-centre thoroughfare where trading or craft activities were probably more important than home-cooking.[1] Here it would be far more convenient to live on take-away food from one of the local cookshops, re-heating if necessary on a chafing dish. This anticipates the widespread modern practice of using the sandwich and office microwave for regular urban meals.

In most other modest urban houses, and in small rural houses, the living area and kitchen were usually combined into a single room, perhaps some 15 feet or 5 metres square. This enabled the woman of the house to maintain a single fire and carry out her multifarious duties with maximum efficiency. It was so effective that in terms of size and function the kitchen/living-room continued in everyday use up to at least the latter half of the twentieth century in most English homes. From numerous excavated examples, such as those at Beere in Devon or Wharram Percy in the East Riding, it is seen that the kitchen/living-room usually formed the central unit of a long, ridge-roofed structure.[2] Variously called the hall, firehouse or housebody, it had a pair of opposed doors providing a through draught, or a means of directing and controlling the draught according to the direction of the wind, to help manage the fire burning in the centre of the room. To reduce the effect of sudden gusts or of driving rain, screens might extend some way across the room just within the doors, simple versions of the elaborate oak screens found in great halls. Beyond the doors, at the lower end of the room, milch-cows and calves might be stalled, providing the house with dairy produce and additional heating. At the upper end, a door led into an inner room or chamber used for sleeping and the storage of more valuable items. The 1481 inventory of William Akclum of Wharram-le-Street provides an excellent picture of such a property in use.[3] On entering the 'house', its central hearth was seen to have a spit and a reckon and a pair of kilps for suspending a pan and a kettle over the fire. By the walls stood an aumbry or cupboard for storing food and other perishables and a 'caul', the local form of dresser, for food preparation. Its base had bars to cage some of his fourteen hens. A chair and a cloth-covered meat-board were provided for dining. These, with a few utensils, linen-spinning equipment and farming hand-tools, completed its contents.

As described earlier, many of the houses occupied by the more prosperous, such as yeomen, minor gentry and merchants, found it rather cleaner and safer to have their kitchens and living-rooms in quite separate buildings. These kitchens might be single square rooms, such as the pyramid roofed (and louvred?) early fifteenth-century example at Little Braxted in Essex. Others were divided into a number of separate units.[4] That at Comphurst, Wartling, Sussex, has a room at each side of a wide entrance passage, which terminates in a square kitchen, the end of which extends up to the roof to form a smoke-bay to carry off the smoke from the hearth. A large chamber occupied most of the first floor, which might have been used either for storage or for accommodation. D. and B. Morris have traced a lease of a property owned by the Abbot and Convent of Westminster to the Vicar of Kelvedon, Essex, in 1356 which appears to describe a very similar building. After dealing with the main residence, it lists: 'also one other house in three parts, namely a kitchen with a convenient chamber in the end of the said house for guests, and a bake-house.' A 1557 reference to Great Worge, Brightling, Sussex, describes its kitchen as having a room to dress meat in, with an oven, an oast to dry malt, a bakehouse, a milkhouse and further rooms above.[5] Such multiple-use kitchen and service blocks would certainly have proved extremely useful and convenient, enabling all food preparation and storage operations to be concentrated and contained in a single unit.

The only major problem when cooking in a detached kitchen was that all food, whether hot or cold, had to be carried for a distance in the open air before it reached the dining areas. Rain, snow, mud and gusts of wind carrying in straw and leaves were best kept out of the house, but this was unavoidable with detached kitchens. The obvious solution was to incorporate the kitchen into the main living quarters. This was certainly happening in early fifteenth-century Kent, where houses such as Hever Brocas, Hever, had its kitchen set beneath a large chamber across the bottom end of its hall, one end extending as a roof-height smoke-bay over the hearths. By the end of the century, the kitchen and its smoke-bay were being entirely contained within the extended portion of the cross-wing, as at Campion House, Benenden, and Lynsted Court. The alternative was to place the kitchen and its smoke-bay on the same axis as the hall, beneath the same ridged roof, as at the Old Rectory House, Northfleet, Gravesend, which was built c.1448/9.[6] Such developments were still quite rare, however, and detached kitchens continued to be used in most houses of this status well into the post-medieval period.

With the exception of low sill-walls of stone, clay or cob used in some areas, virtually all the kitchens so far mentioned were timber-framed and roofed with thatch, slate or tile. Exactly the same materials were used for the much larger kitchens required in major houses, castles and palaces. These were usually at least 25 to 30 feet square, but could be larger and longer for royal and noble households. Being timber-framed, they were relatively quick and cheap to erect, were safe and sound on newly-raised earthworks, and could be readily dismantled and removed if required elsewhere. Wooden kitchens were also ideal for temporary use at great feasts, a practice followed for coronation feasts at Westminster Hall into the post-medieval period. Some of the early timber castle kitchens could be quite small, that serving the hall at Sandal Castle c.1106–30 being only 13 feet square. Its roof, probably thatched, was perhaps supported on A-frame crucks set into post-holes at each corner.[7] A building like this would be capable of serving the culinary needs of a basic garrison and construction crew, but not those of a lord and his full retinue. For them,

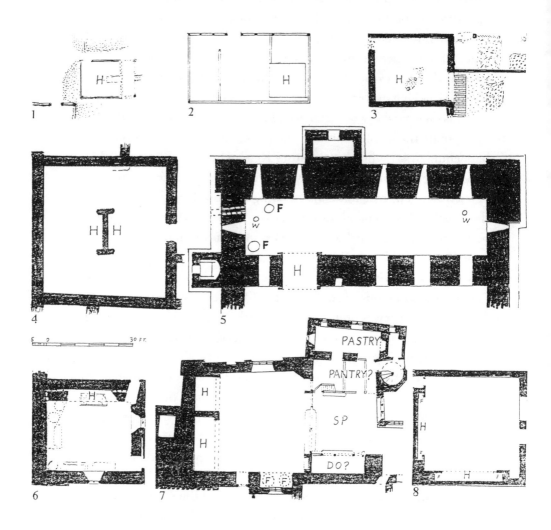

Figure 29. Larger kitchens.

1. Sandal Castle, Yorks., c.1106–30.   5. Middleham Castle, Yorks., 12c.

2. Weoley Castle, Birmingham, pre-1210. 6. Ludlow Castle, Salop, 15c.

3. Northolt Manor, Middx., early 14c.   7. Durham Castle, 1153–95 and 1490s.

4. Clarendon Palace, Wilts., 1176–7.   8. Dartington Hall, Devon, 1390s.

F - Boiler furnaces; DO - Dresser office; H - Hearth; SP - Surveying-place; W - Well.

something like the pre-1210 kitchen at Weoley Castle, Birmingham, would be more suitable. Measuring some 20 by 40 feet, its timber framing was clad in weatherboard and topped with a reed-thatched roof.[8] Not surprisingly, such buildings were frequently damaged or destroyed by fire, and so were largely replaced by permanent stone structures from the twelfth century onwards.

Despite their great expense, stone kitchens proved themselves immensely permanent. That built by Bishop Pudsey (1153–95) at Durham Castle was in almost continuous use from that date up to the present time. Most were square in plan, but other shapes might be chosen to suit local circumstances. For the largest households, they could grow to great rectangles 80 feet or more in length; they might curve to follow the line of a curtain wall, as at Pontefract Castle; or become polygonal to fit an angle in the defences as at Berkeley Castle, or to occupy a projecting tower, as at Raglan Castle.[9] Within their walls, the arrangement of their structure and fixtures was subject to considerable variation, and each element is best considered individually, starting with the hearths and then moving on to the roofs, galleries and dresser hatches.

In the earlier kitchens the hearths were set towards the centre of the floor, away from the walls and easily accessible from all sides. It was almost a continuation of cooking out of doors, but with the advantages of walls and a roof to exclude intruders and the elements. The first stone Sandal Castle kitchen had three separate hearths, a round one for a large cauldron or beef-pot, a long one with gallows-posts for simmering and roasting, and a small stone-paved hearth probably for bakestones, frying-pans and pots supported on brandreths. At Weoley Castle, the hearth occupied a 12 by 13-foot rectangle in one corner of the kitchen, where all these operations could be carried out simultaneously, while at the early fourteenth-century kitchen at Northolt Manor, Middlesex, there was only a small long hearth with gallow-posts, the main hearths being under open-sided lean-to roofs to one side.[10]

Even when burning dry fuel, the unrestrained smoke always caused problems in buildings such as these. On still, foggy days it hung motionless in the roof-space, in stormy weather it billowed down onto the cooks and the food, and when it rained, its accumulated soot was dissolved to form the foul 'hallan drop' which stained everything it fell upon. Most of these problems could be alleviated by moving the hearths from the central floor area to the side walls, and building chimney stacks above to extract their smoke. At Clarendon Palace, the early thirteenth-century household kitchen attempted to retain the central fire by containing two back-to-back hearths within an H-planned central masonry chimney stack.[11] Although this followed an accepted monastic tradition, it must have proved very awkward, effectively dividing the kitchen into two. A similar solution was attempted in the twelfth-century basement kitchen at Middleham Castle in North Yorkshire, where the hearth was accessible from both sides of its spine-wall. Such hearths were rarely, if ever, used in later kitchens.[12]

From the early fourteenth century, most new stone-walled kitchens began to incorporate hearths and chimneys against their outer walls, but it is probable that their central floor areas retained some provision for cooking. It is interesting to note the total lengths of hearths now being provided in kitchens. For example:

1326	Caerphilly Castle	33ft	(Kitchen: 33ft.sq.)
14th century	Sonning Bishop's Palace	18ft	(Kitchen: 35ft.sq.)
14th century	Hull Manor	20ft	(Kitchen: 28ft.sq.)
1370	Haddon Hall	30ft	(Kitchen: 28ft.sq.)
1378	Raby Castle	c.33ft	(Kitchen: c.30ft.sq.)
1390s	Dartington Hall	38ft	(Kitchen: 32ft.sq.)
late 14th century	Cockermouth Castle	18ft	(Kitchen: c.32ft.sq.)
c.1480	Gainsborough Old Hall	31ft	(Kitchen: c.25ft.sq.)
c.1499	Durham Castle	29ft	(Kitchen: 33ft.sq.)
12th century	Middleham Castle	28ft	(Kitchen: 28 x 85ft)
14th century	Kenilworth Castle	78ft	(Kitchen: 28 x 76ft)
15th century	Pontefract Castle	75ft	(Kitchen: 25 x 90ft)
15th century	Canford Manor	52ft	(Kitchen: 20 x 82ft)

It will be seen that although the Sonning, Hull and Cockermouth kitchens are as large as the other square ones, they had under two-thirds of the hearth length. This certainly suggests that some of their hearth capacity was retained on their floors, rather than that they were deliberately built

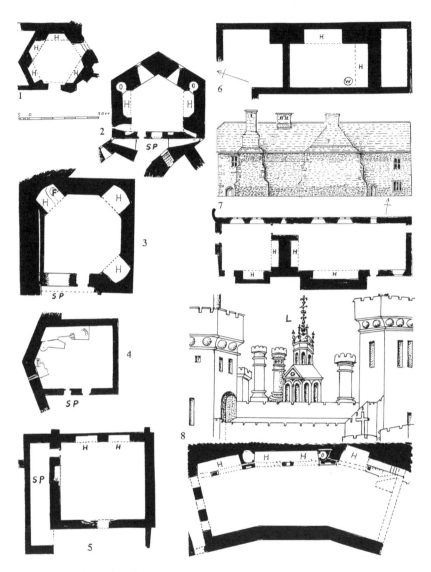

Figure 30. Kitchen plan-forms.

1. Berkeley Castle, Gloucs., 14c.
2. Raglan Castle, Gwent, 1460–69.
3. Caerphilly Castle, c. 1326.
4. Warkworth Castle, Northumb., c. 1400.
5. Sonning Palace, Berks., 14c.
6. Minster Lovell Hall, Oxon., 1430s?
7. Canford Manor, Dorset, 15c. + 16c.
8. Pontefract Castle, Yorks., 15c.

F - Boiler furnace; H - Hearth; L - Louvre; O - Oven; SP - Surveying-place; W - Well.

with a lack of sufficient hearth to serve their households. The size of the hearths in the long rectangular kitchens, particularly those at Kenilworth and Pontefract, clearly shows the difference in scale required when moving from noble to royal catering. It should be remembered, however, that up to half the length of each hearth was probably used for fuel and other storage.

The disposition of the fireplaces around the walls usually placed them close together, either on one wall, or on adjacent walls. This restricted the fuel, heat and smoke to one section of the kitchen, leaving the rest comfortably clean and cool. Some kitchens, such as those at Kidwelly Castle, Hull Manor and Gainsborough Old Hall, placed their fireplaces on opposing walls, but having them on three walls was comparatively rare. Those at Raby Castle were probably arranged in this way to provide the required length of hearth, while still leaving their containing tower strong enough to withstand military action. At Caerphilly Castle, hearths were set diagonally across three corners of the kitchen. Even though its walls now stand only a few feet above floor level, it is obvious that this was a building of exceptional quality, designed to receive a conical masonry roof and louvre. The only comparable polygonally-planned kitchens were those of the thirteenth-century Furness Abbey, St Augustine's Abbey, Canterbury of 1287–91, Charing Palace, Kent, of c.1300 and those of Glastonbury Abbey and Durham Priory of the mid-fourteenth century, all for ecclesiastic rather than lay magnates. Lincoln Palace kitchen of c.1224 also has three diagonally-set corner hearths, as well as two lateral ones, giving a combined hearth length of some 50 feet.[13]

The construction of arched fireplace openings up to 20 feet in width but still strong enough to support heavy chimney stacks, provided a stiff challenge to medieval masons. It would have been easy enough to bridge this with a round-headed or pointed arch, but fireplace arches had to be relatively flat to hold in the smoke and enable the chimney to draw well. The problem with such arches was that they exerted a strong lateral thrust which, if not effectively controlled, would push out the side walls, sending a crack straight up the chimney breast, and bringing the whole structure crashing down. One solution was to keep the hearths quite shallow from front to back, so that they were entirely contained within the thickness of the walls, the mass of masonry on both sides, especially if 20 or 30 feet in height, preventing their arches from spreading. Another method was to incorporate a relieving arch, a strong arch built above the fireplace arch to absorb the bulk of its load. By the late fifteenth century such arches might adopt an inverted V-shape as at Durham Castle, or a shallow four-centred profile as at South Wingfield and Gainsborough Old Hall. The latter were so effective that they allowed horizontal oak beams to provide flat tops to the wide fireplace openings.

In order to extract their smoke more effectively, some kitchen fireplaces had smoke hoods which projected out from their chimney breasts. At Dartington Hall the fireplaces were 20 feet wide by only 3 feet deep, while those at Cockermouth Castle were 11 feet wide by only 2 feet. Clearly these were far too shallow to prevent the smoke from billowing into their kitchens, making the provision of smoke-hoods absolutely essential. It is probable that those at Dartington, being so large and wide, were framed in wood, but elsewhere they were built in stone. A massive corbel was bedded into the wall at the top of each jamb, this being used to support a shallow or even flat arch a few feet in front of the chimney breast, above which rose a pyramidal stone smoke-hood. The kitchen at the Bishop of Winchester's Wolvesey Palace had a magnificent pair of hearths of this type, as did that at Cockermouth Castle, and there are good examples in the kitchen at Kidwelly Castle, but rather smaller in scale.[14]

At roof level, kitchen chimneys usually rose as tall round or rectangular shafts, their height reducing the risk of down-draughts from the gusts which eddied around the adjacent towers and gables. Both manuscript illustrations and excavated examples show them to have frequently terminated in a projecting castellated rim. As well as enhancing the martial roof-line, these may have increased the chimney's updraught, helping passing winds to draw the smoke up and away.

When fires had burned on the kitchen floor, the roof above had usually adopted a pyramid or cone-shaped form to collect the smoke and funnel it out of a central louvre. It might have been expected that such roofs should have disappeared with the adoption of chimneys in the fourteenth century, but this was not always the case. The reasons for their retention probably included ventilation, the provision of top-light, and the removal of smoke from any cooking still being continued on the kitchen floor. Perhaps just

Figure 31. Fireplaces.

1. Kidwelly Castle, Dyfed, c.1300.   4. Herstmonceux Castle, Sussex, c.1400.

2. Dartington Hall, Devon, c.1388–1400.   5. Durham Castle, 1490s.

3. Kenilworth Castle, Warws., c.1388–94 (reconstruction).

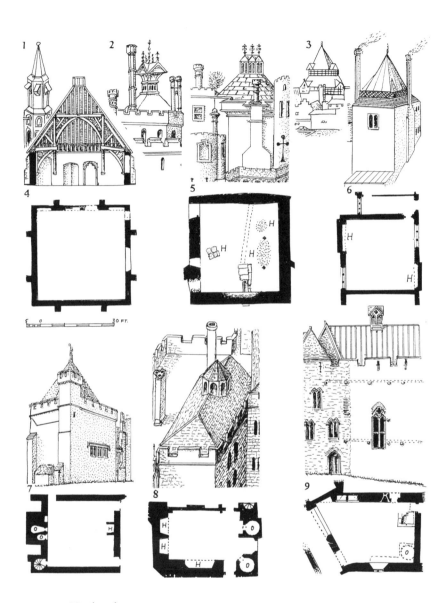

Figure 32. Kitchen louvres.

1. In the Holkham Bible, c. 1320–30.   6. Hull Manor, Yorks., 14c.

2. Melbourne Castle, Derbys.   7. Stanton Harcourt, Oxon., c. 1460–83.

3. Richmond Palace, Surrey, 1498–?   8. Alnwick Castle, Northumb., 14c.

4. Chichester Palace, Sussex, early 13c. 9. Chepstow Castle, Gwent, c. 1282–93.

5. Sandal Castle, Yorks., 1240–70.

as important was their potent external symbolism of great hospitality, equating to wealth, power and influence. They were usually far more than utilitarian roofs, their construction and decoration being of the highest standards. They were the lay equivalent of the chapter houses of great cathedrals, and some of the finest examples of medieval carpentry.

Sometimes these louvred roofs were supported on four stout posts set some 7 or 8 feet in from each corner. The 1245–6 household kitchen at Clarendon Palace and the c.1432 kitchen at Oxburgh Hall, Norfolk, were made in this way, but their posts must always have proved inconvenient.[15] By the late thirteenth century new forms of roof construction made them no longer necessary. The Bishop's kitchen at Chichester was one of the first buildings in England to adopt hammer-beam trusses which raised the bases of the posts high into the air to leave a perfectly unrestricted floor area.[16] Drawings of Hull Manor kitchen suggest that it too had a hammer-beam roof of a rather later date.[17] Most of our knowledge of later medieval pointed kitchen roofs now comes from sketchy early drawings, for only one has survived into the twenty-first century, at Stanton Harcourt, Oxfordshire, which still stands as when first built in c.1460–83.[18] At roof level each of its four corners is spanned by a diagonal arch, to produce an octagonal plan, the springers of each arch having a corbel carved with a human bust to support the wooden superstructure. From each a vertical post rises to frame eight panels of twelve-light louvred openings, eight huge curving ribs then continuing upwards to form a high conical roof.

Major louvre roofs of this kind were very impressive and effective, but similar results could be obtained by setting louvres of smaller diameter on to the tops of much simpler ridged roofs, as at Chepstow Castle, Gainsborough Old Hall, or Alnwick Castle. The finest survival of this type is at St Mary's Guildhall kitchen in Coventry, built around 1400. Here bold stone corbels carved with the Green Man or faces support shallow oak trusses, covered with boarding and lead sheet. In the centre rises a rectangular louvre, topped with a shallow-pitched lead roof, and with two cusped and louvred openings in each wall for ventilation. Whatever their position, louvres were usually topped off with one or more vanes, that for the Eltham Palace kitchen being specifically supplied in 1369 'to see how the wind lies'.[19] Their main function, beyond decoration, was to give the cook

Figure 33. Hammerbeam louvre, the Bishop's Palace, Chichester, early
13c.

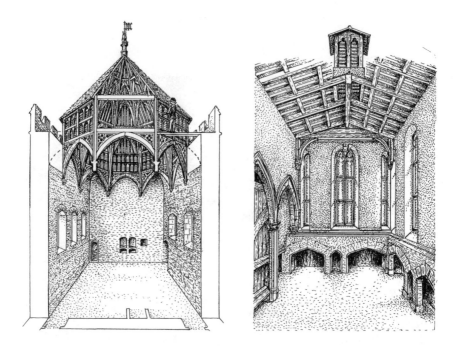

Figure 34. Stanton Harcourt (Oxon.) kitchen, *c.*1460–83 (left). A stair
from the rear door gave access to the roof, from where the louvre-boards
could be adjusted to suit the wind direction as indicated by the vane on
the pinnacle above. At St Mary's Guildhall, Coventry, *c.*1400 (right), the
lead-covered roof retains its rectangular louvre.

all the information he needed to close the pivoted wooden louvre-boards
on one side of the roof and open those on the other, to obtain the best
extraction of smoke and smells from his kitchen. At Stanton Harcourt
and other kitchens with flat walk-ways around their louvres, staircases
were provided so that the boards could be adjusted by hand. Elsewhere
they could be controlled from floor level by means of long cords.[20]

In the greatest of palaces and castles the kitchen's louvred roofs might
be constructed as masonry vaults. Although strong, fireproof and of great
status, these were expensive to erect, requiring the services of a skilled
architect and craftsmen. They showed great originality in design, that
at the Bishop's Palace at St Davids, Pembrokeshire, being particularly
remarkable.[21] From its central column an arch sprang to the centre of

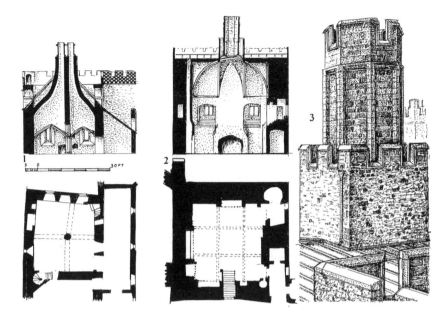

Figure 35. Masonry louvres.

1. St Davids Bishops Palace, Pembroke, 1328–47. Each half of the kitchen has its fumes drawn into a double chimney above each side wall.

2. Raby Castle, Durham, c.1378, its great cross-arches support a square louvre enclosing a narrower octagonal duct (3).

each wall, huge vaulted ducts channelling the smoke rising from any quarter of the kitchen floor into two pairs of chimneys, one against each end wall. This was a considerable technical achievement for the mid-fourteenth century. At Raby Castle, County Durham, the stone vault and louvre probably built by John Lewyn in 1378 still stands intact. Two great semicircular arches spring from each wall, the square formed by their intersection supporting a square louvre within which rises a taller octagonal shaft, both being castellated to improve their performance. Similar vaulted roofs may also have existed at Bolton and Sheriff Hutton castles, but unfortunately their superstructures have been lost through demolition and decay.

The adoption of chimneys to carry smoke away from fireplaces set in the thickness of the walls reduced the need for louvred openings in the roofs or ceilings, so that these could be constructed as simple vaults. About 1170–80 the 85 by 20-foot kitchen in the basement of the great keep at Middleham Castle, North Yorkshire, was built as a plain barrel vault.[22] At the same period, the kitchens in the basements of the keeps at Newcastle upon Tyne and Dover were provided with vaulted roofs; and by the late fourteenth and fifteenth centuries further kitchen vaults were achieving even more impressive proportions. At Ashby de la Zouch Castle, Leicestershire, the almost freestanding household kitchen was provided with a 27 by 50-foot three-bay cross-vault over 30 feet high, providing a fireproof support for a series of chambers above. Even this was out-done by the privy kitchen in the late fifteenth-century Hastings Tower nearby. Here elegant pilasters of contrasting coloured freestone supported an elaborate rib-vaulted roof of the highest quality, once again providing a fireproof floor for the fine chamber on the upper storey.[23] Where this level of fire protection was not required, almost flat timber-framed roofs clad in boarding and sheathed in lead might be used, as at Herstmonceux and Durham castles.

Moving from the roofs to the walls, the main features here were the windows. These were usually either very tall and narrow, or were set around the upper parts of the kitchens so that they could throw the light across the whole room and provide effective ventilation, while maintaining security at floor level. The presence of windows with sills only a few feet from the floor is relatively unusual, and often associated with pastry-working areas, as at Warkworth Castle and Gainsborough Old Hall. Grooves for leaded glass windows are quite rare, completely open lights, perhaps defended with fixed iron bars or grilles, or fitted with hinged wooden shutters, being the norm.

In major kitchens, the clerks of the kitchen and similar senior household officers were enabled literally to oversee the operation of their kitchens from purpose-built galleries. At Gainsborough Old Hall these still remain in place, one apparently being reserved for the clerk of the kitchen, leading from his chamber over the dresser office, and another linking the chambers over the boiling house and pastry. In other kitchens their wooden floors and handrails have disappeared, but the staircases

Figure 36. Vaulted kitchen roofs, Ashby de la Zouch Castle, Leics.
Top. The late-14c. household kitchen has its vault supported on pilasters rising above the gallery. Note the half-glazed windows providing light and ventilation.
Bottom. The privy kitchen of *c.* 1474–83. Note the boiler furnace, well and sink, and the portcullis mechanism.

and doorways which provided access to them still remain, allowing their original dimensions to be accurately reconstructed.

Moving down from the walls to the floors, it would appear that earthen floors were most common, these being reinforced with patches of cobble or rough paving where subject to heat or heavy wear. Only the better kitchens were fully paved, the stone-block paving at Kenilworth Castle's being an impressive survival.

Good drainage was essential in all kitchens, for there were always accidental spillages, or perhaps the need to wash and brush the floors to keep them clean. For these reasons, the floors might be given a pronounced slope. Peasant cottages usually had their living areas higher than their doorways and cattle stalls so that all unwanted liquids would readily drain away. Larger buildings might follow the same principle. The early twelfth-century kitchen at Sandal Castle has a large saucer-shaped sump at one side to receive its liquids (Fig. 29.1). This must have rapidly degenerated into a dirty, stinking, fly-infested puddle, and it is not surprising that better arrangements were rapidly adopted. At Chepstow Castle, for example, the late thirteenth-century kitchen floor was made to slope down several feet away from the serving hatches, a large stone-lined sump in the lowest corner carrying everything away via a duct cut through the adjacent wall.

Kitchens also produced large quantities of waste stocks, washing-up and swilling-down waters and the like. These might be particularly offensive since they included masses of solid or semi-solid matter and fats which would readily congeal and rot down to a foul, unhygienic mess. Even at the Palace of Westminster, the stench of the dirty water being carried through the halls was found to be infecting those who came there. This problem was overcome in 1259 when Henry III ordered his mason, Master John of Oxford, to construct a covered stone conduit to carry all the waste from his kitchen directly into the Thames.[24] Stone sinks for liquids, or sumps for liquids and other waste, are to be found in most medieval castle and major house kitchens, these draining into substantial ducts, many large enough to allow a person to enter should any blockage occur. The accounts of Canterbury College, Oxford, include payments for cleaning the kitchen sink or *gurgitum* (the onomatopoeic Latin for a whirlpool or eddy), and setting iron plates at its opening. A further payment in 1506

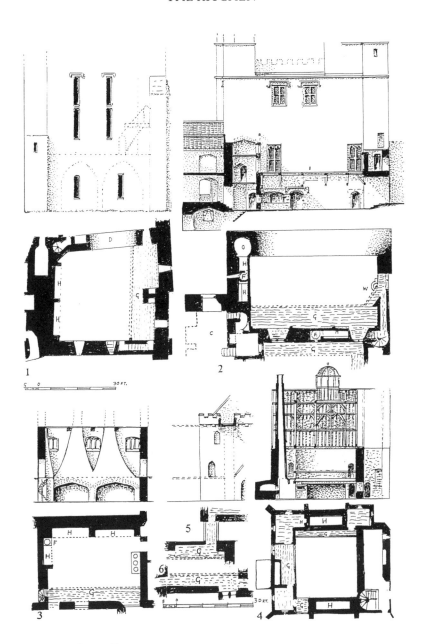

Figure 37. Kitchen galleries.

(1) Cockermouth Castle, Cumbria, 1368–1408; (2) Ashby de la Zouch Castle, Leics.,
late 14c.; (3) Herstmonceux Castle, c.1440; (4) Gainsborough Old Hall, Lincs., c.1480;
(5) Dartington Hall, Devon, c.1388–94; (6) South Wingfield, Derbys., c.1440–59.

enabled two grates to be provided, these keeping back the bones and solids which would have otherwise stopped the flow of water which cleaned the drain passage underground.[25] The Chepstow sump appears to have been designed to receive a large, horizontal floor-level grate of this kind to act as a very coarse strainer for the bucketfuls of kitchen waste thrown into it.

In a number of kitchens, the floor area around the sink or sump was paved and provided with a low kerb. These 'wet areas' would have been ideal for holding the soes and tankards used to bring in water, and also have acted as effective 'draining boards' on which utensils could be rinsed and left to dry off after use. There are particularly good examples in both the bailey and donjon kitchens at Warkworth Castle.

Since the control of raw and cooked foods played such an important part in the management of every household, it was essential that the kitchens should have good perimeter security. Usually there was one door, rarely two, leading out of the kitchen towards the hall and chambers. It was (or they were) invariably inward-opening and lockable. By its side a dresser-hatch also pierced the kitchen wall. Measuring anywhere from a few feet to ten or more in length, and with a flat base at table height, its purpose was to enable dishes of food to be rapidly inspected by the household officers and clerks and delivered to the waiters. To prevent unauthorized entry, such openings were fitted with stout wooden hatches, some hinging upwards internally or externally, or down externally to form a convenient surface for setting out the dishes. One of the latter type is shown in a fifteenth-century English manuscript illustration, with the cook filling dishes from a cast bronze pot on a falling dresser door, supported on two presumably hinged legs.[26] Other doors were hinged from the sides of the hatch, where the holes left by the removal of their hinge-pins still survive. Whichever way they opened, good internal bolts or bars were essential to ensure that they were only opened at the approved times.

In some early buildings, such as Roger Bigod's hall block of 1270–1306 at Chepstow Castle, a room just opposite the dresser hatch may have been used by the officers and clerks when recording the number of dishes being issued, secure cupboards for their accounts being provided in the thickness of the walls.[27] Later dresser offices were placed at one end of the hatches, so that the clerks could get a closer, uninterrupted view. If the building

Figure 38. Dresser hatches and serving-places.
1. John I of Portugal entertaining John of Gaunt, late 15c MS illustration.
2. Gainsborough Old Hall, Lincs, c.1480. 3. Durham Castle, 1499.

allowed it, it was even better for the dresser office to span the thickness of the dresser wall, so that either a doorway or a viewing hatch could enable the clerks to rapidly look down both the internal and external faces of the dresser hatches and to supervise both the kitchen and the waiting staffs simultaneously with maximum efficiency. It is still possible to stand in offices of this type in the late fourteenth-century Ashby de la Zouch Castle kitchen, and in the 1480s example at Gainsborough Old Hall. The efficiency of their plan demonstrates the medieval administrator's pursuit of the very tightest methods of staff management.

In the kitchens described above, most of the cooking was carried out within the main kitchen, perhaps with access to separate pastries, boiling houses and other departments, these being arranged in a haphazard manner in adjacent rooms. In the later fifteenth century, attempts were being made to rationalize this arrangement by combining the separate offices into an integrated whole. Few surviving kitchens demonstrate this development so well as that at Gainsborough Old Hall. Here the central area followed the usual square plan. At one side a deep wide boiling hearth was flanked by a small, separate boiling house, its furnace fired from the main hearth. This was purposely designed as the 'wet' side of the kitchen, probably with access to a well through the adjacent external door. At the opposite 'dry' side lay the wider, narrower roasting hearth, niched seats for the spit-turners being set into each side. By its side the sole ground-floor window lit the table on which pies and pasties were made up for the pastry office and its two large ovens. Although misunderstood and misinterpreted, this kitchen is of the greatest significance, its design and construction clearly demonstrating the high levels of knowledge and skill achieved by late fifteenth-century kitchen planners.

In royal and noble establishments the household kitchen might be left to concentrate on the coarser bulk cookery required for those dining in the body of the hall, a separate privy kitchen being responsible for the finer food served to the lord, his officers and guests dining in the chamber. Privy kitchens appear to have been introduced around the latter half of the thirteenth century, and may be linked to the practice of lords dining in their chambers, rather than in their great halls.

In such households these kitchens could be quite large. That beneath

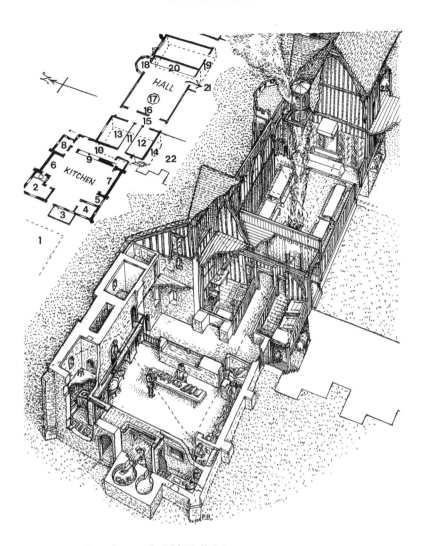

Figure 39. Gainsborough Old Hall, Lincs., *c.*1480.

1. Brewhouse/bakehouse.
2. Boiling house.
3. Pastry ovens.
4. Pastry office.
5. Pastry table.
6. Boiling hearth.
7. Roasting hearth.
8. Dresser office.

9. Dresser hatch.
10. Surveying court.
11. Passage.
12. Pantry.
13. Buttery.
14. Ale cellar below.
15. Screens passage.
16. The towel.

17. Hall fireplace.
18. Dais window.
19. Wine cellar below.
20. Dais.
21. Stair to Lord's chambers.
22. Lodging range.

the royal suite at Conwy Castle c. 1283–7 was over 30 feet long, with a single fireplace, and a doorway cut through the curtain wall. Presumably this last was for waste disposal rather than victualling, since the floor slopes down towards it and it is located beneath a number of latrine chutes. Further internal and external stairs gave ready access to all the royal chambers on the floor above. At the same time that Edward I was building Conwy, Earl Gilbert de Clare was constructing his own great fortress at Caerphilly. Concentric in plan, its rectangular inner ward, enclosed within massive curtain walls defended by great corner towers and gatehouses, was surrounded first by a middle ward some 50 feet wide, and then by a huge defensive lake. The original kitchen was probably in the inner ward, but around 1277–90 Earl Gilbert built a new D-shaped service tower against the curtain wall flanking his great hall. Its basement was built as a malt and brewhouse, and its first floor as a privy kitchen. To provision it, foodstuffs would be barged across the lake to the adjacent postern, and then winched up into a large storeroom, from whence a passage led into the kitchen. Here there was at least one hooded fireplace, probably a boiling furnace and an external drain for waste. When cooked, the food was carried back along the passage, where a dresser office with its own fireplace controlled its delivery through a small serving hatch into the Braose Gallery, a passage in the thickness of the curtain wall leading directly to the Earl's chambers. This arrangement shows that he had particular regard to his own security. Once his c. 40 by 10-foot storeroom had been provisioned, his chamber could be fed almost indefinitely, his privy kitchen being isolated from the inner ward except for the easily guarded serving hatch and a narrow door and stair leading up from ground level.

This was a very unusual privy kitchen, most others being much smaller and closer to the lords' chambers. The early fourteenth-century examples in the keep at Rushen Castle, Isle of Man, and the second floor of the Eagle Tower at Caernarfon are both rectangular, barrel-vaulted chambers, with doors at one end and fireplaces at the other to ensure a good through draught to carry away cooking smells. Both are directly adjacent to the chambers they were to serve, but could be provisioned without entering the chamber, a convenient arrangement which allowed

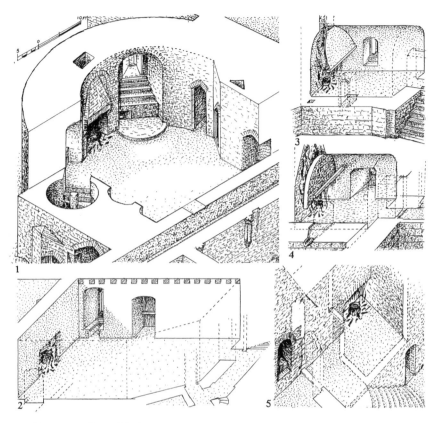

Figure 40. Privy kitchens.

1. Caerphilly Castle, c. 1277–90.   4. Rushen Castle, I. of Man, 14c.

2. Conwy Castle, Gwynedd, 1283–7.   5. Kidwelly Castle, Dyfed, c. 1300.

3. Caernarfon Castle, Gwynedd, post-1300.

The beam across the Rushen Castle kitchen probably represents an earlier timber hood, as at Caernarfon.

the lord to be served with hot food at any time, with minimal trouble. A 1399 reference to 'the Lord's Kitchen' at Kidwelly Castle appears to refer to a room described as 'the little kitchen at the door of the king's hall' in a survey of 1442–3.[28] The surviving masonry of c. 1300 shows that this was a room about 10-foot square set over a basement, with its door just opposite that of the great hall. Here it could be readily provisioned from its external staircase, and its food issued to waiters who would carry it through the hall into the King's Chamber at its upper end.

Not many fifteenth-century privy kitchens have yet been recognized, but those which have appear to be quite large and well-equipped. At Sir John Fastolf's Caistor Castle, Norfolk, built between 1432 and c.1446, his dining-room or winter hall was located on the principal floor of the tall north-western tower. The basement room beneath has a fireplace 13 feet wide, showing that it was designed to serve as a privy kitchen, ideally placed to deliver both food and a degree of under-floor heating to the chamber above.[29] For a truly magnificent privy kitchen, that built in 1474–83 by William, Lord Hastings, to serve his great chamber tower at Ashby de la Zouch Castle is without parallel. Since the tower was virtually freestanding, a remarkably early underground service passage was built from the household kitchen about a hundred feet away, so that its basement storeroom could be provisioned invisibly. There was also a portcullis-defended door at ground level, providing access to two external wells. From the basement store, a spiral stair led up to the privy kitchen, a magnificent rib-vaulted room almost 30 feet square. Its northern 'wet' side had its own well, a sink and a boiler furnace fired from a wide hearth in the west wall. There was probably a roasting hearth further to the south, but regrettably the southern half of the tower was destroyed in the Civil War. From the kitchen door, directly opposite the chamber office (here serving as a dresser office) the food was carried up the next flight of the spiral stair into the great chamber on the floor above. In terms of architectural quality, this kitchen appears to be unique, and demonstrates the importance which Lord Hastings placed upon the food served to those privileged few who dined in his chamber.

Lord Hastings' chamber tower formed a high-status block within a much larger group of buildings which included a huge household kitchen, great hall, chambers and private lodgings. In some lesser establishments the tower had to contain almost the entire household. These tower-houses were still very necessary in border regions, where defence was a matter of primary importance. They might have their stables, agricultural and basic service buildings close by but, in case of attack, they had to be able to function as totally enclosed and self-supporting miniature fortresses. At their most basic, they took the form of tall rectangular towers with one major room on each floor and a variety of small chambers, passages and stairs within the thickness of their massive walls. Their kitchens lay either in the stone-vaulted basements or at first-floor level above secure storerooms/larders. They were quite large rooms, perhaps 25-feet square or around 20 by 30 or 40 feet, with fireplaces 10 feet or more in width, sometimes incorporating baking ovens. Compared to the size of their halls and chambers, these kitchens are exceptionally large, suggesting that they were intended to serve more as general purpose kitchens/living-rooms rather than as professionally-operated kitchens of the aristocratic tradition. This is confirmed by the appearance of bed recesses and small lodging chambers and latrines in the walls surrounding the kitchen at Dacre Castle, Cumbria, for example.[30]

The larger tower-houses might adopt a longer rectangular plan, so their principal floors could retain the conventional linear arrangement of kitchen and pantry/buttery, screens passage, hall and either a chamber, or access to a chamber on a higher level. The early fifteenth-century Hylton Castle, Sunderland, is an impressive four-storey tower of this type.[31] Its kitchen measures some 15 feet square, with a diagonally-set hearth in one corner, a baking oven in the opposite corner, and a large high-level window to provide good illumination. An inventory of 1558 suggests how it may have been equipped in the late medieval period.[32] Then, the kitchen fire had a pair of iron gallows and two crooks on which to hang a great cauldron and a pan for pottages, and an iron spit with two racks for roasting. The culinary facilities here were clearly quite limited, but even so the cooks were regularly using them to cater for a knight's household, feeding those who sat around four tables in the adjacent hall, as well as Sir Thomas Hylton and six of his family and friends dining behind in the great chamber. In other large tower-houses, such as Harewood Castle near Leeds, the kitchens bore a similar proportion to the size of their households.[33] Harewood's measures some 20 feet square, has two 12-foot fireplaces, a large diagonally-set baking oven, a well and a dresser hatch leading into a small servery. However, its hall and chamber are double the size of those at Hylton, so the cooks would still be working in quite a restricted space.

Most of the kitchens described above were intended to serve the needs of an entire household, and so were far too large for feeding the

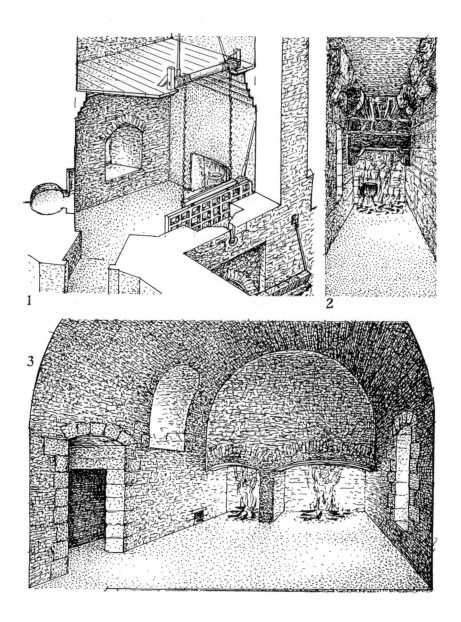

Figure 41. Staff kitchens.
1. Caerphilly Castle, c. 1277–90.
2. Caernarfon Castle, Gwynedd, c. 1295–1323.
3. Bolton Castle, Yorks., c. 1379.

administrative staffs left in residence when the lord and his retinue had departed elsewhere. Management has always prioritized its own comfort, hence many large establishments provided themselves with staff kitchens worthy of prosperous knights. Usually adjacent to dining chambers over gatehouses, they could be quite modest in scale. To cater for Edward I's staff at Caernarfon, their chamber in the Treasury Tower over the service entrance to the castle was little more than a narrow corridor with a hearth at one end, a side window for illumination, and access to the well.[34] The c. 1280s outer gatehouse at Caerphilly Castle has a slightly larger kitchen in its flanking Wassail Tower. It has both a baking oven and a fireplace, as well as the winch for the drawbridge and the portcullis defending the gateway below.[35] In both these examples, it is clear that the scale and quality of the food was to be quite basic, just sufficient to serve minimal needs. Over the following century, staffs' expectations appear to have increased considerably, major households now providing them with substantial cooking facilities. At Bolton Castle, Wensleydale, the staff kitchen built around 1380 was some 20 feet square, with two wide fireplaces, one large, perhaps for roasting and general cooking, and one rather smaller, close to a drain, which might have housed a beef-pot. Well-lit, and with stone vaults above and below to make it completely fireproof, it was ideally designed for its purpose. Another fine example can be seen in the outer gatehouse at Kidwelly Castle. As remodelled in 1408 after being damaged in Owain Glyn Dwr's revolt, it too was stone vaulted, having a deep, 9-foot wide fireplace and a large baking oven, quite sufficient to serve its adjacent 40-foot hall.[36]

Having considered the various forms of medieval kitchen, we can now move on to examine its equipment.

Figure 42. Utensils for food preparation.

1. Dressing knife of William Coke, 1479, and c.1325–40.

2. Chopping knife from Northolt Manor, Middx., and c.1325–40.

3. Leaching knife from London, late 13c.

4–5. Cleavers [and flesh-hook], 13c.

6. The St Mary's Abbey Infirmary mortar, York, 1308.

7–8. Stone mortars with wooden pestles, 14c.

9. Stone mortar as seen at Beverley Minster, Yorks., c.1520.

CHAPTER ELEVEN

Kitchen Furniture and Equipment

The best description of the contents of a medieval kitchen was written by Alexander Neckham in the twelfth century. Despite this early date, comparison with inventories indicates that many fifteenth-century kitchens were equipped in a virtually identical manner.[1]

In the vivarium let fish be kept, in which they can be caught by net, fork spear or light hook, or with a basket. [Sifted bread flour is] used also for feeding small fish. Small fish for cooking should be put in a pickling mixture, that is water mixed with salt... To be sure, pickling is not for all fish, for these are of different kinds. [There should be] a pickling vat and knives for cleaning fish.

Also there should be hot water for scalding fowl. Let there also be a cleaning place where the entrails and feathers of ducks and other domestic fowl can be removed and the birds cleaned. There should also be a *garde-robe* pit through which the filth of the kitchen may be evacuated.

In the kitchen there should be a small table on which cabbage may be minced, and also lentils, peas, shelled beans, beans in the pod, millet, onions, and other vegetables of the kind that can be cut up. The chief cook should have a cupboard in the kitchen where he may store many aromatic spices, and bread flour sifted through a sieve...may be hidden away there.

There should also be pots, tripods, a mortar, a pestle, a hatchet, a stirring stick, a hook, a cauldron, a bronze vessel, a small pan, a baking pan, a meathook, a griddle, small pitchers, a trencher, a bowl, a platter, a pepper mill and a handmill...[and] a large spoon for removing foam and scumming.

It is particularly interesting to read Neckham's description of a small table used specifically for chopping vegetables, for the Luttrell Psalter shows green vegetables being chopped on just such a table in the mid-fourteenth century.[2] The cook is shown holding a long, untapering, pistol-gripped chopping knife in each hand, clearly using them alternately with a rapid rotary motion in order to quickly chop the vegetables for the pottage boiling in the adjacent pots. Pairs of such chopping knives were valued at 4*d*. in the fifteenth century.[3] The blade of one excavated from Northolt Manor measures some 16 inches long by 4 inches wide, on an integral 5-inch scale-tanged handle, closely resembling the Luttrell illustration in both size and shape.[4]

Most general preparation was carried out on another table. This was usually called the dressing board, the kitchen dresser being the hatch through which the food was distributed, and meat-boards being dining-tables. Here the main utensil was the dressing-knife, one of the cooks in the Luttrell Psalter using his to divide a sucking pig. Its convex blade has the end of its back edge cut back in a curve to produce a sharp point. William Coke, the cook to William Cannings, the great Bristol merchant, had the outline of his identical knife engraved on his tombstone in St Mary Redcliffe in 1479. Its blade is 9 inches long, on a 5-inch handle. Such knives were usually valued at 2*d*. each in the fifteenth century.[5]

The third form of knife found in the kitchen was used for leaching, or slicing. This action requires a long, straight blade, one which was fairly narrow, to avoid sticking or dragging when cutting thick pastes or pâtés. It probably resembled one of today's carving knives in size, proportion and construction, some of the 9-inch whittle-tanged sharp-pointed and narrow blades excavated in London probably being leaching knives. These too were usually priced at 2*d*. each in kitchen inventories.[6]

The other cutting utensil was the meat axe. Presumably very large and heavy examples were used for the initial cleaving of carcasses, while smaller ones would be used for trimming and dividing smaller joints on the dressing board. They are occasionally shown on the personal seals of those presumably occupied in the meat trade. Their blades are deep and rectangular, with a heavy rib forged along their back edges and stout cylindrical handles.[7]

In the kitchen in the Blacksmiths' Company Hall in London, which was probably equipped in the same manner as that of a major house, there was one dressing board 10 feet long by 17 inches wide. There were also two 13-inch wide shelves, one 12 feet long, the other 4 feet 6 inches. Such details are quite rare, however, many inventories suggesting that dressing boards and shelves were rarely provided. This is because inventories only listed goods moveable, and not fixtures which formed part of the freehold. This meant that built-in furniture was never mentioned, even though it must have been in widespread use. A list of the fittings of the early to mid-sixteenth-century Bedford House in Exeter illustrates this well;[8]

> One great planck standing in the midest of the kitchen, standing on two
> tressells made fast in the grownd.
> One other short planck...one end made fast in the Wale, the other
> standeth upon tressles made fast in the ground.

A table of this type still survives in the kitchen of Rockingham Castle, Northamptonshire, while evidence of earlier examples has been recovered by excavation. In one corner of a probable boiling house at Newton St Loe Castle, Somerset, C.J. Arnold found the late fourteenth or early fifteenth-century sockets which gripped the four legs of a 5 by 3-foot table, a row of stone slabs beneath its front edge providing a firm footing for the cooks working on its surface.[9] Further evidence survives in the form of the sockets by which woodwork was fitted along the south wall of the privy kitchen at Conwy Castle. These show that its dressing board was some 3 feet off the floor, with a shelf above it 5 feet 6 inches from floor level, and both some 15 feet in length.

Many other dressing boards were similarly large, being made from freshly-cut timber. In 1291–2 the Earl of Norfolk's receiver at Chepstow Castle paid 6d. for a man to fell and cut wood in Wentwood to make large tables for the kitchen, and four carpenters 1s. to plane them smooth.[10] In 1485 two dressing boards of elm, each measuring 10 by 2 feet, were made for the kitchen of Coldharbour Manor.[11] Bishop Fox provided three even larger ones for his Durham Castle kitchen in the 1490s. These remained in constant use for almost four hundred years, and would have been extant today had it not been for the ignorant vandalism of the Warden and Master of Durham University College. In 1886 they destroyed their massive frames, shortened their tops, and had them completely re-planed. Even so, their mutilated remains are still impressive, the tops being formed of two 18-inch planks, 16 feet long by 4 inches in thickness.[12]

One of the simplest ways of making a table was to bore three or four holes through the top, insert the legs, and tighten them in place by driving in a wedge at right-angles to the grain of the top. The Luttrell chopping table was of this type, its construction being ideal to withstand the constant vibration. Alternatively, the dressing boards were mounted on pairs of three-legged trestles, ideal for general kitchen use.[13]

As Neckham stated, a cupboard or aumbry provided a secure store for all the cook's spices and similar expensive ingredients. It might also be used for storing salt beef conveniently ready for use, but still secure from risk of pilfering. These cupboards varied considerably in value, anywhere between 8d., presumably for a small one, to 4s. for something much larger.[14] In the larger and better-planned kitchens, the place of the aumbry was taken by a small lockable room, a good example described as 'The little house within the kitching' still standing complete at Warkworth Castle in Northumberland.

Chests or arks were relatively rare in most medieval kitchens, but coopered tubs and barrels were widely used for the storage of the meal, flour, pearl barley and salt required for everyday use. Some salt kits appear to have been small barrels of around 8 pints capacity, but other late medieval examples were probably plank-built boxes with sloping, hinged lids. One like this is shown on a misericord carving at Manchester Cathedral. Hung on the wall by the fireplace, they kept their contents perfectly dry and convenient for use. Baskets or 'skeps of oscier' would have been ideal for bringing in and temporarily storing fruit, vegetables, fuel and kindling, while hen coops or 'cauls' enabled ducks and hens to be kept in the kitchen, safe from the foxes, while they were fattened up for the table.[15]

For the storage of utensils, kitchens might have shelves mounted against their walls. Being fixtures, they are rarely mentioned in inventories, but series of holes bored at the same height into the uprights of timber-framed kitchens show where pegs were driven in to support the shelf-planks. Scorch-marks a few inches above often show where standing candles might have fallen over when left unattended.

Stools and forms were sometimes found in kitchens, but medieval peasants did not find them as useful as we would today. The skeletal remains of the housewives who lived at Wharram Percy in East Yorkshire show that they spent much of their time with their ankles flexed, squatting on their haunches. We now associate this pose with third-world cookery but, practised from infancy, it was used in these islands too. The stance is ideal for floor-level cookery, keeping the eyes, nose and mouth well below the smoke level in cottages without chimneys.[16]

It is probable that many peasants would have slept on the floor around their hearths on the coldest of nights, sensibly preferring comfort to modern concepts of decency.[17] The same practice was followed in many major kitchens, the royal scullions laying 'in the nights and dayes in the kitchen on ground by the fire-side' up to 1526.[18] At Dartington Hall in 1400, they had two mattresses provided for this purpose.[19] Few of today's population will remember the pleasures of sleeping in a firelit room, warm, well-ventilated, and with everything bathed in a gently flickering rosy glow, but those who can recall the experience will realize that the scullions were suffering no hardship, but were more comfortably housed than many of their lords and masters in their huge and draughty chambers.

In the royal household, it was customary for the kitchen officers to sleep in chambers placed directly above their places of work, such as the pastry or boiling house. The same practice was apparently followed at Gainsborough Old Hall, with chambers over its pastry, boiling house and dresser office for their respective personnel. A chamber in the chimney breast at Warkworth Castle, entered by means of a ladder, may have provided similar accommodation or could have been used to store dry goods. Since the cook was a more important member of the household, he usually had a room of his own, close to those of the administrative officers. At Caistor Castle, for example, Sir John Fastolf's cook was able to retire to his individual chamber each night, there to snuggle down between the sheets of his feather bed beneath a fine red coverlet beautifully embroidered with roses and bloodhounds' heads.[20]

On rising each morning, the scullions might don clothing which, sometimes described as 'garments of such vileness', had become dirty and greasy through prolonged use. On hot days, however, the entirely male staff might prefer to remain naked.[21] Even so, they would need some protection for their more sensitive parts, this being provided a naperoun (the diminutive of *nappa* or tablecloth), a barm-cloth, or a barm-skin, barm being the Old English word for the lap. Those worn by the cook in the Luttrell Psalter appear to be simple squares of soft black leather, the top two corners tucked into their belts at each side, so that they hung down to the knee. In contrast, one described in Chaucer's *Miller's Tale* was of linen 'as whit as morne mylk', and they could also be made of coarse hessian-like harden, or of woollen cloth.[22] If provided with tapes or 'naperoun tabbes', they could be tied around the waist in the modern manner.[23]

In addition to its general furnishings, each kitchen was provided with various utensils required for carrying out each individual cooking operation. Before describing these in turn, it is first necessary to consider the means by which foodstuffs were ground and strained ready for use in many different recipes.

As Geoffrey Chaucer observed in *The Pardoner's Tale*, 'These Cookes, how they stampe, and strayne, and grynde, And turnen substance in-to Accident.' In fact, texture played a major part in the qualities expected of many medieval dishes. To reduce the hardest of ingredients, such as spices, a grate or grater might be used. These might also be found in the buttery or parlour, ready for dusting dishes with freshly grated spices just before they were served. Thomas Marton had one made of silver, weighing just over 5 ounces, for this refined use, but most workaday examples were made of iron, costing about 2*d*. each, ideal for grating bread for thickening pottages or making sauces.[24] Perhaps because of its pungency and relatively general use, pepper was often ground in its own mill, described as 'a pair of pepper querns.'[25] Unfortunately there appears to be no further evidence to suggest whether these were small millstones, mortar mills, or ball-mills, as used at later periods.

Mortars made of cast bronze or iron were particularly useful for grinding hard, dry ingredients. Experience showed that they worked best if their pestles were made of a different material, bronze mortars with iron pestles forming the usual combination, these being used with a smooth, rotary motion. Some examples were quite large, weighing 20–30lb, but few achieved the size and quality of the great bronze mortar made for the infirmary of St Mary's Abbey, York, in 1308.[26] This weighs 76lb, its sides cast in an elaborate tracery design, each panel depicting a lion or mythical beast.

Being made of cheaper materials, masonry mortars were more common. The finest were carved in marble, others in the best available local stone or even local pottery.[27] Used with wooden pestles, the smaller ones, costing from 1d. to around 6d., were ideal for both dry materials, and semi-liquid or firmer pastes.[28] If particularly smooth, moist pastes were required, such pestles and mortars were abandoned in favour of mullers: beehive-shaped blocks of bronze or hard stone, worked with a rotary motion on a flat slab. One fourteenth-century recipe describes how the cook should quickly fetch a muller of brass, and use it to grind together spices of all kinds, including cinnamon, saffron and cloves.[29]

Large stone mortars were generally used in quite a different way, being either set into the floor, or placed directly upon it. Standing or kneeling before them, their users grasped the shafts of long double- or single-ended wooden pestles, pounding them up and down to de-husk grain for frumenty, and for similar basic operations. These are seen in use in English illustrations from the fourteenth to the sixteenth centuries.

After being ground, dry, powdery goods could be further refined by sifting, only particles of a particular size passing through the meshes of cloth stretched across the bottom of a shallow, cylindrical sieve, 'sarse' or 'ring'. In 1459 Sir John Fastolf's cook was using sarses of both wood and brass.[30] The finest of the linens forming their bases was bolting cloth, which had the best reputation for sifting the whitest flour from wholemeal. 'Crees' or 'crest' probably had a more open weave, suitable for rice flour and the like, which had to be passed 'thorow a crees bunte [sieve]…& in defaute of a bunte, take a Ringe'.[31] Shaking the finest flours through such sieves was a slow process, one which could be speeded up by tipping the meal onto a loose square of bolting cloth, rolling it up, grasping the ends in the hands, and jerking it up and down vigorously, as shown in the ordinances of the York Bakers' Company.[32] For the coarsest sieving, the cloth was made of the strong, straight hairs from horses' tails, the hair-sieves of contemporary recipes.[33]

Hair sieves were also used to process wet foods, straining both by gravity, or under pressure. The latter was particularly effective for removing fibres and coarse particles, apple or cherry pulps being rendered especially smooth in this way. 'Frot [rub] hem wel in a seve so that the jus be wel comyn owt' instructs one recipe of c.1381, suggesting that either the hand or the back of a spoon was used to drive the juice through.[34]

The simplest method of separating almost clear liquids from grounds or solids was to pass them through a piece of linen or canvas. 'Then take a fayre Canvas and put it [across the mouth of a pot] & late renne out the water' advises one recipe, cloths also enabling the 'threads' or 'cock-treadings' [umbilicus] from beaten eggs, or the pulp, seeds and skins of mulberries to be totally removed.[35] When mixtures had to be slowly gravity-filtered for maximum clarity, pieces of either bolting cloth or perhaps a coarse worsted cloth called tammy were sewn into the form of long, open-topped cones called strainers or runners. Believed to echo the shape of the sleeves worn by the Greek physician Hippocrates, they were particularly useful for straining the dregs from hippocras, a sweet, spiced wine. From a 1508 recipe for its preparation, we can estimate that the gallon size of such a strainer was about 20 inches deep by 25 inches in circumference (50cm x 64cm), and 13 by 20 inches (33cm x 50cm) for the half-gallon.[36] To suspend them with their mouths open, their tops were hemmed to enclose strong wooden hoops, the Earl of Derby buying forty of these at 3d. each in the 1390s. Cords tied at intervals around the hoops enabled them to be hung from pegs set above the bowls into which their filtered contents fell.[37]

If the liquid could be easily separated from the solid matter, it was much quicker to pass it through a 'sile'. Durham Priory accounts for 1459/60 refer to a sile as 'a bowl with a hole'.[38] This perfectly describes the siles used in north-country dairies up to the mid-twentieth century, 8-inch diameter wooden bowls, each with a wide hole in its base surrounded by a bold foot-rim. In use, a piece of fine linen or muslin was stretched across this hole and secured by a cord around the foot-rim. Its great advantage was that the cloth could be immediately replaced with a freshly-laundered piece ready to filter subsequent batches.

When reading through medieval recipes, the length of time required for any cooking operation is usually absent. Since devices measuring less than an hour were virtually unknown, this is hardly surprising, but it is interesting to note those timings which were in use. The briefest was the 'ave', the recitation of the prayer 'Ave Maria...' which the practised could chant at great speed, but probably represented some 20 seconds.[39] Rather longer was the 'furlongways', the time it took to walk 220 yards, about 2 minutes.[40]

Once a meal had been prepared in the kitchen, the cooks had to make every surface and utensil clean for re-use. This did not mean that the sooty exteriors of the pots were polished to brightness, for as Thomas Tusser stated

> No scouring for pride: Spare kettle whole side. Though scouring be needful, yet scouring too much Is pride without profit, and robbeth thine hutch.

Soot, fats and dirt were not easily removed, even boiling water having little effect unless made soapy. Although not mentioned in medieval culinary sources, it is possible that urine was used for this purpose. There would have been a plentiful supply from the kitchen staff, and its efficacy for dissolving fats and grease was apparently well known. Up to the early twentieth century some English cottagers were still washing their hands and faces in it every morning, before rinsing in cold water, to retain excellent complexions, while as 'lant' it was used to remove natural greases from woollen textiles. Having used it on greasy pots, it was found to be at least as efficient as any modern detergent, a good rinse removing any risk of odour. Alkaline wood ashes from the fires, when mixed with hot water, would produce a strong caustic lye which, similarly acting on the fats within the pots, would make a very effective cleaning agent. The continuing folk tradition suggests that vegetable alternatives were also used, the chief of these being soapwort (*Sapinaria officinalis*), along with 'poor man's soap' or bracken roots.

For particularly stubborn accretions, it was necessary to scour the utensils with abrasives such as sand or fine gravel. Trevisa confirms this

with his remark that 'By frotynge [rubbing] and scourynge of gravel...
bras and yren is made bryght.' One of the best scourers was the horsetail.
Gerard's *Herbal* described how women 'scowre their pewter and wooden
things of the kitchen therewith, and therefore some of our housewives do
call it pewterwort.'[41] Its other names were 'dishwashings' and 'scourwort'.
The favourite variety was the great rough horsetail (*Equisetum hyemenale*),
which grew to 2 or 3 feet in height. The minute crystals of flinty silex
coating its leaves were arranged in extremely fine rows, like a file. Also
called shave-grass, it was imported from Holland in later centuries for
the polishing of both wood and metals.[42] Finally, many households used
worn-out tablecloths and towels for washing up and drying, but sometimes extra supplies had to be bought in. In 1419 Dame Alice Bryene paid
20*d.* for 6 yards of linen cloth for cleaning the windows and vessels in her
kitchen.[43]

Before moving on to consider the various forms of cooking practised
in the kitchens, some contemporary descriptions of the cooks should help
recreate something of their social character. They did not stand high in
popular opinion, having a reputation for drunkenness, cheating tricks
and gluttony. Roger Hodge, a London cook, originally from Ware, twenty
miles north of London, was one of the pilgrims described in Chaucer's
Canterbury Tales. He did have good practical skills;[44]

> For boiling chicken with a marrow-bone, Sharp flavouring powder and
> a spice for savour. He could distinguish London ale by flavour, And he
> could roast and seeth and broil and fry Make good thick soup and bake a
> tasty pie...As for blancmange, he made it with the best.

But his host had no hesitation in suggesting that he

> ...stole gravy out of many a stew, Many a Jack of Dover [hake?] have you
> sold That has been twice warmed up and twice left cold, Many a pilgrim's
> cursed you more than sparsely When suffering the effects of your stale
> parsley Which they had eaten with your stubble-fed goose; Your shop is
> one where many a fly is loose.

These were the tricks of the proprietor of a public cookshop, but cooks in private households were exposed to even greater temptations.[45]

Of foolish cooks
These fools revelling in their master's cost
Spare no expence, not caring for his damage
But they as Caitiffs often thus them boast
In their gluttony with dissolute language
'Be merry, companions, and lusty of courage.
We have our pleasure in dainty meat and drink,
On which things only we always muse and think.

Eat we and drink we therefore without all care,
With revell without measure as long as we may
It is a royal thing thus lustily to fare
With other's meat, thus revell we always.
Spare not the pot! Another shall it pay.
When that is done spare not for more to call,
He merely sleeps, the which shall pay for all.'

The great deceit, guile and uncleanliness
Of any scullion, or any bawdy Cook,
His Lord abusing by his unthriftiness.
Some for the nonce their meat lewdly dress,
Giving it a taste too sweet, or salt, or strong
Because the servants would eat it them among.

And with what meats so-ever the Lord shall fare,
If it be in the kitchen, before it comes to the hall,
The cook and scullion must taste it first of all,
In every dish these Caitiffs have their hands,
Gaping, as it were dogs for a bone.
When nature is content, few of them understands
In so much that, as I trow, of them is none
That die for age; but of gluttony each one.

No wonder that great households had to employ tiers of administrators to prevent such expensive waste. At the other end of the social scale, the cooks were just as keen to make sure that every scrap of edible food came their way. The use of the index finger to scoop the remaining juices from the cooking pot up to the lips gave it the finely appropriate name of 'the lickpot.'[46]

CHAPTER TWELVE

Pottage Utensils

Pottage is a greatly maligned and misunderstood food. It is frequently portrayed and recreated by re-enactors as a single dish. 'This', they exclaim, 'is pottage!' – thrusting forward a bowl of grim, grey and gritty gruel, unskimmed, smoke-flavoured and foul. Any medieval cook who served such a mess would have been soundly disciplined or, perhaps even worse, made to eat it.

In fact, 'pottage' is a simple word having but a single meaning: 'that which is cooked in a pot'. This encompassed hundreds of different dishes, made of every conceivable ingredient, ranging from the simplest plain-boiled cereal gruels to the richest and most flavoursome of game stews. At peasant level, a few small pots would produce the pottages required to serve the complete dietary needs of an entire family, while in noble kitchens a multitude of pots of perhaps 3 to 10 gallons capacity would be used to cook the great variety of dishes served at every meal. Before considering the various recipes, it is first necessary to gain some knowledge of the cooking pots, and the manner in which they were deployed.

Many fireplaces were specifically equipped for the suspension of cooking pots over the flames. Where the hearth lay in the middle of the floor, gallows were frequently the choice. As depicted in the Bayeux Tapestry, these are shown as two uprights with forked tips which hold a horizontal bar, just like a medieval executioner's gallows. Some were of great size. The main hearth in the kitchen at Sandal Castle had a foot-square socket set diagonally at each end of its 10-foot hearth to support a strong gallows-beam, from which hung two large bronze pots.[1] Portable gallows, such as John Cadeby of Beverley's 1430s 'pair of budges called iron gallows', remained in use well into the sixteenth century.[2] By this time, however, they were being replaced by iron bars or wooden beams bridging the throats of kitchen chimney flues. The hearths of the priests' houses at Ashby de la Zouch Castle show how they were fixed, one having a socket cut into each side to receive the ends of the bar, while another had two bars projecting from the top of the fireback, on which the gallows-bar could be supported horizontally. Since the bars were still portable, they continued to be listed in inventories as 'gallow balks', 'bemes of iron' or 'pott beams of timber'.[3]

In order to vary the height of the cooking pots over the fire, and thus their cooking temperature, they were hung from an iron pot-hook or reckon crook. Its upper end hooked over the gallow beam, while its lower end terminated in a hinged narrow loop. This engaged with a long ratchet-like 'rack', allowing the hook at its base to be rapidly raised or lowered at will. Originally described accurately as 'a rack-and-crook', this combination was usually known by its abbreviated forms of 'reckon' or 'reckon-crook'. References to 'two iron chains called reckons' in Yorkshire in 1417, and to a 'pott chayen' at Dale Abbey in the 1530s suggest that a different type was made of loops of chain just like those used up to the twentieth century in the Western Isles of Scotland.[4] The link between the reckon and the cooking pot was provided by loops of chain, hinged bow or 'bail' handles, or by 'potclyppes' or 'pot-kilps', these being bow handles hinged in the middle so that they could fit pots of different sizes.[5]

Instead of being hung over the fire, the pots could also be stood on strong iron stands, their fire-welded joints enabling them to withstand the constant heat of the flames. Today archaeologists call them 'trivets', but this fifteenth-century word was never as widely used as the Old English 'brandise' or 'brandreth' meaning 'burning-iron'. Even in the twentieth century west-country housewives always differentiated between these and 'trivets', which were simple rivetted frames only suitable for supporting vessels at the fireside.[6] Most brandreths were circular or triangular frames mounted on three vertical legs, but others were more substantial. The great brandreth at Durham Priory had two ribs and eight iron bars, Thomas Morton of York's had six feet, and Peterborough Abbey had a pair which together weighed 70lb.[7] Regrettably, there is neither pictorial nor archaeological evidence of their design.

The oldest form of metal cooking pot was made by beating sheets of virtually lead-free, low-tin bronze into deep bowl-shaped or almost spherical forms, their rims being worked over iron hoops fitted with suspension loops. These were known as brass pans, as in Chaucer's Reeve's 'panne of bras' or Eleanor Rummynge's 'good brasse pan'.[8] Being light in relation to their volume, they were ideal for hanging over the fire.

The other major type of cooking pot was made of cast bronze, with three integral legs extending from the base, a flaring rim which provided both strength and an excellent seating for lids, and two suspension loops. The earlier, pre-fourteenth century examples tend to have globular bodies, while the later ones were rather more squat and bag-shaped, these being more stable and presenting a greater surface area to the hotter part of the fire. Major households required sets of these pots, all of different sizes, such as those listed in the 1450 inventory of Thomas Morton, canon residentiary at York Minster. Their volume was recorded in 'lagens' a medieval measure of 14 pints:[9]

Description	Volume	Weight	Value
2-eared	19 gallons 4 pints	62lb	8s.
3-footed	12 gallons 6 pints	38lb	5s.
3 short feet	?	36lb	5s.
iron handled	10 gallons 4 pints	40lb	3s. 4d.
	7 gallons 4 pints	25lb	3s. 4d.
	5 gallons 2 pints	23lb	2s. 6d.
	3 gallons 2 pints	11lb	2s.

Some cooks developed quite familiar relationships with their pots, to the extent of giving them personal names. In Durham Priory kitchen, two pots were called 'Stockton' and 'Wardle', while their accompanying pans included 'Hesildon', 'Moreby', 'Drundale', and 'Eden'. Another in Yorkshire was called 'Gingyll' ('jingle'), meaning to sound like a bell. The pot in St Lawrence's Hospital, Bristol, which held 16 gallons, was called 'Colman' in 1400, either after the great Celtic saint, or appropriately punning 'colmy', meaning sooty. Such names must have been of great service to the cooks, since they could call for a pot by name, and know precisely which would be brought to them.

Smaller pots were more commonly found among lower-status folk, those from 1 to 4 gallons being quite adequate for a family's needs. Some indication of the number and size of pots and pans required by households of different status is provided by the following extract from west-country inquisitions *post mortem* of around 1400.[11]

	Pots	Their weight	Pans
Earl of Huntingdon, Dartington	11	?	4
Abbot of Beaulieu, Tregoning	3	100lb	2
T. Guldesfeld, Vicar of Plymouth	3	120lb	4
W. Bateryng, husbandman, Bideford	3	40lb	–
N. Upton, merchant, Teignmouth	2	20lb	3
W. Symond, tailor, East Budleigh	1	8lb	1
J. Bole, husbandman, Buckfastleigh	1	6lb	–

Two smaller types of bronze cooking pot, having three short legs and a long projecting handle, were called either posnets or skillets. It is

Figure 43 (opposite). Pans, pots and their accessories.

1. Copper alloy raised pan with iron rim and bail handle, from late-medieval London.

2. Copper alloy fabricated pan with iron hanging chain, from late-medieval London.

3–4. Iron rack-and-crook and brandreth from Norwich, 1507.

5–7. Iron brandreths from London, Weardale and Northampton.

8–10. Cast bronze pots from Durham, mid-14c.; West Country, late 15c?; and London, late medieval.

11–12. Cast bronze posnets from Alston, Cumbria, 14c? and London, 15c.

13. Earthenware cooking pot from Sandal Castle, Yorks., 1483–5.

14–15. Earthenware posnets from Sandal Castle, early 15c.

16–17. Earthenware skillets from Sandal Castle, early 15c. and Kingston upon Thames, 14c.

18–19. Earthenware posnet lids from Cheam, Surrey, early 15c. and Castle Rising, Norf.

20. Wooden posnet lid.

Figure 44. Pans, pots and their accessories.

1. A pan in its clay furnace, 1505.

2. A pan on its brandreth, *c.*1340.

3. Food-vessels simmering in a pan and pots, 1338–44.

4. Three standards, a skimmer and flesh-hook, *c.*1320–45.

5. A pot over the fire, second quarter 14c.

6. A cook stirring his pot, St Mary's Minster, Thanet, Kent, *c.*1401–19.

7. Putting a lid on a pot, *c.*1500.   8. A flesh-hook.

9. A cook with flesh-hook and ladle, Maidenhead parish church, Berks.

10. Cooks with bellows and ladle, and a pan hanging on its rack-and-crook, Boston parish church, Lincs.

11. A pan, brandreth, ladle and rack-and-crook, *c.*1500.

difficult to trace their differentiating features. The earliest reference to a posnet is in 1281/2 when one was bought for 6*d.* for Edward I's daughter Elizabeth at Rhuddlan in North Wales.[12] The word is derived from the Old French *poconnet*, meaning a small pot, which precisely describes the vessels still known by this name up to the twentieth century. They have the same body, legs and lid-seating of the larger pots, but are much smaller and are provided with a long handle. Medieval recipes recommend them for simmering small joints of meat, making thick sauces, and for deep-frying.[13] Thomas Morton's small bronze posnet, complete with its bronze handle, weighed 6lb, suggesting a one-gallon capacity.[14]

During the fourteenth century the word 'skillet' described two quite different utensils. When the monks of Durham purchased a hemp rope for their skillet in 1398, they were referring to a small bell, the Old French *eskelette*, while the 'skellet menea' bought for 3*d.* in Nottingham four years earlier was apparently a cooking vessel.[15] Even though this is scanty evidence, it does suggest that the skillet was bronze, like a bell, and quite small, the price suggesting as little as 1lb in weight. In more recent polite and dialect usage, skillets are recognized as almost cylindrical vessels with three short legs and a handle extending horizontally from the rim, a pattern which probably follows that of their medieval predecessors.[16] We may therefore assume that their major difference was that posnets were lidded, and skillets open-topped.

Whatever their form and size, metal cooking pots and pans always represented one of the household's major investments. Even so, there never appears to have been enough of them to meet the requirements of either professional cooks or housewives. In most kitchens earthenware cooking pots continued to play a significant role. Being porous, brittle, poor conductors of heat, and readily shattering under thermal shock, they were far from ideal for cooking over direct heat. Only their cheapness and the superlative skills of the potters made their use feasible. By mixing grit, sand or crushed shells into their clay, throwing them on the wheel so that their walls were exceptionally thin, giving their bases a pronounced sag, and firing them at comparatively low temperatures, they were able to produce very serviceable cooking pots.

In use, they could be set down in or against burning logs, a bed of embers, peat or charcoal, supported over the fire on brandreths, or perhaps even suspended from a reckon-crook by means of hanging loops or a wire passed beneath their rims.[17] From the late tenth century they had been made with tripod feet so that they could stand within the fire like the later bronze pots, posnets and skillets. Potteries throughout the country went on to produce all manner of cooking pots, some with feet, some with hanging loops at the rim, some with a protruding handle, and most quite plain, but all designed to meet the demands of their individual communities.

In wealthier households, and probably the poorer ones too, ceramic cooking pots were certainly treated as disposable cook-ware, sooting found just on one side of excavated examples suggesting that they had only been used once before being discarded. If the contents were to be drained, recipes directed that holes should be pierced through the pot's base. Similar holes converted pots into funnels, while whole pots might be smashed to retrieve their contents.[18] Accidental breakage remained a great and frequent disadvantage however. Some recipes advise 'if hit be an earthen potte, then set hit on the fire; when thou takest hit downe and lete hit not touche the grounde for breaking', or 'set high upon a wyspe of straw that hit touche not the cold grownde'.[19] George Curtis of Littlethorpe, a traditional potter still selling earthenware cooking pots in the 1960s, told me that they should always be tempered before use. This was done by filling them with water, putting them in a cold oven, slowly bringing them up to temperature, and letting them cool again before being withdrawn. Perhaps medieval cooks used similar methods. However, if all precautions failed and a pot did crack in use, there would be an instant riot of anger, recrimination and disappointment, as vividly described in Chaucer's *Canon's Yeoman's Tale* of a broken crucible:[20]

> The pot breaketh and farewell, al is go...
> Whan that our pot is broke, as I have sayd.
> Every man chit and halt him [displeased].
> Somme seyde it was long on the fir makyng;
> Somme seyde nay, it was on the blowyng
> Thanne was I fered, for that was myn office.
> 'Straw', quod the thridde, 'ye been

lewed [uneducated] and nyce [foolish],
It was not tempered as it oghte be.'
'Nay', quad the fourthe, 'stynt and harken me,
Be cause oure fir ne wasnat maad of beech,
That is the cause, and oother noon, so thee'ch!'

When starting to prepare any recipe, it was first necessary to select a pot of a suitable size. A proverb against the short in stature claimed, 'Little pot, soon hot'. A lid might then be required, an open-topped pot wasting heat and allowing soot and smoke to spoil the flavour and colour of the contents. 'Loke thy pott be well kevered that the hete go not owte' advised one late fifteenth-century royal recipe.[21] Pot lids were often of wood. 'Potlede de ligno' are listed in Nottingham records in 1403, and there are recipes which instruct the cook to 'have a lid of tree upon the pot's mouth well closed.'[22] These simple discs of wood have good insulating qualities, their tendency to warp being easily remedied by turning them over from time to time, a square or round hole through their centres enabling this to be quickly done using a prick or a skewer. Earthenware pot lids took the form of inverted domed or shallow conical bowls, central knobs or pronounced foot-rims being provided as handles. Their use was probably restricted to the smallest earthenware cooking pots and to those earthenware posnets which archaeologists mistakenly called 'pipkins', a word unknown in the medieval period.[23]

Lids were essential when braising, a method by which meats were poached in aromatic vapour within a sealed pot. One late fifteenth-century recipe describes how a chicken should be propped on splints within a pot or posnet over a pint or two of herbed wine. Either rolls of dough or strips of paper or linen cloth coated in a flour and egg-white paste were then smeared around the rim, and the lid pressed on top to seal it completely.[24] After perhaps a couple of hours of slow cooking, the chicken emerged moist, tender and finely flavoured, accompanied by its own rich spicy syrup. Alternatively, pots of food might have a double layer of canvas tied across their mouths before being plunged into large pots or pans of boiling water. This very effective method later developed into jugging, as in jugged hare.[25] Other techniques will now be considered in greater detail.

Pottage Recipes

The over-riding purpose of this chapter is to offer the opportunity to study and experience one of the most interesting and varied forms of medieval English food. To do this, it presents a sequence of late fourteenth- and fifteenth-century manuscript recipes in modern form, starting with meat pottages, then on through those of fish, dairy, vegetables, fruits, flowers, cereals, almonds, flour-pastes, bread-sops, caudles, and jellies. It is by no means comprehensive, however, and anyone wishing to study this topic in greater detail is advised to consult the many excellent volumes of transcribed medieval recipes such as C.B. Hieatt and S. Butler's *Curye on Inglysch* (Oxford 1985), C.B. Hieatt's *An Ordinance of Pottage* (London 1988) and G.A.J. Hodgett's *Stere Htt Well* (Adelaide n.d.). For the origins of many of their recipes, M. Rodinson, A.J. Arberry and C. Perry's *Medieval Arab Cookery* (Totnes 2001) is invaluable.

It has often been said that the past is a foreign country, and this concept is particularly relevant to pottages – they are amazingly different to virtually all the dishes with which we are familiar today. Anyone who has demonstrated and served medieval food for any time is acquainted with the public's surprise at the now-unusual combinations of flavours, particularly those of meat and sugar, or meat and fruit, and at the range of colours and textures used to make the dishes more appealing and interesting. When first cooking and eating medieval foods, it is best to disregard preconceived notions of taste, and explore the various flavours and textures in their own right, for most display a knowledgeable and sophisticated use of ingredients and techniques.

When starting a pottage, for example, the meat might be prepared by roasting, frying or parboiling. Not only did this set the texture and flavour of the meat before it was finished by simmering in richly-flavoured stocks, but it also enabled the cooks to transform in a matter of minutes the many plain spit-roast and pot-boiled joints into a range of quite different, individual dishes just before they were to be served. Such pre-cooking could enrich basic flavours too, as when chickens were tossed into the beef-pot before being separately prepared. It might also add to the efficiency of the kitchen, enabling left-over cooked but unbroken joints to reappear in hashed form at succeeding meals.

During the process of cooking, the selection of ingredients, and the order in which they were added were very carefully considered. The recipe for strawberry (p. 270) illustrates this particularly well. In order to restore the slight sharpness and bright colour lost when cooked, this purée of strawberries was enhanced with a little wine vinegar and spices such as pepper, and its colour restored with red wine and the red food colour sanders. The appearance of lard might at first sound rather strange, until it is appreciated that this would give an additional gloss or finish to the completed dish. It was further appreciated that some flavourings mellowed and lost their potency if included at the start of the cooking process, and so the vinegar and food colour were only added after the mixture had been cooked and removed from the heat.

The consistency and texture of pottages was initially determined by chopping, mincing (i.e. finely chopping), teasing, grinding or sieving the principal ingredient. Additional thickening agents might also be employed. These were usually, but not always, added at the final stage of cookery. If added earlier, they would have reduced the circulation of the stock simmering in the pot, causing it to burn if not constantly stirred. By adding them at the end, not only were these problems averted, but it was also possible to adjust exactly the final consistency. The main thickeners were cereal-based; flour (rarely), rice flour, oatmeal, breadcrumbs or amydon. Amydon was pre-prepared by soaking grains of wheat in cold water for eleven days, changing the water daily. After being pounded in a mortar, boiled and sieved, it was allowed to settle, and turned out onto a cloth. Having been regularly turned until dry, it was then used as a very smooth wheat-starch thickener, the medieval equivalent of today's cornflour. Eggs were also used for thickening, either the lightly beaten yolks or whole eggs, or hard-boiled yolks beaten to a smooth paste. For some recipes, whole eggs were mixed into the pottage and then sufficiently cooked to form a granular curd, a texture virtually unknown in modern cookery. Other egg-yolk or whole-egg pottages were gently cooked to form smooth, rich custards, again demonstrating good levels of skill.

The appearance of pottages was greatly enhanced by their colour. In some recipes white meats such as chicken were rubbed with saffron so as to emerge a brilliant deep yellow, while in others the cooking stocks were coloured so as to transfer their hue to the main ingredients. Smoothly ground white chicken pottages were particularly receptive of colouring, and various recipes show how they appeared red, yellow, green and even blue on the table. The art of glazing meat was also practised, cuts being coated in thick spiced honey and wine caramel, on which bands of gold and silver foil could then be mounted (see boar in confit, p. 235). Most of the pottages were simply dished and served, but some recipes give details of garnishing. For example, they might sprinkle the surface with ground spices or sugar, or stud them with raw or fried almonds or pine kernels, decorate them with red or white comfits or even, for jellies, spear them with small branches of laurel or bay-leaves.

All the following recipes have been selected to demonstrate the range of ingredients and methods used to make medieval English pottages. Since they are intended for practical use, they only deal with foodstuffs which are generally available and acceptable to modern sensibilities. Very few people today will have both access to, and a potential appetite for boiled swans' feet, stewed chicken heads, gizzards and feet, sheep tripe and the like; or for lampreys, once so prestigious, but now virtually unknown on English tables.

VENISON

VENISON IN BROTH[1]

2lb/900g venison joint, trussed   ¼pt/150ml red wine
½tsp each, parsley and sage   2tbs [red] wine vinegar
½tsp mixed ground clove and mace

Put all the ingredients in a pan, with enough water to cover them, and simmer gently for 2 hours before serving in a dish with its own stock.

ROE FOR SEWE[2]

2lb/900g venison joint, trussed   ½tsp mixed ground pepper,
½pt/300ml [red] wine   clove and cinnamon
½tsp each, chopped parsley, sage and hyssop

Put the venison into a pan, cover with water, bring to the boil, skim, and simmer for 1½ hours.

Remove the meat from the stock, cut into cubes, put into a clean pan with the remaining ingredients, and simmer for a further 30 minutes until tender. In the original recipe, the raw blood was stirred in at this stage to produce a deeper colour.

STEWED COLLOPS [HASHED IN SPICED WINE][3]

1½lb/675g roast venison, sliced   6 cloves, bruised
½pt/300ml [red] wine   ¼tsp ground ginger
¼pt/150ml meat stock   1tbs wine vinegar
6 peppercorns, bruised   ½tsp salt
piece of stick cinnamon

Put all the ingredients into a pan, cover, and simmer for 10 minutes, shaking the pan from time to time, then serve.

BRUET OF SPAIN [IN A CREAMY SPICED WINE STOCK]⁴

1½lb/675g venison
2oz/50g butter
¼pt/150ml [white] wine
½pt/300ml almond milk

4 cloves, a few cubebs and
blades of mace
1tsp sugar, with a pinch of
cinnamon
1tbs wine vinegar

Cut the venison in long slices, and fry in the butter.

De-glaze the pan with the wine, add the almond milk (see p. 279) and spices, simmer for 10 minutes, stir in the sugar and vinegar, and serve.

BEEF

Beef stews were richly flavoured, some having the meat pre-roasted or pre-boiled before adding the herbs and spices, while others incorporated all the raw ingredients from the start. A 'dry-stewing' method was also employed, in which the ingredients were virtually steamed in closed vessels.

BEEF STEWED⁵

1½lb/675g lean beef, cubed
8oz/225g onion, finely chopped
1tsp each, parsley and sage
2oz/50g white bread, no crusts
4tbs wine vinegar
pinch of saffron

small piece cinnamon stick
6 cloves
a few blades of mace
pinch grains of paradise
a few cubebs
1tbs salt

Stew the beef in 1pt/600ml water for about an hour, strain the stock into a clean pan, rinse the meat and add to the pan with the onion, herbs, and the spices (except the saffron), add a little more water if required, and simmer for a further 30 minutes.

Beat the vinegar and the bread together, rub it through a sieve, and stir into the stew with the salt and saffron when the meat is tender, then pour into a dish and serve.

Variations
Initially roast the beef in a piece for 1 hour at 180°C/350°F/ gas mark 4 before cubing and simmering for 30 minutes with 1pt/600ml red wine instead of water, a little red food colour (for sanders) and 1oz/25g currants.[6]

Initially simmer the beef in [red] wine with a little water, with only 'good herbs' rather than spices, omit the bread, but finish with cloves, mace, cinnamon, red food colour (for sanders), vinegar and currants.[7]

MEAT STEW, FROM A SERGEANT [COOK] TO THE KING[8]

2lb/900g lean beef	½tsp ground clove,
8oz/225g lean chicken	pepper, ginger and mace
8oz/225g onions, sliced	pinch of saffron
1tbs honey	1tsp each chopped sage,
2oz/50g currants	rosemary, thyme,
1oz/25g ground almonds	hyssop and savory
4tbs [red] wine	

Finely chop the meats, put in a pan with the remaining ingredients and sufficient water to barely cover them, then simmer very gently for 45–60 minutes, until the meat is tender.

A DRY STEW FOR BEEF[9]

2lb/900g lean beef joint, trussed	6 cloves
8oz/225g onions, finely chopped	a few blades of mace
½pt/300ml [red] wine	2tbs currants

Place all the ingredients in a heatproof jar or small pan, cover with a piece of a polythene boiling bag and a piece of cloth or muslin, and tie down around the rim – this method is suggested to provide a safe alternative to medieval forms of stopping.

Place the jar or pan in a larger pan, with the water up to an inch from the rim, cover, bring to the boil, and then simmer for some 1½–2 hours until the meat is tender. A metal spoon or similar placed beneath the jar/pan will prevent it from rattling as it boils.

Alternatively, put the onions, wine, spices, currants and a little pepper in a pan, arrange a few clean sticks diagonally from the base to just below the rim, and prop the meat, cut in thick slices, on top of these, before covering and simmering gently for some 2 hours.

LONG WORTS OF MEAT [A THICK STEW WITH GREENS][10]

2lb/900g lean beef joint, trussed   6oz/100g white breadcrumbs
a beef marrow bone   pinch of saffron
8oz/225g cabbage or spring greens   1tsp salt

Put the beef and bone in a pan, just cover with boiling water, bring back to the boil, skim, then simmer gently for 1½–2 hours until tender.

Parboil the cabbage or greens until just tender, then drain, chop coarsely and stir into the beef stock with the breadcrumbs, saffron and salt, simmer briefly, and then serve the beef joint with its stock all in the same dish.

LAMB AND MUTTON

MUNTELATE [STEWED WITH ONIONS, THICKENED WITH EGGS AND VERJUICE][11]

2lb/900g lean lamb, cubed
8oz/225g onions, finely chopped
1tsp mixed ground pepper, clove and mace

3 egg yolks, beaten
1tbs lemon juice [for verjuice]

Put the meat in a pan, cover with water, and simmer for 1 hour.

Add the onions, herbs and spices, and cook for a further 20–25 minutes until the meat is tender.

Beat the eggs and lemon juice together, remove the stew from the heat, beat in the eggs, then pour into a dish and serve.

CHARMARCHAUNT ['MERCHANTS' MEAT'?][12]

2lb/900g lean lamb, cubed
6oz/150g white breadcrumbs
1tsp salt

½tsp chopped parsley
½tsp chopped sage

Put the meat in a pan, cover with water, and simmer for some 1½ hours until tender.

Scald the bread with some of the stock, beat until smooth [rub through a sieve], add the salt and herbs, return to the meat, stir while simmering for 5 minutes, then serve.

STEWED MUTTON [HASHED IN ONION, HERB AND SPICED STOCK][14]

1½lb/675g lean roast lamb, very finely chopped
6oz/150g onions, finely chopped
¾pt/450ml wine
1tbs wine vinegar
½tsp salt

pinch of saffron
¼tsp ground pepper and cinnamon

Put all the ingredients in a pan, cover, and simmer for 10 minutes, shaking the pan from time to time, then serve.

PORK

The pork specified in medieval English recipes was of three types: pig, meaning a weaner or suckling pig; pork, meaning mature sow-meat; and brawn, meaning boar meat, particularly the shoulder, and ideally from a wild rather than a domestic breed. The latter was particularly favoured, being cooked with rich, spicy sauces, and sometimes garnished with bands of gold and silver foil.

STEW LOMBARD
[A RED STEW WITH WINE AND ONIONS][14]

2lb/900g lean pork joint	*6 cloves*
2oz/50g lard	*pinch of saffron*
8oz/225g onions, coarsely chopped	*large pinch ground ginger*
1pt/600ml [red] wine	*red food colour (for sanders)*
1tbs sugar	*1oz/25g blanched almonds*
¼tsp mixed ground ginger, cinnamon and galingale	

Roast the pork with the lard at 180°C/350°F/gas mark 4 for 1 hour, then remove and chop into cubes.

Meanwhile heat the onions, sugar, cloves, saffron, ginger and a few drops of food colour in most of the wine then add the cubed roast pork, and simmer gently for some 15–20 minutes.

Fry the almonds golden brown in the lard in which the pork was roasted, drain, dry, and add to the simmering pork.

Mix the spice mixture into the remaining wine, and stir into the stew just before serving.

BOAR IN EGURDOUCE [A RED SWEET AND SOUR STEW][15]

2lb/900g lean pork joint, trussed
1oz/25g pine kernels
   or blanched almonds
1tbs lard
1oz/25g currants, chopped
1oz/25g dates, chopped
¼pt/150ml [red] wine vinegar

¼pt/150ml ginger wine
   (for clary)
2tbs sugar or honey
½tsp mixed ground ginger,
   clove and cinnamon
pinch of saffron
red food colour (for sanders)

Cover the joint with boiling water and simmer gently for some 1½ hours until tender.

Meanwhile fry the pine kernels or almonds golden brown in the lard.

Grind the currants, dates and clove in half the wine [rub through a sieve into a small pan], add the sugar and spices, simmer for 5 minutes, then stir in the saffron, vinegar and pine kernels or almonds with the remaining wine.

Drain the pork, slice into a dish, pour the hot syrup over them, and serve immediately.

FILLETS IN GALENTINE [A THICK RED STEW][16]

2lb/900g pork shoulder joint, trussed
8oz/225g onions (coarsely chopped)
2tbs lard
1pt/600ml beef or lamb stock
¼tsp mixed ground pepper,
   cinnamon, clove and mace

4oz/100g white breadcrumbs
2tbs [red] wine vinegar
red food colour (for sanders)
½tsp salt

Roast the pork with half the lard at 180°C/350°F/gas mark 4 for 1 hour, then cut into cubes.

Meanwhile fry the onions golden brown in the remaining lard, drain, put in a pan, and add the stock, spices and pork, before simmering for some 15 minutes until the meat is tender.

Scald the breadcrumbs with the stock, stir in the vinegar [rub through a sieve] and stir into the pork.

Stir in the food colour and salt, stir over the heat for a few more minutes to thicken the galentine, then serve immediately.

BOAR IN CONFIT [COLD, HONEY-GLAZED FILLETS][17]

2lb/900g pork fillets [usually 3]	2tbs [white?] wine
2tbs salt	large pinch mixed ground
2tbs lard	pepper and cloves
6tbs clear honey	strips of gold and silver foil

Dissolve the salt in 1pt/600ml water, and leave the fillets to soak in this for 1 hour.

Bring a large pan of water to a rapid boil, put in the fillets, and simmer gently for 20 minutes.

Transfer the drained fillets into a roasting tin with the lard, and bake in a pre-heated oven at 180°C/350°F/gas mark 4 for a further 20 minutes until dry and tender.

Rapidly boil the honey, wine and spices, stirring continuously, for about 5 minutes, until the white froth just shows signs of slightly darkening, then remove from the heat, chill the bottom of the pan in a bowl of cold water, and immediately dip in each fillet, coating the upper side, and leave on a dampened board to cool.

When cold, arrange the fillets on a dish, and decorate with a cross-band of gold foil, with one of silver foil spaced to each side.

BRAWN IN PEVERADE [IN PEPPER SAUCE][18]

2lb/900g lean pork joint, trussed	piece of stick cinnamon
8oz/225g small onions, peeled	¼tsp ground pepper
1pt/600ml [sweet white?] wine	pinch of ground clove and mace

Plunge the joint into a large pan of boiling water, and simmer for 1¼ hours.

Parboil the onions for 10 minutes, then drain.

Simmer the wine and cinnamon for 5 minutes, and strain into a clean pan, with the onions and ground spices.

Drain the joint, cut into cubes, add the wine, etc., and simmer for 10–15 minutes, before serving.

MORTREWS [THICKENED MORTAR-GROUND PORK][19]

1 lb/450g lean pork joint
4oz/100g white breadcrumbs
ground ginger to sprinkle as garnish

pinch of saffron
3 egg yolks, beaten

Plunge the joint in a large pan of boiling water, and simmer gently for 1¼ hours, then drain, retaining the stock.

Chop, then grind the meat to a smooth paste, and place in a pan.

Soak the bread in 1pt/600ml of the stock [rub through a sieve], add to the meat and simmer, while stirring, for 5–10 minutes, then beat in the yolks before pouring into a dish.

Sprinkle with the ginger, and serve.

CHARLET [GROUND PORK SCRAMBLED WITH EGGS][20]

1lb/450g cold cooked pork
¾pt/450ml milk
3 eggs, lightly beaten

1tsp sage, finely chopped
pinch of saffron

Grind the pork to a smooth paste [adding a little of the milk to make this easier].

Stir all the ingredients over a gentle heat until the mixture boils, then serve.

CHICKEN, GAME AND RABBIT

When cooking whole chickens, they were first scalded by immersion in boiling water, plucked, drawn, the heads and feet removed, trussed, placed in a pot of cold water, brought to the boil, skimmed and then simmered. The differences between the various recipes come from the composition of the cooking liquid and the syrups poured over the chickens after they had been drained and placed on a dish.

For 2lb/900g chickens, cover them with water, bring to the boil, skim, and simmer for some 40 minutes until tender, then drain and leave whole for a lord, or chop in halves or quarters for all the others, dish, and add the appropriate syrup or sprinkling.

CHICKEN IN BROTH
[HERB-STUFFED, IN SAFFRON STOCK][21]

Stuff with parsley, sage or other suitable herbs, and grapes, simmer in water with saffron, then drain and serve sprinkled with sugar, cinnamon and salt.

CHICKEN IN CAUDLE[22]

Simmer in stock, stirring in ground ginger, saffron, salt and 3 egg yolks just before serving.

CHICKEN IN COMPOST
[STEWED WITH HERBS, LEEKS AND HONEY][23]

Chop 2tbs each of parsley and sage with 6oz/275g finely chopped leeks, and place half this mixture in the bottom of a pan with 8oz/225g honey. Lay on the halved chicken and 4oz/100g minced pork, add ¼tsp mixed ground ginger and cinnamon, then barely cover with water, and simmer.

CHICKEN IN CONSEWE
[A WHITE STEW WITH HERBS AND ALMOND STOCK][24]

Simmer in water, parsley, savory and salt. Grind the stock with 2oz/50g blanched almonds, strain, stir in 1–2tbs sugar, and pour over the chicken in a dish.

CHICKEN IN KYRTYN
[CHICKEN IN SPICED CREAM SAUCE][25]

Simmer in water, meanwhile make a sauce of 1tbs flour or cornflour [for amydon], ½tsp mixed ground ginger, cinnamon and cumin and a large pinch of saffron beaten into ½pt/300ml single cream. Bring to the boil while stirring continuously, pour this over the chicken in a dish, and sprinkle with sugar.

CHICKEN IN HOCCHEE
[HERB AND GARLIC-STUFFED, IN BROTH][26]

Stuff the chicken with parsley, sage, grapes, and between half and a whole head of garlic, each clove being peeled. Sew up the vent, and simmer in meat stock. When dished, sprinkle with cinnamon.

CHICKEN IN SAGE
[AN UNCOOKED HERB AND EGG SWEET/SOUR SAUCE][27]

Grind 4 hard-boiled egg yolks with ½tsp each of sage and parsley leaves and 5tbs/75ml [white] wine, rub through a sieve, stir in 1oz/25g sugar, a large pinch of ground cinnamon and clove, a pinch of [ground] saffron, and 1tbs white wine vinegar. Pour over the freshly simmered and skimmed chicken just before serving.

CAPON STEWED [BRAISED IN SWEET WINE STOCK][28]

sprigs of parsley, sage, rosemary, thyme and hyssop
1 x 2lb/450g chicken, trussed   *½tsp ground ginger*
1pt/600ml [white] wine   *2tbs sugar*
4tbs currants   *large pinch of saffron*

Bruise the herbs by rubbing between the hands, stuff half within the chicken.

Scald and grind the saffron in 1–2tbs boiling water, and rub into the chicken to give it a good yellow colour.

Arrange a few wooden rods diagonally from the rim to the base of a pan, prop the chicken on top of these, add the remaining herbs around its sides and base, and pour in half the wine.

Make a paste of a little flour and water, coat strips of paper or cloth with this paste, arrange them around the rim of the pan, place the lid on top so that it is well sealed on this paste surround, and simmer very gently for about 1 hour.

Stir the currants, ginger, sugar, and a little more saffron into the remaining wine, and briefly simmer together.

When the chicken is ready, remove it into a dish, skim the fat from the remaining stock, add the wine syrup, and briefly re-heat before pouring over the chicken.

Variation[29]
Add finely chopped dates and a pinch of salt to the wine syrup.

For other recipes, the chicken was boned and cubed in preparation for cooking.

CHICKEN IN EGURDOUCE
[IN RED SWEET/SOUR SAUCE][30]

1lb/450g chicken meat, cubed
2tbs lard
4oz/100g onion, chopped
½tsp mixed ground pepper,
    ginger and cinnamon

½pt/300ml [sweet red] wine
a little red food colour (for
    sanders)
2tbs [red] wine vinegar

Simmer the chicken in water for 30 minutes, then drain, dry, toss in the lard until lightly coloured, then transfer to a pan.

Fry the onions in the same lard until pale golden brown and add to the pan with the other ingredients, and simmer for 10 minutes before serving.

HENS IN BRUET
[A THICK YELLOW SPICED STEW][31]

1lb/450g chicken meat, cubed
1pt/600ml light stock [or half stock and either [white] wine or ale]
¼tsp ground ginger
2oz/50g soft white breadcrumbs

¼tsp ground pepper
large pinch of saffron

Simmer the chicken in the stock for about 45 minutes.

Scald the remaining ingredients with a little of the hot stock, [rub through a sieve], return to the pan, and simmer for a further 15 minutes, stirring occasionally.

Variation[32]
Add 2oz/50g finely minced onion, ¼tsp mixed ground clove and mace, 1tsp salt, and 1tbs [white] wine vinegar to the ginger, pepper, breadcrumbs and saffron.

BRUETTE SAAK
[CHICKEN IN A CLEAR SPICED BROTH][33]

1lb/450g chicken meat, cubed
½pt/300ml white wine
1tsp each parsley and hyssop
3oz/75g dates, stones removed
large pinch of saffron

½tsp salt
¼tsp mixed ground clove,
   cubeb and mace
¼tsp mixed ground
   cinnamon and ginger

Place the chicken in ¾pt/450ml water, bring to the boil, skim, and simmer for 30 minutes.

Strain the chicken stock, rinse the chicken, place in a clean pan with half the stock, ½pt/300ml wine and the remaining ingredients except the cinnamon, ginger and salt, and simmer for a further 30–40 minutes until tender.

Stir in the cinnamon, ginger and salt just before serving.

BRUET DE ALMAYNE
[GERMAN STYLE CHICKEN IN SPICED ALMOND MILK][34]

1lb/450g chicken meat, cubed
1pt/600ml almond milk (see p. 279)

1tsp mixed ground ginger
   and galingale

Stew all together for about 45 minutes.

Variations, before cooking[35]
Add a small chopped and fried onion, with clove and cubeb for spices.

Add grapes, and replace the galingale with cinnamon.

Add a finely chopped raw onion, a little lard, 2tbs raisins, and no spices.

A number of recipes require the chicken to be roasted before being stewed thus greatly reducing the time required for their final preparation to a matter of minutes.

GELYNE IN DABBATTE
[A SLIGHTLY SHARP THICK STEW][36]

1 x 2lb/900g roast chicken
½pt/300ml light stock
½pt/300ml [white] wine
3oz/75g soft white breadcrumbs

4tsp wine vinegar
¼tsp mixed ground pepper,
    clove and cinnamon
¼tsp ground ginger

Remove the meat from the chicken, and cut into cubes.

Stew the wine, chicken and spices (except the ginger) in the stock for 5 minutes

Scald the breadcrumbs with the hot liquid from the pan, stir, rub through a sieve, and return to the chicken in the pan, and simmer while stirring for a further 5 minutes.

Stir in the vinegar and ginger, and serve.

HENS IN GAUNCELYE
[CHICKEN IN A CREAMY GARLIC AND SAFFRON SAUCE][37]

1 x 2lb/900g roast chicken
1pt/600ml milk
4 cloves of garlic, peeled

4 egg yolks, beaten
large pinch of saffron

Remove the meat from the chicken and cut into cubes.

Grind the garlic with a little of the milk, add the remaining milk, the chicken and saffron, and simmer for 10 minutes.

Scald the yolks with a little of the hot milk, return to the pan, and stir, without boiling, until it has thickened, then serve.

COYNES [WITH EGG-YOLK 'QUINCES'][38]

a 2lb/900g roast chicken
½pt/300ml beef stock
¼tsp mixed ground pepper
    and cumin

pinch of saffron
2oz/50g breadcrumbs
3 hard-boiled eggs
1 raw egg yolk, beaten

Remove the meat from the chicken, cut into cubes, simmer in the stock with the spices, scald the breadcrumbs with some of the stock, rub through a sieve, and return to the pan.

Remove the whole yolks from the boiled eggs, finely chop the whites, and stir them into the stock with the raw yolk, and stir until it has thickened.

Pour into a dish, and garnish with the whole yolks before serving.

BOUCE JANE [CHICKEN IN A HERBED MILK SAUCE][39]

1 x 2lb/900g roast chicken	1tbs pine kernels
½pt/300ml milk	1tbs currants
¼tsp each finely chopped parsley, sage, hyssop and savory	

Remove the meat from the chicken, cut into cubes, and simmer with the remaining ingredients for 5–10 minutes.

Pre-cooked chickens were also used to make a number of smooth semi-liquid dishes, ideal to add further colour to the table.

BLANC DE SIRE [THICK, GROUND CHICKEN, ALMOND MILK AND RICE FLOUR WHITE POTTAGE 'OF SYRIA'?][40]

1lb/450g cooked chicken, ground	4tbs sugar
2oz/50g rice flour	pomegranate seeds
1pt/600ml almond milk	

Simmer the chicken, rice flour, almond milk (see p. 279) and sugar for 5 minutes stirring continuously, pour into a dish, and sprinkle with the pomegranate seeds.

Other recipes garnish with almonds, white comfits, mace and cubebs, or cinnamon and sugar.

Vert Desire [a green stew][41]

As above, but with a little red wine and 1tbs finely ground parsley leaves to give a green colour.

Anesere [a yellow stew][42]

As above, coloured with saffron, with fried almonds both stirred into the pottage, and used to decorate it.

Dragone [a red stew][43]

As above, coloured with red food colour [for *sanc dragoun*, probably the bloodwort *Runex sanguinens?*].

Viand de Cypres [a blue stew][44]

As above, spiced with ground mace and clove, and with blue food colour [for *inde*, indigo] and studded with fried almonds or pine kernels.

Or, finally, as above, but without any spices, coloured yellow with saffron, and studded with almonds.

PARTRIDGE STEWED[45]

2 partridge, plucked and drawn
½pt/300ml [white] wine   1 blade mace and 6 cloves
¾pt/450ml beef or lamb stock   pinch of saffron
20 peppercorns   ½tsp ground ginger
2oz/50g butter [for marrow]   1tsp salt

Tuck the legs into the vents, push the butter and half the peppercorns inside and sew up the vents.

Put the partridges, remaining peppercorns, cloves and mace in a pan with the wine and stock, bring to the boil, then simmer for about 1 hour 30 minutes until tender.

Stir in the ginger, saffron and salt just before serving.

PHEASANT [OR CHICKEN] MAWMENE
[POULTRY IN A VERY RICH SWEET SPICED SAUCE][46]

8oz/225g cooked pheasant
¼pt/150ml [sweet white] wine
1tsp ground cinnamon
1tsp ground ginger
2tbs sugar
1tsp rice flour

1tsp currants
1tsp pine kernels
¼tsp ground cloves
½oz/12g quince marmalade
pinch of saffron
1tsp vinegar
2–3tsp brandy

Slice the meat across the grain, spread on a cloth, roll up, and roll with a heavy rolling pin to reduce it to soft fibres.

Mix the cinnamon and ½tsp of the ginger with the wine, bring slowly to the boil, then strain the wine into a clean pan.

Stir in the remaining ingredients except the meat, vinegar and brandy, stir until nearly boiling, then add the meat and the vinegar, stir while cooking for about a minute, then pour into a dish freshly rinsed with [sweet white] wine, and level the surface with the back of a similarly rinsed saucer.

Make a hollow in the centre, pour in the brandy, ignite, and serve flaming.

PHEASANT OR PARTRIDGE
[STEWED IN SPICED ALE STOCK][47]

2 pheasants, plucked and drawn
½pt/300ml light or game stock
½pt/300ml ale
pinch of saffron

½tsp mixed ground pepper,
    cinnamon and ginger
1tsp salt
1tbs plain flour

Tuck the legs into the vents, put the pheasants in a pan with all except the flour, and simmer for 1–1½ hours until tender.

Mix the flour with a little water, stir into the stock in the pan, and cook for a few minutes before serving.

PIGEONS STEWED [A RICH HERB AND GARLIC STEW][48]

2 pigeons, plucked and drawn   ¼tsp ground pepper
1 head of garlic   ¼tsp ground clove
1tbs chopped parsley   pinch of saffron
1½pt/900ml beef or lamb stock   1tbs lemon juice [for verjuice]
2tsp mixed chopped sage, parsley, hyssop and thyme

Peel each clove of the garlic, and stuff inside the pigeons with
the parsley.

Place the pigeons in a pan with all ingredients except the lemon
juice, and simmer very gently for about 1 hour, until tender.

Stir in the lemon juice just before serving.

CONY IN CEVY [RABBIT STEWED WITH ONIONS][49]

1 rabbit, cut in small pieces   3oz/75g soft wholemeal
12oz/350g onions, finely chopped   breadcrumbs
1oz/25g lard   1tbs [red] wine vinegar
¾pt/450ml meat stock   pinch of mixed spice
    ½tsp salt

Stew the rabbit, onions and lard in the stock for about 45 minutes
until the meat is just tender.

Scald the breadcrumbs with some of the hot stock, stir in the
vinegar, and stir this mixture back into the rabbit stew, cook for
a few minutes more, then pour into a dish and sprinkle with the
mixed spice and salt.

CONY IN CLEAR BROTH[50]

1 rabbit, cut in pieces   pinch of mixed spice
½pt/300ml [red] wine   red food colour (for sanders)
½tsp mixed parsley and thyme   large pinch ground ginger
pinch of saffron   1tsp [red] wine vinegar

Bring the rabbit, wine and ¼pt/150ml water to the boil, skim carefully, and simmer gently for some 30 minutes.

Strain the stock into a clean pan, carefully pick every bone etc. from the meat, and put this into the clean stock with the herbs, mixed spice and a little food colour, then continue simmering for some 15 minutes until tender.

Remove from the heat, stir in the ginger mixed in the vinegar, pour into a dish and serve.

FISH

A wide variety of fish was served at fast-day meals, including most of the native sea-fish, shell-fish and freshwater fish available today, as well as lamprey, porpoise, sturgeon and whale. For most fishes, the basic preparation was limited to removing all the innards, and probably the gills too, before plunging them into boiling water usually flavoured with salt, parsley, thyme or other herbs, and sometimes either ale or yeast. Richer sauces might then be poured over them just before serving. In selecting the following recipes, I have chosen only those which were intended for varieties which are still readily available, and which do not require the use of fish offal, blood, or the contents of pikes' stomachs and similar parts which most people would now find unacceptable.[51]

HADDOCK OR CODLING[52]

1 small haddock or cod, about 3lb/1.3kg   *1tbs salt*

Slit the fish from the vent to the head, and remove the innards and gills. [The head may also be removed. It was sometimes stuffed and cooked separately. The fish can also be cut into round steaks before poaching.]

Place in a shallow pan, add the salt, cover with water, cover, poach gently for some 15–20 minutes until tender.

Drain the fish, and serve hot with either garlic sauce or greensauce (see p. 334).

TO STEW HERRING[53]

2 herrings	2tsp currants
1oz/25g soft white breadcrumbs	½tsp sugar
½tsp chopped parsley and thyme	1tbs chopped onion
pinch ground black pepper	

Cut the herring from the vent to the head and remove the innards and gills. Retain the milts or roes. Then cut from the vent to the tail, open the fish, and separate the ribs from each side of the spine, without piercing the skin. Separate the spine from the head, and remove it down to the tail, before proceeding to remove all the ribs. Rinse the fish.

Grind the breadcrumbs, herbs, pepper and onion to a smooth paste, stir in the currants, and use to stuff the fish, securing the belly with either a few small skewers [cocktail sticks] or a needle and thread.

Place in a shallow pan of boiling water, sufficient to cover them, and simmer for some 10 minutes until tender, then drain and serve.

FRESH MACKEREL[54]

1 mackerel	1tsp chopped parsley
1tsp chopped mint	1tbs salt

Pull the gills forward, scoop out the gills, hook the innards out with the little finger, and use a teaspoon to scoop out anything remaining inside. Rinse the fish inside and out.

Part-fill a shallow pan with sufficient water to cover the fish, bring to the boil, add the salt, herbs and fish, reduce the heat and poach for some 10 minutes until tender.

Drain, dish and serve with sorrel sauce.

PLAICE BOILED[55]

1 plaice weighing 1-1¼lb/450–550g
2tsp salt   *½tsp ground mustard*
¾pt/450ml light ale   *2tsp chopped parsley*

Mix the mustard and ½tsp salt into ¼pt/150ml light ale, bring to the boil, and set aside.

If the plaice has not been drawn, prise back the gill, snap it out with the finger and thumb, and use the little finger to hook out the innards, then scoop out with a teaspoon anything left behind. Wash the fish.

Put the remaining salt, light ale, the parsley and ¾pt/450ml water into a shallow pan, bring to the boil, put in the fish, reduce the heat and poach gently for 10–15 minutes until tender.

Remove the fish into a shallow dish, add ¼pt/150ml of its stock to the mustard mixture, bring this to the boil, and pour over the fish just before serving hot.

SOLE IN CYVE[56] [IN YELLOW ONION SAUCE]

1 sole weighing 1–1¼lb/450–550g
4oz/100g onions   *½tsp salt*
2oz/50g soft white breadcrumbs   *pinch of saffron*
⅛pt/75ml [sweet white] wine   *¼tsp mixed ground pepper,*
⅛pt/75ml white wine vinegar   *   ginger and cinnamon*

Peel the onions, boil for some 15 minutes until tender, drain, cool, and chop them very finely.

Add the breadcrumbs, wine, vinegar, salt, ground spices and saffron, and grind together to make a smooth paste.

Draw the sole (as the plaice, above), place dark side up on a board, make a cut across the base of the tail, grasp the flap of skin firmly, and pull it towards the head while holding the tail with the other hand. At the jaws, work the skin over the head, and pull off the white skin down to the tail. Retain the skin for fish stocks or jelly.

Bring 1½pt/900ml water to the boil in a shallow pan, put in the fish, reduce the heat, and simmer for 10–15 minutes until tender.

Remove the fish to a shallow dish, cut away and discard the fins.

Add 3tbs of the fish stock to the onion sauce, bring to the boil, pour over the fish, and serve immediately.

FRUMENTY WITH PORPOISE[57]

This was one of the highest-status fish dishes. Although it could be cooked in broth or in galantine, it was also plain-boiled and served with frumenty, as the fish-day alternative to venison. Today we do not eat porpoise, but its place may be taken by fresh tuna.

1½lb/675g fresh tuna
frumenty, prepared to the recipe on p. 273

Plunge the tuna into a pan of boiling water, reduce the heat, and simmer for some 15–20 minutes until tender.

Drain the tuna, serve in a dish half-filled with hot water, and accompanied by a dish of hot frumenty. The carver cut it into pieces for the lord as he dined.

CONGER EEL[58]

2lb/900g conger eel   *chopped parsley*
white wine vinegar

Chop off the head, cut out the vent, remove all the innards from the throat end, and wash clean inside and out before cutting the eel into round steaks some 1 inch/2.5cm thick.

Bring a pan of salted water to the boil, put in the steaks, and poach for 10–15 minutes until tender.

Drain, dish, and sprinkle with the parsley and vinegar just before serving.

TO DIGHT A CRAB[59]

1 dressed, cooked crab, with its shell
2tbs [red?] wine vinegar
1tbs sweet red wine

½tsp sugar
pinch ground ginger and
    cinnamon

Soak the picked crabmeat in the vinegar and wine for some 30 minutes, then chop finely, and rub through a sieve. Add a little more vinegar and wine in the same proportions if necessary to produce a very soft paste.

Mix in the spices and sugar, replace the meat in the shell, place over a gentle heat, and stir gently until it boils, then serve, with a sprinkling of sugar mixed with a little ground ginger and cinnamon.

SHRIMPS[60]

8oz/225g raw shrimps
    [alternatively buy the shrimps ready-boiled and picked]
[white?] wine vinegar

Plunge the shrimps in boiling salted water for 3–4 minutes, cool, drain, then snap off the heads, and pull off the shell to leave only the tail meat. [The instruction that the lord may eat the shrimps without waste confirms that they were picked in this way.]

Half-fill a saucer with the vinegar, and arrange the shrimps around the rim.

MUSSELS IN SHELLS[61]

3lb/1·4kg mussels
6oz/150g onion, finely chopped
¾pt/450ml white wine

4tbs white wine vinegar
¼tsp ground black pepper

Discard any open shells which do not close when tapped, snap off any encrustations and protruding beards, scrub thoroughly, and rinse to remove all grit.

Place all the ingredients in a pan, bring rapidly to the boil, simmer for 5 minutes, shaking the pan occasionally, until the mussels have opened, then pour all into a dish and serve.

MUSSELS IN BROTH[62]

Cook as above, then pick the mussels out of their shells, return to 2pt/1·2l of their stock, and stir in 6oz/175g soft white breadcrumbs, ¼tsp ground ginger, ½tsp salt. Return to the boil, then dish and serve.

OYSTERS IN GRAVY[63]

6oz/150g onion, peeled
12 oysters
½pt/300ml almond milk made
    with white wine (see p. 279)
½pt/300ml light stock

2tsp sugar
1 blade mace
4 cloves
¼tsp ground ginger

Simmer the onion for 15 minutes, then chop finely.

Scrub the oyster shells, open them, saving their liquor. Rinse the oysters in cold water.

Place all except the oysters in a pan, simmer for 10 minutes, then add the oysters and simmer for 2 minutes before serving.

TO BOIL WHELKS[64]

2lb/900g live whelks
   (preferably professionally harvested to avoid polluted sources)
salt, parsley and white wine vinegar

Put the whelks in a pan, cover with cold water, bring to the boil, and simmer for 2 hours. When cold, drain, remove from the shells, remove all the darker innards, the adjacent thin tissue, and the horny outer lids, to leave only the cylindrical muscular part.

   Rinse in salted water, and garnish with parsley rinsed in vinegar.

POTTAGE OF WHELKS[65]

Prepare the whelks as above, then chop very finely. Return to their stock with 2tsp cornflour [for amydon], 4tbs almond milk (see p. 279) and pinches of saffron, ground black pepper and ground cumin. Stir well until almost boiling, and serve hot.

SALMON FRESH BOILED[66]

4 round salmon steaks   *a few sprigs of parsley*
2tsp chopped parsley   *1tbs white wine vinegar*
2tsp salt

Grill the steaks for 2–3 minutes on each side in order to slightly brown and part-cook them.

   Remove the steaks to a shallow pan, add the chopped parsley and salt, cover with boiling water, and simmer very gently for 3–5 minutes until still tender, but cooked through.

   Drain the steaks, leave to go cold, then garnish with the sprigs of parsley freshly rinsed in the vinegar.

   Alternatively, a large section of salmon may be boned, simmered to tenderness with the ground bones, pepper, ginger, cinnamon, saffron and a little flour, then cut into gobbets and a little cumin stirred in just before serving.

TROUT BOILED[67]

2 trout	2tsp salt
2tsp chopped parsley	

Cut the head off the trout and draw out the innards.

Simmer the salt and parsley for 5 minutes in sufficient water to cover the fish, strain it into a clean pan, add the trout, and simmer for a further 10–15 minutes according to size, until just tender. Drain, and serve with greensauce (see p. 334).

Alternatively, leave the head on, draw out the innards and gills from the gill openings, and make six cuts half-way through one side of the spine, three behind the head, and three more along the spine. This will enable the trout to be formed into a circle, [sewing the head to the tail?] so that it can be simmered as above, but in a round cooking pot, and convenient for serving on a round dish with greensauce and sprigs of parsley.

EELS IN BRUET[68]

1lb/450g freshwater eels	⅛pt/80ml white wine
8oz/225g onions, finely chopped	2oz/50g white breadcrumbs
2tsp parsley, finely chopped	pinches of ground black
1tsp sage, finely chopped	pepper and cinnamon
	salt

Cut through the skin just behind the fins, pull back for about an inch, then, grasping the head in a cloth, unpeel the whole skin, as if removing a stocking, before pulling away any remains of the spinal fins. Remove the head, cut the eel open from throat to vent, and remove all the innards. Cut the eel into 1–2 inch/2·5–5cm lengths.

Cover the eel, onion, parsley and sage with water, bring to the boil, and poach for 10–15 minutes.

Soak the breadcrumbs in the wine, stir these into the eel when just tender, cook for a few minutes more, until thickened, then season to taste with the pepper, cinnamon and salt.

BALLOC BROTH[69]

This rich fish broth was very popular, as indicated by its many recipes, one being entitled 'Pik and ele in ballok brothe that muste our dame have, or els she will be wrothe'. Eels appear in every recipe, along with either stockfish or pike, either a whole pike for a lord, or a quarter pike for commoners, all cooked in a herbed and spiced stock.

Ingredients, as in the recipe above, replacing half the eels with prepared pike or soaked salt fish. Omit the breadcrumbs, add ground ginger, galingale and saffron to the spices, and a few drops of red food colour (for sanders).

Prepare the eels as in the first two paragraphs above.

Bring the onions, herbs, and 1½pt/900ml water to the boil, and simmer for 5 minutes.

Add remaining ingredients, and poach for 10–15 minutes until the fish is tender, then dish and serve.

DAIRY POTTAGES

Eggs and cream or milk were the basic ingredients for a number of sweet and savoury pottages. Most were quickly made, but required some skill to ensure that they were not overheated, which would have caused them to change from smooth creamy mixtures into hard curds. Those who do not make custards frequently are recommended to add 1–2tsp cornflour to all but the first recipe.

PAPYNS [A PLAIN CUSTARD][70]

1pt/600ml milk   3tbs sugar
2tbs plain flour   pinch of salt
3 egg yolks, beaten

Beat the flour into the milk, simmer for 5 minutes, stirring continuously, then leave to cool.

Beat in the remaining ingredients, bring to the boil while stirring, and pour into a dish.

ARBOLETTYS[71] [A CHEESE/HERB CUSTARD]

1pt/600ml milk   2tsp chopped parsley
1oz/25g butter   2tsp chopped sage
4oz/100g cheese, grated   ¼tsp ground ginger
4 eggs, beaten

Mix all the ingredients in a pan, heat gently, stirring continuously, until it has thickened like a custard and pour into a dish.

BRUET OF EGGS[72] [A WHOLE-EGG CHEESE CUSTARD]

3 or 4 eggs   1 tbs cider vinegar (for
¾pt/450ml water   verjuice)
1oz/25g butter   ½tsp sugar, with a little
3oz/75g cheese, grated   ground cinnamon

Lightly beat the eggs and vinegar, and pass through a strainer into a bowl.

Heat the water, butter, cheese, sugar and cinnamon, stirring continuously until the cheese has virtually dissolved.

Pour the hot liquid over the eggs, return to the pan, and continue stirring over a gentle heat until smooth and thick (but not curdled), and pour into a dish. Serve piping hot.

CREAM BASTARD[73] [A CUSTARD WITHOUT YOLKS]

1pt/600ml milk
4 egg whites, lightly beaten
2tbs honey

1tbs sugar
¼tsp salt

Cook as arbolettys above.

POTTAGE OF EGGS[74]
[POACHED EGGS IN A SWEET SAUCE]

4 eggs
½pt/300ml milk
2tbs plain flour
pinch of saffron

2tsp sugar
2tsp honey
1tbs sugar mixed with
　½tsp ground cinnamon

Beat the flour, saffron, ginger, sugar and honey into a little of the milk, then beat in the remainder to form a smooth mixture.

Slowly bring to the boil, stirring continuously, and set aside.

Poach the eggs in simmering water until lightly set, arrange on a dish, pour the sauce over, and sprinkle with the sugar and cinnamon mixture.

BUTTERED EGGS[75]

¼–½ oz/10–15g butter per egg.

Gently melt half the butter in a small pan, pour in the beaten eggs, and stir over a low heat until just cooked, but still soft. Stir in the remaining butter, dish and serve immediately. This is the traditional method of making the dish served to the Earl of Northumberland's family and chief officers every Saturday except during Lent.

SALADS

Although uncooked, salads are considered here for convenience. The eating of raw fruits and herbs was not recommended, John Russell warning diners to, [76]

> beware of saladis, grene metis, & of frutes rawe
> for they make many a man haue a feble mawe [stomach].
> Therfore, of suche fresch lustes set not an hawe,
> For suche wantoun appetites ar not worth a strawe.

Considering the well-known virtues of herbs, this was an apparently paradoxical opinion, but probably based on experience. With the partial exception of fruits, virtually everything eaten or drunk in medieval England was sterilized by the heat of cooking, and therefore safe to eat. Herbs gathered from the fields, and perhaps rinsed in unboiled water, did not have this protection, and so may well have caused stomach upsets, and 'make your sovrayne sike'.[77]

SALADS[78]

These were made by composing mixtures of any of the following herbs:

alexander buds	dandelion	primrose buds
borage and its flowers	fennel, red	purslane
calamint (wild basil)	garlic, green	radishes
chibols (spring onions)	leeks, young	ramsons (wild garlic)
chickweed	mint, red	rocket
chives	nettles, red	rosemary
cress	onions	rue
daisies	parsley	violet flowers

Wash them clean, pick away any coarse stalks or blemishes, tear into small pieces, toss with olive oil, turn into a dish, and sprinkle with vinegar and salt.

VEGETABLE POTTAGES

Pottages made of various mixtures of green herbs were very popular. Their ingredients included avens, beet-tops, betony, borage, briar (blackberry leaves), clary, town cress and water cress, coles (spring greens or cabbages stripped from their stalks), red cabbage, fennel, langue-de-boeuf, lettuce, mallow, red nettles, orach, parsley, patience-dock (*Rumex patientia*, or passion dock, *Polygonum bistorta*), primrose, savory, thyme and violet.[79] Blending these to produce the most appealing flavours must have been a matter of skill and experience, but the recipes give no indication of how they were expected to taste. However, their universal method of preparation by being parboiled, drained, chopped and then simmered in various fresh liquids, shows that the cooks were deliberately removing the strongest flavours, in order to obtain more delicate results.

JOUTS[80]

8–12oz/225–325g mixed herbs, from the above list

Boil the herbs in plenty of water for 10 minutes, drain, press dry, chop, and grind to a smooth paste.

For meat-days grind 4oz/100g soft white breadcrumbs with the herbs and a little stock, stir into 2pt/1.2l beef stock, and simmer until thickened.

For fish-days, replace the beef stock with salmon or eel stock.

For jouts with almond milk (see p. 279), add the ground herbs to 2pt/1.2l almond milk and stew until the herbs are tender.

WORTS[81]

8–12oz/225–325g mixed herbs from the above list

Boil the herbs in plenty of water for 10 minutes, drain, press dry and finely chop them. After that, you may do one of the following.

Simmer in 2pt/1200ml beef stock until tender;

or, for buttered worts, simmer as above, then stir in 2oz/50g butter, with ½tsp salt, and serve on sliced or cubed white bread;

or, for white worts, simmer in 2pt/1200ml almond milk (see p. 279), 2tbs rice flour, 1tbs honey, ½tsp salt, and a pinch of saffron;

or, you may simmer in a gruel made of 2pt/1200ml stock, 4oz/100g oatmeal and ½tsp salt simmered for 30 minutes before the herbs are added;

or, you can simmer in 2pt/1200ml meat stock with 4oz/100g ground cooked pork and 1 tbs olive oil;

or, you can make a fish-day version of the above, using fish stock and 4oz/100g ground cooked eel;

or, boil 1 quart/1l mussels for 5 minutes, strain their water into a pan, stir in the prepared herbs, cook until tender, then stir in the de-shelled mussels.

Other vegetable pottages were made with individual varieties.

Beans

Broad beans (*Vicia faba*) were a major field crop in medieval England. Presumably they were eaten fresh in July and August, being boiled with bacon as they were up to the mid-twentieth century.

BEANS YFRYED[82]

1lb/450g broad beans	*1–2 cloves garlic, chopped*
1 large onion, finely chopped	*olive oil or lard for frying*

Simmer the beans in water for some 20–25 minutes until they burst, then drain.

Fry the beans, onion and garlic in the oil or lard for 5–10 minutes, until pale golden brown, pour into a dish and sprinkle with a little sugar and cinnamon.

When dried, and known as 'canabeans', the beans became an important winter and springtime food. The method of preparation involved soaking them in cold water for over 48 hours, drying them in an oven, grinding and winnowing off the hulls at the mill, breaking them into two to four pieces in a mortar, and finally frying them for long-term storage.[83] In this form they were ideal for pottages, coarse breads and bean butter: 'used moche in Lente, it is good for plowmen to fyl the panche; it doth ingender gross humours; it doth replete a man with ventosyte.' [84]

CANABEANS[85]
[PLAIN-BOILED TO ACCOMPANY BOILED BACON]

8oz/225g dried broad/butter beans   1 tsp salt

Soak the beans in cold water for 24 hours and strip off the hulls (strong thumb-nails are an advantage).

Put the beans in 1½pt/900ml cold stock in a pan, slowly bring to the boil, simmer very gently for 90 minutes, adding salt 10 minutes before draining and serving, like frumenty, beneath a hot boiled bacon joint.

CANABEANS[85] [SWEET]

Cook as above, using milk instead of stock, and adding 2tbs honey and ½tsp salt 10 minutes before serving.

CANABEANS[86] [IN LENT]

Cook as above, using almond milk (see p. 279) instead of milk, and sugar instead of honey.

DRAWN BEANS [87]

Cook as in the first recipe, adding 2 large onions, finely chopped, and a large pinch of saffron.

Cabbages

Medieval cabbages appear to have had a much stronger flavour than those of today, and lacked the large compact hearts of more recent varieties. Perhaps the nearest modern equivalent is spring greens. One recipe recommends laying them in a bag in a running stream overnight before being thrown into a pot of boiling water. This particularly interesting account suggests that the use of netted string bags to hold cabbages together in boiling pots was of medieval origin, rather than an invention of Georgian times.

CABBAGES[88]

1–1½lb/450–700g cabbage	*1tsp salt*
1pt/600ml beef stock	*3oz/75g grated white bread*

Remove the coarser outer leaves, enclose in a net bag if possible, plunge into boiling water, and simmer for some 45 minutes, then drain, press dry, chop in pieces, and discard any tough stems.

Bring the beef stock, salt and saffron to the boil, add the cabbage and cook for a further 5–10 minutes until tender, then thicken with the breadcrumbs before serving. For a lord, replace the breadcrumbs with 4 beaten egg yolks scalded with some of the stock and returned to the pan.

One version cooks marrowbones with the cabbage, knocking out two or four pieces of marrow on top of the dished cabbage, while another replaces the bread with oatmeal gruel made with meat stock. The cabbage could also be quartered and simmered in meat stock with finely chopped onions, leeks and saffron.

Fennel

See page 285.

Garlic

In addition to being used as a flavouring for meats, salads, sauces and similar preparations, garlic, known as aquapates, was served as a vegetable in its own right. Its more pungent wild alternative, ramsons, *Allium ursinum*, was eaten, being mentioned in Andrew Boorde's *Brevyary of Health*, but is too strong for recipes such as the following.

AQUAPATES TO POTTAGE[89]

6 heads garlic	¼tsp ground mixed spice
1tbs olive oil	1 tsp salt
large pinch of saffron	

Separate the garlic into cloves, peel them, cover with water in a small pan, add the oil, spices and salt, cover, and simmer for 25–30 minutes until tender and the flavour has mellowed.

Gourds

'Gourds' were described as 'cucumer' in medieval glossaries, John Wyclif's Bible also explaining that gourds were commonly known as 'cucumeres'. The young gourds required for the following receipes would therefore resemble small cucumbers, i.e. courgettes.[90]

GOURDS IN POTTAGE[91]

1lb/450g courgettes	4oz/100g cooked lean pork
½pt/300ml meat stock	2 egg yolks, beaten
4oz/100g onions, finely chopped	½tsp salt
large pinch of saffron	

Peel the courgettes, cut them in large pieces, and simmer them with the onions in the stock for some 10 minutes until tender.

Mince and grind the pork to a smooth paste, and stir into the now-cooked courgettes with the saffron and salt.

Scald the yolks with a little of the stock, return to the pan, stir in, remove from the heat, and pour into a dish. Sprinkle with a little sugar mixed with cinnamon.

Leeks[92]

Leeks were a popular food, being used in salads, sops (see p. 285), mixtures with other vegetables, and particularly in a white vegetable pottage called blanch porre

BLANCH PORRE[93]

1lb/450g of the white part of leeks, finely chopped
1 large onion, finely chopped   pinch of saffron
1pt/600ml light stock   ½tsp sugar with a little
           cinnamon

The original recipes all parboil the leeks before adding the onions, but today's leeks do not require this preparation.

Simmer the leeks and onions in the stock for some 15 minutes until tender; add the saffron, stirring for a few minutes to dissolve its colour. Pour into a dish and sprinkle with the sugar and cinnamon.

Variations
The above recipe was enriched by having small birds simmered in it. Others simmered leeks alone in almond milk (see p. 279) sweetened with sugar or honey, serving them in a separate dish to accompany long pieces of boiled salt eel.

Mushrooms

FUNGES[94]

8oz/225g mushrooms, peeled and diced
4oz/100g leeks, very finely chopped
½pt/300ml stock
pinch of ground pepper and clove
pinch of saffron

Stew all together for 10 minutes.

Onions

Although onions were widely used in a variety of meat, fish and vegetable dishes, there are relatively few with onions as their main ingredient. These include sops of onions (see p. 284) and the following.

BRUET DE ALMAYNE[95] ['GERMAN BROTH']

1lb/450g onions, chopped
1pt/600ml almond milk

¼tsp mixed ground cloves
 and cubebs
2tbs olive oil

Fry the onions in the oil until golden brown, stir in the almond milk (see p. 279) and spices, and simmer for a further 10 minutes.

An alternative version, porrey chaplain, made rings of [flour and water] pastry, fried them in olive oil or lard, and boiled them with the onions in the almond milk.

CHERBOLACE[96]

1lb/450g onions, chopped
½pt/300ml stock
pinch of saffron

½tsp salt
½tsp sugar mixed with a
 little cinnamon

Simmer the onions in the stock, saffron and salt for some 15 minutes until tender, pour into a dish and sprinkle with the sugar and cinnamon mixture.

Parsnips

The medieval word for the parsnip in Old High German and Dutch was *pastinak*, derived from the Latin *pastenaca*. It is by this name that they appear in medieval English recipes for composts and fritters. They were scraped, cut into pieces, rinsed in hot water, and simmered 20 minutes in either stock or water with a little olive oil and saffron. [97]

Peas

The peas specified in medieval English recipes were of two kinds; young/green, or freshly-gathered, and old/white, which had been dried, and therefore required prolonged boiling and blanching to remove their tough hulls. The following recipes represent the main groups of pea pottages.

GREEN PEAS WITH HERBS[98]

1½lb/675g green peas   2tbs chopped mixed parsley,
1pt/600ml beef stock   sage, savory and hyssop
pinch of saffron

Simmer all together for some 10 minutes until tender.

GREEN PEAS TO POTTAGE[99]

Ingredients as above, plus 2oz/50g soft white breadcrumbs

Simmer all the peas for 5 minutes, grind the herbs to a paste with the bread, add half the peas to the mortar and grind to a smooth paste, then return all to the remaining peas and stock.

Return to the boil, and simmer for some 5 minutes more until the peas are tender.

YOUNG PEAS ROYAL[100]

Make up the previous recipe, using half game stock and half almond milk (see p. 279) for the stock, and parsley and mint for the herbs. When ready, stir in 2tbs sugar or honey with 1tsp salt and a beaten egg yolk. Remove from the heat, pour into a dish, and sprinkle with a little sugar.

PORRE OF PEAS[101]

1½lb/675g green peas	1tbs sugar
12oz/350g onions, finely chopped	½tsp salt
1tbs olive oil	pinch of saffron

Just cover the peas in water and simmer for some 10 minutes until they begin to burst, then drain (retaining the stock), plunge into cold water and rub or rinse off the hulls, then return to the pan with the stock and the other ingredients.

Continue simmering for a further 10 minutes until the onions are tender, then serve.

Variations include adding chopped parsley and sage, ground pepper, a little wine and wine vinegar with the onions, and stirring in small slices of toast just before serving. [102]

OLD PEAS WITH BACON[103]

8oz/225g dried peas	1 x 3lb/1350g bacon joint
meat stock	

Soak the peas in water overnight

Place the peas and bacon in a deep pot, cover with meat stock and simmer, the joint taking some 20 minutes per lb/450g plus 20 minutes.

When almost cooked, strain the peas, pound them to a smooth paste, and return to the pot with the stock and bacon.

Add a little water if necessary to form a thick pottage, and serve by pouring over the bacon in a dish.

PEAS OF ALMAYN[104]

8oz/225g dried peas	1–2tsp salt
¼pt/150ml almond milk	pinch of saffron
2tbs rice flour	

Soak the peas overnight, then simmer for about 1 hour until they begin to burst, then drain, plunge into cold water and rub or rinse off the hulls.

Stir the rice flour and saffron into the almond milk (see p. 279). Add to the peas, with sufficient water to just cover them, and stir and simmer until the rice flour is cooked out and the peas are tender. Add salt to taste just before serving.

WHITE PEAS IN GRAVY[105]

Make as in previous recipe, replacing the rice flour and saffron with 1tbs sugar, 4oz/100g chopped onions fried in olive oil, and 2tsp olive oil.

Skirrets[06]

The roots of this variety of water parsnip (*Sium sisarum*) were cooked like parsnips or turnips.

Spinach[107]

Rinse the spinach, cook with no added water in a covered pan for 10 minutes, drain, chop, fry in a little olive oil, and sprinkle with a little sugar and cinnamon.

Turnips[108]

The small white turnips, known as rapes in medieval recipes, were either cooked like parsnips, or could be washed, quartered, parboiled for 10 minutes, drained, and boiled for a further 10 minutes with finely chopped onions, saffron and salt. When dished, they were sprinkled with a little sugar and cinnamon.

FRUIT POTTAGES

Apples

Moiled, or softened apples were made using either boiled apple pulp, or finely chopped fresh apples which retained their original flavour and texture.

APPLE MOISE[109]

1lb/450g cooking apples, peeled, cored, and coarsely chopped
¼pt/150ml almond milk   *pinch of saffron*
2tbs honey   *pinch of salt*
4oz/100g soft white breadcrumbs or 3tbs rice flour

Simmer the apples slowly with some ¼pt/150ml water for 10 minutes until soft, rub through a sieve, and return to the pan.

Beat the breadcrumbs or rice flour, honey, saffron and salt into the apple purée, stir continuously until it has boiled for 5 minutes, then pour into a dish. Sprinkle with a little sugar and ground pepper and cloves.

For flesh-days replace the almond milk (see p. 279) and honey with the same quantities of beef stock and sugar, with 1tsp lard.

For a fish-day alternative, replace the honey with sugar and add 1 tsp olive oil.

APPLE MOYLE[110]

4oz/100g eating apples, peeled and chopped very finely
3tbs rice flour   *2tbs sugar*
½pt/300ml almond milk   *pinch of saffron*

Beat all but the apples into the almond milk (see p. 279), boil together for 2–3 minutes until thick, stirring continuously, remove from the heat, stir in the apples, pour into a dish, and sprinkle with a little sugar and ground cinnamon.

Bullaces

See confectionery on page 347.

CHERRIES[111]

1lb/450g cherries	4tbs honey or sugar
¼pt/150ml sweet red wine	2tsp wine vinegar
1tsp lard	1 egg yolk
3tbs rice flour	large pinch cinnamon and
pinch of saffron or a few drops red food colour (for sanders)	galingale

Reserve a dozen cherries, remove the stalks and stones from the remainder and pound to a pulp with the wine, before squeezing the juice through a cloth into a pan.

Stir in the rice flour, saffron or food colour, lard, spices and honey or sugar. Simmer, stirring continuously, for 5 minutes.

Beat the egg yolk into the vinegar, and rapidly stir into the mixture before pouring into a dish. Decorate with the reserved cherries.

Pears

See confectionery on page 346.

STRAWBERRY[112]

8oz/225g strawberries	⅛tsp each of ground pepper,
¼pt/150ml almond milk	ginger, cinnamon and
3tbs red wine	galingale
4tbs rice flour	2tsp wine vinegar
4tbs sugar	a few drops of red food colour
1tsp lard	(for alkanet)
large pinch of saffron	1 pomegranate for decoration

Pulp the strawberries with the wine, and rub through a fine sieve or muslin

Stir in all but the vinegar, food colour and pomegranate, and simmer for 5 minutes until thick, stirring continuously, then remove from the heat and stir in the vinegar and food colour.

Allow to cool until tepid, spoon onto a dish in separate lumps, stud with pomegranate seeds, and serve when cold.

DRIED FRUIT POTTAGES

FIGEY[113]

6oz/150g dried figs, stalks removed   1tsp pine kernels
¾pt/450ml sweet wine or ale   pinch each of pepper, saffron
2oz/50g white breadcrumbs   and salt

Simmer 4oz/100g of the figs in ½pt/300ml of the wine or ale for some 20–30 minutes until soft, then stir in the wine, bread-crumbs, spices and salt, and rub the whole through a sieve.

Finely chop the remaining figs, stir into the mixture with the pine kernels, and pour into a dish.

POTTAGE OF RAISINS[114]

4oz/100g raisins   1tsp rice flour
8oz/225g apples, peeled and cored   pinch of ground ginger and
½pt/300ml almond milk   galingale

Simmer the apples and raisins in the almond milk (see p. 279) for some 15 minutes until tender, add the rice flour, and beat to a smooth paste while simmering for a further 5 minutes.

Pour into a dish and sprinkle with the spices.

PAYN REGUSON[115]

4oz/100g raisins
2oz/50g white breadcrumbs
½pt/300ml [sweet] wine

⅛ tsp ground pepper
¼ tsp ground ginger
¼ tsp salt

Grind all the dry ingredients together with a little of the wine to form a smooth paste.

Stir in the remaining wine, bring to the boil while stirring continuously, and pour into a dish.

FLOWER POTTAGES

The perfume and colour of flowers was incorporated into a number of sweet pottages of almond milk (see p. 279) thickened with rice flour, amydon, breadcrumbs or egg yolks. Most were suitable for fast-days, but meat-day versions included cooked meats ground to a smooth paste. Boiled hen or capon were most usual, but 'great flesh', i.e. boiled beef, mutton or pork, also appear to have been used. [116]

HAWTHORN ['SPINETTE'], PRIMROSE, RED ROSE, AND VIOLET[117]

¼pt/150ml loosely packed petals of the above flowers
1pt/600ml milk or almond milk   3 tbs sugar or honey
6tbs rice flour or 4tbs cornflour (for amydon)

Reserve a few hawthorn blossoms, primrose flowers, rose petals or violets on their stalks to decorate the finished dish.

Boil the remaining petals in a little of the milk or almond milk (see p. 279) for a few minutes, drain (retaining the liquid), grind to a smooth paste, and return to the liquid with the remaining ingredients, and a little food colour to enhance the original colour of the flowers.

Stirring continuously, bring to the boil and simmer 2–3 minutes. Pour into a dish and [when cold?] decorate with the reserved flowers.

ROSY[118] [WITH MEAT]

4oz/100g cooked chicken, ground to a smooth paste
2oz/50g white breadcrumbs   1tsp lard
½pt/300ml almond milk   ¼pt/150ml red rose petals
pinch of saffron   1 egg yolk, beaten
1tbs cornflour (for amydon)

Reserve a few petals for decoration
Mix the chicken, breadcrumbs, almond milk (see p. 279), saffron and lard in a pan, and simmer for 5 minutes, stirring continuously until thickened.

Chop the petals very finely, rapidly stir into the mixture with the egg yolk, remove from the heat, pour into a dish, and decorate with the rose petals.

CEREAL POTTAGES

Cereal pottages were made in two main forms, those of fairly stiff whole-grain being used as accompaniments to meats, while those of ground meal were ideal for both almost solid pastes, or semi-liquid spoonable gruels.

FRUMENTY

Taking its name from *frumentum*, the Latin word for corn, this was the principal accompaniment to venison or porpoise. It was made from whole threshed wheat, from which the outer layer of bran had been removed, gently stewed until it formed a soft glutinous mass. Appearing in *The Form of Cury* of *c.* 1390, it probably had much earlier origins, representing a method of converting hard wild grain seeds into an easily digested, nutritive and comforting food. In England, it has probably been made continuously for some 12,000 years, for some families in North and East Yorkshire still prepare a batch every Christmas. Here, the traditional methods were either to have the bran ground off in a commercial pearling mill, or to soak the grain in water, place it in a sack, beat it with a stick, and then rinse off the loosened bran. Medieval cooks preferred to place the wheat in a stone mortar, sprinkle it with a little water, and pound it with a wooden pestle to remove the bran, but still leave the grains intact. I can remember the same implements being used in the same way in Yorkshire farms, the mortars or 'knocking stones' effectively de-husking oats for sick horses.[119]

Having prepared the wheat, it was rinsed, boiled slowly until the individual grains burst, simmered with milk or light stock, flavoured and coloured with saffron, and finally thickened with egg yolks for meat-days.[120] For fish-days the milk and the stock were replaced with almond – or hazelnut – milk, and the eggs omitted.

6oz/150g whole wheat grains	*½tsp salt*
¼pt/150ml milk or almond milk	*large pinch of saffron*

Place the wheat in a deep stone mortar, cover with water, and work with a wooden pestle to grind off the bran, rather than pulp the grain.

For a modern alternative, place the grain in a food processor with ¾pt/450ml water and process for about 5 minutes.

Alternatively, use pearl barley instead of wheat.

Pour the grain into a coarse sieve and rinse with water to remove the bran.

Put the drained grain and the saffron into a pan with 1½pt/900ml water or light stock, bring to the boil and simmer gently for about an hour, stirring occasionally, until it has formed a thick glutinous mixture.

Add the milk/almond milk (see p. 279) and salt, cook for a further 5 minutes, stirring continuously, then serve hot.

Alternatively, stir in 1tbs sugar beaten with 2 egg yolks when you add the milk/almond milk and salt.

Rice

Rice production originated in prehistoric Asia but during the fifteenth century the North Italian plains were growing much of the rice imported into England by the Venetian and Genoese spice-ships. For this reason the short-grained 'pudding' varieties should be used, these presumably being in their polished rather than brown forms, since this was a high quality food, in which whiteness and purity were of some importance. A number of recipes closely follow those for frumenty, the grain being rinsed three or four times and blanched by being covered with cold water, brought to the boil and then drained. This would effectively remove all dust and dirt used to adulterate the grain, but may be omitted when using today's cleanly-processed rice. The following recipes represent the four main varieties of rice pottages.

RICE[121]

8oz/225g short-grained rice *large pinch of saffron*
2pt/1200ml light meat or fish stock *1tbs sugar*
1tsp salt (omit if using stock cubes or salted stock)

Place all the ingredients in a pan, bring to the boil, and simmer gently for a further 15–20 minutes, stirring occasionally until the grains are cooked and most of the liquid has been absorbed.

POTTAGE OF RICE[122]

8oz/225g short-grained rice
½pt/300ml milk or almond milk (see p.279)
1tsp salt or 2tbs sugar or honey *large pinch saffron*

Cover the rice with water, bring to the boil, and simmer for some 10–15 minutes until the rice has softened.

Drain the rice, add the remaining ingredients, and simmer for a further 5 minutes, stirring continuously, until it is completely cooked and thickened.

RICE LOMBARD STANDING[123]

Make up the first rice recipe above, with meat stock, rapidly stir in 3–4 beaten egg yolks, remove from the heat, and form into a flat-topped round on a dish. Sprinkle with a mixture of 3 mashed hard-boiled egg yolks, 2tsp sugar, and ½tsp mixed ground ginger, clove and mace, and serve.

RICE MOYLE[124]

2oz/50g ground rice	*large pinch saffron*
1pt/600ml almond milk	*2tbs sugar*
2tbs almonds, pre-fried golden brown in lard [or oil]	

Place the rice, almond milk (see p. 279), saffron and sugar in a pan, simmer and stir continuously for some 5–10 minutes until the mixture is cooked and thickened, adding a little water if necessary.

Pour into a dish, shake level, and decorate with the almonds.

BLANCMANGE[125]

There are a number of recipes for this 'white food', all including rice cooked to softness, ground with almond milks of varying degrees of richness, and either hen/capon, or fish such as lobster, haddock, carp, dace, ray, pike, perch or tench, the whole then being ground to a smooth paste, dished and garnished. The following version is typical,

2oz/50g rice	*1tbs lard*
1oz/25g ground almonds	*1tsp salt*
4oz/100g cooked lean chicken or white fish, free of bones	
8 almonds, fried golden brown in lard, a few aniseed comfits, or a little sugar, perhaps mixed with ground ginger	

Simmer the rice in ½pt/300ml water for 30–40 minutes until the grains are very soft, then drain and grind to a smooth paste with

a little strained almond milk made by grinding the almonds with
¼pt/150ml of either plain water or chicken stock.

Mix the rice, chicken or fish, remaining almond milk, salt and
(only if using chicken) lard together, grind to a smooth paste, and
pour into a dish.

Decorate the blancmange with the almonds, the comfits, or
the sugar perhaps mixed with a little ground ginger.

Oats

Oats can be grown in any part of England, but were particularly suited
to the colder and wetter areas of the north and west. Perhaps because the
finely-ground meal soon became sour, particularly if damp, the form of
oatmeal generally used in the kitchen appears to have been groats, where
the grain was coarsely milled, probably a little larger than today's pinhead
oatmeal.[126] For thickening, these could be ground to dust in a mortar. In
peasant households, oatmeal was ideal for making a variety of different
pottages, such as flummery, sowans, llith, siot, crowdy and brewis which
continued to be made well into the twentieth century, as well as for gruel,
the medieval word for oatmeal porridge. [127] There are no medieval recipes
for this staple food, since methods of its preparation were so well known.
The traditional method of making it involved bringing a pot of water to
the boil before stirring in the groats, thus reducing the time for which it
had to be stirred.

GRUEL

6oz/150g oatmeal (groats or pinhead)   2tsp salt

Bring 1½pt/900ml water to the boil, and sprinkle in the salt and
the meal through the fingers of the left hand, while stirring with
a wooden spatula ('thivel' or 'spurtle') held in the right.

Stir until evenly mixed, without any lumps. Reduce the
heat, and allow to simmer very gently for 30 minutes, stirring
occasionally, and adding a little water if necessary, then serve. It
may be made beforehand and re-heated.

Boiled onions, sliced, or boiled nettles, chopped, may be stirred in before serving. Gruel may also be made with milk.[128]

GRUEL OF FORCE[129]

Follow the first two paragraphs of the recipe above, replacing the water with beef broth. Thin it with a little water, and rub the gruel through a coarse sieve.

Grind 6oz/150g lean cooked pork to a smooth paste. Add saffron to the gruel, and bring to the boil, while stirring. Stir in the ground pork, cook for a further 5 minutes, and serve hot.

GRUEL OF ALMONDS [130]

Follow the first recipe, replacing 2oz/50g of the oatmeal with blanched almonds, and grinding them together to a fine mixture before stirring them into the water with a large pinch of saffron.

POTTAGES OF ALMONDS

Almonds were imported from southern Europe in large quantities, the royal household consuming almost 13 tons in 1286, and even modest households such as that of Dame Alice de Bryene buying 40lb in 1418–19.[131] One of their major uses was to produce almond milk, the main vegetable alternative to cow's milk for fast-day cookery. This involved shelling them, blanching them in boiling water to remove their brown skins, and then grinding them with wine, water or light stock. If dry blanched almonds were simply pounded in a mortar, they emerged as a useless oily mass, rather than a smooth emulsion, and so it was essential that they were blanched immediately before use. Some recipes specify 6½oz/180g almonds to each pint/600g of liquid, but the following proportions give good results.[132] Some recipes specify white wine or light meat stock instead of water, to enhance their flavour.

ALMOND MILK[133]

3oz/75g blanched almonds   *¼tsp salt*
1tbs sugar or honey [or muscavado sugar plus 1tsp white sugar]

Place the ingredients into a jug, pour in 1pt/600ml boiling water, and leave for an hour to cool.

Strain off the almonds (retaining the liquid), and either pound in a mortar or grind in a food processor with a little of the liquid to produce a smooth paste. Add the remaining blanching liquid, pound or grind once more, and then strain off the milk through a piece of freshly-rinsed muslin, squeezing it to produce about 1pt/600ml almond milk.

ALMOND CREAM/BUTTER[134]

Here, the aim is to make a curd by the addition of vinegar. Start by making up four times the quantity of almond milk specified in the previous recipe.

Pour into a saucepan, bring to the boil, and as it rises add 1tbs white wine vinegar and remove from the heat. Allow to cool for some 10 minutes, then pour into a double layer of freshly-rinsed fine muslin or linen cloth. Gather the corners together into a noose of twine, and hang up to drain over a jug for 2–3 hours.

Turn the drained almond cream/butter into a bowl and mix in 2tbs finely ground sugar. Transfer to a small serving dish, level the surface, and garnish with either red comfits or borage leaves.

GRAVIES

Almond milk was an essential ingredient in medieval recipes such as chicken, rabbits, eels or oysters 'in gravy'. 'Gravy enforced' was almond milk flavoured and coloured with ginger and saffron before being enriched with boiled egg yolks and gobbets of fat cheese, while white peas in gravy were finished with almond butter, sugar, fried onions and olive oil.[135]

BRUET OF ALMONDS[136]

1 x 3lb/1·6kg chicken or 2 partridges
1pt/600ml almond milk   *⅛tsp mixed ground ginger,*
1·5tbs plain white flour   *cinnamon and galingale*
large pinch saffron

Truss the prepared bird(s), cover with salted water, and simmer the chicken for some 50 minutes, the partridges some 30 minutes, until tender.

Beat the flour and spices into the almond milk, bring to the boil while stirring, simmer for 5 minutes, and pour over the drained and quartered birds in a dish.

POTTAGES OF FLOUR-PASTE

Pasta, in the form of simple flour and water pastry, was made in two main forms, either small flat diamonds called lozenges [or makerouns], or round stuffed tartlets called ravioles.

LOZENGES[137]

8oz/225g plain white flour   *4oz/100g grated white cheese*
4pt/2.2l light stock   *(Cheshire or Cheddar)*
1tsp sugar mixed with ¼tsp ground cinnamon or 2oz/50g butter

To make the lozenges, put the flour into a bowl, make a well in the centre and work in just sufficient cold water (about ¼pt/150ml) with a knife blade to form a stiff dough. Turn on to a floured board, knead until smooth, then roll out to a thickness of approximately one-sixteenth of an inch or 2mm.

Cut into diamond shapes some 2 inches/5cm long, and either use fresh or, for long-term storage, leave on a floured cloth in a warm place for one or two days until dry.

Bring the stock to the boil, stir in the lozenges, and simmer, uncovered, for some 10–15 minutes until tender.

Drain the lozenges, and place on a dish in two or three layers with the cheese and either the sugar/cinnamon mixture, or the butter in between and on top.

LOZENGES ON FISH-DAYS[138]

a batch of lozenges made as in the recipe above
½pt/300ml almond milk   *pinch of saffron*
1tbs sugar   *¼tsp salt*

Plunge the lozenges into boiling water and simmer for some 10 minutes until tender, then drain.

Meanwhile bring the remaining ingredients to the boil, stir in the lozenges, and pour into a dish.

RAVIOLES[139]

a batch of dough made as above, cut into rounds some
    2 inches/5cm in diameter
6oz/150g grated white cheese such as Cheshire or Cheddar
2 raw egg yolks   *pinch of saffron*
2oz/50g butter

Grind two-thirds of the cheese and half the butter with the yolks and saffron to make a smooth paste.

Place about ½tsp of the mixture in the centre of half the pastry rounds, damp the edges with a little water, and cover with the remaining rounds, excluding all air, and pressing the edges tightly together.

Plunge the ravioles into boiling water, and simmer for some 10 minutes until tender, then drain.

Layer the ravioles in a dish with the remaining cheese and butter.

RAVIOLES[140] [OF SPICED PORK]

a batch of dough as for lozenges above

8oz/225g lean pork	⅛tsp mixed ground clove and
4 dates, chopped	black pepper
2 dried figs, chopped	1tbs sugar
1 egg yolk	1tbs currants
1½pt/900ml chicken stock	2oz/50g grated cheese
large pinch of saffron	⅛tsp ground ginger

Chop and then grind the pork, dates, yolk, saffron, clove, black pepper and sugar to a smooth paste, moistening it with a little of the chicken stock, then stir in the currants.

Roll out the dough, and cut into eight 4-inch/10cm rounds. Spread the mixture on four of the rounds, leaving the edges clear. Dampen the edges, cover with the remaining rounds, and seal the edges, excluding all air.

Bring the remaining stock to the boil in a large pan, put in the ravioles, boil for 10 minutes, put into a deep dish with the stock, and sprinkle with the mixed grated cheese and ginger.

BREAD POTTAGES, SOPS

In their earlier form, sops appear to have been small pieces of bread dipped into cups of wine at table, where they could be eaten with a spoon, or possibly the fingers. St John's Gospel describes how Jesus predicted his betrayer as 'He it is to whom I shall give a sop, when I have dipped it'. From a practical point of view, sops were one of the most useful adjuncts of pottages. The combination of hot flavoursome broths with oatcakes, bannocks or leavened bread produced tender, nourishing and virtually instant meals such as everyday brewis, and the high quality sops. Some sop dishes were made with simple cubes of white bread.

ALLAYED MILK[141]

3–4 thick slices of white bread, crusts removed,
    and cut into 1in/2.5cm sops
¾pt/450ml milk   3tbs sugar
4 egg yolks, lightly beaten   pinch of salt

Arrange the sops in a dish.

    Beat the remaining ingredients in a pan, heat gently, while stirring, until it has thickened, but not boiled, and pour over the sops just before serving.

SOPS CHAMBERLAIN[142]

Since early recipes for this dish make no mention of heat or cooking, it appears to have been a simple, cold dish which a chamberlain could easily make for his lord or lady using the ingredients kept in the livery cupboard, rather than in the kitchen.

½pt/300ml hippocras [or red or white wine in which 1tsp ground
    cinnamon and ginger and 1tbs sugar have been soaked
    for 3–4 hours, and then filtered out]
3 slices white bread prepared as sops above

Arrange the sops on a dish, douse with the hippocras or wine, sprinkle with mixed sugar and cinnamon, and serve.

For most other sops, the cubed bread was lightly toasted on a grid-iron, but a modern grill works just as well. It is best to grill the whole slice on both sides before removing the crusts, cutting the rest into 1in/2.5cm cubes, and perhaps arranging these to grill the cut sides. [143]

SOPS CHEAT[144]

3 thick slices wholemeal bread, prepared as toasted sops, above
½pt/300ml almond milk made with light stock
¼tsp mixed ground clove, mace and ginger
3tbs pine kernels   *3tbs sugar*
2tbs currants

Arrange the sops on a dish.

    Simmer the remaining ingredients for 5 minutes, pour over the sops, and serve.

SOPS DORY[145] [WITH ONIONS]

3 thick slices white bread, prepared as toasted sops, above
8oz/225g onions chopped to some ¼–½in/1cm pieces
2tbs olive oil   *½pt/300ml white wine*
¼pt/150ml almond milk

Fry the onions in the oil until pale gold in colour, then add the wine, bring to the boil, and simmer for 5 minutes.

    Heat the almond milk (see p. 279), pour over the sops in a dish, and pour the onions on top.

SOPS DORY[146] [WITH SAFFRON, ON WHICH POACHED CAPONS MIGHT BE SERVED]

3 thick slices white bread, prepared as toasted sops, above
¼pt/150ml almond milk   *1tbs sugar*
½pt/300ml white wine   *pinch of salt*
large pinch of saffron
2 tsp sugar mixed with ¼tsp mixed ground ginger,
   cinnamon, clove and mace

Douse the sops in a dish with half the wine.

    Mix the remaining wine with the almond milk, saffron, sugar and salt in a pan, bring to the boil, pour over the sops, and sprinkle with the spiced sugar mixture.

SLIT SOPS[147]

3 thick slices white bread, prepared as toasted sops, above
1½lb/675g trimmed leeks　　　　*3tbs olive oil*
1pt/600ml white wine　　　　*1tsp salt*

Quarter the white of the leeks lengthwise and cut into lengths of some 1 inch/2·5cm to enable them to be spooned up.

Simmer the leeks in the wine, oil and salt for 15–20 minutes until tender, then pour over the sops in a dish.

SOPS IN FENNEL[148]

3 thick slices white bread, prepared as toasted sops, above
2 heads of fennel, sliced　　　　*large pinch of saffron*
1 medium onion, finely chopped　　*1tsp salt*
2tbs olive oil
2tsp sugar mixed with ¼tsp ground cinnamon

Simmer the fennel, onions, oil, salt and spices for some 30 minutes, until tender, then pour over the sops in a dish.

OIL SOPS[149]

3 thick slices white bread, prepared as toasted sops, above
1lb/450g onions, chopped in some ¼–½in/1cm pieces
1pt/600ml mild ale　　　　*1tsp salt*
2tbs olive oil　　　　*½tsp ground black pepper*
3tbs sugar　　　　*large pinch of saffron*

Simmer the onions in the ale and oil for some 20 minutes until tender, then stir in the remaining ingredients, simmer for a further 2–3 minutes, then pour over the sops in a dish.

TOASTS

In contrast to sops, toast dishes were based on thick slices or 'trenchers' of toasted white bread which had various rich, sweet mixtures either spread onto them, or soaked into them.

TOAST TO POTTAGE[150]

4 thick (3–4in/8–10cm) slices of white bread, toasted
3tbs clear honey
½pt/300ml sweet red or white wine
pinch of salt

¼tsp mixed ground black
    pepper and ginger
1 piece preserved ginger

Mix the wine and honey, bring to the boil, skim, and stir in the ground pepper, ginger and salt.

Pour on the toasts, and stud with vertical strips of the preserved ginger.

POKEROUCE[151]

Make as above, replacing the wine with an additional 4tbs honey, and the pepper and salt with cinnamon and galingale. Stud the toasts with pine kernels.

SOPS IN DOUCE

4 small slices of white bread, toasted
¼pt/150ml almond milk
1tbs sugar

⅛tsp salt
¼pt/150ml sweet [white?]
    wine

Douse the toast in half the wine and place beneath a low-heated grill to warm through.

Bring the almond milk, sugar and salt to the boil, stir in the remaining wine, and pour over the hot toasts in a dish.

CAUDLES AND POSSETS

These were warm comforting drinks served either at the end of supper to close the stomach or to those who were ill or in childbed. They were usually made with cow's – or almond – milk, wine or ale, sugar, spices and thickening in the form of egg yolks, flour, or fine white breadcrumbs, but there are many variations between the individual recipes.[152] The following demonstrate something of their range.

CAUDLE OF ALMONDS[153]

Make up as 1pt/600ml almond milk (see p. 279) using either blanched or unblanched almonds and white wine or ale-and-water instead of water, with a pinch of saffron. Serve hot.

CAUDLE OUT OF LENT[154]

1pt/600ml almond milk made with sweet white wine
4 egg yolks, lightly beaten   *pinch of salt*
2tbs sugar   *red food colour*

Beat the yolks, sugar and salt into the almond milk (see p. 279), and stir over a gentle heat until it begins to thicken but does not boil. For a thicker version beat in 1tbs wheat flour or rice flour and a pinch of saffron with the eggs etc., before cooking.

Turn into a dish, decorate by dropping on a little watered-down red food colouring (originally alkanet).

CAUDLE FERRY[155]

¾pt/450ml sweet white wine   *¼tsp mixed ground mace,*
3 egg yolks, lightly beaten   *cinnamon, and galingale*
1tbs sugar   *1tsp sugar mixed with a little*
pinch of salt   *cinnamon*

Beat all but the sugar and cinnamon mixture together, stir over a gentle heat until it begins to thicken, but does not boil.

Pour through a strainer into a dish and serve hot, sprinkled with the sugar and cinnamon.

POSSET[156]

1pt/600ml milk   large pinch ground ginger
1pt/600ml sweet white wine or ale

Boil the milk, remove from the heat, pour in the wine or ale from a height and leave for 5–10 minutes, to form a soft curd. Then scoop up the curd, transfer into a dish, and sprinkle with the ginger. [The whey may be drunk separately.]

Alternatively drain the curd in a fine muslin, rub through a sieve with ⅛pt/75ml sweet white wine, stir in a little ground ginger and 2 tsp sugar, transfer to a dish, and strew with caraway comfits.

A COLD POTTAGE[157]

Make up 4 times the quantity of almond milk as in the recipe for a caudle of almonds, replacing the water with sweet white wine.

Divide in two, boil one half plain, the other with ¼tsp ground ginger and cinnamon and a pinch of saffron.

Strain each almond cream separately as in the final paragraph of the preceding recipe for posset and, when drained, turn into separate small dishes before serving cold.

JELLIES

Since jellies could be spooned from dishes, as well as being cut in slices, they occupied a half-way stage between pottages and leaches. Some menus include 'pottage callyd gele', for example, while jelly recipes might be entitled 'viand leach'.[158] Medieval cooks had noticed that the stock left after boiling certain meats and fish turned into a set or semi-set jelly as it cooled. Those with plenty of sinew and skin, i.e. collagen, were found to give the best results, and so calves' feet and hock-joints and pigs' trotters, ears and snouts were often used, as well as poultry, for meat jellies. For fish jellies, the 'sounds' or swim-bladders of stockfish, which later generations would process into isinglas, were probably the most effective ingredient, but eels or eel-skin, plaice, pike, tench and turbot could give usable results. According to the recipes, it was merely necessary to simmer the fish in white wine to produce a crystal-clear jelly, but anyone who tries this with most white fish will find that a pound/450g of fish will only make about a tablespoon of rather glue-like jelly after prolonged simmering and reduction.[159] Many of the recipes incorporate into the finished dish the fish or meat used to form the basic jelly, which shows that they must have been subject to a very long, very gentle simmering, rather than a brief period of hard boiling, which would have rendered them extremely tough. As the old proverb says, 'a stew boiled is a stew spoiled'. Even though some recipes discarded the jelly-making ingredients, and poached fresh fish and meat in the jelly stock, nothing can detract from the realization that the medieval cooks were masters of their craft, skilled in temperature control and the extraction of clear jellies without recourse to any methods of clarification beyond simple straining. To compensate for this loss of skill, and lack of access to unprocessed swim-bladders, some of the following recipes incorporate gelatine as a convenient substitute.

JELLY DE CHARE[160] [MEAT JELLY]

2½–3lb/1·1–1·4kg calves' feet [or pigs' trotters] cleaned and
*   chopped*
1 prepared chicken weighing 3lb/1·4kg or 4 pork chops
3pt/1·8l [sweet]white wine   1tsp salt
¼tsp ground pepper   4tbs [white] wine vinegar
blanched almonds, cloves and   large pinch of saffron
*   sliced ginger to garnish.*

Bring the feet or trotters and the wine to the boil, skim, then gently simmer, barely any steam escaping from the lid, for 3 hours.

Pour the liquid into a measuring jug, make up to 2pt/1·2l with more wine if necessary, pour into a clean pan, add the chicken or chops, pepper, saffron, salt and vinegar, cover, bring to the boil, skim and simmer gently for a further 30 minutes or more until the meat is tender.

Remove the skin from the chicken and detach the legs, arrange these or the chops in a dish, pour on the stock, and leave in a cool place to set before garnishing the surface with the almonds, cloves and ginger.

Variations

Instead of making a jelly with trotters or feet, dissolve 4tbs gelatine in 2pt/1·2l wine.

If you would like to make a pink jelly, replace the white wine with claret.[161]

Remove the cooked meat from the bones, cut into 'small morsels', cover with the stock, sprinkle with galingale, and when set, decorate with sprigs of laurel or bay leaves.[162]

MEAT JELLY[163]

1lb/450g chicken or lean pork, cubed
½pt/300ml [white] wine   pinch of saffron
½pt/300ml water   4tsp gelatine
¼tsp mixed ground clove and ginger

To form a good jelly from meat alone, as in the original recipe, requires the presence of quantities of skin and sinew. To replace these the modern version uses gelatine.

Bring the meat, wine and water to the boil, skim carefully. Add the spices. Simmer very gently for about an hour until tender.

Stir the gelatine into 3tbs cold water, and stir this into the pan, until dissolved, then turn all into a dish and leave to set.

Variations for preparing jellies

Make the jelly by briefly simmering ½tsp each of whole cloves and chopped ginger in 1pt/600ml sweet white wine. Remove from the heat, strain, and stir in 2tbs gelatine mixed in ¼pt/ 150ml cold water until dissolved, then drain and leave to set.[164]

For an opaque white jelly add the gelatine in ¼pt/150ml almond milk (see p. 279) instead of the water.

For other colours, a few drops of food colour may be added to produce red (for sanders or alkanet), blue (for indigo) or yellow (for saffron).[165] These coloured jellies may be dressed in the following ways:

Colour half the jelly white, pour into a dish and leave until set, then colour the other half red, and allow to cool before pouring over the layer of white.[166]

Erect a circular wall of pastry in the centre of a dish, pour one colour of jelly around it, leave it to set, remove the pastry, and fill the void with jelly of another colour.[167] These would have been the party or parted jellies listed in menus.

Pour a batch of the white jelly into a dish, allow to set, then cut away the surplus to leave the form of a plaice, pike, sole or tench. [168]

The practice of using meat jellies to produce fish for fish-days extended to the conversion of either a veal hock or calves' feet, hearts and lungs into a stiff, sliceable mass, which could be passed off as sturgeon.[170] In a similar manner, stiff fish-based almond milk jelly could be moulded in egg-shells, left to set, and then have the shells peeled away to leave realistic 'boiled eggs' in jelly. These were decorated with gilded cloves, and used to garnish slices of leach lombard.[171]

JELLY OF FISH[172]

1lb/450g white fish, such as turbot, plaice, tench, eel or pike
1pt/600ml white wine, or half white wine/half vinegar, or one
    third vinegar/half white wine/one-sixth water
2tbs gelatine

Simmer the fish in the liquid for some 10 minutes until tender, then lift out on to a plate (reserving the stock). Remove the skin and bones and divide into pieces, arranging these on a dish.

Stir the gelatine into ¼pt/150ml cold water, add the hot, strained stock, stir until dissolved, pour over the fish, and leave in a cool place until set.

CHAPTER FOURTEEN

Leaches

Derived from the Old French *lesche*, the medieval leach was simply a slice. It might be cut from a joint of meat, but there were numerous recipes for binding various ingredients into a solid mass which could then be sliced, dished, coated in a piquant sauce, and garnished ready for the table. Some recipe manuscripts have whole sections dedicated to these 'Leche Vyaundes' or 'sliced foods', some being of meat or fish set with their own juices, or combinations of various foods set with eggs, rice flour, breadcrumbs, curds, cheese, or blood.[1] For the cook, they had the great advantage of being able to be prepared well before a meal was to be served, most being cold dishes, sometimes 'revived' with a hot sauce just before being sent to the table. For the diner, meanwhile, they provided a whole range of well-flavoured, delicate dishes, all easy to cut, masticate and digest, even with poor teeth. The following recipes include meat, fish, egg and cereal leaches, those for posset and curd leach being in the dairy chapter (p. 84) and for sweet leaches and gingerbreads in the confectionery chapter (p. 343).

MANGE MOLEYNNE[2]
This title probably comes from the French *manger*, 'food', and *moleine*, 'soft', which describes its consistency, when compared to that of cooked meats.

8oz/225g raw chicken, finely chopped/minced
2tbs ground almonds   *1tbs lard*
3tbs rice flour   *1tbs sugar*
                                        9 blanched almonds

Grind the almonds with ¼pt/150ml water, strain off the almond milk, mix with the chicken, the rice flour and lard, and simmer gently for 10 minutes, while stirring continuously.

Remove from the heat, stir in the sugar, pour into a rinsed dish, and leave to set.

Cut the pâté into slices, and stud each with three almonds fried golden brown.

BLANCHE BRAWN [3] [PORK PÂTÉ]

1lb/450g pork shoulder	1tbs sugar
2oz/50g ground almonds	1tsp salt

Grind the almonds in ¾pt/450ml water, and strain the almond milk through a cloth into a pan.

Finely mince the pork, stir into the almond milk along with the sugar and salt, then simmer for some 30 minutes, stirring continuously until it is so stiff that if pushed against the side of the pan, it will not flow back again. [Two teaspoonsful of gelatine sprinkled in with the pork helps to compensate for the lean, tender nature of modern pork.]

Press into a freshly-rinsed bowl, leave to cool and set, then slice and serve.

BRAWN IN CONFITE[4] [SPICED PORK PÂTÉ]

Follow the above recipe, but simmer the pork for 1¼ hours, before mincing it. Add ½tsp ground clove and 1tsp each of ground cinnamon and ginger at the same time as you add the sugar. After that, hang up in a muslin to drain for a few hours before slicing.

CHARLET FORCED[5]

8oz/225g cooked pork
1pt/600ml milk
4 eggs, lightly beaten
pinch of saffron

5tbs ground almonds
1tbs rice flour
1tbs sugar
2tbs parsley, finely chopped

Grind the almonds with ½pt/300ml water, strain off the almond milk, and mix a little of this with the pork, before grinding it to a smooth paste.

Thoroughly mix the pork, milk, eggs, saffron and parsley in a pan, bring to the boil while stirring continuously, simmer for 5 minutes, then leave to cool a little, before hanging up in a cloth until completely drained, cold and set firm.

Slice the charlet, arrange in a dish, and pour over it a sauce made by simmering the rest of the almond milk, rice flour, sugar and saffron together for a few minutes.

CHARLET COUNTERFEITED OF FISH[6]

8oz/225g cooked haddock or cod
8oz/225g ground almonds
2tbs sugar
pinch of saffron

2tbs white wine vinegar
2tbs [sweet white?] wine
¼tsp mixed ground ginger,
    mace and cinnamon

Grind the almonds with 1pt/600ml water, and strain off the almond milk through a cloth.

Beat the fish to a smooth paste, having removed all bones, stir in ½pt/300ml of the almond milk, 1tbs sugar and the saffron, and heat to boiling, stirring continuously.

Remove from the heat, stir in the vinegar, leave to stand for 10 minutes, then pour into a piece of muslin, and hang up in a cool place to drain for an hour or two, then press it into a deep dish, and leave for a further hour.

Turn the charlet out of its muslin onto a clean board, cut across into slices, and arrange in a dish.

Heat the remaining almond milk and sugar with a little more saffron. Bring to the boil, remove from the heat, stir in the wine, and pour this sauce over the sliced charlet.

Mix the spices into a further 2tsp sugar, and sprinkle on top just before serving.

POTTAGE WASTERE [WHELK LEACH][7]

8oz/225g cooked whelks	a few drops red food colour
2tbs ground almonds	(for sanders)
1tbs honey or sugar	2tbs rice flour
pinch of saffron	a little ground ginger & sugar

Grind the almonds with ¼pt/150ml water, then strain off the almond milk.

Grind the whelks to a smooth paste with the almond milk, and stir in the sugar or honey, saffron, red food colour and rice flour, then bring to the boil, stirring continuously, until quite thick.

Press the mixture into a freshly-rinsed basin, leave in a cool place until cold and firmly set, then turn out onto a board, and slice with a freshly-rinsed knife.

Arrange the slices on a dish, sprinkle with a little ground ginger mixed into sugar, and a few red comfits, if available.

HAGGIS

Haggis was made in England from at least the 1420s through to the middle and late nineteenth century. Its supposedly unique Scottish character was invented as part of that country's Romantic revival in the reign of George IV. Traditional English versions recorded from the seventeeth century onwards are based on oatmeal, mutton-suet, dried fruits and herbs such as parsley and thyme all cooked in a sheep's stomach, and it is probable the medieval peasant versions were of similar composition.[8] Those appearing in fifteenth-century recipe books contain richer and more delicate ingredients, such as eggs, breadcrumbs, cream and ground pork. To make them could apparently be a full-time occupation, the *Catholicum Anglicum* of 1483 translating 'An Hagas maker' as a *tucetarius* (sausage-maker). Texts such as the *Liber Cocorum* and *The Noble Boke of Cookery* describe chopping sheep's hearts, parboiled gut and the like for their haggis, but since these ingredients are now generally unavailable, the following medieval recipes are more suitable for today's use. The sheep stomachs originally used may be replaced by fine linen or muslin pudding-cloths or bags as specified in the ffraunt hemelle and leach Lombard recipes below. These are of particular interest, since they show that the pudding-cloth was of early fifteenth century date, if not even earlier, rather than being a late-Tudor English invention, as often stated.

FFRAUNT HEMELLE[9]
[AN EGG, MEAT AND BREADCRUMB PUDDING]

4 eggs, lightly beaten	*pinch of saffron*
5oz/140g minced cooked meat	*¼tsp mixed ground pepper,*
5oz/140g white breadcrumbs	*ginger and clove*

Mix the dry ingredients, make a well in the centre, pour in the eggs, and stir to make a smooth mixture.

Take a piece of fine linen or muslin, rinse it, squeeze it, shake it out flat, and dust with plain flour.

Heap the mixture in the centre, draw up the cloth around it, tie tightly, plunge into a deep pan of boiling water, and simmer for 45 minutes.

Drain the pudding, turn out, and grill or broil to give the exterior a light colour just before serving.

AN ENTRAIL [A PORK, CHEESE AND EGG PUDDING][10]

1lb/450g lean pork, finely ground	*pinch mixed spice*
4oz/100g grated cheese	*¼tsp salt*
4 eggs, lightly beaten	

Cook as above, simmering for 1 hour.

LEACH LOMBARD[11]

1lb/450g lean pork	4 dates, stoned & chopped
3 eggs	¼tsp ground pepper
2tbs sugar	¼tsp ground cloves
4oz/125g raisins	¼tsp salt
2oz/50g currants	

Finely mince the pork, mixing in the beaten eggs and other ingredients, tie in a cloth which has been scalded, squeezed, shaken flat, and dusted with flour, and boil for 30–40 minutes, until firmly set and cooked.

Turn the meat out onto a board, carve in the manner 'of a peskodde', and arrange on a dish.

To make the accompanying sauce take:

4oz/125g raisins	pinch of saffron
¼pt/150ml red wine	a few drops red food colour
¼pt/150ml almond milk	(for sanders)
pinch of ground pepper & clove	

Grind the raisins to a smooth paste with the wine, add the remaining ingredients, and simmer for 2–3 minutes.

Stir in:

¼pt/150ml red wine
¼tsp mixed ground ginger and clove

Bring almost to the boil, pour over the leach, and serve.

PUDDINGS

Medieval ox and sheep puddings were made by enclosing their fresh blood, chopped internal fat and oatmeal groats in short lengths of their large intestine, these being boiled until cooked. They were virtually identical to today's black puddings, except that the groats may now be replaced with pearl barley, or omitted completely. They were broiled [grilled] just before being served, and probably eaten with mustard.

EGG LEACHES

Eggs were particularly useful for making leaches. At their simplest, they merely enriched thick starchy cereal leaches, but many leaches were either very thick egg custards, or pressed masses of enriched scrambled eggs.

CUMIN[12]

2oz/50g ground almonds	*1 raw egg yolk*
6tbs cornflour (for amydon)	*1 hard boiled egg yolk*
1tbs ground cumin	*1tbs sugar mixed with pinches*
2tbs sugar or honey	*of ground ginger, mace*
½tsp salt	*and clove*

Grind the almonds with ¾pt/450ml water and strain off the almond milk into a pan.

Slake the cornflour in a little cold water then stir it into the almond milk with the cumin. Simmer slowly for 10 minutes, stirring continuously, before removing from the heat and beating in the raw egg yolk, sugar or honey, and salt, and pouring the mixture into a freshly-rinsed dish.

When cold, slice the leach into a dish, and sprinkle with the crumbled hard-boiled yolk, the sugar and the spices.

CREAM BOIL[13] [A SLICED BOILED CUSTARD]

½pt/300ml single cream
4 egg yolks
[1tbs cornflour]

pinch of salt
borage flowers for decoration

Beat the yolks, salt and cornflour into the cream [the original recipe has no cornflour, but its presence will help the inexperienced cook to produce a smooth custard, rather than a mass of hard egg curds].

Heat the mixture gently, stirring continuously, until just boiling, then dip the base of the pan into cold water, and pass the custard through a sieve into a freshly-rinsed bowl. Leave to set in a cool place.

Wet the top surface of the custard, turn it out onto a freshly-rinsed dish, cut into slices with a wet knife, and decorate with the flowers.

MILK ROASTED[14]

Follow the above recipe, replacing the cream with milk, and omitting the cornflour, boiling the mixture until curdled, then hanging the curds in a piece of muslin until they have drained and set into a solid mass.

Cut the curd into thick slices, grill on a greased grid-iron, and serve.

LET LARDES[15]

This was similar to the above recipe, except that the egg curds were enriched with small cubes of fat cut from boiled bacon joints, and usually built up in layers of different colours and flavours, perhaps just green, red and yellow, or, as here, with black, white and purple too. The coloured curds might also be mixed to give a marbled effect. The curds were probably pressed firm and dry in a small wooden or pottery curd mould lined with muslin, but a similar utensil may be obtained today by drilling a number of holes around the sides and base of a plastic box some 4 inches/10cm across, similarly lined with muslin.

12 eggs, beaten
2pt/1·2l milk
1tsp salt
2oz/50g fat from boiled bacon

2tbs chopped parsley
2tbs fried black pudding
a few drops of red and purple
*   food colour (for sanders*
*   and turnsole)*

Chop the fat very finely, beat into the milk with the eggs and salt, and divide this mixture into six separate pans. Mix the saffron into one, grind the parsley into another, the black pudding into the third, the red and the purple into the fourth and fifth respectively, and leave the sixth plain.

Heat each pan in turn, stirring the contents until they have formed a firm curd, pour off the whey, and pack each coloured curd in turn into the box, finally putting a weight on top, and leaving them to set into a solid mass.

Turn the curds out onto a board, cut into thick vertical slices to show stripes of all the colours, and either arrange on a dish, or grill or fry and serve hot.

VIAND DE LEACH[16]

These recipes are characterized by the mixing of a soft posset-curd of milk with ale or wine with rather firmer egg-curds or fresh curds from the dairy.

1pt/600ml white wine
8 egg yolks, beaten
pinches of ground clove, ginger,
*   cinnamon and saffron*

1pt/600ml full cream milk
½pt/300ml ale
2tbs sugar

Beat the yolks, clove, ginger and saffron into the wine and gently heat, while stirring, until it forms a curd. Strain off the whey through a fine cloth.

Heat the milk almost to boiling, pour in the cold ale from a height, leave for a few minutes to cool, then strain off the whey through a fine cloth.

Mix both curds together with the sugar, cinnamon and ginger. Tip into a muslin bag, hang up to drain, then press to firmness under a weight.

Turn out the curds, slice and arrange on a dish.

CHAPTER FIFTEEN

Roasting

Purely radiant heat provided the best means of cooking tender joints of meat, game and poultry. It gave succulent and delicately-flavoured results, but only at the expense of considerable labour. If a joint was placed in front of the fire, the surface facing the flames would quickly char, insulating the remainder, and ruining the meat. It had therefore to be constantly turned, so that the burst of heat received from the fire was absorbed into the joint during the remainder of its rotation. Even so, it was best to start with the meat perhaps 18 inches away from the fire until it heated through, only then moving it closer, as a well-cooked exterior would still insulate the interior, and leave it almost uncooked, even if roasting continued for several hours. Since this rotation was time-consuming, roasting appears to have formed little or no part of peasant cookery, none of the necessary equipment being listed in inventories of cottage households, even those supplied with metal cooking pots and similar goods.[1]

Wooden spits were used even by the prosperous, these being long poles sharpened at one end, their Latin name *veru*, a spear, being accurately descriptive. Some were made of hazel, but from the late twelfth century the manor of Ashwell, Essex, was held from the Crown by the service of providing a spit of maple to roast the King's meat on the day of his coronation.[2] Iron spits were pointed at one end and forged as a cranked handle at the other. They were probably easier to turn, harder-wearing and strong enough to carry heavier loads. Being highly conductive, they were able to transfer their heat into the core of the joints, speeding cooking time. They were both round and square in section, the latter giving a better grip on the meat. The largest were huge. The *c.*1450 inventory of Thomas Morton of York lists square ones weighing 49lb and 46lb, and round ones of 48lb, 38lb, 25lb and 21lb.[3] Given a 1-inch cross-section, this implies

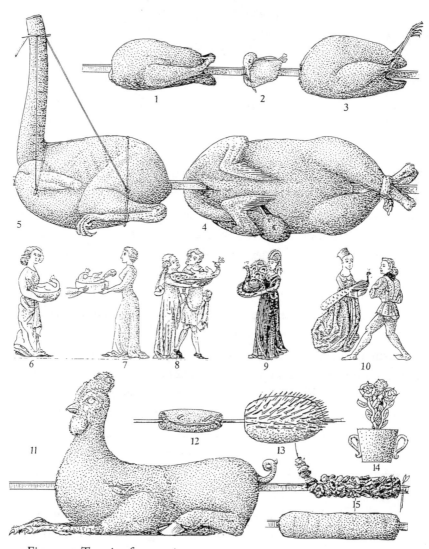

Figure 45. Trussing for roasting.

1. Pheasant.

2. Snipe.

3. Chicken.

4. Bittern.

5. Peacock.

11. Cockatrice of capon/pig.

12. Aloe ('olive').

13. Urchin (hedgehog).

14. Pot-wise (flowerpot).

15. Train roast or hastelet.

6–10. serving peacocks at King's Lynn, 1364 (6 and 7), c.1350, and 15c.

Note the short tails indicating young, tender birds.

that the square spits must have been some 12 or 13 feet in length, ideal for the great arched fireplaces of the period. Aside from these large examples, smaller ones were used, right down to eel spits and lamprey spits, just long enough for a single fish.[4] The usual term for a small spit was either a 'hastelet', from the Latin *hasta*, a spear, or a 'broach', Sir John Fastolf having 'two little broaches round' in 1495, and Thomas Dalby one which weighed just 1lb in 1400.[5] These were ideal for small roasts, such as tongues, the meatballs called pommedory, and also for disposing of unwanted kings. It was 'A broche of burning fire was put through a horn that was put in his fundament into King Edward II's body' that was used to murder him at Berkeley Castle in 1327.[6]

In some west-country kitchens, low blocks with grooved tops were used to support the spits, these being shown in the mid-fourteenth-century Luttrell Psalter; actual examples made in the local pottery up to the seventeenth century are displayed in the Museum of North Devon at Barnstaple. Iron racks or cob-irons were much more common, only one being needed if the other end of the spit was cradled in the spit-turner's lap, 'one spit with one cobbard' listed in Nottingham in 1495 being typical.[7] Manuscript illustrations show them as tripods, some with a number of hooks to hold spits at different heights, while others form part of brandreths holding pots over the fire. Inventory evidence suggests that larger households relied on pairs of racks, these being essential where long and heavily-laden iron spits were in regular use.

In John of Gaunt's great kitchen at Kenilworth Castle, the hearths built around 1361–99 were originally provided with foot-thick walls at each end. These appear to be the earliest examples of what became the standard form of spit-rack-cum-fireguard used in the royal household. The Lord's Side kitchen at Hampton Court shows how they looked when complete.[8] Their front edges sloped back to support large inverted T-shaped bars, from which projected up to eight notched racks to hold numerous spits. Since the Kenilworth spits must have been about 16 feet long, with a working length of about 12 feet, and since one standing and one sitting spit-turner could shelter behind each end-wall, winding a spit with each hand, these hearths each provided up to 96 feet of spit space. This truly reflects the cooking capacity required in a great medieval kitchen.

The alternative names for those who turned the spits were hasteler or turn-broach. The lord of the manor of Finchingfield, Essex, no doubt considered it an honour to turn the spit for the coronations of Edward III and his successors, but this was exceptional since it was a most undesirable task.[9] 'The cook's knave, that turneth the spit', had a bad reputation, but his temper and cleanliness can hardly have been improved by spending long hours turning the spits, his front roasted by the fire, his back chilled by the strong draughts which fed its flames, and its heat giving him a perpetual thirst. One fourteenth-century manuscript shows him sheltering behind a circular straw target, but tellingly depicts him as an ape.[10] This 'son and chief heir of Dame Idleness' was thus described by John Lydgate,[11]

A precious knave that cast him never to thrive

His mouth well wet, his sleeves right threadbare

A turnbroach, a boy for Hogge of Ware [Chaucer's Cook]

With louring face, nodding and slumbering...

Nor hath he no joy to do no business,

Save of a tankard to pluck out the lining.

Contrary to popular belief, meat was always roasted in front of the fire, never over it. No sane person would wish to burn good joints, or coat them in soot and ash thrown up by dripping fat. Instead, the fat and juices were collected in a shallow utensil placed before the fire, under the joint, there to be basted back over the meat to keep it moist. In a number of large kitchens the dripping was collected in stone vessels sunk into one end of the hearth. The bailey kitchen at Warkworth Castle has a 2-foot by almost 10-foot stone-slabbed channel across the front of its roasting hearth, this sloping down into a stone mortar ready to collect the dripping from the numerous spits used here for great feasts. At the York Bedern, a cooking pot was used in the same way, a hole pierced through its base being plugged with clay.[12] The Conisbrough Castle roasting hearth was provided with a shallow stone dripping-trough set just in front of its kerb. Some three and a half feet long, it has a shallow slope at each end, so that the juices could be readily scooped up for basting.[13] Survivals of this kind are rare today, but presumably they were once quite common, since their portable equivalents are relatively scarce in medieval inventories.

Being tough, heat-proof and easily forged, wrought iron was an ideal material from which to make dripping-pans. The fourteenth-century Queen Mary's Psalter shows a long, rectangular example, one end forming a spout from which the dripping could be poured either into a vessel set into the hearth, or some other vessel deep enough to receive the basting ladle.[14] A small rectangular iron dripping-pan excavated from Coppergate, York, has a spout in each corner for the identical purpose.[15] Few cast bronze dripping-pans have survived, but a very fine one was discovered in Hanning Bog near Otterburn in Northumberland in 1872. Presumably it had been deposited here in troubled times, like a number of other medieval bronze cooking vessels found in the north Pennines. Twenty-one inches long by nine wide, it was mounted on three legs for stability, with strong bar handles at the front and the right-hand end, so that its contents could be tipped from the spout at its left end.[16]

Due to their widespread use, and frequent recovery from excavations, we have considerably more knowledge of earthenware dripping-pans. In 1419 Dame Alice de Bryene bought '4 earthen pans... to catch the dripping 6d.', and '2 iron pans bought at Steresbrigge for taking the dripping fat 3s. 4d.'[17] These entries clearly show the difference in price between earthenware and iron pans, and hence the popularity of the former in smaller households. Some of the earliest might include the leaf-shaped and semi-circular lead-glazed examples made in Surrey whiteware in the mid-fourteenth century, but others were made in various English potteries in the fifteenth and sixteenth centuries.[18] All have either spouts or hollow tubular handles for the dripping to be poured into deeper vessels ready for basting.

Manuscript illustrations from the early fourteenth century show long wooden spoons being used to pour the juices collected in the dripping-pan back over the roasting joints. Today this is known as basting, but to medieval cooks it was 'dropping'. Meat fat must have been the usual medium, but red wine, salt and pepper was recommended for venison.[19]

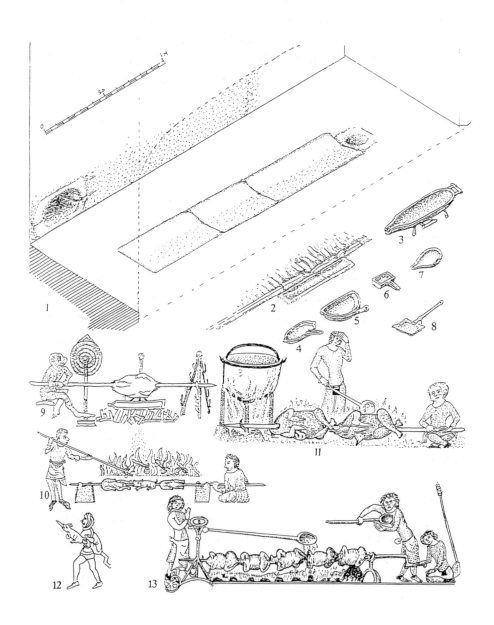

THE SIDES OF A DEER OF HIGH GREASE ROAST

1 joint of venison	*1tsp salt*
1pt/600ml red wine	*½tsp ground black pepper*

Weigh the joint, calculate the cooking time at 30 minutes per lb (450g). Spit it, continue to turn it before the fire until tender, regularly basting it with the remaining ingredients. Alternatively oven-bake in an oven pre-heated to 170°C/325°F/gas mark 3, placing the joint on a grid in a roasting tin containing the wine and seasoning, and basting it from time to time.

When cooked, place the joint on a hot dish, adding the liquor from the pan just before serving.

Batters such as spiced beaten egg yolks or almond milk and wheat starch could also be dropped over roasts in order to seal them. These were difficult to apply evenly when poured over the meat, much falling down into the dripping-pan. The practical alternative was to use a thicker mixture which could be painted on using a feather or a stick. This was one

Figure 46 (opposite). Roasting utensils.
1. Masonry dripping channel and collecting pot, Warkworth Castle, Northumb., *c.*1400.
2. Masonry dripping-pan, Conisbrough Castle, Yorks.
3. Bronze dripping-pan from Hanning Bog, Otterburn, Northumb.
4–7. Earthenware dripping-pans from London, 13–14c, Surrey, mid-14–mid-15c, Lyveden, Northants, 15c. and Malvern Chase, Worcs., late medieval/16c.
8. Wrought iron dripping-pan from York, late medieval?
9. A wooden spit, iron dripping-pan, cob-iron and wet straw screen, 14c.
10. A wooden spit on earthenware supports, and a fire-fork, *c.*1320–45.
11. Bittern or crane? on a wooden spit, supported by a brandreth, and a wooden basting ladle, *c.*1340.
12. An iron? spit with cranked handle, 15c.
13. An iron spit on tripod cob-irons, and wooden basting ladles, *c.*1340.

of the methods used to endore ('gild') roasts with flour, sugar and egg-yolk batters, the whites being used in the same way to produce paler tones.[20]

FILLET OF PORK ENDORED

1 large pork fillet	*½tsp mixed ground ginger,*
2 egg yolks	*black pepper and saffron*
½tsp salt	*1tsp plain flour*

Spit-roast the fillet, or oven bake at 180°C/350°F/gas mark 4, on a grid in a roasting tin, for some 40 minutes until tender.

Beat the remaining ingredients together, adding a little water as necessary to produce a thick, paintable paste. Brush this over the fillet, return to the heat until set, then brush on succeeding coats until the batter is used up, then serve.

Before certain meats were roasted, some form of preparation was required to ensure that they did not dry out. Fillets of venison, breasts of veal and rabbits might be parboiled, for example, and some game birds might be larded. This involved inserting strips of fat bacon or pork into the meat, so as to baste and flavour it internally as it cooked. [21]

PARTRIDGE ROASTED

2 partridges, oven-ready	*¼tsp mixed ginger and salt*
4oz/100g fat bacon or pork	*¼tsp mixed ginger and*
¼pt/150ml red wine	*cinnamon*

Cut the bacon or pork into ¼ inch/5mm-wide strips 1½ inches/4cm long. Use a larding needle to stitch each one into the breasts of the birds in rows, both ends projecting outwards.

Truss (see p. 313 below) and spit-roast or oven bake at 180°C/350°F/gas mark 4 for about 25 minutes, until tender.

Simmer the ginger and salt with the wine.

Dish the partridges, pour the hot wine over them, then sprinkle with the ginger and cinnamon just before serving.

Poultry, game and sucking pigs might be forced or stuffed. Geese or capons were packed with suet, chopped hard-boiled egg yolks, parsley, herbs, ginger, cinnamon, salt, pepper and either grapes or boiled onions. Sucking pigs, meanwhile, were stuffed with a mixture of fresh breadcrumbs, saffron, ginger and suet all bound with beaten eggs. Another most effective method was to stuff under the skin as in this recipe.[22]

CHICKENS FARCED

1 large oven-ready free-range chicken
3 hard-boiled egg yolks
1oz/25g currants
1tsp salt
1tsp mixed ginger, pepper and saffron

1 small tin chopped pork
1tsp each chopped parsley,
    sage and thyme

Insert the fingers at both ends to separate the skin from the flesh. Originally this was done by blowing into a cut in the neck, to inflate the skin.

Mix the remaining ingredients to form a smooth paste, and insert this evenly between the skin and the flesh, then truss for roasting (see p. 312 below and Fig. 45, no. 3).

Spit-roast gently for about 20 minutes per lb (450g) plus 20 minutes, checking that the internal temperature is at least 70°C (160°F). Alternatively, oven-bake at 200°C/400°F/gas mark 6 for the same time.

This technique gives excellent results, since all the moisture and flavour is trapped within the skin; it also carves well, the stuffing falling away to leave the succulent chicken intact.

Marinating was practised, the meat being stabbed and then soaked in flavoured liquors, a typical example being the following.[23]

CORMARYE

1lb/450g pork fillet
¼pt/150ml red wine
2tsp salt
¼tsp ground black pepper

1tsp ground coriander
1tsp ground caraway
1 clove garlic, crushed

Stab the fillet with a sharp knife, and cover with the remaining ingredients.

Leave to marinate for up to 12 hours, turning and rubbing the meat from time to time.

Spit-roast, or oven-bake on a grid in a roasting tin at 180°C/ 350°F/gas mark 4 for 30 minutes.

De-glaze the dripping-pan/roasting tin with a little light stock, and serve this around the roast.

For basic roasts, the first task was to truss the joint so that it would never fall to pieces as it cooked and, most importantly, that it would rotate with the spit. Since forked holdfasts were unknown, it was all too easy for the joint to hang stationary before the fire as the spit turned uselessly within it. One basic aid was the prick, a sharp-pointed splint of wood which we would now call a skewer, ideal for securing the stuffing within a roast pig, or beef olives.[24] Another was twine, seen in Luttrell Psalter binding the forelegs of a roast pig to the spit. It was also possible to use necks and beaks of plucked and drawn poultry and game as bindings and skewers, for example:[25]

Bittern
The legs folded up, the spine removed from the neck so that the skin could be wound around the spit, and the bill stuck into the breast.

Chicken
The head removed, but the feet left on.

Curlew
As bittern, but the lower bill removed.

Heron
As bittern, but with the wings removed. Alternatively, long legs could have their bones removed below the knee, so that their skin could bind the birds to the spit. This method is seen in the Bodleian Library's *Romance of Alexander*, c.1340.

Partridge

As chicken.

Pheasant

Remove the head, neck and part of the lower legs, leaving sufficient to tuck into the vent.

Plover

Remove the legs and wings.

Quail

As chicken.

Snipe

Remove the wings, fold up the legs, wind the neck around the spit, and use the bill to skewer it to the shoulder.

Woodcock

As snipe, but skewer the bill through both thighs.

Peacock

This required a distinctive style of trussing, explained below.[26]

PEACOCK ROASTED

1 peacock, under 18 months
3 egg yolks
ground cumin

Lay the peacock on its back, cut the skin across from the joint of one thigh to the joint of the other, and around the joints of each thigh, and peel the feathered skin from the thighs.

From that last cut, cut down to the vent, peel back the skin on both sides, and cut across the base of the 'parson's nose', so that the tail and surrounding skin are separated from the carcass.

Turn the bird breast-down, ease the skin, tail and the rest up the back, cutting the inner ends of the pinions so that the wings remain part of the skin.

Pull the skin up the breast and neck, as if removing a stocking, until the neck is exposed up to the top vertebra. Cut through this, to separate the entire skin from the carcass. Dust the flesh side of the skin with cumin.

Draw the peacock through the vent, rinse, and dry with cloths.

Spit the peacock from the vent through the top of the breast (see Fig. 45), push one skewer through the breast, just below the wings and spit, and another through the thighs below the spit. Using twine, truss the neck vertically against a wooden or metal skewer, and the legs up as if the bird was sitting on a perch.

Roast or oven-bake at 180°C/350°F/gas mark 4, allowing 20 minutes per lb (450g), plus 20 minutes (or until tender). It may be basted with wine, spices and salt, or endored with beaten egg yolk. When cooked, remove from the heat and allow to rest for 10 minutes.

Originally, the skin was replaced over the roast carcass, 'on a targe, and sprade the tayle abrode, and serve hym fort as he war a quyk pekok', with the comb gilded. Today, it should be mounted on a chicken-wire substitute for presentation at the table, then returned to the kitchen, where the real peacock is now ready for carving and serving with sauce ginger.

Today, peacock has an undeservedly bad reputation. 'Those who have tried it...do not really recommend the experience,' advises one authority. This is because *aged* birds are tough. Medieval illustrations of peacocks being served all show them with fairly short tails, hence under eighteen months old, and thus very tender and succulent. The flesh tastes something between chicken and pheasant, the two great breasts and drumsticks being ideal for carving.

As well as roasting real birds, the cooks were skilled in producing replicas to excite their masters' tastes for all things novel and curious. At their simplest came *aloes* (the Old French for 'larks', and today's 'olives'): artificial larks made by enclosing a rich stuffing within a slice of raw meat.[27]

ALOES OF BEEF OR LAMB

4 thin slices of raw beef or lamb, about 4 inches/10cm diameter

for beef	for lamb
½tsp thyme	1tsp parsley
½tsp sage	1 hard-boiled egg yolk
2oz/50g suet	pinch ginger and saffron
1 medium onion, chopped	2oz/50g suet
pinch pepper and salt	1 medium onion, chopped
	large pinch salt

Lightly beat the steaks, then season.

Mix the remaining ingredients, spread over the steaks, roll them up, and secure them with either small skewers or a few stitches of thread.

Mount on small spits and roast, or prop across the rim of a roasting tin and oven-bake at 170°C/325°F/gas mark 3 for about 30 minutes, basting with a little fat from time to time.

When tender, remove the thread, and place on a hot dish. They may be sprinkled with vinegar, ground pepper, cinnamon and ginger, and a crumbled hard-boiled egg yolk.

More complex methods were used to turn one capon into two. This was accomplished by filling its removed skin with forcemeat, and roasting it alongside the skinless carcass on the same spit. Counterfeit kids were made in the same way, their front and back legs being slotted into cuts made at each side of the neck to replicate the traditional method of trussing. [28] Both pomme dorryse [golden apples], and hirchones [urchins or hedgehogs] were made of finely ground meat, usually simmered until cooked, then mounted on the spit to be endored. The following recipes used the same basic mixture, but others are of ground beef, or of pork and partridge ground together. [29]

POMME DORRYSE [GOLDEN APPLES]

2 eggs
1½lb/675g ground pork
large pinch ground black pepper
   and clove

1oz/25g currants
2tsp plain flour
2tbs fresh parsley
pinch saffron

Separate the eggs and mix the whites thoroughly into the pork, spices and currants.

Divide the mixture into balls of about 2 inches/5cm in diameter, drop into boiling water, and simmer for some 10–15 minutes until firm.

Meanwhile beat the flour into the yolks, adding 2tsp water to make a smooth batter, and divide this into two. Grind the parsley into one half to produce a green colour, and saffron into the other to produce a yellow colour.

Drain the meat balls, and either mount on a small-diameter spit and roast, or skewer and prop across the rim of a roasting tin. Brush with either the green or the yellow batter, and bake at 200°C/400°F/gas mark 6 for a few minutes until it has set.

HIRCHONES [HEDGEHOGS][30]

2 eggs
1½lb/675g ground pork
large pinch ground black pepper
   and clove
1oz/25g currants

2tsp plain flour
pinch saffron
20 blanched almonds
1tsp lard
1tsp sugar

Prepare the meat mixture as in the recipe above.

This time, form the mixture into a short, thick cylinder. Roll this in a square of scalded and flour-dusted muslin (a substitute for the pig's stomach), tie the ends tightly, plunge into boiling water, and simmer for some 30 minutes until cooked.

Make the saffron batter as before.

Meanwhile, scald the almonds, allow them to cool then cut into slivers to act as hedgehog spines, and gently stir-fry in the lard and sugar until just browned, then drain.

Drain the meat roll, remove the cloth, dry the roll, and, making holes with a small skewer, insert the 'spines'.

Mount on a small spit/skewer, brush with the saffron batter, and bake as in the previous recipe. The sugar-fried spines make an excellent accompaniment to the pork.

'Potte wys' ('pork devised as flower-pots') was a delightful way of using the same mixture to produce pint-size flower pots, their handles or 'ears', and their minature rose trees being made of fried pastry. 'Sac wis' had the mixture boiled in small canvas bags, which were then removed so that the 'sacks' could be roasted and endored.[31]

POTTE WYS

2 eggs	1oz/25g currants
1½lb/675g ground pork	2tsp plain flour
large pinch ground black pepper and clove	2tbs fresh parsley
	pinch saffron
for the flowers	
4oz/100g plain flour	8oz/225g lard
1 egg, beaten	

Prepare the mixture as instructed in the recipe for pomme dorryse, and pack into a greased 1pt/600ml charlotte mould or similar heatproof container. Stick a thick wooden skewer or rod down through the centre.

Place the mould on a grid in a large saucepan, fill to half its height with boiling water, cover the top of the mould with a piece of greaseproof paper overlapping its edges, and simmer for some 30 minutes until cooked.

Meanwhile, construct the 'flowers'. Mix sufficient of the beaten egg into the flour to form a stiff dough. Roll out half an inch/1cm thick, and model into miniature rose stems, each 4–5 inches/10–12cm long , with leaves, and a flat 'Tudor' rose on each. Leave enough dough to fashion a pair of handles for the 'flowerpot'. Fry these in the lard to a light brown and leave to cool.

Make the saffron batter as before.

Drain the mould, turn out the 'flowerpot' and brush it with the saffron batter. Roast or bake it as in the previous recipe.

Remove the 'pot' from the spit, insert the 'roses' into the spit-hole, fix the handles to each side and serve.

The identical mixture was also one of those used to make a much more exotic dish, the cockatrice. This mythical creature, believed to hatch from a cock's egg incubated by a venomous snake, had the reputed ability to kill by its mere glance. To make one, a rooster was plucked and skinned, leaving the head and legs attached. The skin of the back end of a sucking pig was then sewn on to it, the whole being stuffed with ground pork flavoured with spices, saffron, currants and salt. After parboiling to set it in shape and cook the stuffing, it was spitted and endored a bright yellow using egg yolks and more saffron. Finally decorated with gold and silver leaf, it was served, complete with its beaked, combed and wattled head, sharp claws, trotters and curly tail. In an alternative version, the front end of the pig was sewn onto the back end of the cock, to produce a similarly startling beast. [32]

The final counterfeit roast was intended to replace a probably offal-stuffed large gut called hastelette, or haslet. This took its name from the Old French *hastelet* and Latin *hasta*, a spear or spit. For fish-days, the spit was wound with a variety of dried fruits and nuts threaded onto linen yarn to form a compact cylindrical mass. Once this had half-roasted, and the natural sugars had begun to caramelize, it was basted with a thick batter, until it resembled a large, smooth sausage. [33]

TRAYNE ROAST

4oz/100g blanched almonds	*10oz/275g plain flour*
6oz/150g dates, halved	*2tbs sugar*
10oz/275g dried figs, quartered	*½tsp ground clove*
3oz/75g raisins	*½tsp ground ginger*
¾pt/450ml white wine or ale	*pinch of saffron*

Drill small holes through each almond, then, using a needle and up to six feet of strong linen thread, thread the fruit and almonds alternately to form a long 'necklace'.

Tie one end on to a spit, and wind it round in a tight spiral, without any spaces, to form a compact cylinder of fruit and almonds.

Roast until the fruit starts to caramelize.

Meanwhile, mix the wine or ale into the remaining ingredients to make a smooth batter.

Holding the batter in a dish beneath the roast, ladle some over it, and continue turning. Once this first layer is cooked, add subsequent layers in the same way until they have formed a cylinder, without any visible trace of the fruit and nuts.

Remove from the spit and serve hot, one or two 9-inch lengths being required for each dish.

In order to be spit-roasted, foods had to have sufficient bulk and strength to withstand piercing with the spit, and to take the strain of continuous rotation. It was for these reasons that most fish, with the exception of eels and lampreys, were hardly ever cooked in this way. Instead, along with steaks and a few egg-curds and pastries, they were cooked on roasting-irons or grid-irons. These were horizontal frames of parallel bars, supported a few inches above beds of glowing embers or charcoal on three or four short legs. Most were made of iron, such as the 'roste iron with 7 staves' mentioned in the Paston letters, but the finest were of highly conductive and non-rusting silver.[34] Sir John Fastolf had one of these, as did Lady Elizabeth Clifford, probably at Skipton Castle.

Hers weighed 5lb 4oz, and was valued at some £8 16s. 4d., a massive sum for a kitchen utensil.[35] There are a few excavated examples of medieval grid-irons, but their usual design of a rectangular barred frame with a long, loop-ended handle extending from the middle of one side, is shown in those carried as the personal symbol of St Laurence. According to popular tradition, he was martyred in Rome in AD 258 by being roasted to death on a massive gridiron.

This form of roasting was ideal for making toast and cooking fish.[36] Since it was so simple and effective, it had no need of complicated recipes. One appears to suggest a marinade of sweet red wine, mixed spices, cinnamon, cloves and cubebs, this being quickly boiled and poured over the fish after it had been cooked.[37] Similar ingredients were used as a hot sauce for grid-roast sole, pike, tench cut down the spine and spread flat, turbot fillets, and salmon steaks.[38]

SALMON ROAST IN SAUCE

½pt/300ml sweet red wine   ¼tsp ground black pepper
¼tsp ground cinnamon   ¼tsp ground ginger
1 medium onion, finely chopped   ½tsp salt
1tsp lemon juice (for verjuice)
4 thick round salmon steaks, cut through the body

Simmer the cinnamon in the wine for 2 minutes, strain, then treat the onions in a similar manner, in the same wine, for some 15 minutes. Remove from the heat, and stir in the lemon juice, pepper, ginger and salt.

Grease the bars of a grid-iron, and grill/cook the salmon steaks for 15–20 minutes, turning them over when half cooked. Put onto a dish, and pour the re-heated sauce over them.

Most vegetables were unsuitable for cooking on the gridiron, but mushrooms could be parboiled and larded with thin strips of fat bacon or pork before being grilled. When tender, they were brushed with beaten egg yolk and had a little ground clove and cinnamon sprinkled onto their undersides.[39]

CHAPTER SIXTEEN

Frying

One of the great advantages of frying is its relative speed. For working people, shallow-fried eggs and bacon, pancakes and similar foods produced virtually instant, satisfying meals, with little expenditure of time and fuel. In great households, meanwhile, more time could be spent in the preparation of batters, pastries and fritters which could be rapidly fried off and served crisp and hot at the appropriate stage of a meal. The frying media were either white grease, which we now know as lard, or olive oil. They were used in two distinct ways. For shallow frying – of pancakes, bacon or omelettes for example – the main function of the grease or oil was as much to prevent the foods from sticking to the pan as to cook them. Froyse, a spiced mixture of chopped, cooked beef and beaten eggs, provides a good example of a shallow-frying technique:

> then take a fayre Frying-panne, & sette it over the fyre, & caste ther-on
> fayre freysshe grece, & make it hot, & caste the stuf ther-on, and stere it
> wel in the panne tyl it comes to-gederys wel; cast on the panne a dysshe &
> presse it to-gederys, & turne it onys, & thanne serve it forth[1]

For this kind of frying, a shallow pan with an almost flat bottom is necessary. Those shown in contemporary Continental manuscript illuminations are virtually identical to early twentieth-century examples, with a round iron pan mounted on a long handle. Presumably these were used in England, but to date there is no archaeological evidence for them. Their earthenware equivalents are relatively common however, from the late twelfth century through to the sixteenth. Their bases were only slightly concave, to enable them to receive the heat without cracking, while their handles were either pulled and tapering, or thrown hollow to form a

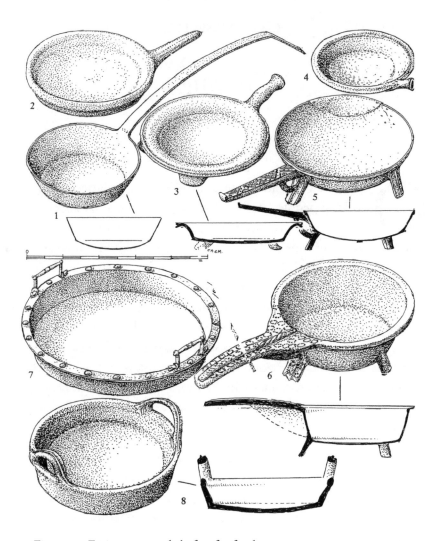

Figure 47. Frying-pans and chafers for food.

1. Wrought iron, from Pottergate, Norwich, 1507.

2–4. Earthenware, from Sandal Castle, Yorks., early 15c; Low Countries, imported into Norwich, 1507; and Surrey, late 14–early 15c.

5. Cast bronze, from Stanford in the Vale, Oxon., c. 1300?

6. Earthenware copy of one of the above, from Upper Heaton, West Yorks., late 13–early 14c.

7. Chafer for food.

8. Chafer for food, earthenware, Sandal Castle, c. 1483–5.

spout for pouring off the fat.[2] Since shallow-frying requires the pan to be kept horizontal and directly over the heat, they must have been used on brandreths.

For most deep-frying, in which the food was totally immersed, a deeper pan was essential, one holding perhaps a couple of inches of boiling fat. These were ideal for fritters, lozenges, cruste rolls and so forth. Very few have been excavated, but one wrought iron example from Pottergate in Norwich is 10 inches broad by 3½ inches deep.[3] Having a convex base and a long handle, it was ideal for having its front edge shoved into the fire, setting up convection currents in the fat which would cook the contents evenly. The other utensil recorded for deep frying was called a chafer. Recipes instruct to 'set wyte grece over the fyer in a chaufour'; dribble batter into 'a chaufer with oile and frye it wel'; and even 'have a chaufer under to kepe that [which] fallys down' when roasting.[4] Inventories describe them as having two ears, a bow handle, a lid, and one as weighing 7lb.[5] Sir John Fastolf had '1 grete Chafron of brasse, 2 Chafernes of a lase sorte' and '4 Chafernes of French gyse for sewys [broths]'. This body of evidence suggests that these chafers for food were broad, round bronze vessels, a few inches deep, sometimes having a lid, sometimes 'ears' or handles at each side, and sometimes a bow handle for suspension. Exactly such a vessel formed part of the Nant Col hoard found in Wales. Probably made in the fourteenth century, it measured just over 15 inches diameter by 2½ inches deep, with a handle at each side.[7] The same form is known in earthenware from the eleventh century in Devon, Wiltshire, Northamptonshire and Norfolk, perhaps indicating that most chafers for food were originally ceramic, and only later copied in bronze.[8] A later example, used at Richard III's Sandal Castle in 1483, was probably heated either on a brandreth over the fire, or on a cooking chafing dish filled with burning charcoal.[9]

The usual form of chafer appears to have had a deep, convex-based round pan with a handle projecting from the side, and three short legs from the perimeter of its base. In the late thirteenth or early fourteenth centuries these were being made at the Upper Heaton pottery in West Yorkshire. A virtually identical one, but cast in bronze, has been found at Stanford in the Vale in Berkshire.[10] The latter had clearly been used by having the side opposite the handle thrust into the front of the fire. This had caused it to crack, and be repaired with a large rivetted patch. From a practical point of view, this form of chafer was also ideal for deep frying.

Shallow-frying, in which the fat or oil acted more as a means of preventing food from sticking to the pan than as a cooking medium, was ideal for thin sliced meats such as bacon and ham, as well as fried eggs and pancakes. The following recipe provides an interesting variation on the fried egg.[11]

TOWRES

4 eggs, separated
pinch of saffron
large pinch of salt
1tbs lard

¼tsp mixed ground black pepper, mace & clove
1tbs ground pork (optional)
1tsp melted butter

Lightly beat and strain the egg whites, mix them with the saffron and salt.

Beat together the yolks, mixed spices, pork (if used) and butter (to replace bone marrow).

Melt the lard in a shallow frying-pan, pour in the egg whites, running them round the centre to form a large disc.

When the egg white has set, pour the yolks in the centre, and as they set, fold the sides of the white circle over it, to form a square 'pasty' enclosing the yolks.

Fry until cooked through, then dish and serve.

Shallow-frying was also good for making a variety of vegetable dishes such as parboiled and drained spinach, or mixtures of boiled beans, boiled and chopped onions and garlic stir-fried in olive oil, as well as for stirred egg dishes we would now recognize as omelettes.[12]

MESELADE

6 eggs
1oz/25g butter

1 slice of white bread
sugar for sprinkling

Beat the eggs, strain them, and pour them on to the butter melted in the pan.

As the egg sets on the bottom of the pan, remove this to the sides with a saucer, allowing the raw egg to take its place. Continue cooking gently in this way until all the egg is gathered in the centre and just set.

Put the slice of bread on the eggs, turn the whole over, so that the bread absorbs any remaining butter, and has heated through, then remove onto a dish, and serve sprinkled with sugar.

If this recipe was flavoured with the juice of the flowering wild plant tansy (*Tanacetum vulgare*), it became rather bitter, and so became traditionally associated with Easter, recalling the bitter herbs of the Passover.[13]

TANSY

Grind a few stems of tansy in a little water, strain the juice, and add sufficient to flavour 6 beaten and strained eggs.

Cook as in the previous recipe, but omitting the bread. Turn over the cooked eggs when they are set, and cook the other side for a few minutes. Dish, sprinkle with sugar and serve.

If the same basic recipe was enriched with finely ground cooked meat, it became a froise.[14]

FROISE

Finely chop or mince 3oz/75g cooked beef or veal, beat into 6 eggs, with ¼tsp salt and a large pinch of ground black pepper.

Fry in a little lard, as in the meselade recipe. Place a dish over the pan, turn both over, and slide the froise back into the pan with a little more lard, and cook for a few minutes more.

Dish, slice and serve.

In yet another version, the eggs were stirred into fried onions to give a fine savoury dish resembling buttered eggs rather than omelettes.[15]

HANONEY

8oz/225g onions, finely chopped   *4 eggs, beaten*
1–2tbs clarified butter or lard

Gently fry the onions in the butter or lard until a pale golden brown.

Reduce the heat, pour in the eggs, and stir gently, as if scrambling eggs, until the mixture has formed into rough lumps. Dish and serve.

When deep-frying in a few inches of oil or fat, the food was cooked by being completely enveloped in its hot cooking medium. It was therefore important to maintain a moderate, rather than a smoking-hot temperature, in order to allow the food to cook through. Food which looked a fine brown on the outside, but remained raw within, was far from palatable. Due to the rapidity with which they could be cooked, egg and flour batters formed the basis of numerous recipes for frying. Today we tend to think of this as pancake batter, but, although pancakes were being made in the fifteenth century, there are no contemporary recipes.[16] Presumably they were so well known that there was no need to write them down. The following selection show how various batters were either fried on their own, mixed with other ingredients, or used to coat or enclose various sliced foods.

LONG FRITTERS[17]

4oz/100g cottage cheese   *3oz/75g plain flour*
1 egg, beaten   *lard for frying*

Beat the egg and cheese together to form a smooth paste, beat in the flour, and use a spatula to form into a half-inch (1cm) thick rectangular slab on a freshly-scalded and rinsed board. This was 'no broader than the hand'. This might mean either a 4-inch or 9-inch 'hand', but is here assumed to be 4 inches/10cm.

Heat the fat until hot, but not boiling. Using the edge of a wet spatula (to replace the medieval ox-rib), divide off a slice approximately 1½ inches/4cm wide. Slide it into the fat, and cook 3–4 minutes until golden brown. Repeat until all has been used up.

Drain, dish, and sprinkle with sugar.

SAMARTARD[18]

Make the batter as above, adding ¼pt/150ml single cream and a further 2oz/50g plain flour.

Scoop up a portion of batter in a saucer, start pouring it into the lard at one edge of the pan, drawing the hand back to finish pouring at the opposite edge, and fry to a pale colour.

CRYSPES[19]

½pt/300ml milk
1tsp dried yeast
1tbs sugar
½tsp salt

2 egg whites, beaten
4oz/100g plain flour
lard for frying

Beat the yeast, sugar, salt and egg whites into the milk, pour into a well in the flour, and beat to form a smooth batter. Leave in a warm place for 30–60 minutes.

Test for consistency by dipping your finger in the batter, lifting it out and watching to see whether the batter runs off in a thin stream, as it should. If it forms droplets, beat in a little more flour, and check again.

Heat the lard to frying temperature.

Originally the batter was run in from the fingertips. Today it is much safer to use a piping bag with a very small nozzle, moving this continuously to form long strands of fritter.

As the batter cooks and rises to the surface, use a bone-dry skimmer to remove the fritters on to a dish. Sprinkle with sugar, and serve.

Similar fritters were made with a bread and almond batter. Their name, cyuele, may have been derived from the Old English *cyule* meaning keel-boat, perhaps from their appearance when floating in the hot fat.

CYUELES[20]

2oz/50g ground almonds	*pinch of salt*
2oz/50g fresh white breadcrumbs	*1 egg, beaten*
2tbs sugar	*oil or lard for frying*

Mix all the ingredients, grind to a smooth paste, pat into round cakes on a floured board, and fry.

Drain, dish, and sprinkle with sugar.

HERB FRITTERS[21]

Make as cyueles, using 3oz/75g breadcrumbs, 2tsp chopped fresh herbs, ¼tsp salt and 1 egg.

APPLE FRITTERS[22]

3 dessert apples	*pinch ground black pepper*
1 egg	*pinch of saffron*
4oz/125g flour	*1tbs sugar*
¼pt/150ml water or milk	*lard or oil for frying*

Sift the dry ingredients into a bowl, make a well in the centre, break in the egg, begin to beat in the flour, adding the water or milk little by little to form a smooth batter. Set aside for 30 minutes or more.

Peel the apples, cut in ¼-inch/5mm slices, dip in the batter, and deep-fry in the lard or oil at 180°C/350°F for 2–3 minutes, until golden brown.

Remove, drain, dish, and sprinkle with sugar.

Alternatives

Replace the pepper with ½tsp salt.

Beat fresh yeast into the batter, and leave in a warm place for up to an hour before using.

Replace the sliced apples with freshly parboiled parsnips, carrots (both 'pasternakes') or whole apples. Dip, unsliced, into the batter, and deep-fry.

BRAWN FRY[23]

Make the batter as above, replacing the pepper with ½tsp salt. Slice cooked brawn thinly, dip in the batter, fry, drain, dish, and sprinkle with sugar.

BROWN FRIES[24]

As brawn fries, but using thin-sliced wholemeal bread instead of the brawn.

In one of the most popular of medieval fried foods, the batter was replaced by beaten egg yolks. Pain perdu, 'lost bread' or, as it is better known today, 'eggy bread', was simply a slice of bread with the crusts cut off, dipped in strained, lightly salted egg yolks, fried in clarified butter or lard, and sprinkled with sugar.[25] Plain fried bread was also used as the basic ingredient for making 'pain foundow', dissolved or mixed bread. For this, the fried bread was soaked in red wine, ground with raisins, and mixed with clarified honey, sugar, ground cloves, mace and ginger to form a stiff paste, which was garnished with either aniseed or coriander comfits.[26]

Deep-frying was ideal for frying pastries too. In their simplest form, they were nothing more than discs of very thin pastry, which rapidly puffed up and crisped in the hot fat. Today we would call them poppadoms, being more familiar with their Indian chickpea equivalent.

CRISPELS[27]

8oz/225g plain flour	¼pt/150ml cold water
2tsp sugar	lard or oil for frying
pinch of saffron	clarified honey

Mix the dry ingredients, make a well in the centre, pour in half the water, and work it in with a spoon, adding the remaining water little by little to form a stiff dough.

Roll pieces of dough out very thinly, allow to rest for a few minutes, then cut into 4-inch/10cm rounds. Fry in the hot lard or oil, turning them over to cook on both sides.

Drain, drizzle with clarified honey, and serve immediately.

If cut in diamond shapes, the same recipe produced lozenges. If three or four were to be served on a dish, these were 'as broad as a hand or less', but those about 2 inches long prove more convenient if they are to be served in thick sauces, such as savoury hare broths, or sweet spicy ones.[28] The latter include brydons, prenade or breney, the 'bren' element perhaps coming from the Middle English brenne, to burn, reflecting their hot taste and temperature.[29]

BRYDONS, PRENADE OR BRENEY

½pt/300ml sweet red wine	pinch of saffron
5 dried figs, chopped	3 dates, finely chopped
2tbs clear honey	1tbs pine kernels
1tsp mixed ground black	1tbs currants
pepper, clove, mace and cubeb	2tbs vinegar

Simmer the figs in the wine until tender, grind them, and strain the liquids into a saucepan. Add the remaining ingredients (with a little more wine if necessary to make the sauce runny).

Simmer briefly, and pour over a batch of lozenges made from the previous recipe, dish, and serve hot.

The other method of flavouring fried pastries was to stuff them. Most were either diamond-shaped ('lozenges') or pie-shaped ('chewets'), but others were made from either rounds of pastry folded over to resemble miniature Cornish pasties ('rissoles'), or long ovals folded to look like the pods of field beans. Recipes for their fillings include some mainly of meat, some of fish with fruit, and others of fruit alone. The following selection includes one of each type.

LOZENGES DE CHARE[30]

8oz/225g ground pork	3 dates, finely chopped
2 raw egg yolks	2tsp sugar
2tbs currants	pinches of ground ginger,
pepper & saffron	

Make a batch of pastry as for crispels, above.

Thoroughly mix the other ingredients, reserving one yolk.

Divide the pastry into two and roll out each portion to measure 12 inches (30cm) square. Spread the pork mixture over one square and lay the other one over it.

Cut the square into lozenges, using either a wet knife (with a vertical, rather than a slicing action) or, as one recipe suggests, the edge of a saucer. [31]

Brush the remaining yolk, beaten with a little salt and sugar, around the edges of each lozenge to seal it, and fry gently for about 5 minutes until the filling has cooked.

REYNOLLE[32]

Follow the above recipe using 4oz/100g each of ground cooked pork and finely grated cheese, with ¼tsp mixed ground pepper, cinnamon, ginger, cloves and mace.

NESE BEKYS[33]

Follow the lozenge recipe, but using 8oz/125g boiled and boned salmon and eel, 3 ground dried figs, with ¼tsp mixed ground ginger and cinnamon.

RISSCHEWES DE FRUTE[34]

Repeat the lozenge recipe once more, but this time using 10oz/275g dried figs, 2 tbs olive oil, 3tbs pine kernels, 3tbs currants, 12 finely chopped dates, 1 tsp mixed ground pepper, clove, mace and cinnamon, a pinch of saffron, ½tsp salt, and a few drops red food colouring. Finely chop the figs, grind to a smooth paste in the oil, and mix with the remaining ingredients. Roll the pastry into (say) 3-inch/8cm rounds, put a little of the filling into the centre, fold the pastry over and seal the edges with the egg yolk to form 'rissoles' before frying.

This concludes the main group of medieval fried dishes, but there were other individual recipes of interest, ranging from deep-fried chicken and chunks of sausage with sage-flavoured eggs, to pork-stuffed sage leaves, demonstrating the great versatility of this simple technique.[35]

CHAPTER SEVENTEEN

The Saucery

Medieval sauces may be readily divided into two distinct types. The first to be considered here were cold, strongly flavoured and very long-lasting, rather like modern ketchups; the second were usually hot, well-flavoured, and freshly-made to accompany a particular dish. The first type might be made by a domestic cook, but was often the work of either a professional, town-based sauce-maker, such as John Romby of York, or of the saucery or 'salsery' division of a major household.[1] Edward III's saucery was staffed by a single sergeant, but by 1455 Henry VI's had a sergeant, a clerk, a yeoman and a groom making sauces for the King, and four others making those served in the hall.[2] The spices they needed were delivered every day from the spicery, whose clerk recorded their quantity, and reported them to the counting house. Much of their vinegar was produced from unserviceable wines remaining in the cellar, while their bread presumably came from the bakehouse or pantry.[3] Since they were probably busiest at meal times, the saucery staff tended to eat in their own office, rather than in the hall.[4]

Due to its widespread use with beef, pork, mutton, some gamebirds and most salt fish, mustard was by far the most important of all the store-sauces. The Earl of Northumberland's household of 166 people used 140 gallons a year, averaging just over 2 teaspoonfuls per person per day.[5] This was all bought from professional suppliers, men such as Caxton's 'Nicholas the mustard maker'.[6] To make mustards, the seed was washed, oven-dried, ground, and sifted through a sieve to produce the pungent yellow powder we are still familiar with today.[7]

LUMBARD MUSTARD

3tbs mustard powder	*1tsp (sweet white?) wine*
1tbs clear honey	*2tsp (white?) wine vinegar*

Mix these thoroughly, and store in a covered jar.

The mustard was originally packed into mustard pots or jars for use or sale.[8] Their rims must have had projecting edges similar to those of traditional jam jars so that parchment or paper covers could be tied over them, to prevent spillage or drying out. In 1380 John Wyclif apologized that some of his 'lettris mai do good to cover mustard pottis'. [9]

Most of the other store-sauces used a basic mixture of breadcrumbs for consistency, vinegar for sharpness and preservation, and various other ingredients for flavour. They include:[10]

SAUCE GINGER

8oz/225g fresh white bread, crusts removed
½pt/300ml white wine vinegar

4tsp ground ginger	*1tsp salt*

Soak the bread in the vinegar until soft, then rub through a sieve three times.

Stir in the ginger and salt, bottle and seal.

SAUCE PARSLEY[11]

As sauce ginger, but replace the ginger and salt with 2oz/50g fresh parsley leaves (not stalks) ground to a smooth paste.

SAUCE VERT [GREENSAUCE][12]

As above, but replace the parsley with approximately equal quantities of parsley, mint, sorrel and chives.

SAUCE CAMELYNE [13]

8oz/225g white bread, sliced and toasted golden brown
¼pt/150ml (white?) wine vinegar   *¼tsp ground cinnamon*
¼pt/150ml (white?) wine   *¼tsp ground ginger*
4tsp sugar   *¾tsp ground cloves*
pinch of saffron

Soak the bread in the vinegar and wine until soft, then rub through a sieve three times.

    Stir in the spices, bottle and seal.

SAUCE ROUS[14]

As sauce camelyne, but omit the sugar and ginger, and add ¼tsp each of ground nutmeg and black pepper.

SAUCE GALENTYNE[15]

8oz/225g wholemeal bread   *1tsp salt*
½pt/300ml wine vinegar   *1tsp ground black pepper*

Prepare as for sauce ginger above.

SAUCE ALIPER[16]

8oz/225g wholemeal bread, sliced and toasted
½ bulb garlic, finely chopped and ground
½pt/300ml wine vinegar   *1tsp ground black pepper*
1tsp salt

Prepare as for sauce ginger above.

    In addition to the sauces, there was a chutney-like pickle of vegetables preserved in a sweet-and-sour spiced vinegar, called compost: [17]

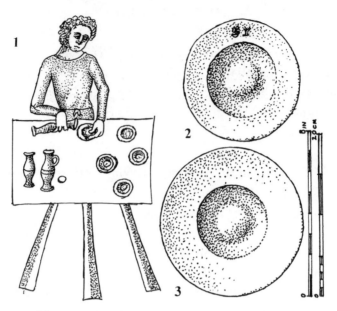

Figure 48. The saucery.

1. The saucers are filled with pre-prepared sauces stored in jugs, *c.*1320–45.

2 and 3. Pewter saucers, with narrow and broad rims, *c.*1500.

COMPOST

4oz/100g radishes, topped and tailed
8oz/225g parsnips, scraped and cut in large pieces
8oz/225g turnips, scraped and cut in large pieces
8oz/225g cabbage, coarsely chopped
3 medium cooking pears, stalks removed

1tbs salt	*¼tsp ground cinnamon*
½pt (white?) wine	*¼tsp aniseed*
½pt/300ml (white?) wine vinegar	*¼tsp fennel seed*
3oz/75g clear honey	*large pinch saffron*
2oz/50g raisins	*½tsp ground mustard*

Place the vegetables in a saucepan, cover with water, bring to the boil and simmer for 10 minutes.

Add the pears, return to the boil, and simmer for 10 minutes, until the pears are parboiled.

Drain the vegetables and pears, lay them on a few layers of clean cloth to drain, then sprinkle them with the salt and leave them overnight in a cool place.

Mix the remaining ingredients, and leave to mature overnight.

Use the cloth to wipe the salt and brine from the vegetables and pears, place in a stoneware or glass jar, cover with the spiced wine vinegar, etc., seal and leave for at least a week before using.

These eight store-sauces and the compost, each with its own strong and distinctive flavour, added considerable interest to any medieval meal, those based on herbs permitting the fresh tastes of spring and summer to be enjoyed throughout the entire year. I now keep them all in glass jars for use at everyday meals, but tall jugs served this purpose in the medieval saucery. If made of the impervious Siegburg or Langerwehe stonewares imported from Germany, they would have kept their contents in perfect condition for long periods, the porous or lead-glazed English earthenware presumably allowing their sauces to dry out, or even absorb the lead from their glazes. The mid-fourteenth-century Luttrell Psalter shows a servant filling saucers, presumably with sauce ginger since it was to accompany the roast pig being dished on the adjacent table.[18]

Sorrel sauce, made by grinding sorrel leaves to a smooth paste with a little salt, may have been made in the saucery, but most of the hot, fresh sauces served with specific dishes would have been made by the cooks in the kitchen.[19] These were particularly useful for adding flavour to plain boiled and fried fish;

STOCKFISH SAUCE (1)[20]

½pt/300ml strained fish stock   1tbs finely chopped parsley
3tbs lemon juice (for verjuice)   ¼tsp ground ginger

Bring to the boil and pour over the cooked fish.

STOCKFISH SAUCE (2)[21]

½pt/300ml strained stockfish stock
2oz/50g walnut kernels, chopped
1 small clove garlic, chopped

4oz/100g white breadcrumbs
¼tsp salt
large pinch ground black
    pepper

Grind the dry ingredients to a smooth paste, stir in the hot stock, and pour over the fish.

EGURDOUCE FOR FRIED FISH[22]

6oz/150g onions, finely chopped
1tbs lard or olive oil
¼pt/150ml (white?) wine
¼pt/150ml (white?) wine vinegar

1tbs sugar
¼tsp ground clove
¼tsp ground mace

Fry the onions golden brown in the lard or oil.

    Add the remaining ingredients, cover and simmer for 10 minutes, before pouring over the freshly fried fish.

SOBYE SAUCE FOR FRIED FISH[23]

3oz/75g grated white bread
1oz/25g raisins, chopped

½pt/300ml (sweet white?)
    wine
¼tsp mixed spices

Grind the bread and raisins to form a smooth paste, mix in the wine and spices, and pour over the fried fish just before serving.

Both boiled and fried fish might have a hot cive sauce poured over them, its main ingredient being minced onions, *cive* being the Old English for onion, along with wine, vinegar, bread, spices and colourings such as saffron yellow.[24]

CIVEY FOR BOILED FISH

1 unpeeled onion (about 6oz/150g)	⅛pt/75ml (white?) wine
2oz/50g white breadcrumbs	vinegar
¼pt/150ml stock the fish was	½tsp mixed spice
cooked in	½tsp salt
⅛pt/75ml (white?) wine	large pinch saffron

Put the onion in a pan of cold water, bring to the boil and simmer for some 20–25 minutes, until tender.

Peel the onion, chop, and grind to a smooth paste with the stock. Mix in the remaining ingredients, boil together, and pour over the fish in a dish just before serving.

For roast meats, the simplest sauces were uncooked, their ingredients being merely finely chopped or ground together, and sprinkled over the minced or finely chopped meat. Since these are cold sauces, and the meat is minced, they probably represent a practical way of making left-overs interesting and palatable, without having to get the kitchen fires back into operation. They certainly eat well when used in this way.[25]

SAUCE FOR MINCED SHOULDER OF MUTTON

2oz/50g onion, chopped	¼tsp ground ginger
2tsp parsley, chopped	¼tsp salt
1tbs (white?) wine vinegar	

Chop all together finely, and sprinkle over finely chopped cooked shoulder of mutton.

SAUCE FOR ROAST PIGEON

As above, but replace the ginger with a small clove of garlic, ground to a smooth paste.

For hot meats, there were specific sauces for capon,[26] duck,[27] goose[28] and venison, but the chief of these were:

PEURATE [PEPPER] SAUCE FOR VEAL AND VENISON[29]

3oz/75g white bread, sliced	¼pt/150ml meat or game
2oz/50g lard	stock
1tbs wine vinegar	1tsp ground black pepper
	¼tsp salt

Fry the bread in the lard, and grind to a smooth paste with the remaining ingredients.

SAUCE GAUNCELI OR SERMSTELE FOR GOOSE[30]

2 large cloves garlic	½tsp salt
1oz/25g plain white flour	large pinch saffron
½pt/300ml milk	

Chop and grind the garlic to a smooth paste, mix with the milk, and beat into the flour, salt and saffron.

Simmer for a few minutes, stirring continuously until thickened and cooked, adding a little more milk if necessary to produce a good pouring consistency.

For geese and swans there were two sauces made in particularly distinctive ways. The simplest of these was a rich, thickened giblet gravy, an ideal accompaniment to the roast or simmered meats. Its name, chawdron, meant entrails. In the household of George, Duke of Clarence in 1469, the staff of the saucery were allowed to keep the waste parts of the swans, so long as sufficient chawdron was left to make this sauce.[31] There are a number of recipes for its preparation, but all take the giblets and often the cleaned intestine, boil them and chop them, and then thicken them with the bread made into a smooth paste with the bird's blood and broth, the whole being seasoned with ginger and spices, and wine or vinegar.[32] The other sauce, sauce madame, was an interesting combination of stuffing and sauce, designed to flavour the flesh as it roasted, as well as providing an excellent accompaniment.[33]

SAUCE MADAME FOR ROAST GOOSE

1 x 9–11lb/4–5kg goose, oven-ready
½ bulb garlic, the cloves peeled and coarsely chopped
1lb/450g quinces and/or pears, peeled and cored
1tbs mixed chopped sage, parsley, hyssop and savory
1 batch of galentine, made to the recipe on p. 335
8oz/225g grapes   *½tsp ground ginger*
½pt/300ml (sweet white?) wine   *large pinch saffron*

Stuff the goose with the garlic, quinces or pears, grapes and herbs. Sew up both ends, truss, and either mount on a spit or place on a rack in a roasting tin and bake in an oven pre-heated to 200°C/ 400°F/ gas mark 6 for 15 minutes per lb (450g) plus 15 minutes at the end, basting frequently.

When the goose is tender, remove from the heat, joint it into large pieces, and remove the stuffing. Arrange the meat on a dish, and leave in a warm place.

Chop the stuffing, add to the galentine and spices in a saucepan, and stir while bringing up to the boil, adding sufficient wine to give a pouring consistency. Pour over the goose just before serving.

Figure 49. St Catherine sugar mould.

Used for casting figures in grained sugar, from the Old Bailey, London,
15c.? This mould shows St Catherine crowned to indicate royal status,
holding her martyr's sword in her right hand, and the wheel upon which
she was executed in her left.

CHAPTER EIGHTEEN

The Confectionery and Wafery

Sugar, the staple ingredient processed in the confectionery, was first experienced by English people during their first major incursion into the Mediterranean as part of the First Crusade of 1096–9. Within a few years, small quantities were being imported as an expensive luxury, the amounts then being gradually increased to several tons by the late thirteenth century. Household accounts provide evidence for its places of origin, the monks of Durham buying sugar 'Marrokes' and 'Babilon', the Earl of Derby sugar 'Candy' (Candia being the contemporary name for Crete), whilst recipe-books list sugar 'Cypre' (Cyprus) and sugar 'of Alysaunder' (Alexandria). All these were brought into our southern ports by the galleys of Venice and Genoa. Much of the sugar arrived in the largely refined form of conical sugar loaves, those purchased by Bishop Swinfield of Hereford weighing about 8lb at 6d. to 8d. the pound in 1289, for example. Other sugars arrived 'black', which we would now call muscovado, or else 'rock' or 'rupe', large-crystal, highly refined sugar candy. Sugars which had been boiled and mixed with finely powdered flower petals at source were held to be particularly good for colds and other ailments, promoting warm and moist humours. In 1287, Edward I's Great Wardrobe accounts record the purchase of 667lb of sugar, 300lb of violet sugar, and a massive 1,900lb of rose sugar. The same had been prescribed to his sickly son Henry, who had died in 1274 when only six years old. Such medicinal use only accounted for a small proportion of the imported sugar however, the bulk being diverted to the confectionery for the royal table.

Separate confectioneries and waferies existed only in the greatest households, their function being to produce the spiced and sweetened compounds or confections served as digestives at the close of dinners, suppers, and also at more intimate and luxurious entertainments. Considered hot and moist in nature, such sugary foods helped to break down the food received into the body's cauldron, the stomach, a practice we still follow with our after-dinner mints and liqueurs. In the fifteenth century the clearing of the table was called the void, this word then being transferred to the sweetmeat course served at this time. Its contents are listed in a number of contemporary menus:[1]

1.   Blandrelles [white apples] and pippins with caraway comfits, wafers and hippocras.
2.   Apples and pears roasted with sugar candy, figs, raisins, dates topped with minced ginger, wafers and hippocras.
3.   Apples and pears with spices, spiced cakes and wafers, braggot and mead [for a franklin].
4.   Apples and pears with sugar candy, minced preserved ginger, wafers and hippocras.
5.   Blandrelles or pippins with caraway comfits, wafers and hippocras.

To provide these in the royal household, Henry VI and Edward IV had the services of a sergeant as head of the confectionery department.[2] This officer's duties included a considerable administrative element: recording the receipt of the required sugar, spices and dried fruits obtained from the spicery, the apples, pears, cherries, wardens, quinces and nuts from the royal garden, and the blandrelles and pippins bought in as required. He also took responsibility for the pans, basins, ladles and other tools required by his staff, as well as the spice plates of precious metals and pewter, and the fine towels used to serve the confections to the King, his chamber and hall. Along with his yeoman, he was also expected to be a skilled practising confectioner, making comfits, sugar plate, chardequince (quince marmalade) and all manner of preserved fruits as they came into season. Their general assistant, the groom, helped to make the confections too, as well as keeping everything clean, bringing in the department's food, fuel, lighting and raw materials, and collecting, washing and drying the spice plates after they had been used each day. This must have been a busy office, for on great days of estate the King's spice plate contained a pound and a half (675g) of sweetmeats, and that of the dukes, earls and barons, one pound (450g).

The royal wafery was headed by a yeoman.[3] He collected his flour from the bakehouse, recording the quantity with a tally, and his sugar, eggs, towels and boxes for storing and serving his product from the spicery. To assist him he had a groom who also made wafers, and a page when it was necessary to train someone new to practise this skilled craft. Wafers were only served to the King, dukes, earls, the chief officers of the household and important visitors each day, more widespread distribution being restricted to the principal feast days.

Such departments were only to be found in the greatest establishments. Most nobles expected their cooks to perform these functions themselves, buying in ready-made confectionery to supplement that which they could make. This would certainly include imported 'green' ginger in syrup, and perhaps the quince and sugar *marmalade* made in Portugal, as well as supplies of the necessary sugar, spices, dried fruits and colourings. There are also references to the purchase of ready-made comfits, used both as sweetmeats and for garnishing other dishes.[4] Such purchases made good practical sense. Sugarcraft required both specialized knowledge, and specially selected working areas. In an ordinary kitchen or food storage area, the humidity rapidly causes comfits, sugar plate and other confections to degenerate into a syrupy mass, fit for nothing but sweetening other foods. At Hampton Court, the confectionery was arranged on the first floor over the pastry ovens to avoid this problem, a practice which had been found essential during previous centuries.

The principal fruits to be prepared in the confectionery were apples, quinces, wardens (an old variety of baking pear), and pears. These could be either plain roasted, or simmered and cut into large pieces, or thinly sliced before being briefly boiled in sweet spiced wine to become pears in syrup, or pears in confite.[5]

PEARS IN SYRUP

1lb/450g cooking pears
½pt/300ml sweet red wine
½tsp ground cinnamon

2tbs sugar
¼tsp ground ginger
pinch of saffron

Cover the unpeeled pears in water, bring to the boil, and simmer for some 30 minutes until tender.

Simmer the spices and sugar in the wine for 2–3 minutes.

Peel the pears, cut into two or three pieces, add to the wine, boil briefly, and pour into a dish. Serve hot or cold.

Alternatively they could be cooked, pulped, and thickened by boiling, using egg yolks or breadcrumbs to produce chardewarden or, with other fruits, chardequince, chardedate, or chardecrab.

CHARDEWARDEN[6]

½pt/300ml muscat wine (for bastard)
1lb/450g cooking pears
5oz/125g fresh white breadcrumbs

½tsp mixed ground clove, cinnamon, cubeb and black pepper

Simmer the pears in the wine in a covered pan for some 30 minutes until tender, then peel, mash and rub through a sieve with the wine.

Add the spices and breadcrumbs to the pear pulp, mix thoroughly, and heat to boiling while stirring continuously. When thick, pour into a dish and serve hot or cold. The original recipe kneads the breadcrumbs into the pear pulp, but the above method gives virtually the same, but far less messy, results.

CHARDEQUINCE[7]

1lb/450g quinces, quartered and the pips removed
12oz/350g clear honey
1tbs ground ginger

Cover the quinces with water, simmer until tender, drain, and rub through a sieve.

Boil the pulp and honey together until a small sample sets like thick jam, then remove from the heat, stir in the ginger and pack into a shallow box from which it may be cut as required.

CHARDEDATE[8]

8oz/225g dates, stones removed   1tbs ground ginger
4oz/100g clear honey

Grind the dates to a smooth paste (it is easier to chop them finely and then knead them smooth).

    Boil the honey to 120°C/250°F on a sugar thermometer, pour into the dates in a small bowl, and rapidly work in with the ginger. Pack into a shallow box from which it may be cut as required.

The last two recipes were written at Spalding Priory in Lincolnshire early in the fifteenth century. They are unusual in giving precise quantities for the ingredients. For preserving around 70lb of pears it states that a massive 2lb (900g) of pungent spices were necessary. Using modern spices, carefully harvested and packed to preserve their full flavour, this authentic quantity would make pears virtually inedible, the levels of spicing in these modernized versions has therefore been reduced considerably.

    It is probable that many of the thick fruit pottages such as apple moise (see p. 269), normally made in the kitchen, would also have been made in the confectioneries of the largest households. One of the richest of these was the following.[9]

ERBOWLE

1lb/450g bullaces (or damsons)   ¼tsp ground ginger
½pt/300ml sweet red wine   3tbs rice flour
3tbs honey   small pinch salt

Simmer the fruit in the wine for 10–15 minutes until tender, then rub both fruit and wine through a sieve.

    Stir the honey, ginger and rice flour into the pulp and simmer, stirring continuously, to produce a smooth, thick maroon mixture.

    Pour into a dish, allow to cool, and garnish with a sprinkle of salt and white comfits.

The gingerbreads made in the confectionery were quite different from anything we now recognize by that name. Instead of being baked ginger-cakes, they were thick, sticky pastes, honey-sweetened and with the ability to release their flavour a few moments after they had been placed in the mouth. The simplest were made as a straightforward blend of honey, ginger and bread.[10]

GINGERBREAD (WITH BREAD)

8oz/225g clear honey
6oz/150g white bread crumbs
2–3tsp ground ginger

a few drops red food colour
(for sanders)
sugar and cloves to garnish

Boil the honey, stir in the food colour, ginger and breadcrumbs, and work in the pan over a low heat with a spatula for a few minutes, then leave until cool enough to handle.

Knead the gingerbread to form a smooth dough and either pack into a shallow box, or roll out to around ⅜ inch/10mm thick in a square slab. From this, small squares may be cut for serving at the 'void'.

The other type was made by boiling honey to a thick caramel-toffee-like consistency, mixing in ground ginger, and again moulding it in a shallow box, from which pieces could be cut.[11]

A note here on honey: unlike sugar, honey is not a standard product. Its boiling properties vary greatly. Some honeys will boil up to 150°C/300°F in a few minutes; some burn before reaching this temperature; while others produce a deep and almost unmanageable froth. For these reasons, the honey may be initially clarified using the same recipe as for sugar on the next page.

GINGERBREAD (OF BOILED HONEY)

1lb/450g honey
1tbs ground ginger

¼tsp ground pepper

Boil the honey to 130°C/265°F, pour out on to a lightly oiled marble slab, and sprinkle with the spices.

Use a lightly oiled metal spatula to work the spices into the honey then, when just cool enough to handle, form into a roll. Grasp this at each end, stretch it, double it, and stretch it again, repeating the process ten times.

Pack into a shallow box, sprinkle with more ground ginger, and cut out as required.

In the original recipe, the boiled honey is worked in a soaked wooden bowl, and pulled over a wooden or hart's-horn peg fixed onto a vertical wooden beam, but these methods make an already difficult process even more awkward.

Honey remained a good sweetener for preserving and gingerbreads, but for all the finer processes of confectionery, sugar was essential. It had been imported in substantial quantities from Alexandria, Cyprus and Morocco from the thirteenth century, some perfumed, and some in tall sugar cones. Despite its high cost, perhaps five times that of honey, it frequently had to undergo a final stage of clarification in the confectionery before it was fit for use.[12]

TO CLARIFY SUGAR

10oz/275g sugar	*1 egg white*
⅔pt/400ml water	

Lightly beat the egg white into the water in a pan until it just begins to raise a froth, then add the sugar.

Heat the water, stirring gently, until the first sounds of simmering are heard, then stop stirring, and reduce the heat so that the syrup just bubbles. Then leave until the froth has risen to the surface, breaking in the middle to reveal the clarified syrup.

Strain the syrup into a clean pan, and discard the froth. This produces a clear syrup, but if the original sugar was brownish, it will still retain a golden colour. In this case, the syrup should be allowed to go cold, a fresh egg white beaten in, and the process repeated until all trace of brown-ness has disappeared.

The syrup produced by clarification could be used in various ways, including the production of comfits: strongly-flavoured seeds repeatedly coated in layers of dried syrup until they resembled small white peas. This was one of the longest and most tedious tasks in the whole kitchen repertoire, for it could not be rushed. Any attempt to build up the layers by using stronger syrups rapidly converted the desired smooth surface into one extremely rough and crystalline.[13]

COMFITS

2tsp aniseed, caraway seed or fennel seed
  (or you can use root ginger, soaked overnight in water and cut
  into ⅛ inch/3mm cubes)
1lb/450g white cane sugar   *½pt/275ml water*

Place the sugar and water in a saucepan and heat gently, stirring with a wooden spatula until completely dissolved.

Stop stirring, bring to the boil, and cook until it reaches 110°C/225°F on a sugar thermometer. Remove from the heat, and dip the base of the pan briefly into cold water to stop further cooking.

Place the seeds or the chopped ginger in a shallow pan and stir them with the flat of the hand over a gentle heat until perfectly dry. Add 1tsp of the syrup, and continue stirring with the hand so that they stick neither to each other nor to the pan. Continue stirring until each seed is hot, dry and evenly coated.

Repeat the above process numerous times, adding a little more water to the syrup if the sugar-coating starts to become rough.

Once the seeds have been sufficiently coated to make a sweet about an eighth- or a quarter-inch (3–6mm) diameter – which takes hour upon hour – remove the pan from the heat, but continue to stir with the hand in the pan until perfectly cold, otherwise they will discolour.

Pack into boxes and keep in a thoroughly dry place until required for use.

The final coating of the comfit might be made with the syrup stained red, perhaps using turnsole, to produce red comfits. These might be used to decorate light-coloured dishes such as blancmange or almond creams, as well as for accompanying the fruit served at the end of meals.[14]

The pure boiled-sugar confections made from the end of the fourteenth century or earlier in England are, quite remarkably, still being mass-produced here today, available from every sweet-shop. Only their names have changed in the intervening seven hundred years. What we now call humbugs, were originally 'penides', from *panid*, refined sugar in Arabic, this being one of the numerous preparations introduced from the Middle East after the Crusades.[15] Their reputation for easing coughs continued well into the nineteenth century. 'Edinburgh Rock' meanwhile, was virtually identical to sugar plate, the hard, brittle consistency of the sugar being made far more palatable by being converted into a mass of fine, frothy crystals.

Note well that great care should be taken when boiling sugar. Its high-temperature scalds are especially dangerous.

TO MAKE PENIDES[16]

8oz/225g white cane sugar   *¼pt 150ml water*

Rub a marble slab with a little olive oil. Dampen a pair of clean gardening gloves to protect the hands when handling the hot boiled sugar.

Lay a cloth dusted with rice flour beside the marble slab.

Stir the sugar into solution in the water in a small saucepan, until it is dissolved. Stop stirring, and leave the syrup to boil until it reaches 143°C/290°F on a sugar thermometer.

Remove from the heat and pour as a broad strip down the length of the marble slab. Using a lightly oiled spatula, both sides of this ribbon are turned over into the middle. At this point, grasp both ends with the gloved hands and pull the sugar into a long strip. Double it by folding in half lengthwise, and stretch again. Repeat this stretching and folding, working rapidly, until it has turned a silky white. Originally this was done by pulling the sugar over an iron hook fixed on a wall at head height.

Once you have the desired consistency and colour, roll the sugar into a short cylindrical rod of about ¾ inch/20mm diameter on the floured cloth. With a pair of scissors, cut the cylinder into lengths measuring just under 1inch/25mm. Keep in an airtight container until required.

TO MAKE SUGAR PLATE[17]

Assemble the ingredients as for penides. This time, dust the marble slab with rice flour shaken through a cloth.

Boil the sugar as in the previous recipe. If red rather than white sugar plate is required, add a few drops of food colouring (instead of the original turnsole) before boiling.

Remove the syrup from the heat and stir rapidly with a wooden spatula until it lightens in tone, as small crystals form.

Return to the heat for a few moments, still stirring, then pour out onto the slab as thinly as possible. Leave it to cool.

Divide into pieces and pack into an airtight container until required.

Instead of being poured out as a flat, frothy crystalline slab, this opaque sugar plate could be cast into moulds to make three-dimensional fruits and figures. Since the moulds were either soaked in water or coated in almond oil to prevent the sugar from sticking irremoveably to their interiors, they might have been made of wood, plaster or pottery. Such moulds, fashioned in two or three parts, could have been taken from real apples and pears, leaving a funnel-shaped pouring hole at one end for the boiling sugar to be poured in. A clove inserted at the bottom represented the 'blossom', while a strip of cinnamon bark provided the 'stalk'. To complete the illusion, they were then painted in vegetable colours bound with raw egg-white. Saffron made a strong yellow, saffron and woad varying shades of green, and brazil-wood boiled with gum arabic a fine red.[18]

For making figures, an actual fifteenth-century mould still survives, excavated from the Old Bailey in the City of London (Fig. 49).[19] Made of unglazed red earthenware, it is the front half for a figure of St Catherine with her wheel, about 5½ inches (140mm) high. The figures it produced may have been painted in naturalistic colours, or gilded by applying real gold or silver foil over a thin coating of raw, lightly beaten egg white.

'Marchpane', today's marzipan, was also used to make figures. Fabyan's *Chronicle* of 1494 describes 'A march payne garnysshed with dyverse figures of aungellys.'[20] There appear to be no English recipes for its preparation, but a number of sixteenth-century versions suggest that it was a compound of blanched almonds, sifted white sugar and rosewater all ground to form a thick dough, very similar to that still widely available.

Due to their heavy use of honey and spices, the sweet wines such as hippocras, clary and piment would probably have been made in the confectionery, their recipes appearing alongside those of sugar plate and other confections in culinary manuscripts.[21] In most households, however, they were made by the butler in the buttery.[22]

HIPPOCRAS[23] (RICH, UNIFORM SPICE FLAVOUR)

2pt/1·2l sweet red or white dessert wine
½tsp each of ground cinnamon and ginger
¼tsp each of ground grains of paradise and long pepper
½tsp mixed ground cloves, galingale, caraway and spikenard
1tbs sugar or clear honey

CLARY[24] (SLIGHTLY DRY GINGER/PEPPER AFTERTASTE)

2pt/1·2l sweet red or white dessert wine
3ins/7.5cm cinnamon bark
1½tsp each of chopped root ginger and (bruised) black pepper
1tsp mixed (bruised) nutmeg, clove, galingale, caraway seed, mace,
*   coriander seed, long pepper and grains of paradise*
4tbs brandy
2tbs clear honey

PIMENT[25] (SUBTLE HERB FLAVOURS)

2pt/1·2l sweet red or white dessert wine
½tsp each of (bruised) cloves, galingale, nutmeg, grains of paradise,
    long pepper and elecampane (Horse-heal or Inula helenium)
    root, if available
¼tsp each of dried rosemary, mint, sage and chopped bay leaf
8oz/225g clear honey

For each of the above, soak the spices in the wine for 1–2 days or more. Strain through fine cloth (or filtration paper), stir in the sugar or honey until dissolved, then bottle ready for use. It is better to use whole but bruised spices and leave them in the wine for longer periods. Finely ground spices can form a colloidal mass which is virtually impossible to filter.

To filter these wines, they were passed through conical bags made of bolting cloth, a very finely woven linen, their rims being hemmed to receive thin wooden hoops. Their shape was believed to resemble the sleeve of Hippocrates, the celebrated Greek physician, this name being transferred to the spiced wine filtered in this way. Instructions for its preparation start with grinding the spices separately and keeping them airtight in dried pig or sheep bladders.[26] Having been mixed into the wine then frequently stirred overnight, it was allowed to settle. In some recipes the clear was then poured off, and only the dregs strained through a single filter bag hung between two trestles. Others follow a much more complicated process, hanging a row of six filter bags from a pole or perch, each over its own pewter bowl. Having been passed through the first bag, it was tasted and the balance of flavours adjusted by adding further spices to the second bag. Only having gone through the final four bags was it ready for storage in a closed cask, the spices remaining in the bags being retrieved for flavouring sauces. For making clary and piment, it was found to be much simpler to put the whole spices into a cask of wine, roll it around or stir it to help extract the flavour, then just leave them to settle. As well as being used as digestives, spiced wines such as clary were considered to be medicinal, five spoonfuls soaked in three sops of bread being the daily morning dose for old men to warm their stomachs and clear their heads.

It is interesting to find aqua-vite, brandy, included in the clary recipe above. Distilled spirits began to be imported from Genoa and Holland from the mid-fourteenth century, and then to be produced along with other medicines in monastic still-houses in this country. They were rarely made in domestic still-houses until after the Dissolution, most supplies for the medieval kitchen usually being bought in. Recipes for its preparation describe how a blend of pungent spices were ground up, mixed into wine lees along with pounded herbs, and passed through a glass still.[27] Earthenware stills were also used, their remains having been excavated from a number of mainly monastic sites.[28] Although useful for strengthening spiced wines and braggot, the distilled spirits variously known as aqua-vite, aqua-fortis or ew ardaunt were chiefly used for flambé effects. Major dishes were thus enabled to make spectacular entries into the dining chamber, with flames rising from the towers of subtlety castles or slices of mawmeny. 'Putte thereon a litel aqua vite and qwen hit is dresset in dysshes… thenne light hit with a wax candel and serue hit forthe brennynge', reads one recipe.[29]

The wafers served with the spiced wines were made by pouring a small pool of batter on to one flat round face of a pair of hot iron wafer-tongs. As the faces were clamped close together, the batter expanded rapidly, sending spurts of surplus mixture and jets of steam from their perimeter. Once cooked to a deep cream colour, the tongs were opened, and the wafer removed. After drying out briefly, wafers were then stored in closed containers, for they soon became soggy in a damp atmosphere. There are few medieval English recipes for wafers, but one describes a batter made of white flour, egg whites, sugar and ground ginger, mixed with soft cheese and the ground stomach of a pike.[30] They can be made succesfully without the pike, however, but still take considerable practice to bake successfully using either traditional iron wafer-tongs or the aluminium versions still available in France and Holland.

WAFERS

2oz/50g plain flour	*1oz/25g curd or cream cheese,*
½tsp ground ginger	*ground or beaten smooth*
3 egg whites, lightly beaten	*1oz/25g butter*

Sift the flour and ginger into a bowl, make a well in the centre, pour in the eggs and cheese, and beat to produce a smooth batter.

Heat the closed irons on one side and then the other over a stove. Wrap the butter in a piece of cloth, and use to lightly grease the inner faces of the irons.

Pour a pool of batter on to one face of the irons, close them together, and hold until the steam subsides and before there is any smell of scorching.

Trim any surplus batter from the edges of the tongs, open them, remove the wafer, and leave for a few minutes to dry on a cooling rack before storing in an airtight container.

Wine, wafers and sweetmeats were not only served at the close of meals but, requiring no further preparation and being of high status, they were ideal for more intimate entertainments in the chambers. At the Green Knight's castle, Sir Gawain was taken[31]

> To a side-room, where first of all, they call
> For spices, which men spread to bring them unstintingly,
> With beakers of warming wine at each return.

In fine weather, they were also served in bowers, arbours or herberers, luxurious summer-houses erected in parks or gardens a short distance from the main residence. In July 1502, Henry VII's queen, Elizabeth of York, had one specially built for one of her sweetmeat banquets: 'To Henry Smyth clerc of the Castell of Windsore for money by him payed to a certain labourers to make an herbour in the little parke of Windsore for the banket for the Quene 4s. 8d.'[32] Such parties became very popular in succeeding centuries.

Returning to the dining chamber, the confectionery was usually responsible for producing the 'subtleties' served to introduce or more usually terminate the courses of great feasts. Their purpose was not to be eaten, but to provide allegorical, patriotic or symbolic table-sculpture, each being designed to promote a particular theme. Some were made of edible materials such as sugar plate, marchpane or pastry, but others were of mere wax, paper, tinfoil or wood. In the late fourteenth century, Chaucer recorded 'bake-meats and dish-meats, burning of wild fire and painted and castled with paper'. The monks of Durham bought 'Tinfoil... for the decoration and painting of the subtleties for the feast of the Nativity of the Lord' in 1467–8.[33] At the enthroning of Archbishop Warham of Canterbury in 1504, the painting of his throne and the 'work of the Subtleties in sugar and wax' cost the huge sum of £16, a clear indication of the high cost of their materials and workmanship.[34]

Some subtleties were relatively straightforward. John Chandler, Bishop of Salisbury, had the Agnus dei, a leopard and an eagle terminating each of the three courses of his 1417 enthronement feast. The Bishop of London had devices including a castle standing in a broad custard, its centre having a wench and a demon drawing a green-robed doctor from his pulpit, a scroll on his head declaring *in deo salutare meo*. John Russell's *Boke of Nurture* provides details of themed subtleties for particular feasts. One for Christmas, for example, featured:[35]

> *First Course* The Annunciation, with Gabriel greeting the Virgin Mary with an Ave.
> *Second Course* An angel singing to three shepherds on a hill.
> *Third Course* The Virgin Mary presented by the three Kings of Cologne, as the Wise Men were then known.

Another used the ages of man as a means of symbolizing the seasons and their respective humours;

> *First Course* A gallant young man called Sanguineus or Spring, piping and singing while standing on his cloud, inscribed,
> *Largus, amans, hillaris, ridens, rubie que coloris*

    Cantans, carnosus, salis audax, atque benignus

    [Abundant, loving, cheerful, laughing, rosy and beautiful,

    Singing, full-fleshed, sufficiently courageous, and also kind].

Second Course A rough, red, angry warrior called Estas or summer, standing
    in fire, inscribed for choler;

    Hirsutus, Fallax irascens prodigus, satis audax

    Astutus, gracilis Siccus crocei que coloris

    [Rough, treacherous, abounding in anger, sufficiently bold,

    Cunning, lean, tearless, gold in complexion].

Third Course A weary middle aged man called Harvest, standing in a river,
    wound in weeds, and wielding a sickle. He was inscribed for autumn
    and phlegm;

    Hic sompnolentus piger, in sputamine multus,

    Ebes hine sensus pinguis , facie color albus

    [Here sleepy, tedious, slavering,

    the senses fade into stupidity, white faced].

Fourth Course Winter, a feeble old man with grey locks of hair, sitting on a
    cold, hard stone. He was inscribed for melancholy;

    Invidus et tristis Cupidus dextre que tenasis

    Non expers fraudis, timidus, lutei que coloris

    [Envious and melancholy, avaricious, careful and frugal,

    Not without deceit, fearful, the colour of clay].

The story of St George and the dragon was also told in patriotic subtleties:

First Course The shield of St George, and an angel.

Second Course St George on horseback, slaying the dragon.

Third Course A castle with the King and Queen coming in to see how St
    George slew the dragon.

    Subtleties for royal feasts were even more impressive. For Henry IV's
marriage to Joan of Navarre in 1403, they included a crowned panther
and a crowned eagle, a suitably imperial symbol.[36] His feast for a French
delegation had an emphatic theme of sliced brawn decorated with St
George's cross and the Garter ribbon.[37] Henry V's coronation feast

featured his father's badges of the swan and the antelope. At the end of the first course, there appeared a great white swan sitting on a green base, a scroll in its bill announcing '*Regardez la droit voy*' (Behold the right way), while the surrounding cygnets bore '*Theney la ley/Gardez la fey/Hors de cours/Sort bannez tort/Eyez pele/des comunalte*' (Keep [hold] the law/ Protect the faith/ Let wrong be banished from your heart/ Have pity on the commons [i.e. the poor]). This was followed by a procession of 24 swans, each with 'noble honour and joy' in its bill. Further swans, cut out of brawn to decorate a jelly, started the second course, an antelope inscribed '*sauvez plus maynteyn dieux*' (save more, uphold God) finishing it. The third course subtlety closed the whole feast with a display of eagles in gold with '*dest jour notable est honorable*' (this auspicious day is honourable).[38] When Henry married Catherine of Valois in 1420, the theme of her namesake St Catherine was adopted, along with a variety of other symbols in a series of decorations that ran as follows:[39]

First Course St Catherine discussing with doctors, a book in her left hand, and a scroll '*Madame le Royne*' (Madam the Queen) in her right. A pelican in her nest with chicks, representing redemption through Christ's blood, since she reputedly gave her own blood to save her offspring, bore the answer '*Ce est la signe, et du Roy, pur tenir, joy, et a tout sa gent elle mete sa intent*' (It is the Kings' wish, that all his people should be merry, and in this manner makes his intentions public).

Second Course 1. A flampoint flourished with the royal arms, with three gold crowns decorated with fleur-de-lis and flowers. 2. a panther, and St Catherine holding her wheel in one hand and a scroll '*La Royne ma file in cest ile per bon reson aves renount*' (The Queen my child, shall meet with deserved renown in this island).

Third Course 1. A white leach flourished with hawthorn leaves and berries. 2. St Catherine with numerous angels, and the scroll '*Il est escrit par voir est eit, per marriage pur, cest guerre ne dure*' (It is written, as is heard and seen, that by a sacred marriage, war shall be terminated). 3. An armoured knight on horseback (Henry V), holding a tiger cub (representing Catherine) throwing mirrors at a great tiger (her father, Louis) and with a scroll '*Par force sanz reson je ay pryse cest beste*' (By force, without cunning, I have taken this beast). The tiger, meanwhile, still looked in its mirror, *'Gile de mirrour ma fete distour'* (The deceitfulness of the mirror, hath been my destruction).

The St Catherine images displayed here reflected scenes from her life, demolishing the arguments of fifty philosophers promoting idolatory, and being carried to Mount Sinai by angels. These had been adapted, by their scrolls, to celebrate the King's great victory at Agincourt, his triumph over France, and this union with the French royal family, whom he expected to succeed. It is tempting to link the Museum of London's St Catherine sugar mould with this great feast.

When Henry VI was crowned at only nine years old in 1429, the subtleties for his coronation feast continued to promote his claim to the French throne.

> *First Course* This included viand royal planted with lozenges of gold, a boar's head armed in a castle of gold, a red leach with crowned lions, a custard royal with golden leopards sitting up to hold fleur-de-lis, and a fritter as a sunburst, with fleur-de-lis at its centre. The subtletly featured St Edward the Confessor of England and St Louis of France, both wearing their coats of arms, holding the King as he stood between them, his coat of arms probably displaying St Edward's arms impaling those of France. A scroll between the two saint-kings read 'behold 2 parfight kinge under one cote armour', while beneath them was written:
>
> Holy seyntes, Edwarde and seynt Lowyce,
> Concerve this braunche, borne of your blessyd blode,
> Lyve amonge Cristen, moste soveraygne of pryce,
> Inherytour of the flour delyce so gode.
> This sixte Henry to reygne and to be wyse,
> God graunte he may, to be your mode,
> And that he may resemble your knygthode and vertue,
> Pray ye hertely unto our Lord Ihesu.
>
> *Second Course* A jelly of two colours with the motto *'Te Deum laudamus'*, a peacock in its skin, and a leach planted with a red antelope, crowned and chained in gold, surrounded by golden leopards and fleur-de-lis.

There was also a fritter garnished with leopards' faces and two ostrich feathers, etc. The subtlety showed the King kneeling before the Emperor Sigismund and his father Henry V, with the verse:

> Agayne myscreants, the emperour Sygysmunde
> Hath shewed his myght, whiche is imperyall.
> And Henry the V a noble knyght was founde
> For Cristes cause in actes marteyell,
> Cheryshed the churche to Loller's gave a fall,
> Gyvynge example to kynges that succede
> And to theyr braunche her in especyall,
> While he doth reygne to love good and drede.

Third Course Blancdesire scattered with gold quatrefoils, a pie like a shield quartered red and white, set with golden lozenges and borage flowers, etc. The final subtlety showed St George of England and St Denys of France kneeling before the Virgin and Child, as they presented the King to her. In his hand, a scroll bore:

> O blessyd Lady, Crists moder dere,
> And thou seynt George, that called art her knyght,
> Holy seynt Denys, O marter most entere,
> The sixte Henry here present in your syght,
> Shedyth, of your grace, on him your hevenly lyght,
> His tender youth with vertue doth anounce,
> Borne by discent, and by tytle of ryght,
> Justly in reygne in Englande and in France.

Elaborate as they were, Henry V's and VI's subtleties appear modest when compared with those of later generations. This might be illustrated by describing those made for Archbishop William Warham's enthronement in March 1504.[40] At his own table, a subtlety called a warner, since it 'warned' or preceded the serving of the main course, was first carried up to his table in the great hall. Mounted on a round board, it had an octagonal base with a tall tower made of flowers rising from each corner to an embattled parapet, each one of which displayed the figure of a beadle with his staff. Although the contemporary description is not entirely clear, it appears that the towers supported three 'boards' or floors, each with a mass of figures and captions. On the first, St William in the robes of an archbishop sat next to the King in parliament, as the Chancellor of Oxford and other doctors presented the kneeling William Warham to his majesty. The Chancellor's scroll read:

> *Deditus a teneris his noster alumnus*
> *Morum, and doctrinae, tanum profecit, ut aulam*
> *Illustrare tuam, curare negotia regni*
> *Rex Henrici, tui, possit honorifice*
> (The customs and knowledge of this our foster child
> [the archbishop?] are yielded and surrendered, for what
> they are worth, so that, King Henry, they may enlighten
> your hall [or court, or college] and may do honour to the
> government of your realm).

The King answered:

> *Tales esse decet, quibus uti sacra majestas*
> *Regni in tutando debeat imperio.*
> *Quare suscipiam quem commendastic alumnum*
> *Digna daturus ei praemia pro meritis*
> (Such things are fitting, to whom is due power through
> guarding the holy majesty of the realm. How shall we
> receive what is entrusted to our foster-child [the archbishop?],
> to be worthy of that which is given, privileged for merit).

On the second board Warham in doctor's gown was shown in a tower piled with rolls, as the King presented him to Our Lady at rolls, with the verse:

> *Est locus egregius tibi, virgo sacrata, dicatus,*
> *Publica servari quo monumenta solent.*
> *Hic primo hunc situ dignabere, dignus honore,*
> *Commendo fidei serinia sacra sua*
> (This place is especially favoured by you, holy virgin,

dedicated, kept safe by the people as an accustomed
remembrance, who first made this place worthy,
commend this shrine of faith consecrated to you, as worthy of honour).

The third board showed the Holy Ghost, presumably in the form of a white dove, projecting bright beams of grace towards Warham, with:

> *Gratia te traxit donis cœlestibus aptum*
> *Perge, parata manent uberiora tibi*
> (Grace is ready to hastily bring down heavenly gifts
> to you, remaining prepared to do so more abundantly [to you]).

The second and third courses were also introduced with warners of equal magnificence, with masses of saints, the Pope and cardinals, angels, a church and choir, and a full depiction of the archiepiscopal enthronement ceremony. After the first course had been served, the Duke of Buckingham, steward of the feast, retired to the dining chamber, where his dinner was served with further subtleties:

First The King enthroned amid the Lords, and with knights and others
  standing behind a barrier, watching two white-harnessed knights
  jousting on horseback.
Second The conversion of St Eustace, showing the saint kneeling in a park,
  beneath a great tree full of roses, a servant holding his horse as the vision
  of a white hart appears, a shining crucifix between its antlers.

Duplicates of these were served at the end of the Archbishop's table in the great hall, with more subtleties at the lower tables there, including the Brothers' board:

First St Augustine, his monks and doctors, arriving before King Ethelbert
  in AD 597, asking permission to preach to his people and convert them
  to Christianity, all amid towers and weathervanes. The doctors' scrolls
  read *Ergo vigilate super gregem* (Therefore keep watch over the people).
Second A throned doctor sitting like a judge of the Arches, with doctors and
  proctors pleading the causes of church law, all before the main altar of
  an abbey church with numerous altars.

At the Mayor of Canterbury's tables, the subtlety showed a castle bristling with soldiers, all in a town populated by the Mayor, members of his council, and its citizens. The subtlety for the Barons of the Cinque Ports' table was similarly appropriate. It showed them holding light shields bearing their arms of three half-lions, half-ships, all on the decks of a great warship, its sail painted with the same arms.

Work of this quality was extremely costly, the £16 paid for the subtleties and for painting the throne representing over £7000 in modern terms.[41] Being particularly complex, they must have taken much time to prepare and, since wax is easier to work and is far more robust than sugar, it is probable that this material predominated. The great drawback of sugar is that it rapidly absorbs water from the atmosphere and unless the air is extremely dry, will start to weep syrup within a matter of hours, wasting the workmanship put into its moulding, modelling and painting. Wax, meanwhile, has none of these problems, remaining firm even on the hottest days, and lacking the brittleness of sugar. In an age when the spectacle of the feast was perhaps the most effective public expression of wealth, power and status, the provision of memorable subtleties was an important political investment.

CHAPTER NINETEEN

Planning Meals

Deciding what to cook and in which order each dish should be served were decisions which could only be taken in the more prosperous households. In many peasant and poor urban homes, it was more a matter of eating whatever became available. Real hunger always stalked the poor, especially when there was no work in the months before harvest, and particularly when the harvest failed.

Although not well represented in medieval records, there is substantial evidence for a continuous tradition of gathering wild foods through to the early twentieth century. Nettles were widely used for making broths and pottages, along with bistort ('passion dock' or 'Easter ledges'), sorrel, wild garlic ('ramsons'), mushrooms and many other herbs. In the spring, the fresh leaf-buds of the hawthorn were nibbled – I still do this, being taught by my grandfather; they were known as 'bread and cheese' – as were the sweet bases of clover flowers. Late summer and autumn then brought wild strawberries, blackberries, bilberries ('whortleberries') and a variety of nuts. Wild birds are likely to have been eaten too, using nets or bird-lime made from holly-bark to take anything from a sparrow to a rook. Wild birds' eggs were also eaten, especially those of seabirds collected from the high east-coast cliffs. Even so, it would have been difficult for anyone to have survived as a hunter-gatherer in medieval England; without, that is, recourse to farmed animals or crops, and prohibited the game they might otherwise have pursued. In *Piers Plowman*, when the established resources failed, Hunger fiercely attacked the unprepared Waster:[1]

Hunger in haste thoo [sieze] Wastour by the mawe [stomach]
And wrong hym so by the wombe [belly] that

al watrede hise eighes [watered his eyes]
He buffeted the Bretoner aboute the chekes
That he loked lik a lanterne al his lif after
He bette hem so bothe, he brast [burst] ner hise guttes.

The basic foods used to keep hunger at bay included bran-mash, peas, beans, and coarse bread made of pea-meal, bran and bean-meal, or of the rough blends usually baked only for horses and hounds.[2] The unemployed might be willing to accept these as payment for work before harvest, but when it began and their services were in great demand, they expected nothing but the finest wheat bread, the strongest ales, fresh meat, fish baked or fried, and the highest of wages.[3] In 1424, the harvest workers at Sedgeford in Norfolk were being typically well fed, each man receiving, on average, some two pounds of wheaten bread, an ounce and a half of oats in his pottage, a pound of meat, three and a half ounces of fish, and four ounces of dairy produce, all washed down with over six pints of ale.[4] Such plenty would be short-lived, however. Those who harvested the crops and tended the herds and flocks had to use a substantial part of their produce to pay their tithes to the church, their multure to the miller and rents to their lord. The residue had to feed their dependants throughout the coming year. It is not surprising that Piers Plowman found himself short of food:[5]

'I have no penny', quod Piers, 'pulettes to bugge [buy]
Neither gees nor grys [pigs], but two grene cheses,
A few cruddles and creme and a cake of otes,
And two loves of benes and bran ybake for my fauntes [children]
And yet I say by my soule, I have no salt bacon
Ne no cokeney [egg], by Crist, coloppes to maken!
As I have percile and porettes [leeks] and manye plaunte coles [greens].
And eke a cow and a calf, and a cart mare
To drawe afeld my donge the while the droghte lasteth
By this liflode we mote lyve til Lammesse tyme [1 August]
And by that I hope to have hervest in my crofte,
Thanne may I dighte thi dyner as me deere liketh

Al the pouer peple the pescoddes fetten [fetched];
Benes and baken apples thei broghte in hir lappes,
Chibolles [spring onions] and chervelles and ripe chiries manye,
And profrede Piers this present to plese with Hunger.'

The poor old widow in Chaucer's *Nun's Priest's Tale* lived in a similar manner, having the produce of three cows, a sheep, three sows, a cock and seven hens. In her sooty hall and 'kitchen melancholy':[6]

...there she ate full many a slender meal;
There was no *sauce piquante* to spice her veal...
She drank no wine, nor white nor red had got.
Her board was mostly served with white and black,
Milk and brown bread, in which she found no lack;
Broiled bacon or an egg or two were common,
She was, in fact, a sort of dairy-woman.

A good impression of the festive foods enjoyed at this level comes from the texts of the shepherds' scenes written for the Nativity section of the annual mystery plays. In the Chester cycle, they dine on bread and oatcake, onions, garlic, leeks, smoked ham, a pig's foot, a sheep's head soused in ale, a pudding (of the black- or hogs-pudding type), hot meat, butter, curds and a green cheese. Their contemporaries in Wakefield made similar preparations:[7]

1ˢᵗ *Shepherd* Lay forth all our store, Lo, here! Brawn of Boar,
Here's a foot of a cow well sowsed, I ween,
The shank of a sow that spiced has been,
Two black-puddings, I vow, with liver between,
Let gladly, sirs, now, my brothers, be seen
What more?
Both beef and mutton
Of an ewe that was rotten
Good meat for a glutton
Eat of this store.

2nd *Shepherd* I have in my bag no kale, but boiled and roast

Even an ox-tail that would not be lost;

Ha-ha, good-hail! I stop for no cost,

A good pie or we fail; that is good for a frost

In the morning:

Of two pigs the groin

All hare but the loin

No spoons we enjoin

Here at our feasting.

3rd *Shepherd* Here is to record the leg of a goose,

Basted for our board, pork or partridge to chose,

A tart for a lord, how the gravy doth ooze.

A calf's liver stored with verjuice

Good sauce

A restorative right

For a good appetite.

Perhaps the most interesting aspect of these lines, probably composed in the early fourteenth century, is their reliance on the trimmings and offal of animals, rather than on the good joints required for noble and gentry cookery. There was a piece of boar-brawn, but the mutton came from a diseased sheep. From at least the thirteenth century and on into the nineteenth, sheep which died in this way were soaked for a few hours, drained and salted, before being boiled up for the workers.[8] Most of the other meat was offal: heads, feet, knee-joints, groins, tails, livers, blood. Even the hare had had its only decent meat removed, leaving nothing edible but the legs. Presumably the cottagers' pigs were killed throughout the year, and the offal or 'fry' shared out around the community, as in the post-medieval period. The presence of butter, curds and green cheese confirms the importance of 'white meats', or dairy produce, as mentioned in the previous quotations.

These sources certainly provide us with an accurate overview of the foods eaten by the English medieval peasant, but it would be mistaken to believe that they represent a single uniform diet. Regional differences, influenced by soil-type, altitude, climate, fuel and culture would have been very pronounced, as we can tell from later records. In some communities oats were the preferred bread-corn, in others barley, in others wheat. In some diets, fish might predominate, while in another region people would enjoy using weighted squails to knock squirrels from their dreys, ready for the pot. Many of the practices recorded in books such as William Howitt's *Rural Life of England* of 1840, F.G. Heath's *The English Peasant* of 1893 and H.M. Neville's *A Corner in the North* of 1909 were probably already centuries old by the fifteenth century, helping us to interpret the regional significance of documentary and archaeological evidence. The meal times of different groups of medieval workers were probably similarly diverse. While most crafts were pursued during the hours of daylight, agricultural workers had to work around the requirements of their livestock, and mariners those of wind and tide. It is not surprising that even Parliament could not specify their diet with any exactitude. In the sumptuary ordinance of 1363, it was able to order that 'grooms, as well as the servants of great men as of traders and craftsmen… shall be served once a day with meat or fish, the rest with other food, as milk, cheese, butter and other such victuals according to their estate'. In contrast, men and women engaged in husbandry or with goods worth under £2 were merely to 'live upon such food and drink as is suitable, and then not to excess', hardly definitive legislation![9]

Moving on to the households of those who employed labour, food habits become much more regular. As a general rule, there were two meals each day, dinner served at 10 a.m. and supper at 4 p.m., although these could be moved an hour forward or back depending on the season, or the particular preference of the head of the household.[10] These meal-times were obviously determined by practical considerations. Since dinner was usually the main meal of the day, when hot meats were generally served, it was essential that sufficient time was allowed for them to be issued from the larder, trussed and cooked during daylight hours. Cooking by firelight and traditional wax lights is an extremely dangerous and inefficient operation, fraught with difficulties. Having tried it from time to time, I can confirm that the tiny flames of a dozen candles cannot penetrate the overwhelming black darkness of a great medieval kitchen, even the first rays of dawn bringing a vast improvement in visibility. For this reason alone, dinner was impractical before 10 a.m. for much of the year.

After dinner had been served, time had to be allowed for washing
and cleaning the cooking plant, utensils and tableware ready for re-use,
for the kitchen staff to have their dinners, and for the food to be planned,
prepared and cooked for supper. Considering the time required to clear the
hall and dining chamber, feed the kitchen staff and make everything ready
for next morning, all before the onset of dusk, 4 p.m. was the optimum
supper-time for most households.

Even though this standardized two-meals-a-day system was most
efficient both from a management point of view, and as a means of keeping
everyone well fed, it meant that no food was served during the eighteen
hours between 4 p.m. and 10 a.m. This was a long period for particular
groups, such as youths. The six henchmen of Edward IV's court shared
a mess of boiled meat, two loaves and a gallon of ale to break their fast
each day, an essential preparation for their riding, jousting and dancing
exercises, and tuition in manners, music and language.[11] Edward's son, one
of the Princes in the Tower, similarly had breakfast just after mass, and
before his lessons.[12] One fifteenth-century schoolboy remembered how
'My brekefast was brought to my beddys side as ofte as me liste to calle
therfor, and so many times I was first fedde or I were cledde [before I was
clad]'. Like many others, he found this indulgence disappeared within a few
years; 'Now at fyve of the clocke by the monelyght I must go to my booke
and lete slepe and slouthe alon… brekfastes that were sumtyme brought
at my biddynge is driven oute of contrey and never shall cum agayne.'[13]

The provision of breakfasts enabled a further layer of visible social
distinction to be introduced into the household. The regulations drawn
up for the King's mother, Princess Cecily, Duchess of York, state that
'Breakfasts be there none, savinge onely the head officers when they be
present; to the ladyes and gentlewomen, to the Deane and to the Chappell,
to the Almoner, to the gentleman ushers, to the Cofferer, to the Clerke
of the Kitchin, and to the Marshall' as well as the officers brieving in
the counting house.[14] In other words, they were only to be served to
the aristocracy, for prestige, and to those officers who would be working
when dinner was being served, and so required food in their offices well
before dinner-time. This general policy is confirmed in a number of other
contemporary records, from the ordinances of the royal households to the

expenses of much smaller establishments. Those of the widowed Dame Alice de Bryene in Suffolk typically show that whereas about twenty people had dinner every day, breakfast was restricted to between three and eight individuals on most days.[15]

Other food and drink was consumed informally throughout each day. For agricultural and craft workers who needed to keep up their intake of liquids, there were nuncheons ('noon-cups') or 'drinkings', usually of bread and ale, eaten in the early afternoon. These were provided by their master or employer and formed part of their wages.[16] The *Oxford English Dictionary* records that in 1422–3 Robert 'the dawber' received his 'noonchyns' when daubing, while eight labourers in 1500 were paid 3*d.* a day, with nuncheons valued at 6*d.*, reflecting their importance. In medieval households, the daily allowance was called a livery. The size and quality of a livery, and any restrictions on who might be entitled to it, were exploited to emphasize differences in rank and status. In Edward IV's court, the nobility and servants in attendance received the following, which might be consumed at any time, but apparently excluded that which was served at dinner and supper;[17]

Title	Number of servants	Loaves	Wine (pitchers)	Ale (gallons)
Duke	9	10	3	6
Marquess	7	7	2.5	5
Earl	5	6	2	5
Viscount	3	4	1	3
Baron	2	3	0.5	2
Knight + 1 companion		2	0.5	2
10 Grooms of Chamber		4		2
4 Pages of Chamber		1		0.5
6 Henchmen		3		2
Steward	8	8	2	6
Treasurer	5	7	2	6
Controller	2	5	1	3
Cofferer	1	4	0.5	3

This approximates to 1 loaf and 5 pints of ale per person, plus a third of a pitcher of wine for those allowed it. In the Northumberland household, the Earl and Countess's livery was 2 manchets, a loaf of household bread, 2 pints of wine, and 8 of beer; their head officers received 1 manchet, half a household loaf, 2 pints of wine and 4 of beer each; and most other servants a half or quarter of a household loaf and 2 to 4 pints of beer.[18]

Having described the sequence of meals served each day, we can now follow the planning processes which preceded them. The practice of the royal household, recorded in 1469, was for:[19]

> The Steward, the Tresorer, the Countroller, the clerke of the kichyn, the marshalle [of the hall], the usher [of the chamber], pantlers, butlers, cookes, lardeners, catourers, and suche other officers, at twoe of the clocke at aftyrnoone, assemble in the halle, and there ordeigne the fare of the said Duke and his household, for the souper the same nighte, and the next daye's dynner; and the marshalle or ussher to bringe brede, wine, and ale, to the said ordinaunce, accordinge to the olde custome of the courte.

The agenda of an identical reporting/planning meeting held at 1 p.m. in the Northumberland household is given on page 31. Here all shortcomings experienced over the previous twenty-four hours would be noted, and samples of bread, ale and wine collected by the marshal and the usher from the hall and chamber respectively, checked for size and quality. The chequer-roll would then have been consulted to confirm the number of people who had been served, and to note any predictable additions or subtractions for the following day. This would enable the number of 'messes' to be calculated. This word had a number of distinct meanings. Here it meant a small unit of diners, usually four in number, and hence the dished portions of food which they would share at table. It was an extremely practical concept. At its simplest, the appearance of a hundred diners on the chequer-roll meant that the pantler would have to provide 25 loaves, the butler 25 pots of ale, and the cooks 25 dishes of pottage, of meat, and so forth at dinner and supper, as well as 25 liveries of bread and ale. In practice, however, some people got more food to reflect both their status and the number of servants and other followers they would be expected to feed. These were allowed as, for example: [20]

Rank	Messes
Duke, Marquess, Earl	4 messes boiled meat and roast
Viscount	3 ditto
Baron	2 messes boiled meat and some roast
Steward, Treasurer	4 ditto
Controller, Cofferer	2 ditto
2 Clerks of Greencloth	2 ditto

Having calculated the number of messes and how many were to be roast, rather than boiled, the appropriate officers could be instructed, provided with their supplies from the larder and other departments, and all practical preparations put in hand.

For the royal table, the number of messes varied from day to day, according to the king's particular needs, but they would certainly have outnumbered those of dukes and higher nobility. Edward III always had at least eight dishes on his table at every meal. Their content was determined for the king, as advised by his doctor of physic, working with the steward, chamberlain, sewer, and master cook for the mouth.[21] The required food would then be drawn from the larder and elsewhere, and taken to the privy kitchen for cooking.

The foods which could be selected for meals varied from one season to another, as fruits, vegetables and dairy produce became available, but meat, fish, butter, cheese and cereals were always present, thanks to various methods of preservation. The governing factor for changes in the daily fare was not the raw ingredients, however, but state-enforced religious practice. For the good of their souls, everyone was expected to reduce their diet for almost half the days of the year.[22] Every Friday (the day of the crucifixion), Saturday (dedicated to the Virgin Mary), and Wednesday (when Judas accepted the thirty pieces of silver), meat was forbidden, and as an additional penance on Friday the only meal of the day was dinner. Then there were the Ember Days of fasting and prayer held on the Wednesdays, Fridays and Saturdays following the first Sunday in Lent, Whitsunday, Holy Cross Day (14 September) and St Lucia's Day (13 December), when dairy produce was allowed, as well as fish. This gave rise to special dishes such as tarts for Ember Day, made with boiled onions bound with cheese and eggs.[23] Numerous saints' days were celebrated in a similar manner, but the great fasts of the year were Lent, commencing on Ash Wednesday, and Advent, starting on the fourth Sunday before Christmas. The cooks made these fish-days much more interesting by producing a whole series of culinary deceptions. One was to use almond-milk jelly 'in the manere of playsse [plaice], or of codlynge, or of eles, or of pykes, or of soles, or tenches', and another to pour it into egg-shells to make 'boiled eggs'.[24] Pieces of skewer-roast meat coated in batter, called hastelettes were similarly replicated using dried fruits, to produce 'hastolettes on fisshe days'.[25]

After the sliced bacon had been eaten on Collop Monday, and the eggs as pancakes on Shrove Tuesday, Lent started in earnest, with its six weeks when neither meat nor dairy produce was permitted. To modern minds, this restriction is perfectly clear, but medieval scholars found it open to debate. 'Men of relygyon eat barnacles [fowles lyke to wylde ghees, which growen wonderly upon trees] upon fastynge dayes bycause they ben not engendered with flesshe', for example.[26] The Duke of Clarence served one of these at a fast-day dinner in Salisbury in 1465/7.[27] Beavers, being furry, were obviously meat, but their tails being scaly (and, incidentally, weighing up to 4lb, and being very good eating) were obviously fish![28] The cooks also used substitutes for meat-based ingredients, the most common being almond milk to replace cow's milk, and deployed all their skills to make fish as appetizing as possible. When Sir Gawain arrived at the Green Knight's castle on the last day of Advent, he was appropriately served with:[29]

> dishes of various fish;
> Some baked in bread, some broiled on embers,
> Some boiled, or stewed with spices, in their juice,
> All served with delicate sauces that he relished,
> And he politely proclaimed it as a feast...

The provision of such foods was an expensive exercise. As everyone fasted at the same time, fish and dried fruits would be in great demand. However, there were nuances to universal observance. It was recognized that fasting could be unwise for certain vulnerable groups. The poor, the young, the old and the infirm might therefore be allowed to follow their usual diets. Even in prosperous establishments, the degree of fasting could be modified to meet different aspirations of piety. Some might fast on Mondays and Tuesdays as well as on the three accepted days of denial. By contrast, certainly from the fourteenth century, there were some households which might allow meat for one meal on Wednesdays.

Having taken account of all the above factors, the cooks and household officers could now draw up bills of fare for the continuing sequence of daily meals, commencing with the breakfasts.

The appearance of 'Roger atte Becche *cocus de gentaculo* [cook for breakfast, L. *janticulum*] in the accounts of Edward I shows that this peripatetic monarch enjoyed cooked breakfasts in the decades around 1300, but this was unusual.[30] The few people who might take breakfast in the fourteenth and early fifteenth centuries probably had no more than a little bread and cheese, only the monarch and great nobles having anything more substantial. Edward IV had four manchet and two *pain de main* loaves, a mess of unspecified food from the kitchen, and four pints of ale for breakfast, while in 1501 the Duke of Buckingham was having perch, plaice and roach, butter and eggs.[31] Three years later, the Archbishop of Canterbury sat down on the morning of his enthronement to a breakfast of hot ling, herrings, pike in sage, carp in ferry, grilled salt eel, fried tench in sauce, and slices of salmon, stuffed, rolled and roast. Most breakfasts were much plainer, of course, as we can see from the declining scale and quality of those served to the various ranks within the Northumberland household. These included:[32]

BREAKFASTS ON FLESH DAYS

	pieces boiled beef	boiled mutton	chicken	trencher loaves	manchet	house- hold bread	wine	beer
Lord & Lady	½ chine or chine			1	2		2pt	2pt
2 sons		3 bones	1		1	½		4pt
Head officers	2	2 bones			1	2		8pt
Others, per mess	1					1		4pt

BREAKFASTS ON SATURDAYS OUT OF LENT

	pieces salt fish	buttered eggs	dish of butter	trencher loaves	manchet	household bread	wine	beer
Lord & Lady	1 or	1	1	1	2		2pt	2pt
2 sons	1 or	1	1		1			4pt
Head officers	2	1 or	1		1	2		8pt
Others, per mess	1					1		4pt

BREAKFASTS IN LENT

	pieces salt fish	smoked herring	pickled herring	dishes of sprats	dishes of butter	[bread, wine & beer as above]
Lord & lady	2	6	4 or	1		
2 sons	1		3 or	1	1	
Head officer	2		4			
Others, per mess	2					

There are few bills of fare for flesh-day dinners served in the hall, but their content may be ascertained from runs of daily accounts. Those of Dame Alice de Bryene's household of around twenty people in 1412–13 provide an excellent example.[33] Throughout most of the year a quarter of a beef carcase and a quarter of a bacon pig were cooked each day, these being supplemented or replaced with mutton and lamb joints during the second half of each year, and pigeons from Easter to November. There was one of these home-bred birds for each person every flesh-day in summer and autumn. This constitutes, with the beef and pork, a high level of meat consumption. Neither vegetables nor cereals were recorded in the accounts, since they would have come directly from the gardens and home farm but, by adding these to the stock remaining in the beef pot after the meat had been boiled, they would have provided an ample supply of pottage to precede the meat.

On fish-days, one stockfish and half a salt fish appear to have replaced the beef and bacon in the beef-pot, with anything between two and five red and/or white salted herrings for each person from December, throughout most of the following year. Red herrings went out of use in July, and white herrings in October, these being supplemented by smoked herrings (i.e. kippers) between September and November. Occasional purchases of perhaps a score of plaice, or a few large haddock, probably indicate welcome additions to this plain diet. Even at great feasts, those sitting in the hall could still only expect more white herring, plaice and haddock, along with whiting, ling, and eels.[34]

Despite plentiful information regarding the range of foods carried into the dining chambers, and the complex rituals attending their service, it is still very difficult to determine their actual numbers and content. In the royal court, dukes, marquesses and earls were given four messes of boiled and roast meat, viscounts three, and barons three messes of boiled meat including some roast. Both the steward and treasurer of the household had four messes of boiled meat and two 'rewards' of roasts from the royal table, the controller receiving half this amount.[35] It is possible that this might represent the number of dishes they expected to be served at their own dinner tables, but there is evidence that their menus were more extensive.

Even on the 'Scramlynge Days' in Lent, when catering was minimal, the Earls of Northumberland supped on forty sprats, two pieces of stockfish, a quarter of salt salmon, two slices of turbot, a dish of flounders, baked turbot or a dish of fried smelts, a total of six dishes. Similarly, their Rogation Day supper included a cake of butter, two pieces of salt fish, a quarter of a fresh cod, the same of ling, two slices of turbot, a quarter of soused 'byrt' (turbot?) and a dish of either flounders or roach, again six dishes.[36] These suggest that a nobleman would have at least six dishes for his dinner and supper, perhaps eight or even ten not being unreasonable.

For feasts, many more dishes would be served, but modern readers must always remember that many of the dishes listed in feast menus were just single dishes, not multiple identical dishes as listed in today's banquet menus. When a franklin, a freeholder just below the rank of gentleman, held a feast, he would provide: [37]

First Course   brawne with mustard
            bacon with peas
            boiled beef or mutton, boiled chicken or capon
            roast goose and roast sucking pig
            capon bakemeat or baked custard of eggs & cream

Second Course mortrews and jussel [eggs and broth]

roast veal, lamb, kid, cony, chicken or pigeon

bakemeats and dowcets

fritters

a leach

spiced apples and pears

bread & cheese

Void spiced cakes and wafers

braggot and mead

Although varied and plentiful, everything listed here is home-grown, except for a few spices, the only 'luxury' items being the goose, pig and wafers. In its general arrangement of courses, and the order in which the individual types of food appear, it closely follows the much more lavish feasts provided in the chambers of the nobility and gentry.[38]

The first course at a great feast was usually introduced by either the garnished and garlanded boar's head, or brawn accompanied by mustard or pepper sauce. This was followed by either venison with frumenty, or one of the richer pottages such as bruce, bruet of almaine, or viand royal. Then came bakemeats of capon and probably small game birds, chewets, 'graund chare' (i.e. great or boiled meat or salt venison), and roast bittern, curlew, cygnet, goose, heron or pheasant. The second course commenced with a number of roasts, including great birds, small game birds, venison and sucking pig, accompanied by rich pottages such as caudle ferry, murray or blanc desire. Bakemeats such as tarts and flampoints might also be served, but these were usually reserved for the third course. This again started with roast game, cockatrice, hastelettes, potwyse, sackwyse or urchins, before moving on to the richer bakemeats of castelettes, malaches, custards lombard and royal, doucets, flampoints and the like. Some forms of fritter, jelly, leach, or baked fruit completed this course, after which the table was cleared, ready for the serving of the void.

For fish-day feasts, some bills of fare reserved the cheaper fish such as stockfish or smoked herrings for the first course, but most had good quality fish throughout, lamprey appearing in the first and third courses, for example. As regards methods of cookery, baking, boiling and frying featured in each course, while roasting tended to be reserved for the second course, and perhaps the third too, as in the flesh-day menus. In order to complement the delicate flavours of the various fish, their accompanying pottages and pastries were kept appropriately sweet and bland. Those for the first course included rice moyle, various sweet leaches, custards and almond butter, while for the second and third there might be further leaches, jellies, frumenty, tarts, fritters, baked quinces and marchpanes. By the opening of the sixteenth century, there could even be baked oranges and orange fritters too, marking the introduction of this exotic fruit into the English culinary tradition.[39]

The following sample menu for a flesh-day comes from John Russell's *Boke of Nurture* of c.1440–50:[40]

First Course brawn with mustard
        pottage of herbs, spice and wine
        boiled beef, mutton, pheasant, swan with chawdron
        capon, pig, baked venison
        leach lombard, fritter vaunt
        a subtlety

Second Course blancmange, jelly (pottages)
        roast venison, kid, faun, or rabbit
        bustards, stork, crane, peacock in its skin, heron
            or bittern, partridge, woodcock, plover, egret
        sucking rabbits, great birds, larks, and bream
        dowcets, pain puff
        leach, amber jelly, fritter pouch
        a subtlety

Third Course cream of almonds, maumeny (pottages)
        roast curlew, snipe?, quail, sparrows, house-martins
        perch in jelly, crayfish
        petty peruant, baked quinces, leach dugard, fritter
            sage
        a subtlety

Void branderells or pippens, with caraway comfits
        wafers with hippocras

And for a fish-day:

First Course muscelade or minnows, with salmon, eels and lampreys

porpoise and peas (pottage)

baked herring sprinkled with sugar, green (fresh-salt) cod,
      roast (grilled) pike, lamprey, and sole

baked gurnard and lamprey

a leach, a fritter

a subtlety

Second Course dates in syrup, red and white jelly (pottages)

conger eel, salmon, john dory all in syrup

bret (brill?), turbot or halibut, carp, bass, soft roes?, trout,
      chub, bream, sole, eel, roast lamprey

a leach, a fritter

a subtlety

Third Course cream of almonds, maumeny (pottages)

fresh sturgeon, bream, perch in jelly, whelks, minnows,
      shrimps, grilled herring

pety peruant, a fritter, a tansy

a subtlety

Void apples and pears with sugar candy and minced preserve
      ginger

wafers with hippocras

These are general menus, but others were specifically designed for particular times of the year. Wynkyn de Worde's *Boke of Keruynge* provides separate menus for the periods between Easter Day to Whitsunday, Whitsunday to Midsummer (the feast of St John the Baptist, 24 June), Midsummer to Michaelmas (29 September), and Michaelmas to Christmas.[41] These included appropriately symbolic dishes, Easter featuring a blessed calf, boiled eggs with greensauce, and a tansy, the bitter herbs representing those of the Passover. John Russell also provides a menu for a Christmas feast, with scenes from the Nativity depicted in its subtleties.[42]

Before feasts of this quality could be served, extensive preparations had to be made by the gentleman usher of the great chamber and the usher of the hall, working with the butler, pantler, and ewerer.

CHAPTER TWENTY

The Buttery and Pantry

It is uncertain when butteries and pantries first began to be set up at the lower end of the hall. The first appearance of these words according to the *Oxford English Dictionary* is in 1389 and 1300 respectively, but archival evidence suggests a much earlier date. In the twelfth century, Alexander Neckham provided an excellent description of their contents; [1]

> In the cellar or storeroom [i.e. buttery] should be casks, tuns, wineskins, cups, cup cases, spoons, ewers, basins, baskets, pure wine, cider, beer, unfermented wine, mixed wine, claret, nectar, mead, pear wine, red wine, wine from Auvergne, clove-spiced wine for gluttons whose thirst is unquenchable.... In the pantry let there be shaggy towels, tablecloths, and an ordinary hand towel which shall hang from a pole to avoid mice. Knives should be kept in the pantry, an engraved salt cellar, a cheese container, a candelabra, a lantern, a candlestick, and baskets [for carrying the bread?].

There is also good archaeological evidence. At the King's Hall in Scarborough Castle, for example, the north-west end of this large early to mid twelfth-century hall was reconstructed in the first half of the thirteenth century as a fully developed buttery and pantry, separated by a service corridor leading from the external detached kitchen. [2] Similar arrangements appear in most halls from this time and for the rest of the medieval period. Examples are too numerous to mention, but the drawing of Gainsborough Old Hall (Fig. 39) illustrates the layout perfectly.

In the smallest peasant houses, the functions of the buttery and pantry were reduced to a simple aumbry or cupboard in the 'hall', the multi-functional living-room of these two- or three-room dwellings. Within were stored a few harden or linen tablecloths, spoons, a salt cellar, dishes and saucers of pewter or wood, wooden cups, and the candlesticks and rushlight holders ready for use on dark winter evenings.[3]

In rather more prosperous houses, those of husbandmen, craftsmen, merchants, minor gentry and clerics, a separate room was provided for this purpose. It might be called either a storeroom (L. *promptuarium*) or a buttery, but these were in reality of identical function, as shown by inventories of their contents.[4] They might be furnished with an aumbry, ark or chests for table linen and tableware, a trestle table for general preparation and for slicing wholemeal loaves into trenchers, and stands to support large ale pots at a convenient height for filling the ale jugs. At the most basic level, farmers such as John Hall of Holgate might have only six dishes, two salt cellars, one linen and three harden tablecloths and a twill towel in their storerooms, worth only 3s., whereas a York mason such as Hugh de Grantham had the following in his:[5]

5	vessels [beer casks]	3	mazers
1	tuntree [stillage to hold the casks]	1	aumbry
1	tunmell [mallet to tap the casks]	1	casket for spices
1	tundish [funnel]	2	salt cellars
1	tynelyn [brewing tub]	17	silver spoons
10	beer jars	1	lamp
2	stands [for the above?]	3	bronze candlesticks
2	measures	1	pr. pepper mills
2	4pt jugs	6	tablecloths
1	pewter pint pot	6	towels
1	pewter quart pot	3	surnaps
3	leather cans [ale jugs]		a brass mortar
3	silver cups		

Total value £2 3s. 4d.

One of the practical problems experienced in single storeroom/buttery/pantries of this type was that they were combining two functions which had completely different requirements. Ale, beer and wine all needed to be kept cool, where dampness and spillage would cause few problems, but bread and table linen needed to be kept relatively dry, being spoiled by any contact with moisture. The obvious answer was to separate them into butteries devoted entirely to the service of drinks, and pantries for bread and tableware. Pairs of such rooms are a common feature in most surviving medieval houses, all the way through from those of yeoman and gentry to those of royalty, ideally with the buttery to the cool, damp north, and the pantry to the warmer, drier south, both at the lower or service end of the hall. Following the same logic, we might expect the buttery and pantry to be listed separately in inventories, and to be placed under the charge of separate officers, the butler and the pantler, but this was not the case in any but the greatest noble and royal households. In the fifteenth century, the butler was effectively absorbing the duties of the pantler in most establishments; the 1508 edition of *The Boke of Keruynge*, based on earlier sources, assumed that the same person would take on both roles. [6]

By way of contrast, the largest and most prestigious households found it most convenient to divide their buttery and pantry facilities into separate units. Once nobles had ceased to dine in their great halls and retreated into their chambers (an early to mid fourteenth-century phenomenon following earlier royal practice), it became obvious that chamber suites should now have separate services from those at the low end of the hall. As early as 1283–5 Edward I had a service room of this type adjacent to his great chamber in the state apartments at Conwy Castle (Fig. 68). Sophisticated in design, it had direct access to the ale and wine cellar, a squint for visual and oral communication to the chamber, and a staff latrine. Here could be assembled the precious tableware, table linen, dismantled tables, ale, wine and bread required for each meal, all quite separate from the facilities provided for the household staff in the great hall. Similar chamber-suite butteries and pantries can be recognized in other, later buildings. At Wressle Castle of *c.*1380, for example, the architect, probably John Lewyn, provided one set of buttery and pantry at the low end of the hall, and another linking the lord's chamber and the chamber used for dining (Fig. 69). This had direct access to the cellars for drinks, to the dais end of the hall for the service of food from the kitchen, and to the courtyard, so that bread and other foods could be brought in from the outer offices.

The other divisions in royal and major establishments included the separation of the bread and tableware services of the pantry from those of hand-washing and table linen. The latter were consigned to a department called the ewery, and will be discussed in the following chapter. As for the service of drinks and drinking vessels, the buttery was divided into the cellar, butlery of ale, pitcher-house and cup-house, as described in the royal ordinances of Edward IV.[7]

The chief officer overseeing these departments was the sergeant of the cellar. He ensured that all supplies brought in by the purchasing officers, the purveyors of wine and the ale takers, were measured, adjudged for quality, safely stored, and details of their distribution and accidental loss carefully recorded. In addition, he had overall responsibility for all the necessary equipment and utensils, including the fine silver and gold vessels provided by the counting-house and the jewel-house for serving the drinks into the chambers. He personally served the King with wine and ale, collaborating with the yeoman of the cellar for the King's mouth to decide which were best, and assisted by a groom for the King's mouth. The drawing of the wine from the casks and its delivery up to the buttery bar for the hall, the chambers, and for liveries to individuals, was carried out by a yeoman and two groom trayers. To do this they used quart, half-pitcher, pitcher [gallon?] and sester measures. Finally, there was a page of the cellar, who had to wash out the barrels, tubs and pitchers, as well as the drinking pots and cups, presumably drying the latter with cup-cloths. The distribution of ale was organized in a similar manner, a yeoman versoure measuring and recording the incoming supplies and their delivery by two yeomen versoures, with a page to do the washing and cleaning.

The pitcher-house and cup-house were headed by a chief yeoman, again responsible to the sergeant of the cellar. With three yeomen colleagues, two attending each sitting at meal-times, he supervised his two grooms as they brought up the measured pitchers of wine and ale, counting their number, and recording this on a tally which was split with the yeomen trayers and versoures. He also took charge of all the pots made of silver or pewter, the leather pitchers and wooden tankards used for carrying up the drinks, and the cups of silver, turned ash-wood and other materials used at meal-times. Each evening the grooms also set out the livery pots for those allowed overnight refreshments, collecting them and returning them to the cup-house each morning for washing and re-filling, the washing forming a large part of the page's duties.

In total, a permanent staff of eighteen was retained for buttery duties in the royal household, some noble houses employing perhaps just four, a yeoman and a groom in the cellar and in the buttery, while gentry families would have proportionately less. This reflected the scale of their respective operations, however, rather than any real differences in their practical work.

Since barrels were heavy, and their contents had to be kept cool, it proved most convenient to store them in cellars either below ground or in basements at ground level. Quite often they were divided into two units, the main ale cellars being accessible from the low end of the hall, and the wine (and strong ale?) cellars accessible from the dais or chamber end, as at Gainsborough Old Hall. In other establishments, the cellars occupied single large rooms, especially those sited beneath great halls. Few adjacent cellar/buttery offices have yet been recognized, but there is a good fourteenth-century example at the southern end of the great hall at Kenilworth Castle. With ready access to the main cellar and to staircases up to both the dais and the chambers, it is well lit, the window-sill being cut broad and flat so as to provide either a good writing surface for cellar-books, and/or an ideal place to fill the pitchers ready for service, ledges in the walls opposite supporting the stillages holding the barrels. In the room next door there is a convenient fireplace and a latrine for the comfort of the cellar staff.

From a number of manuscript illustrations it is seen that most ale and wine barrels were bound with wooden bands, and were stored horizontally, although some, known as stands, were open-topped and vertical, predecessors of the later bell-casks.[8] To tap them, the cellar staff selected either their gimlet or one of two different-sized augurs called terriers and began to bore an upward-sloping hole some four-fingers' height above the lowest part of the barrel rim.[9] This ensured that the sediment or dregs always remained undisturbed. Immediately after piercing the staves, the augur was withdrawn and a faucet [tap], a tampion [bung] or a 'canel of box' driven into the hole with the aid of a mallet. The 'canels'

Figure 50. The buttery.

1–3. Carrying up the pitchers, and drawing off the ale or wine, 13c.

4. Filling a wine-pot, Friskney, Lincs., 14c.?

5–6. Using wooden cups for drink taken from a standard and from a barrel, 14c.

7. Filling a pitcher from a cask on the buttery bench, Ludlow, Salop, 15c.

were bungs bored with a small central hole so as to receive a smaller, more easily-removed bung. Most illustrations of cellar or buttery staff show them held in one hand while a pitcher is held in the other as it fills.

Since the barrels were prone to leakage or secondary fermentation, they had to be checked by candlelight every night and, as a precaution, have their heads washed down with cold water. Should there be a leak, strips of linen cloth were driven into the joints using a 'chinching iron' and the butt end of an adze.[10]

In addition to the strong, ordinary and small ales and beers in the ale cellars, the following wines were usually stored in addition to ordinary imported red and white wines:[11]

Bastard: sweet Spanish wine, resembling muscadel;

Campolet: a white wine;

Hippocras: sugar-sweetened and spiced red or white wine prepared in the buttery (see the recipe on p. 353);

Claret: yellowish or light red wine from the Bordeaux region – part of the English crown lands in France for some 300 years;

Clary: honey-sweetened spiced white wine, with a hot, gingery flavour, prepared in the buttery(see the recipe on p. 353);

Malmsey: a strong sweet wine from the neighbourhood of Monem-vasia at the southern tip of Morea in Greece;

Muscadel: a strong sweet wine from the muscat grape;

Osey: a sweet French wine, *vin d'Aussai,* from Alsace;

Piment: red or white honey-sweetened herbed and spiced wine prepared in the buttery (see the recipe on p. 354);

Respis: according to Andrew Boorde, 'All maner of wynes be made of grapes excepte respyce, the whiche is made of a bery' – it appears to have been a sweet red wine made of raspberries;[12]

Rhenish: the characteristic white wines of the Rhine valley;

Romney: sweet red or white wine from Greece;

Tyre: originally a strong sweet wine from Tyre in Syria, but also imported from Calabria or Sicily;

Vernage: strong, sweet Italian wine;

Vernage wine cut: 'cut', or 'cuit', was new wine reduced by boiling and

given added sweetening; it was used both as a drink on its own, or as an addition to weaker wines in order to improve their keeping qualities.

When serving any ales, beers or wines, the barrels were tapped, and their contents run directly into large pots or vessels called pitchers or pots, the word jug being unknown in the medieval period. From their baluster shapes, it appears that many of the pitchers shown in drawings were large earthenware vessels, probably the same as the '12 earthen pitchers for beer 3s.', '8 gallon pitchers for beer 1s.', or '4 earthen pitchers for beer 8d.' listed in contemporary buttery inventories.[13] Most of them had tall bodies, frequently bulbous, single handles, and either a plain rim, or one pulled forward to form a pouring lip. Some adopted tall conical bases, narrower necks and grooved sides, to copy pewter or silver pots as closely as possible.[14] From the late fourteenth century a rather different shape began to be made, one with a wider neck, a rather more cylindrical or bulbous body, two, or occasionally three or four strong handles, and sometimes a hole near the base for a faucet or tap. Significantly, they have no means of sealing their mouths, and so were not intended for the storage of either drinks or other foodstuffs. Holding about a gallon, they were ideal for carrying drinks from the cellar into the buttery, or even on into the hall, for immediate use. [15]

Figure 51, opposite. Pitchers, tankards, pots and cups.
(1–3) earthenware pitchers for carrying ale from the barrels to the buttery and on into the hall etc., from Lyveden (Northants), Norwich and Doncaster, all 15c.; (4) a coopered can for the same purpose; (5–6) pewter pots to carry drinks from the cellar to the chamber or elsewhere, from near Tonbridge Castle (Kent), late 14c., and Deptford (Kent), c. 1500; (7) a red glass wine pot for the same purpose, from Eynsham Abbey (Oxon.), 13–15c.; (8–9) a wooden cup, and a mazer with silver-gilt rim, 15c. (10–12) an earthenware drinking pot and two stoneware cruses imported from Siegburg and Langerwehe, all from Sandal Castle Yorks., 15c.; (13) green and yellow-glazed lobed cup from west Surrey, 14–early 15c.; (14–15) green glazed cups made in west Surrey, from Sandal Castle, mid–late 15c.; (16) bluish-green glass cup, from Middle Pavement, Nottingham, 1400–80.

Wooden vessels for the same purpose were known as both cans and tankards, those supplied to the navy in 1495 being of one-gallon capacity, ideal for supplying one mess at table.[16] Presumably these were identical to those recovered from the wreck of the *Mary Rose*, cooper-made and bound with wooden bands. Other cans or pots were made of leather. Sir John Fastolf had four one-gallon pots and three pottle or four-pint leather pots in his buttery, and Thomas Greenwood of York had a gallon can and eight pottles in his.[17] There is little archaeological or visual evidence of their appearance, but a pitcher-house groom in the 1545 painting *The Field of the Cloth of Gold* is seen to hold two leather gallon pots, each tall and cylindrical, tapering towards the wide neck, and with one handle.

Gallon and pottle pots of metal might, in modest households, be made of pewter, and of silver or silver-gilt in those of higher status. Of the finest workmanship, they might be enamelled with their owners' coats of arms, daisies, flowers or other appropriate devices.[18] As shown in depictions of the marriage feast at Cana and the feast at Bethany, such as those on the roof bosses at Norwich Cathedral dating from the 1460s or 1470s, they could be of a restrained baluster shape, with flat lids hinged from the top of their single handles. Others had their much more pronounced baluster-shaped bodies mounted on a tall foot, and their lids raised as flattened domes. One of this type being filled is seen in a mural painting in All Saints Church, Friskney, Lincolnshire, and a late fifteenth- or early sixteenth-century example has been recovered from the Thames at Deptford.[19]

Glass bottles or jugs were quite rare, but do appear in a number of inventories, Elizabeth Sywardby having a particularly fine jug, enamelled and gilded, valued at 4d. in 1468.[20] Others found in excavations have been plain, or decorated with moulding, bands of coloured trailing, or dramatically swirling red spirals called marvering. Their rims were usually provided with a pouring lip, and their handles given a raised thumb-piece for a sound grip.[21]

In addition to receiving wine and ale at meal-times, members of large households were provided with further supplies for drinking ad lib during the rest of the day. The buttery therefore had to use some of the pots described above to issue 'liveries' each day, ensuring that each person was served the regulation quantity of liquor in a pot of appropriate quality. For example, the Kings' steward, as head of the domestic household, and presumably all nobles too, had to be served in silver pots.[22] The quantities for some individuals initially seem very high, until it is remembered that they were expected to be shared among that person's servants or staff. In Edward IV's court, the following liveries of drink were issued each day: [23]

	Pitchers of wine (4pt.?)	gallons of ale
The King	5	4½
Duke	3	6
Marquess	2½	5
Earl	2	5
Knight	½	1
Squire	½	
Steward	2	6
Treasurer	2	6
Controller	1	4
Cofferer	½	3
Sergeants	1	
Grooms	1	
Pages	½	

Come the end of the day, the pots had to be retrieved from their recipients, washed, dried, and refilled ready to be issued once more.

In major households, drinking cups were provided at meal-times, then collected, washed and wiped dry by the buttery staff. This meant that each person had to have a personal cup from which to drink their liveries at other times. In the royal palaces, any man of worship could exchange his 'old soyled cuppes of ayshe' for new ones at the cup-house.[24] These lathe-turned ash cups are shown in a number of manuscript illustrations and in carvings such as 'The Last Supper' boss in the nave of Norwich Cathedral. They are also well represented in the archaeological record, but since archaeologists persist in calling them bowls, they usually go unrecognized. They are saucer-shaped, some 6–7 inches in diameter by

1½–2 inches high, their rims turned to a narrow edge for ease of drinking. Handles were unnecessary, since in order to keep the rim perfectly clean, an important factor when cups were used communally, [25]

> The cup should be held between two fingers;
> The thumb should not touch the sweet wine…
> Drink and then turn the bowl to thy neighbour,
> So that his lips are not placed where thine were.

Cups of superior quality were made of mazer, the closely-knotted wood from burrs growing on maple trees. They were identical in form and function to the ash cups but, to confirm their higher status, were strengthened and enriched with metal rims and feet. The earlier 'mazers' as they were called from the early fourteenth century, had relatively plain, narrow rims, and a decorative disc called a frounce set into their centres.[26] From around 1450 their rims began to grow much taller, virtually doubling their capacity, and their frounces transformed into 'prints' or 'bosses', embossed and engraved discs held in place by a surrounding frame. The latter offered great scope for decoration, themes including personal coats of arms, monograms, merchants' marks, and religious emblems such as the Trinity, the Majesty, Our Lady, IHS, IHC. The gentry's best mazers could be quite elaborate, Lady Euphemia Langton having one with a tall silver foot, a silver-gilt rim and three lions. But these were modest when compared with those in royal use. Henry IV's included a huge example which contained three gallons, while Henry V had mazers garnished with three angels in silver-gilt and other enrichments of gold, pearls, sapphires and balanites.

Another prestigious form of wooden cup was made from the shell of the coconut. Since these only grew around the tropical shores of the Indian and Pacific Oceans, it is surprising to find them appearing in London as early as 1337, where one with a foot and cover of silver cost 30s. By the fifteenth century they regularly appear in the inventories of well-to-do houses, twenty being listed in the York registry between 1394 and 1487.[27] Cups made of the shells of the ostrich were much rarer, but Nicholas Sturgeon, a priest, was able to leave two in his will of 1454, while in the 1390s four owned by the Duke of Lancaster, later Henry IV, had a specially-made carrying case to ensure their safety in transport.[28]

Earthenware drinking vessels are rarely mentioned in medieval records, but the numerous small pitchers of about a pint capacity made throughout the country were most probably used for informal drinking. Others were imported from the Rhineland potteries at Siegburg and Langerwehe, their great attraction being that they were made of salt-glazed stoneware, hard, tough, impervious and well glazed.[29] This trade started in the early fourteenth century, but accelerated from the middle and late fifteenth century. Accounts record the Howards paying 8d. for drinking 'crewses' for their household in 1481, for example, while the Northumberlands were buying 240 'stone crusis' each year at the rate of a halfpenny each.[30]

A number of English potteries, influenced by the success of these cruses, began to make earthenware copies finished with glossy lead glazes.[31] They also began to make vessels we recognize clearly as cups.

The earliest had the same shallow form as wooden cups or mazers, with a narrow foot, but had the rim pinched into a number of lobes, interspersed with two or more handles.[32] Clearly this enabled different people to drink from them, each using a separate section of the rim, as described previously when discussing wooden cups. To create additional interest, these cups, made from the late thirteenth century onwards, had miniature stags, dogs, trees or human figures set in their bowls so that they would gradually emerge as the liquor was consumed. In the latter decades of the fifteenth century, deeper, narrower two-handled cups were introduced into the repertoire, the most significant potteries to produce these being on the Hampshire/Surrey border, where they were glazed yellow or green, and in West Yorkshire, where the local red clay was glazed to produce a range of dark browns to metallic blacks.[33] Craftsmen in the latter place specialized so heavily in cups that they were known as 'cuppers' rather than potters, their product probably replacing the traditional wooden cups of that region shortly after 1500.

Since they were chiefly made in Europe, Egypt and Spain, the glass cups used on English tables from the thirteenth century onwards were always restricted to relatively high-status families. The native glasshouses

Figure 52. Cups.

1. Silver, with gilt knop and trefoil bands, from Lacock Church, Wiltshire.

2. The Royal Gold Cup, Paris, *c.* 1380, later owned by the Duke of Bedford.

3. Silver gilt, *c.* 1480–1500, from Kimpton Church, Hampshire.

already well established here by the early fourteenth century appear to have concentrated on window glass rather than on tableware.[34] Records such as the 1463 Hull port books show how cargoes including baskets of drinking glasses were being imported from the port of Middleburg in the Netherlands.[35] From here they would be carried by ship up the river systems to cities like York, where shopkeepers such as Thomas Gryssop had six glasses valued at 4*d.* and two large glasses at 6*d.* in 1466.[36] Similarly, a barrel containing 240 glasses valued at 10*s.* was imported into Southampton in 1469, and one and a half 'skoke' of drinking glasses into Newcastle upon Tyne in 1499–1500 by the *George* from Denmark.[37] Examples excavated from a variety of high-status sites show that the tall-stemmed goblets popular in earlier periods were largely replaced by beaker-shaped cups in the early fifteenth century. Some 3–5 inches high, they were made of clear or green glass, either plain or decorated with applied ribs, roundels called prunts, moulded motifs, enamelling or gilding.[38]

Glass drinking vessels might be elegant and attractive but unless of exceptional quality and enriched with enamelling and gilding they never approached the status and magnificence of those made of precious metals. In royal households, they might be of solid gold enhanced with enamels of unsurpassable design and craftsmanship such as the Royal Gold Cup made in Paris in c.1380 for the French royal household and acquired by John, Duke of Bedford some twenty years later. They could be very large and heavy, Sir John Fastolf having some silver-gilt cups bearing his crest in enamel, others looking like fountains with columbine flowers, still more with roses, or knops like pearls, their weights ranging from some forty to sixty ounces.[39] Most were provided with covers terminating in decorative finials, these being essential for the cupbearer to use when tasting a few drops of wine from the main cup as part of the assaying ceremony carried out when serving a great lord.

Some indication of the numbers of vessels required to enable a buttery to serve its ale and wine efficiently is given by the 1505 accounts for the Lord Mayor of London's Feast. For this meal alone it was necessary to purchase 24 great stoneware pots, 184 earthenware pitchers, 720 earthenware pots for ale and wine, and 800 'asshen cuppes', all of which would have occupied a considerable length of shelf-space.[40]

The Pantry

Having completed this survey of the 'wet' area of the butler/pantler's domain, the 'dry' areas will now be considered, starting with the pantry of the middle to late fifteenth-century royal household.[41]

This department was controlled by a sergeant called the chief panterer to the King's mouth. His was a largely administrative post, responsible for taking delivery of the bread by tally from the bakehouse each morning, reporting the quantity to the counting house, while his yeoman brever separately reported how many loaves were actually distributed each day, to ensure that none was wasted or stolen. The practical work was

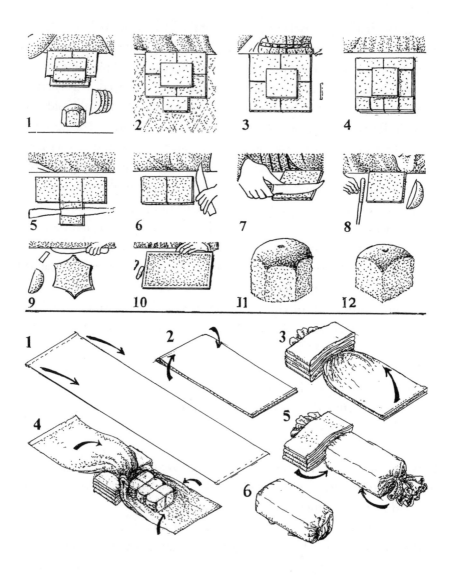

Figure 53, above, opposite. Trenchers.

1. Trenchers for a prince? 14c.

2. For a king, with a salt in front, 1360–80.

3. For a king, 15c.

4. For an archbishop, with four salts in front, 1466.

5. For a Knight of the Garter, c. 1360–80.

6. For a knight, c. 1325–40.

7–8. For ordinary people, at St Kew, Cornwall, 1490s, and the Earl of Warwick, c. 1483.

9–10. Silver? trenchers for a peacock feast, 1364, and Richard II, the Dukes of York, Gloucester and Ireland.

11–12. Loaves 'chipped' for general use, and squared for wrapping in a portpain.

Figure 54, below, opposite. The portpain.

Having been laid out flat, the fine linen portpain was (1) doubled end-to-end, (2) the folded end grasped tightly and twisted like a toffee paper, and (3) held down beneath folded towels, over which the loose top end was folded back. Having placed six or seven loaves bottom-to-bottom on the lower end, (4) fold its sides over them, then fold the top back over them, (5) twist the loose end like the folded end, and finally (6) tuck these underneath to form a neat package.

undertaken by three yeomen panterers, two grooms and two pages, who brought in the loaves from the bakehouse cart, stored them in clean bread-bins, pared them for use, and packed them in containers called porters in which they were delivered to the hall and chamber. They also made salts for the hall, these probably being identical to those made for Archbishop Neville, salt spread over a square bread trencher with a knife, then cut into four (square) pieces.[42] A separate page for the mouth prepared the loaves for the King's use, and carried his porter up to the chamber.

In noble houses, a much smaller pantry staff was required, the Earl of Northumberland, for example, having just one yeoman and one groom to prepare his bread.[43] Lesser pantries stored their bread in bins, such as the two 'bredd binges' still in the Gainsborough pantry in 1625, or in aumbries, old wine barrels called pipes, or lidded chests called arks or garners.[44] Before 8 a.m. each day, the pantler donned his linen apron and brought out the required number of loaves: the lord's being new, other fine bread one day old, coarse household bread three days old, and wholemeal bread for trenchers four days old. For the round white loaves, he used a special knife called a chipper to cut away the tougher sides of the crust, being careful not to remove too much of the fine inner crumb.[45] This probably explains the hexagonal faceted sides of loaves frequently seen in contemporary stained glass and carvings. For the lord's table, the loaves had to be treated in a rather different manner, six or seven being carefully chipped until square in plan and identical in size.[46] These were then wrapped in a linen cloth called a portpain ('bread-carrier') a yard wide by 7 feet 6 inches long, and doubled to half that length. Having grasped the folded end, it was tightly twisted like a toffee-paper, and held in place beneath a couple of folded towels. The topmost loose end of the portpain was then folded back over the towels, so that the loaves could be placed in a row, bottom to bottom, along the length still lying on the table. Having folded the sides of this length over the sides of the loaves, the topmost loose end was used to cover the loaves, the opposite end now being twisted like the other, and finally both twisted ends tucked under the loaves to produce a neat, box-like wrapping (Fig. 54). Since the Earl of Northumberland's portpain was only 3 feet 9 inches long, it must have been used in a similar way, but to wrap perhaps only three or four loaves.[47]

The bread trenchers of wholemeal bread were squared slices, perhaps half an inch in thickness, used as personal cutting boards on which portions of solid foods were placed – once they had been cut out of the joints on the dishes – so they could be cut into smaller pieces and lifted to the mouth. They also held small quantities of salt or sauce, but they were not plates. Food was never piled on them, and sloppy foods never placed on them (being eaten directly from the dish). Their function was to preserve the tablecloth from knife-cuts and any form of soiling, not to hold the whole of a person's entire course before them. At informal meals, diners might make their own trenchers, Chaucer recording how 'They sette hemselfe atte dyner, & made trenchers of brede to putte theyr mete upon', but usually they were prepared in the pantry.[48] To make them, one pantry knife was used to cut the trencher loaves into square blocks, and another particularly sharp blade produced perfectly smooth surfaces as it cut the blocks into square slices. All the waste bread trimmed off both the white and the coarser loaves was carefully collected, for it provided a good food supply for the lord's hounds. [49]

Trenchers of permanent, hard materials were also used at both ends of the social scale, the wealthy using them to demonstrate their status, and the poor to economize on the use of bread. Silver examples were very expensive, the Prior of Durham's matching pair costing 12s. in the 1360s.[50] As shown in manuscript illustrations, they might be rectangular or hexagonal, and there are descriptions of trenchers with the head of St John the Baptist, as owned by Alice Langwath in 1467.[51] For ordinary use, wooden trenchers were imported into this country from Denmark in large quantities.[52] In 1499/1500, for example, the *George* and *James* of Newcastle upon Tyne shipped in over two and a half thousand, valued at between 16 to 25 for a penny, showing just how cheap they were.[53] Some may have been purchased in quantity for communal use too, the London Blacksmiths' Company having a stock of 72 ready for use in their hall in 1496.[54]

The pantler was also responsible for keeping, preparing and serving salt for the tables. This was received in the form of solid blocks which had to be reduced to a smooth, fine powder, ideally by shaving it with an ivory plane that measured 2 inches wide and 3 inches long.[55] If the

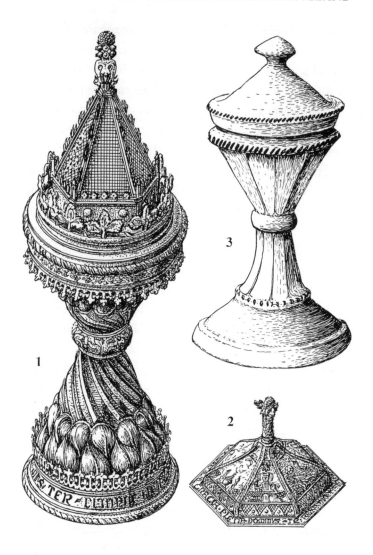

Figure 55. Salts.

1. The New College, Oxford, salt, 1493.

2. Lid of a pewter salt, with the Annunciation, Virgin and Child, and Adoration in the panels, the 'Ave' round the rim, and the Virgin as its finial.

3. Yellow-glazed earthenware salt, from Sandal Castle, Yorks., late 15–early 16c.

salt had been delivered in a stained or unrefined state, the pantler might dissolve it in three times its volume of water, boil it, strain it through a towel or sieve, boil it again, skim off any scum, and continue the boiling until the brine evaporated to the point of crystallization. Tipped out on to a cloth, it was finally spread out to dry in the sun, ready for use.[56]

For the most impressive meals, the salt cellars were made of solid gold, the finest being of amazing magnificence. In 1439 Henry VI had two such salts, one shaped as a man and the other a woman, each effigy holding salt cellars in their hands. Garnished with 26 rubies, 14 sapphires, 96 pearls, and 14 bosses each of three additional pearls, they weighed almost 6lb, and were valued at £140.[57] Most of the nobility used silver-gilt for their best salts, some being made in the form of a lion, a dragon, towers (or even towers with a palace), or some personal motto or device. Sir John Fastolf had 'Me faunt fere' on a wreath around the top of one of his salts, and his arms and a double rose engraved on two others.[58] They were usually provided with covers, the pantler making sure that the salt within never touched them in order to avoid any spillage onto the table. Large households might also having matching sets of perhaps six or twelve silver salts for less important place settings.[59] Other salts for more general use were made of pewter, tin, latten or glass.[60] Visual evidence for the appearance of English fifteenth-century salts appears in the Beauchamp Pageant manuscript, this being confirmed by the recovery of the lids of two fourteenth-century pewter examples from the Thames foreshore.[61] These have shallow ogee domes and tall knobs, one now in the Museum of London having panels depicting the Annunciation, the Virgin and Child and the Magi with '[GR]ACIA. P[LENA]. DOMINUS. TE:+REX...' [... full of grace, the Lord is with thee], all surmounted by a figure of the Virgin. Similar salts made of lead-glazed white earthenware were probably made from the late fifteenth century in a number of north-country potteries, their conical bodies, bases and lids being knife-cut to reproduce the faceted shape of contemporary silverware. Examples have been excavated from Sandal Castle and Haselden Hall in Wakefield, as well as from the nearby Potovens pottery kilns.[62]

Since many high-quality dishes had to be sprinkled with powdered spices after being carved, the well-equipped pantry could have a pestle and

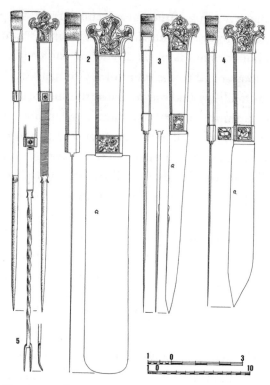

Figure 56. Carving set, late 15c.

This Continental set, with hardstone handles and gilt finials, is perhaps rather more complete than most used in England. It includes (1) a steel; (2) a serviteur, with one sharp edge and tip for serving the carved food; (3) a narrow knife for holding firm 'noble' foods; (4) a broad knife for carving; and (5) a small fork, probably to accompany the serviteur.

mortar or a pepper-mill to grind them, or a small grater. The resulting powder was then tipped into a silver casket ready to be carried to the table. One owned by Thomas Morton of York in 1449 was engraved 'strew on powder', to confirm its use. Weighing almost 5oz, it may have had internal divisions so as to hold a selection of the required spices. [63]

A number of dishes had to be finished by being re-heated when actually on the table. Partridges, for example, had to be minced, seasoned and then 'set upon a chaufing-dishe of coles to warme', while lampreys were to be lifted from their pastry onto a dish lined with slices of fried bread, seasoned, mixed with jelly from the pie, and placed on 'a chaffire hoote' ready for the lord.[64]

The chafing dishes for table-use had to be of very high quality were they destined for a royal table. James III of Scotland had one of silver-gilt while that used by the Archbishop of York contained just over a pound of solid silver.[65] Most other people used bronze chafing dishes – such as Margaret Pigott's 'brass chauffer for the table' – either English-made or imported from the Low Counties, or they owned cheap earthenware copies made locally or imported from the Continent, especially from the Saintonge region of France.[66] Each chafer had a shallow bowl-shaped body mounted on a tall hollow foot which effectively insulated it from the tablecloth as well as providing draught for the glowing charcoal above and catching its fine grey ashes. Three knobs rising from the rim enabled metal dishes of food to be placed on top without smothering the fire, while handles around the sides allowed the whole vessel to be moved to and fro as required.

The pantry also appears to have been responsible for knives used by the lord and perhaps his principal guests, as well as those employed by the carver. In 1503, for example, Richard Brampton, gentleman of the pantry to Queen Elizabeth of York, paid 8s. for a pair of enamelled knives for the Queen's own use, and 13s. 4d. for a pair of carving-knife blades.[67] The latter, if following the usual English practice, comprised a broad blade and a narrow one to act as a skewer to steady the joints when carving venison or other 'nobel' meats (see figure opposite).[68] Such knives were usually of very high quality, as was indicated by their price. Those used by Sir John Fastolf included a set of three, all with ivory handles secured by gilt rivets, and contained within a single purpose-made sheath.[69] The personal knives used by the lord would be of similar quality, their blades probably inlaid with precious metals, and their handles beautifully enamelled and garnished. The pair of knives made for John Baret of Bury St Edmunds shortly before 1463, for example, were inlaid with his personal motto of *Grace me governe* in silver.[70]

The reason why only a few knives were stored in the pantry was that virtually everyone, male and female, carried their personal eating knives in sheaths hanging at their belts at all times. These had sharp, single-

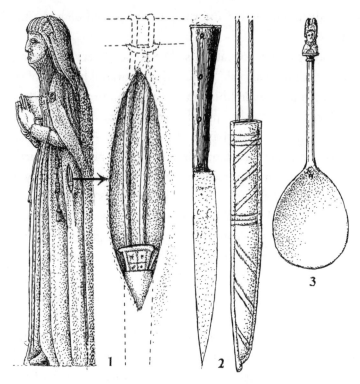

Figure 57. Knives and spoons.

1. Everyone carried their personal eating knife in a sheath hung from their belt, as seen in this effigy of Margaret, Lady Gascoigne, in Harewood parish church, *c.* 1461–6.

2. An early–mid-15c. knife and late 14c. sheath from London.

3. A pewter spoon with a woman in horned head-dress as its finial, 15c.

edged and pointed blades, most up to the early fifteenth century being whittle-tanged, with a rectangular shaft extending through the centre of the handle. These were then largely superseded by scale-tangs, each side of the flat tang having panels of stained wood, usually boxwood, horn or bone riveted to each side.[71] Decorated with silver, they cost up to 1*s.* or 2*s.* each, in contrast to ordinary ones at only a 1*d.*, 2*d.* or 3*d.*[72] Their close-fitting leather sheaths were frequently decorated with a variety of creased or stamped motifs, and incorporated thongs by which they could be suspended.[73] Manuscript illustrations show men with them either tucked into or hung from their belts, while funerary effigies of clerics and women sometimes show slits cut into the left sides of their habits or gowns, with the knife handles and suspension cords conveniently hung within.

Spoons could be carried in the same way, or perhaps tucked into a purse or into the hat.[74] The simplest were carved out of wood, the eighth-century word 'spon' actually meaning a splinter of wood. They were best made of smooth-grained, water-tolerant and virtually tasteless timber such as maple (later sycamore), which was used for this purpose up to the middle of the twentieth century in Wales. The other cheap alternative was shaped and pressed cattle horn, one owned by a Beverley mason in 1430 being valued at 2d.[75] Their advantage was that they were 'neither so in use no[r] rough to the lips as wood is, but lyght plyaunt and smooth, that with a little licking will always be kept as clean as a dy.'[76]

Next in quality came those of pewter, cast with shallow fig-shaped bowls, long, narrow polygonal or round shafts, and terminals in the form of acorns, lions, apostles, jesters, or the busts of aldermen, maidenheads or those with horned head-dresses.[77] Silver spoons were made to exactly the same designs, and also with folding shafts so that they could be doubled up and perhaps slipped into leather sheaths by which they could be hung from the belt.[78] These were clearly personal items, like many other silver spoons, but matching sets of six, twelve, twenty-four, thirty-six or even forty-eight were kept in some butteries, ready for setting the tables in the chamber and perhaps on the dais too.[79] Such spoons usually cost around 2s. 6d. each, but if gilded and decorated the price might rise to almost 7s. and, if gold, to as much as £2.[80] Clearly such spoons were those which were reserved solely for the use of a great lord. Forks were similarly exclusive, since they were only used for eating the sweet, syrup-preserved green ginger, and presumably other sticky confections, when they were served at the 'void' at the end of the meal. Sometimes, forks were combined with a spoon, while others were more decorative, having their stems supported by dragons' heads.[81]

Such forks would have been used in conjunction with the spice plate, the greatest and most impressive of all medieval serving vessels. In these the comfits, green ginger, marmalades and other preserves were carried before the lord and his chief guests as they stood for the void. Sir John Fastolf had three. The largest, a massive 110-ounce silver-gilt example, was shaped like a double rose, with his helmet or crest picked out in bright enamels in the centre. The others each weighed over 70 ounces, both silver-gilt, one bearing his coat of arms, and the other writhen decoration.[82]

The other serving vessels stored in the buttery/pantry included chargers, large enough to carry a swan or other large joint; platters with flat bottoms and low rims, ideal for carving; dishes with flat or convex bottoms and deeply curved sides leading up to their rims, designed for pottages; and saucers, like miniature dishes, to hold mustard and other piquant sauces. Their physical dimensions are rarely recorded, but their size may be estimated both from their weights and a number of surviving examples, for instance:[83]

chargers	c. 40–50oz.	c. 16–18ins.
platters & dishes	c. 20–25oz.	c. 10–11ins.
saucers	c. 7oz.	c. 5 to 7ins.

In a household of any size the accumulated value of all the silverware represented a substantial part of its capital assets, the equivalent of its deposit account in an age without modern banking. In a prosperous craftsman's house, it might amount to £10–£15, a gentry house around £30, and for a great lord or churchman, perhaps £300, truly vast sums for that period.[84] These figures are approximate, but they do demonstrate the need for the tightest security. In the royal household, the jewel-house held most of the plate, issuing it to the service department as and when it was required. The same procedure must have been followed in noble houses. The cofferer's vaulted strongroom was the obvious place to store it, but at Bolton Castle John Lewyn provided Lord Scrope with a separate concealed strongroom adjacent to the buttery and pantry, ideal for storing his plate, yet convenient for serving the hall and chambers. Within butteries and pantries of any scale, the provision of lockable aumbries and lockable doors would have been essential, both to prevent deliberate theft and to ensure that honest servants remained honest.

The value of silver always restricted its use, but those who could not afford it, or were not of sufficient status to be served with it, such as

Figure 58. Lighting.

1. Pewter candlestick from London, *c.* 1400.

2–4. Iron pricket-cum-socket, pricket-cum-rushlight, and rushlight holders, all from medieval York.

5. A beeswax torch held by a chamber-servant, used to provide ambient lighting, early 15c.

most of those dining in the hall, pewter provided an excellent substitute. It was made in the identical shapes, was kept highly polished to look as silver-like as possible, and was purchased by the 'garnish', this comprising two chargers, and a dozen each of platters, dishes and saucers.[85] Other pieces, such as spoons or salts, would have been bought individually.

Further down the social scale came wooden dishes, platters and saucers, these too following silver shapes, but being described as being wooden, treen, or 'of tree'. They were usually made from ash, with others of field maple or alder, all of which could be lathe-turned to produce smooth-finished, moisture-tolerant and relatively non-absorbent vessels.[86] Perhaps rather surprisingly, earthenware versions of these tablewares were virtually unknown in the fifteenth century, only being introduced in the early 1500s.

For most of the year there was no need for any illumination on the table since meal-times were designed to take the best advantage of natural light, being held between 10 a.m. and 4 p.m. Even so, candles or rush lights were essential in the darkest days of winter. The largest were probably of pricket form, with a spike on which to stick the base of the candle, but most appear to have had sockets, these being far more suitable for the usual wax or tallow candles which had a diameter of just under one inch. The usual metal form, either in gilt, silver, brass/latten or pewter, had a narrow cylindrical shaft some 4 to 6 inches high, rising from a deep, flat-topped round base.[87] In less prestigious locations, wooden candlesticks were also used, these being fitted with pairs of iron 'flowers'. Although their wooden bases have rotted away, the ironwork flowers have been recovered from excavations, some having candle sockets, some pricket-spikes and some V-shaped holders for rushlights, while quite a number combine two or more of these features.[88]

The provision of tableware and lighting equipment described here formed only a part of the responsibility of the buttery and pantry, for in most households these offices looked after all the table linen and utensils for hand-washing too.

CHAPTER TWENTY-ONE

The Ewery

The ewer was the vessel from which water was poured over the hands when washing before meals, but the ewery, as a domestic office, dealt with a much larger range of duties. The fullest account of a major ewery appears in Edward IV's Black Book of the Household. Its chief officer, the sergeant, received all the silver and silver-gilt ewers, basins and cups he required from the controller, the weight of each piece being carefully recorded. He received all the table linen by measure in the same manner, had it marked (rather like modern laundry marks), and was personally responsible for its care. Any items which became badly worn had to be submitted to the controller's inspection and, only if he agreed, be disposed of to the scullery, saucery, confectionery, or the surgeons. Every day, before each meal, the sergeant and his staff had to prepare the hall and chambers for use, carrying in the wood and coals for the fires, the rushes to cover the floors, and the water for hand-washing. Having wiped the tables, they covered them with tablecloths, and set out their wares on similarly covered ewery tables and cupboards. After meals, they collected their wares and the chamber table linen and kept it safe until it was required again. Only the hall tablecloths remained in use for days at a time, being changed but twice a week unless they had become particularly soiled.[1] Similar procedures were followed in most households. Although they might be on a smaller scale, they used a comparable range of artefacts.

'No man schulde take mete but that he anoon before waished him', instructed Reginald Pecock in 1499.[2] This was an important preliminary, since fingers were used to handle food throughout every meal. The standard equipment for hand-washing was an ewer, a vessel from which water was poured over the hands, and a basin, which caught the water, and might have been used for rinsing before drying the hands on a towel. In peasant houses, earthenware ewers and basins, or even coopered vessels, may have been used, but husbandmen, craftsmen and all prosperous members of society had metal ewers. Thus we learn from the probate inventories of the diocese of York that T. Walmsley, a rector in 1479, had 3 stone ewers valued at 6s.; J. Cadeby, a mason in 1430, a hanging tin ewer worth 3s. 4d.; and R. Barber in 1497, two basins, a laver and pewter pots priced at 3s. 4d.[3]

The cheapest ewers were of pewter or tin, the better latten or brass, and the best of silver, or even gold. Most held under a pint of water, and were provided with a spout to produce a fine stream, and a handle which allowed a steady, constant flow. In the early thirteenth century, cast bronze ewers were made in the form of mounted knights, lions or deer. Their main area of production appears to have been north Germany and the Low Countries, but much cheaper earthenware copies were made by English potters for those unable to afford the beautiful and accurately modelled originals. Some of these bronze 'aquamaniles' (a collectors' term introduced in the late nineteenth century) remained in everyday use for centuries. At Durham Priory, 'the ewer pourtrayed like a man on horseback, as he had been riding or hunting, which served the sub-Prior to wash at the [refectory] top table' was still being used in the 1530s.[4]

Around the first quarter of the fourteenth century, London founders began to make pear-shaped cast bronze ewers, each standing on three tall legs and bearing inscriptions around their bodies, such as:[5]

+IE:SVI:APELLE:LAWR/IE:SERF:TVT:PAR:AMVR CF
(I am called a laver, I serve all for love)
+IESVI:LAWR:GILBERT:E/T:MEMBLERA:MAL:IDEDERT
(I am the laver Gilbert, who carries me off, may he obtain evil from it)

Their spouts were similar to those of modern jugs, but others shown in fourteenth-century manuscripts had tubular spouts braced to their bodies by horizontal bars. Examples of this slightly later type have been found in various locations from the Scottish borders down to the south coast, some being datable to the fifteenth century by accompanying coin hoards.[6] They are most probably the lavers listed in fifteenth-century

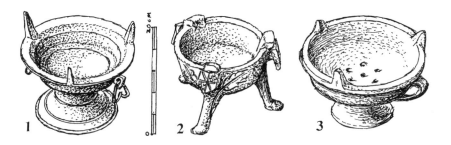

Figure 59. Chafers for the table.

1. Cast brass, 15c.

2. Earthenware, with Bishop Despenser's arms, from North Elmham, Norfolk, late 15–early 16c.

3. Earthenware, from Sandal Castle, Yorks., early 15c.

inventories, where they were accompanied by wash basins probably made in the same metal. Again from the diocese of York, in 1409 Robert Schylbotyll of Scarborough was noted as having '4 old basins, 3 lavers', and in 1497 Richard Barber of Hull owned '2 basins, [and] a laver'.[7]

It is interesting to consider why these vessels had three legs. These are more difficult to cast than flat bases, and are only found on pots and posnets designed to stand within a fire. It is unlikely that they were placed in the hearth fire to warm their hand-washing water, for their sooty bases would introduce unwelcome dirt into the chamber. However, they could have been stood over a charcoal fire, perhaps in a chafing dish (above), for that would only leave a fine dusty ash, easily brushed off to leave the bronze bright and clean. The other form of cast bronze ewer also had a pear-shaped body, now mounted on a short conical foot, but its tubular spout was much shorter, emerging just below the rim.[8] This too is shown in fourteenth-century manuscripts (Fig. 60.13), and was replicated in the green-glazed Surrey whitewares then being made at Kingston upon Thames.[9]

Due to the practice of melting down and modernizing old-fashioned pieces of pewter and silverware, hardly any medieval ewers of this quality

Figure 60. Ewers.

1 and 2) Cast bronze, North German, found at Hexham, Northumb., and a stag, 13c.; (3–5) Earthenware ewers from Norfolk, Nottingham and York, 13c.; (6) Earthenware, from Saintonge, France, found at Exeter, late 13c.; (7) Cast bronze, bearing, in translation, 'I am the laver of Gilbert, he who carries me off, may he obtain evil from it', found on the Gower, early 14c.; (8) Cast bronze, from Strata Florida, Ceredigion, c. 1300?; (9) Earthenware copy of cast bronze, Kingston upon Thames ?late 13c.; (10) Silver-gilt, 15c.; (11) Cast bronze, found in York, 14–15c.; (12) Earthenware, made in Scarborough, Yorks., found in Dartford, Kent, 13–14c.; (13–15) Ewers and a hanging laver in use, 14c.; (16) A hanging laver, basin and towel, c. 1500.

have survived. Even so, considerable evidence for their appearance may be gained from archival sources such as inventories. They seem to have been frequently made in pairs to match their basins, and in the largest households were of great size and quality, as in the following instances:[10]

> 1439: Henry VI, 'a pair of Basyns of silver over gilt, chaced with double roses and pounsed… weyng 20lb 8 unc.'
>
> 1449: Thomas Morton, two silver basins with gilt roses weighing 6lb. Two ewers of one set for the same weighing 2lb 10oz £15.
>
> 1459: John Fastolf, '2 Basyns, the verges gilt with popy leves, enameled with my maisters helmet in the bottom weing 169 unces [10lb 9oz], 2 Ewers gilt, enameled in the same wise weiyng 80oz [5lb]', [plus a similar set weighing 231 ounces, (4lb 8oz) 8 other ewers and a basin weighing 177oz (11lb 1 oz)].

Only the wealthiest could afford ewers of solid gold, such as the Duke of Exeter's 'ewer of gold, with a falcon taking a partridge with a ruby in its breast'.[11]

Special forms of ewer were also produced to serve specific functions. For informal meals, diners might wash their hands beneath a hanging laver, this being a cast bronze cistern resembling a legless cooking pot suspended from a hinged bow handle and having two (rarely four) teapot-like spouts. Many of these were imported from the Low Countries, Richard III's Act of 1483 decreeing 'That no merchaunt straunger bring into this Realme … Chafynge disshes [or] hangynge lavers.'[12] In manuscripts they are seen hanging from either wall-mounted brackets or from tall wooden pillars, their towels hanging above and their basins below.[13] In 1415 Robert Talkan, a York girdler, had an iron standing basin and a hanging ewer worth 12s. in his hall, presumably for communal use.[14]

Where large numbers had to wash quickly, as at the entrance to a great hall, the ewers would have to be particularly capacious. It is most probable that many of the finest decorated fourteenth- and fifteenth-century earthenware jugs, particularly those with tubular spouts, made in Scarborough and North Yorkshire, were intended to serve here as ewers.[15] Their materials would ensure their cheapness, but their quality would reflect the aspirations of the household.

Figure 61. Lavers for screens passages.

These were provided for hand-washing utensils etc. for the use of those dining in the halls at:

1. Cockermouth Castle, Cumbria, 1368–1408.

2. Little Wenham, Suffolk, early 15c.   4. Battle Hall, Kent, c. 1330.

3. Dacre Castle, Cumbria, early 14c.   5. Borthwick Castle, Midlothian, 15c.

For washing in hall, the ewers, lavers and basins were usually set out on a table or cupboard just within the entrance, in the screens passage. The basin was placed below the ewer cupboard against the centre of the screen at the Bishop's Palace at Wookey, Somerset, in 1461, for example.[16] In well-fitted establishments, lavatories for hand-washing were actually incorporated into the structure. In 1288 Master Robert the Goldsmith was paid £2 'for working of five heads of copper, gilded, for the laver of the small hall [and] for the images of the said laver, and for whitening the laver and gilding the hoops' at the Palace of Westminster. Perhaps his work influenced the laver built in the hall of Battle Hall near Leeds, Kent, around 1330.[17] This has a pair of castellated cisterns with leopard- or lion-headed spouts set into a magnificent crocketed and traceried niche, with a sink below to carry away the water. There are much plainer fourteenth-century examples at Cockermouth Castle and Dacre Castle in Cumbria, which have provision for shelves to hold either ewers or towels; and good fifteenth-century ones at Borthwick Castle, Borders, South Wingfield, Derbyshire, Little Wenham, Suffolk, and at Kirkham House, Paignton (now in the vicar's vestry at Paignton parish church).[18]

Here the ewerer set out the ewers, lavers, basins and towels:[19]

An ewere in halle there nedys to be
And chandelew [candles] schalle have and all napere
He schalle get water to gentilmen,
And als in alle yomen.

The same officer also warmed the water in cold weather, heating it over a chafing dish of charcoal. This is implied by the entries in the inventories for T. Crayke, gentleman (1488), for 6 basins and ewers 5s. and a chafer for heating water 3s. 4d., and for T. Morton, canon, for 3 brass basins and ewers 6s., a large chafer 10s., and a small chafer 1s. 4d.[20]

Throughout every meal, the ewerer sat at the bottom end of the hall, in an area known as 'the towelle', in order to ensure that clean water and towels were always available, the latter being changed at least twice a week unless they had been soiled by ill-mannered servants and guests who were unaware that,[21]

In the water wasschith so clene youre hands
That youre towell never ensoyled be
So foule that hit be loathly unto see
Wasschith wyth watire till your handes be clene,
And in youre cloth there no spotte be sene.

The quality of the towels reflected the prosperity of the house. Husband-men such as William Atkynson of Helperby (N. Yorkshire) used a pair made of harden, a very coarse cloth made from the roughest 'hards' left after heckling flax or hemp.[22] These were valued at 8*d*. in 1456. Next came plain-woven linen, twill linen probably woven with fine diagonal lines, and diaper linen woven in diamond patterns, as seen in various manuscript illustrations.[23] The finest were imported from Rennes in Brittany and from Flanders, two short towels of 'Rennes ware' costing 6*s*. 8*d*. in 1423.[24] In the hall, it is unlikely that anything better than the plainer linens were provided for everyday use, usually measuring around two ells (7 feet 6 inches) in length.

For those dining in the chamber, the ewerer took especial care in preparing their hand-washing water. To perfume it, and warm it in cold weather, he used a silver pan called a chafer. One glossary describes this as a 'Chawfore to make whote a thynge, as water'.[25] One owned by William Duffield of York weighed 16.5oz and was valued at £2 2s. 7½d. in 1452.[26] This was held over the glowing charcoals in a chafer of a firebasket type, such as Sir John Fastolf's 93oz silver 'chaufer to sett upon a table for hote water', and used for recipes such as this one which dates from the early fifteenth century:[27]

> To make water for washing at table
> Boil some sage, and pour off the water, and let it cool until it is as little
> more than warm. Add to it camomile or marjoram or rosemary, and boil
> it with orange peel. Laurel leaves are also good.

Alternatively rosewater could be used, this being distilled from rose petals to extract their fragrance and cordial qualities, comforting the heart and the brain.[28] Presumably the perfumed water would have been transferred into some of the impressive silver pottle pots, either enamelled or gilt, which stood on the ewery table at great feasts. Here they could be mixed with supplies of hot and cold waters, filtered through clean napkins, and assayed by tasting before use.[29] The cups used for this ceremony were variously described as, [30]

> 1420: 'A tastour of selver wyth myn owne marke ymade in the bottom';
> 1423: '1 little taster of silver for rosewater 1½oz. 4s.';
> c. 1430–40: 'A qwyte cuppe of tre [a cup of white wood]'.

For chamber use, the quality and size of the towels was usually superior to those in the hall. Those used before dining measured some 7 feet 6 inches by 9 inches, and were carried to the lord or master by a servant, along with the ewer and basin. By contrast, the washing at the end of the meal was a far more formal ceremony, for which the towels were required to cover the entire table top, drop at least half-way to the floor at each end, and still be long enough to have two broad pleats folded across them, all as a double thickness. The rough formula for calculating their length appears to have been length of table plus some 6 feet, all multiplied by two. This means, for example, that a 10-foot table would require a 32-foot towel. A well-equipped household would have a range of towels to fit its various tables, the following being used by William Kexby of York in 1410:[31]

> 4 ell towel = 15ft for a 3 to 4ft table
> 6 ell towel = 22ft 6in for a 5ft table
> 8 ell towel = 30ft for a 9ft table
> 9 ell towel = 33ft 9in for a 11ft table
> 15 ell towel = 56ft 3in for a 17ft table
> 20 ell towel = 75ft for a 31 ft table

Usually these were of white linen, but they might also be woven with blue borders or other embellishment.[32]

When preparing these towels for use, they were first doubled end-to-end, and placed on top of a surnap, a single piece of cloth half the length of the towel, but of identical width. In modest homes, it might be made

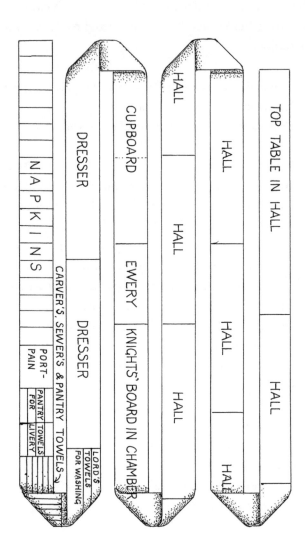

Figure 62. Napery.

This shows how the Northumberland household divided up its 87 yards of yard-wide linen each year.

from rough harden and simply placed on top of the table-cloth to protect it from splashes of water, but it was usually of white linen.[33] Only rarely were coloured surnaps used, Robert Schylbotyll having one of 'puce lewyn', a purple-brown linen imported from Leuven in the Low Countries, in 1409.[34]

Having described the utensils and fabrics employed for hand-washing, we can now move on to tablecloths, which were found almost universally. Even in relatively poor husbandmen's homes, the table was covered with a piece of harden, while a canvas cloth might provide long and practical service in some halls.[35] White linen, however, was the usual material for tablecloths, its quality reflected in its weave: either plain, twill, diaper, of Reine- (Rennes), or Paris-work. The standard width was one yard, most inventories acknowledging this by mentioning only their individual lengths. Broader cloths, such as the eight by two and a half yard example woven with fleur-de-lis listed in York in 1452, were exceptional, this one being valued at £3 6s. 8d.[36] In most large households the cloths were made up from bolts of linen, the clerks calculating what they should produce, even down to the last inch. In the Northumberland household, 70 ells or just over 87 yards (an ell measured 45 inches in England, 37.2 inches in Scotland and 27 inches in the Low Countries) of yard-wide linen were bought each year at 8d. the ell, a total cost of £2 6s. 8d. This produced:[37]

Top tablecloth for hall	1 at 21ft 8·75in	x	36in
Side tablecloth for hall	7 at 15ft	x	36in
Knights' tablecloth for great chamber	1 at 21ft 8·75in	x	36in
Ewery tablecloth	1 at 7ft 6in	x	36in
Cupboard cloth, double	1 at 7ft 6in	x	72in
Cupboard cloth, single	1 at 7ft 6in	x	36in
Kitchen dresser cloth	2 at 16ft 8·75in	x	36in
Lord's washing towels	2 at 7ft 6in	x	9in
Carvers' & Sewers' towels	4 at 7ft 6in	x	5·7in
Bearing towels for pantry	2 at 7ft 6in	x	5·7in
Pantry towels for livery	8 at 3ft	x	9in
Portpain for pantry	1 at 3ft 9in	x	36in
Napkins	18 at 1ft 6in	x	36in

Figure 63. Towels of office.

Waiters' towels on the left arm or shoulder: (1) c. 1230; (2) 14c.; (3) 14c.;
(6) 15c.; (11) 1490s.

4 and 5. Towels used for carrying stacks of dishes, Germany, 1490s.

6. Sewer, with towel over right shoulder, 15c.

7. Marshal, with his staff of office, 15c.

8. Carver, with towel over left shoulder, 1483.

9 and 10. Butler, with towel round the neck, 1483 and 1490s.

The relationship between the size of the tablecloths quoted above and that of the tables they were to cover, may be estimated using the 1496 inventory of the London Blacksmiths' Hall which lists:

Table	Size	Cloths	End Overhang	Side do.
Top	13ft x 3ft	17ft 6in x 3ft 9in	2ft 3in	4½in
		16ft 6in x 4ft 6in	1ft 9in	9in
Hall	16ft x 2ft	18ft x 3ft 2in	1ft	1ft 1in
		18ft 9in x 3ft 2in	1ft 4½in	1ft 1in
Cupboard	?	3ft 9in x 3ft 9in		
		8ft 3in x 3ft 4½in		

This suggests that the Northumberlands' hall had a top table around 17 feet long, its side tables about 13 feet, and its knights' table in the great chamber 17 feet, all about 2 feet or, perhaps, 2 feet 3 inches in width.[38]

The ewery cloths and cupboard cloths were used to cover the ewery table and the cupboard on which tableware was set out for both use and display in the room where the lord or master dined. In some royal and noble houses, the cupboard cloths were made of red worsted material, impractical as a table covering but ideal for draping the ascending shelves of the court cupboards where masses of magnificent gold and silverware were displayed.[39] Here its rich colour and soft surface would provide an ideal foil to the glistening metalwork.

The lord's washing towels have already been described but other towels served different functions. Those for the carvers and sewers were primarily badges of office. Since these individual members of the household usually had their duties allocated to them on a daily basis, perhaps performing a different role each day, it was important that everyone knew just who was doing what. When at the ewery table, the carver had a towel placed over his left shoulder and knotted at his right hip, his office was immediately recognizable. Similarly, the sewer had his over his right shoulder and knotted at his left hip, and the waiters tied theirs around their left biceps, the loose ends ready to be used to grip dishes held in both hands. The bearing-towels for the pantry, being identical in size, probably performed the same function for the pantler. In the fifteenth century his duties had been largely absorbed into those of the butler. He wore his towel around his neck like a stole, so that he could use it when carrying the bread, cutlery, salt and napkins to his master's table.[40] Pantry towels for livery would have been used by the pantry staff when dispensing the daily allowances of food, drink and lighting materials to those members of the household included in the detailed list of liveries. The Earl and Countess of Northumberland, for example, received two manchet loaves, a household loaf, a gallon of beer, a quart of wine and a pound of white wax candles each evening, this probably being kept in a livery cupboard for their use. By contrast, a gentleman of the household was given half a household loaf, two quarts of beer and two white wax lights; the porter, a quarter loaf, one quart of beer, and three white wax lights.[41]

Since the use of fingers and spoons to eat food was a relatively neat and tidy process, there was little chance of any moist or greasy food falling onto a diner's clothes. For this reason, napkins were generally unknown, except at the tables of the great, and even here they were only used in small numbers. The eighteen made each year for the Earl of Northumberland's table represents a substantial quantity in the medieval period. Their size, at 36 inches long, appears to be average, others listed elsewhere ranging from 27 to 45 inches. Here they were of plain-woven linen, but they might also be of twill, diaper, or of work.[42] There is little evidence to show how they were used. Since the carver had to pass one to his lord on the flat of his knife, they must have been neatly folded, perhaps lengthwise into four, and then into four again to form a 9 by 4½-inch stack. This would be easy both to serve, and to open across the lap, their most likely position, as they are not seen on the upper body in any depictions of dining.

CHAPTER TWENTY-TWO

Table Manners

Manners were one of the most important indicators of status and education in medieval England, and so were carefully formulated, taught and observed across most levels of society. This chapter will deal with those of ordinary people, who took their everyday meals in the hall.

The word 'hall' today conjures up a huge banqueting-room hung with brilliant textiles, heated by roaring log fires, lit by hundreds of candles, and inhabited by silk- and velvet-clad lords and ladies dining off great gold and silver chargers. Such images, promoted in the works of film-makers and those who publish guides to ancient monuments, are almost entirely fictitious. In reality, the hall had already become a servants' hall in most fourteenth-century great households; in farmhouses it was where the farm servants fed; and in cottages it was the single kitchen-living-room in which all domestic activities took place, often with cattle and hens under the same narrow roof.

Reconstructing the manners of medieval peasants is far from straight-forward, for poverty in contemporary descriptions is usually seen in terms of poor food and poor tableware, not in coarse habits. Even though in *c.* 1475 well-bred young children were being warned, [1]

> Cut not your meat as it were Field men
> That to their meat have such an appetite
> That they don't care in what ways, nor when
> Nor how ungodly they on their meat twyte [pluck],

there is sound evidence to suggest that most peasants had good basic manners. Among Chaucer's Canterbury pilgrims, for example, the

Figure 64. Simple meals.

1. Feeding the poor as an act of corporal mercy, with barefooted guests politely eating with their right hands in fourteenth-century France.

2. English pilgrims at table, early 15c.

3 and 4. Canterbury pilgrims dining communally, probably using their own knives and spoons to help themselves to the bread and dishes of meat, late 15c.

ploughman had little difficulty in sharing the common table with the knight, the merchant, or even the elegant prioress who,

> …let no morsel from her lips fall,
> Nor wet her fingers in her sauce deep,
> Well could she carry a morsel, and well keep,
> That no drop never fell upon her breast,
> In curtasy was set full much her lest.
> Her over-lip wiped she so clean
> That in her cup no farthing [of grease] was seen.

Similarly, manuscript illustrations of barefoot, poorly-dressed pilgrims at table show them using their hands and utensils in the correct way.

The basic principles of medieval dining were straightforward and hygienic: the hands must be washed before approaching food and, since the left hand was used for toilet purposes, it should never convey food to the lips. Furthermore, food should never be bitten, for only animals [and modern actors] bit instead of cutting or breaking their food into mouth-sized portions.

Fortunately, English popular folk culture provides ample evidence of how food was eaten in fields and cottages. Along with regional patterns of speech, custom and belief, the minutiae of correct behaviour seem also to have persisted through several generations. For solid food, such as bread, meat and cheese, the standard method used up to current living memory was to grip the food in the left hand, while holding the knife in the right. 'He must have a snack of bread and cheese, so he takes his knife, cuts a massy fragment of the rich kissing-crust … from the upper half of the loaf, and places it between the little finger and the thick [palm] of his left hand; he cuts a corresponding piece of cheese, and places it between the thumb and two forefingers of the same hand, and alternating cutting his bread and cheese with his clasp knife … he wipes his mouth and says "Well, Jack, we must be off lad".[2] This account of a farm labourer's meal was written in the 1840s, but the holding of food between the thumb and forefingers of the left hand and the knife in the right is just as described in books of manners and seen in woodcuts of the fifteenth century. It is

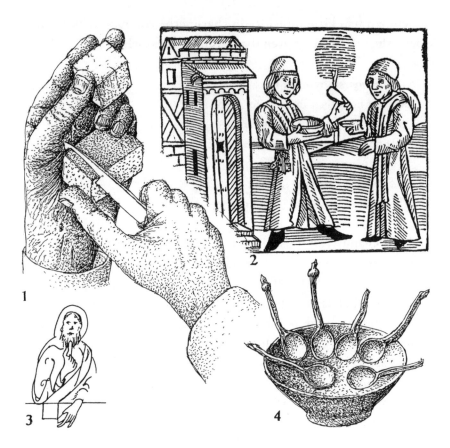

Figure 65. Basic food handling.

1. Cutting a piece from a hunk of bread grasped between the third and fourth fingers and the palm, before cutting a piece from the block of cheese grasped between the thumb and first and second fingers. This was still practiced by outdoor workers up to the mid-twentieth century.

2. A polite traveller shows his good manners by advancing his first two fingers and thumb to grasp his dole of bread.

3. This early-14c. apostle on the wall of All Saints Church, Friskney, Lincolnshire, uses his left hand to hold food by his square trencher, and his right hand to raise a portion to his lips.

4. This pewter badge, found at Bankside, Southwark, shows a mess of pottage, complete with the spoons of those who were to consume its contents.

also as I was taught in Hampshire in the 1960s. Traditionally, the morsels of food cut off and eaten in this way were called thumb-pieces, the same word being used in Hertfordshire to describe pieces of wood with which labourers held their food when their fingers were dirty. 'Thumb buckas' (West Yorkshire), thumb buttercakes (Lancashire) and thumb shags (Cumbria), meanwhile, were slices of bread or oatcakes on which butter had been spread with the thumb.[3]

If pottages were to be eaten in the open air, the dish was set into a hole in the ground, its rim level with the surface, so that it could not be accidentally knocked over. Each person then took out their own wooden spoon and, in order of social precedence, took turns in scooping up a mouthful. Shepherds on Hutton Conyers Moor were still eating their New Year's Day frumenty in this way in the 1820s.[4] If the more liquid pottages were to be enriched with sops of bread, these were usually cut from the loaf using a knife, only the most unmannerly biting them off as 'gob-sops' before dropping them into the dish.[5]

Within the smallest dwellings, many must have eaten their food using these outdoor methods. Even in the mid-nineteenth century many households were still using their small, single tables merely to support their dishes of food, the family standing around them, since there was no further room on the table, and neither space nor seating to accommodate them. In Leeds in the 1730s,[6]

> Ere clock strikes eight their call'd to breakfast
> And bowls of milk are brought in haste.
> Good water-pudding [porridge] as heart could wish,
> With spoons stuck round an earthen dish.

A fifteenth-century pewter badge found in Southwark shows just such a pottage dish, with six acorn-knopped spoons set around its rim, ready to be used in an identically communal manner. John Wood of Bradford recalled around 1810, 'The porridge ... were served up in one dish or bowl placed in the middle of the table, the family placing themselves around, some sitting, some standing, each one being supplied with a spoon or knife without the use of fork or plate. They proceeded to help themselves in the best way they could, the most active getting the best share. I just remember a bright youth who, in order to secure the use of the largest spoon, was in the habit of carrying it all the day, stuck in one of his buttonholes.'[7] Earlier, fifteenth-century youths were probably carrying their wooden spoons or 'gobsticks' in precisely the same way, ready to compete at table, dining in the same way too.

Although many medieval peasants must have eaten their meals using these basic methods, others would have adopted more refined practices. In the more prosperous cottages and the communal halls of farmhouses, manor houses and castles, most people would have sat at cloth-covered tables furnished with appropriate tableware, and eaten their meals with varying degrees of polite decorum.

Halls could differ enormously in quality and scale, from the magnificence of the hall at the Palace of Westminster measuring almost 240 feet by 70 feet, to those of many smaller manor houses, no more, perhaps, than 20 feet by 30 feet. Their construction and architecture have been subject of much study in books such as Dr Margaret Wood's *The English Medieval House*, so they will only be considered here as locales for meals.[8] Each hall might display its own distinctive features, but a typical fifteenth-century example would have three doors leading to its lower end wall: that in the centre formed a service passage from the kitchen dresser-hatches, while those to the sides led into the pantry and buttery. Directly adjacent to the end wall, broad external doorways in each side wall provided access for all those coming to dine in the hall, a screen-wall between them forming a passage which, except for one or two strategically-placed openings, prevented strong gusts entering the hall itself, and obscured the view from the hall down into the service rooms. It was in this passage that the 'towel' was set up, with ewers, basins and towels for hand-washing before meals. If it was given an upper floor, it also provided a convenient gallery for musicians, their loud music announcing the imminent service of dinner or supper in an age which lacked personal timepieces. Next came the body of the hall, lit with tall windows, and floored with either beaten earth, boarding, ceramic tiles or stone flags.

For heating, most halls had a hearth in the centre of the floor, perhaps paved with stone or tiles set on edge to resist the heat of the burning wood.

Figure 66. A setting for one mess on the lower tables in the hall.

In north-eastern counties, the use of coal fires demanded an iron grate set over an ashpit. Directly overhead, a louvre was built on the ridge of the roof to allow the smoke to ventilate to the open air. Fireplaces built into the side walls, as at Conwy in the 1280s, remained quite unusual in halls until the post-medieval period.

The furniture in the body of the hall was simple, merely tables and long forms or benches. In virtually all modern reconstructions, these are built of massive, thick and wide slabs of oak, requiring the muscle of at least four burly labourers to move them. Their design and construction is based on the concept that everything medieval was coarse and thick, but not on real evidence. In the *Promptorium Parvulorum sive clericorum* of c. 1440 a table is defined as a 'mete boord that ys borne a-wey when mete is down'. Tables were put up just before each meal, then dismantled to leave a clear sweepable floor. For this reason they had to be as conveniently light and portable as possible. The 1413 ordinances of the York Joiners' Company state that a dining-table should be 'of the length of one wainscot [imported oak plank], good one-inch boarding, and into a table of five quarters [45 inches?] good half-inch boarding, and for the legs of the said table which is made of half-inch boarding, good one-inch boarding.'[10] The 1496 inventory of the Blacksmiths' Company's possessions describes a dining-table 16 feet long by 30 inches wide extending down one side of its hall, standing on just two trestles.[11] This shows that these tables were relatively lightweight, just long inch-thick planks on a couple of trestles, sufficient to support the weight of the tableware, but springy and bowing if leant on to any degree.

The design of the trestles probably followed that shown in the contemporary illustrations such as the 1450s wall-paintings in Pickering parish church, or those tables recovered from the wreck of the *Mary Rose*.[12] These have a horizontal rail with one tenon cut vertically into one end, and two splaying out at an angle at the other, into which rectangular legs could be inserted, to form a firm support for the table top. Kept in place merely by their own weight, they could be quickly erected when required, then instantly collapsed into neat stacks of uniform rails and legs once the meal was finished.

For seating, long benches were used, these having either frames, vertical planks reinforced with brackets, or probably legs wedged into holes drilled through the tops.[13]

Although part of the same physical space as the remainder of the hall, the upper or inner section furthest from the kitchens was furnished, and actually functioned, as if it were a separate room. Up to the fourteenth century this had been the site of the lord's table, but thereafter it was usually occupied by his chief household servants, being the direct predecessor of the stewards' rooms of the seventeenth to twentieth centuries.

In order to emphasize its status, its floor level might be raised by a single step to form a dais, while a high, curving timber-framed canopy might project over it from its back wall. The same wall might also house a wide fireplace for extra comfort. Added brilliance, almost like stage-lighting, was provided by the erection of a large semi-polygonal window to one side. Architectural historians call these 'oriels', a name which no medieval person ever applied to them. An oriel was, in fact, an enclosed porch, lobby or gallery, identical to the Cornish *orrel*, a porch, or balcony, or Welsh *oriel*, a gallery. If an oriel existed in a medieval hall, it was a musicians' gallery, such as the 'new oriel for the lord's trumpets in the hall', erected for Henry VI in 1450–51, and not a bay window.[14] Some oriels took the form of a small retiring room off the dais/chamber end of the hall, where meals might sometimes be taken. References to this practice, combined with the mistaken use of the word 'oriel', has led modern guidebooks to show great lords dining in the bay windows of their servants' halls, a ludicrously inaccurate situation.

The main feature of the dais end of the hall was a long table. This might be virtually identical to those in the body of the hall, perhaps with superior trestles, but still designed to be removed from in front of the diners so that they could easily rise from their seats once the meal was over. Alternatively, tables might be dormant, that is 'sleeping' or motionless, since they were fixtures. Chaucer's Franklin had a table dormant in his hall, always standing ready-covered, and Thomas Morton of York 'two boards called dormoundes with two long benches for the same' in his hall in 1449, all valued at 5s.[15] Tables for the dais could bear painted decorations, such as grey, green, or black and grey schemes with roses.[16]

Behind the table, there might be chairs, perhaps accompanied by stools, or else a single long bench covered in a rich textile 'banker'. Behind either chair or bench rose a tall strip of cloth called a dosser, the wall-hangings to each side being known as costers. In major halls, such as the Archbishop's hall at his palace in York, these textiles could be of great size, one set in blue say, a fine woollen serge, comprising:[17]

> 1 banker, 24ft x 2ft 3in;
> 10 feather cushions for the bench;
> 1 dosser, 42ft x 9ft;
> 2 costers, 33ft x 7ft 6in;
> 1 coster for the wall above the cupboard (no dimensions).

Presumably the dosser was 9 feet longer than the costers to allow for its top end to project horizontally and then drop vertically, to form a cloth of estate, or canopy over the Archbishop's place at the table. Other materials used for these hangings included tapestry of Arras showing morris dancers, or borders of birds and boars, coats of arms, stripes of red and black, red and green and so forth, or with painted decoration.[18]

Figure 67. Built-in cupboards.

1. At the side of the dais in the hall of Harewood Castle, Yorkshire, *c.* 1367.

2. In the same position in the donjon of Warkworth Castle, Northumberland, *c.* 1380.

As they were so expensive, hangings of this quality would only be installed for special events. At other times, they would be housed in the storeroom or wardrobe. At the Earl of Northumberland's northern castles, for example, the Arras tapestries were put up at Christmas. To avoid damaging them with foul smoke, the usual coal fires were replaced by those of charcoal.[19]

The furnishing of the dais was completed by a number of features designed to hold tableware and other necessary items. The most important of these was the cupboard, originally a simple table on which to set out the cups, but then developing into a more complex structure, the York joiners making them of two wainscots (oak boards) formed into four posts and a 'main body' of half-, three-quarters and one-inch boards.[20] A 1485 description of 'an aumbry with a cupboard above the same' suggests that they had enclosed sections with doors, surmounted by a flat top, and perhaps a shelved and canopied extension rising above for the display of silver and gold tableware.[21] This arrangement is seen in a number of Continental manuscript illustrations. Most cupboards were only a few feet long, their cupboard-cloths measuring 7 feet 6 inches by 3 feet. These were usually made of linen, but in great households red worsted or red say would provide a particularly rich effect.[22] In some high-status halls, the cupboard was constructed as part of the primary masonry structure. Perhaps the finest of these, dating from of c.1367, lines the right side of the dais area in Harewood Castle. Surmounted by a fine cusped and crocketed arch, the interior is provided with its own window to illuminate the contents. Another occupies a similar position in the donjon hall of c.1377–90 at Warkworth Castle, while that at Alnwick Castle was in the wall behind the dais.

Having described the hall and its dais, we can now return to the body of the hall to trace its staffing and use. In any large household, this was controlled by the marshal of the hall. His office and duties had been introduced from France before the thirteenth century, having developed from early origins in the lord's stables where a *mareschal* was a farrier or horse-servant. As a senior gentleman servant, he carried a rod as symbol of his authority, this being 27 inches long, the diameter of an arrow.[23] Such staffs once had a very practical purpose. William II armed 300 ushers of his hall and kitchen with rods to protect the guests from the unwelcome attentions of the *garçons* and the waiters from the *lecheours* who tried to snatch their dishes. At the coronation feast of Henry V's queen, Catherine of Valois, in 1420 the Earl Marshal rode around Westminster Hall on a great charger, 'with a multytude of typped stavys aboute hym, to kepe the rome in the halle.'[24] In the fifteenth century, the marshal policed the whole house and its environs, suppressing fights and affrays, the drawing of knives, theft, arguments, and the 'oreble chydings' of all present. He had full authority to deal with offenders by imprisoning them under the charge of the porter to await the lord's judgement, or setting them in the stocks for a period.[25]

On entering the hall each morning, the marshal supervised his yeoman usher and groom of the hall as they turned out the dogs (who would only be allowed back indoors after supper), cleaned all the ashes from the fires, shook or beat the wall-hangings with rods, and swept the bare floor.

Next, the groom of the hall, who usually took charge of the woodhouse and coal-house, brought in the fuel and lit the fires every day between All Saints' Day (1 November) and Candlemas Eve (2 February), when heating was permitted.[26] For every load he brought in, a notch would be cut across a split tally-stick, the groom and the marshal each keeping half, to maintain an accurate account. Next, the tables were put up, their tops wiped clean, and the forms or benches set out down on both sides.

Having been told how many 'messes' or groups usually of four people were to dine in the hall, the tables could now be laid. First came coarse linen or canvas tablecloths from the ewery, then a trencher of either bread or wood for each person, a household loaf for each mess from the pantry, and cups and a pitcher of ale or beer for each mess from the buttery.[27] The ewery also set up 'the towel' with its ewers, basins and towels in the screens passage, ready for use. By 10 a.m. all had to be in place, as the household servants and less important guests now entered the hall doors, summoned by the minstrels' drums, woodwind and brass sounding from the gallery.

Regular members of the household would know from experience where they were to sit, each in descending rank from the dais-step down towards the screens. The only exceptions were the marshal, clerks of the kitchen, and the ewery staff who sat at the lower end of the hall to control its doors, to supervise the dispatch of food from the dresser, and service the 'towel' respectively. Well-mannered strangers and visitors knew that, having washed, they should stand in front of the centre of the hall screen, where they would be greeted by the marshal and directed by him or his usher to their appointed place in the hall, on the steward's table on the dais, or to the knights' table in the chamber, according to their status. This task demanded great knowledge and discretion, since each level of the nobility, clergy, officers of the law, civic dignitaries and servants was subject to a long-established and rigid order of precedence. Great offence could be caused if individuals were seated where they, or the rest of the household, considered they were out of place, for this was the most public demonstration of a person's status in a society skilled in observing such matters.

When everyone was standing where they ought to be, grace was said, its form varying according to whether it was for dinner or supper, meat-day or fish-day, Easter Eve or Easter Day and so on. [28] It usually began with the priest or chaplain crying 'Benedicite' (Bless you) and receiving the response 'Dominus' (Lord), before going on to recite a psalm, the Pater Noster (Lord's Prayer) and blessings, all in Latin. Only then did everyone sit down.

If a folded napkin was provided, this was placed on the lap, ready to wipe the lips if moist or greasy.[29] Drawing his knife from a sheath hanging from his belt, slices of household loaf would probably have been cut by each person in order of seniority within the mess, and set to the left of the trencher. Such slices had been used as a combination of comestible and utensil in England from at least the thirteenth century. [30]

The first dish to be set down before each mess was a pottage. To eat this each person dipped their spoon into the communal dish, being careful not to overfill it, and risk soiling either their clothes or the tablecloth. On no account was anyone to drink directly from the dish, put their fingers into it, blow it if it was too hot, or leave their spoon in it. Small pieces broken or cut from the slice of bread could be dropped into the pottage and eaten with the spoon, but they should neither be crumbled in, nor dipped in twice, since this would foul the pottage with grease and saliva.[31]

Once the pottage was finished, the spoon was wiped clean with a morsel of the slice of bread, this then being eaten, leaving the spoon clean and ready for succeeding pottages and suchlike.

If a solid food, such as boiled or roast meat and fish, or leach, was served next, good manners dictated that the worthiest in the mess should cut his portion first, always ensuring that enough of the best parts were left for others, especially if there were strangers present. Using the thumb and two forefingers of the left hand, each person in turn grasped only that part which they wanted, cut it off using their knife held with the thumb and forefingers of the right hand, the haft within the palm, and placed it on his trencher. Still holding it firm with his left hand, he cut it into mouth-sized pieces, set down his knife, propping its greasy blade on his trencher to keep the tablecloth clean, before using the thumb and two forefingers of his right hand to raise the pieces up to his lips.[32] This neat procedure ensured that only the right hand ever approached the lips and that the meat in the dish was never contaminated with saliva.

If salt or sauce was required, a little was taken up on the point of the knife and placed on the trencher, probably towards one corner:

> Touche not wyth mete salt in the saler
> Lest folke appoynt you of uncunningnesse,
> Dresse hit apparte uppon a clene trenchere

where the meat could be dipped into it.[33] This kept the salt and sauce clean for everyone else. Eating solid food in this way was an elegant performance if carried out with sufficient skill, and eliminated all need for biting or gnawing:

> Burnish no bonys wyth yor tethe, be ware
> That houndis teethe fayleth of curtesie,
> But with your knyff make the bonys bare.

This was sound advice. These bones, along with all other waste, were to be retained on the trencher until they could be transferred to a voider, a dish specially provided for this purpose.[34] Keeping the trencher tidy, uncluttered and clean was a mark of good manners. If a bread trencher became soiled or moist with juices, however, it too could be placed in the voider, and a fresh one obtained, perhaps from a stack provided for each mess.[35] Other important details included keeping the knife clean by regularly wiping its blade on a morsel of bread, which was then eaten, keeping the knife away from the face, eating only a small quantity at a time, and keeping the mouth closed when eating.[36]

Drinking took place throughout each meal, commencing after the first dish had been served. Probably everyone helped themselves in order of seniority from the communal pitcher of ale or beer set at each mess. Since it was customary to offer one's companions drinks from one's cup as a mark of friendship, cleanliness was imperative. Before drinking, the mouth and fingers were wiped on the napkin to remove any trace of grease or dirt. The cup was proffered to the friend, while facing him; he took it with both hands, drank part of it, as quickly as possible, and returned it part-full, after which it could be returned to the table.[37]

At the close of the meal, each person cleaned his knife, took a fresh trencher, and ate a little cheese as a digestive, finally standing for grace. Then would he go about his business until repeating the whole process at supper, at 4 p. m. or thereabouts.[38]

Since meals were essentially semi-formal social events, good manners went far beyond the handling of food and drink. To show courtesy to one's master or host, a little of each dish should be tasted. Only the meat which was to be eaten immediately was to be cut from each joint, in order to preserve the remainder in good condition for passing on to the poor, and eating should only be sufficient for necessity, not purely for pleasure or gluttony. If the portions were rather small, or were whisked off the table prematurely by hungry waiters, no complaint was to be made, for this too would be discourteous.[39]

In order to be companionable at table, and promote the harmony of the household, it was recommended that conversation should cover pleasurable topics, everyone being permitted to tell their stories without distractions or interruptions, quarrels, grimaces, raucous laughter or fidgeting with the tableware. Table-talk was not to be repeated, however, for gossip could soon breed discord within the closed community of any household.[40] For similar reasons, all diners were expected to sit up straight with neither elbows nor fists on the table, and avoid loosening the girdle, picking the nose, ears, teeth or nails, scratching the head or crutch, stroking cats or dogs, spitting, vomiting, belching, or 'thy hynder part from gunnes blastynge', 'and thyn ars be natte carpyng'.[41]

Up on the dais, food of better quality was likely served and manners observed in an almost identical manner, but there are few details of how these upper servants dined.[42] The steward, controller, treasurer, perhaps with others of similar gentlemanly rank, would have been provided with pots of wine rather than solely ale or beer, and fine manchet loaves rather than coarser household bread. Each person would prepare his loaf by first using his knife to cut it through horizontally, to separate the top from the bottom. The upper half would then be cut into four 'fingers' and re-assembled as if whole by the left side of his place and the lower half cut into three 'fingers' and re-assembled alongside, crust uppermost, ready for being used just like the household bread described above.[43]

CHAPTER TWENTY-THREE

Dining in the Chamber

T he chamber was the everyday living-room of the lord and his family, together with the senior members of his household and many personal servants. Access to this room was denied to lower servants and visitors of low status but, by modern standards, it was still a relatively communal, rather than strictly private space. Up to around 1300 the chamber might lead off either the upper or the lower end of the hall, but then the lord and his family began to abandon the high table in the hall as their usual dining-place, and retire into their chamber for all their meals.[1] This desire for an increasing degree of separation between the nobility and the bulk of their households, and all their banal operations, was quickly reflected in the planning of domestic buildings. Those chambers at the low end of the hall, usually over the buttery and pantry, or a cellar, and close to the entrance doors and the noise, bustle and smells of the kitchen, were no longer constructed for family use but, like the high table in the hall, were usually left in the occupation of the steward, the head of the domestic administration. From now on, the lord's chamber was always either off the upper end of the hall, or in its own courtyard or tower even further removed from the household servants.[2]

'The Chamber', being a singular rather than a plural noun, gives the impression that it was always just a single room. In some early buildings, such as the White Tower in the Tower of London, built around 1100, this was probably the case. The room in question here was some 30 by 63 feet, rising through two storeys. The chamber also remained a single room in many minor-gentry houses throughout the medieval period.[3] In most royal, noble and upper-gentry houses, however, 'the chamber' rapidly expanded to become a complete high-status residential suite. Certainly by the reign of Henry II (1154–89) royal castles such as Nottingham and

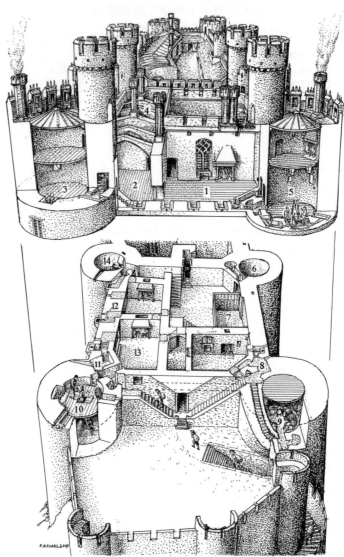

Figure 68. The chamber suite, Conwy Castle, 1283–7.
(1) great chamber; (2) King's chamber; (3) head officer's chamber; (4) Queen's chamber; (5) chapel with chamber for chapel staff above.
Ground floor: (6) larder?; (7) granary; (8) buttery; (9) cellar; (10) counting house or greencloth with concealed strongroom beneath; (11 and 12) wardrobes of beds and robes for King and Queen respectively; (13) kitchen; (14) privy bakehouse.

Scarborough were built with at least two chambers, a great chamber for some public use, and a much more private King's chamber.[4] In the late thirteenth century, Edward I's master-mason Master James of St George was planning royal chamber suites of great sophistication, exemplified by that in the inner bailey of Conwy Castle, built between 1283 and 1287, which has survived to a remarkable degree until the present day.

This was a virtually self-contained unit, with its own granary, bake-house, larder (?) and kitchen for food preparation; a cellar and a buttery for drinks; a strong-room, counting house/greencloth and head officer's chamber for administration; and a chapel with sacristy, vestry and clerks' lodgings for worship. All these were designed to serve a suite of great, King's and Queen's chambers arranged as a consecutive sequence of first-floor rooms. For security and maximum efficiency the service-rooms and chambers were linked by a complete system of backstairs corridors concealed in the thickness of the walls. To facilitate serving meals in different locations, there was one passage from the kitchen to the low end of the great chamber, and another from the kitchen, past the greencloth door for surveying, through the King's wardrobe to his own chamber. A third permitted wine to be carried from the cellar to the same chambers. Yet a fourth, carefully concealed at the back of a window seat in the King's chamber, where it would be totally invisible behind a wall-hanging, gave access to the head officer's and greencloth chambers. This would enable the King to enjoy apparently confidential discussions with his visitors, in the certain knowledge that his clerks, and probably his bodyguards too, were listening to every word, just a few feet or even inches away.

Up to around the mid-fourteenth century, most chambers appear to have been multi-functional. If a meal was to be served, a trestle table and seating would be set up, used, and afterwards put back into store in a buttery or other room; if the King wished to go to bed, the officers of the Wardrobe of Beds would bring in his bed, make it up, and then remove it back into the wardrobe next morning; if the King wished to dress, his officers of the Wardrobe of Robes would attend him here, along with the Wardrobe of Beds, who carried his close-stool (commode) in and out whenever he wished to go to the toilet. From this time, there is increasing, if sparse, evidence for some of these functions being allocated

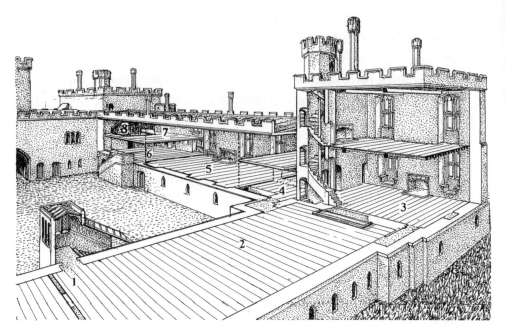

Figure 69. The hall and chamber suite, Wressle Castle, *c.* 1380.
(1) screens passage; (2) hall; (3) lord's chamber over buttery[?]; (4) service
rooms, buttery and pantry for the chamber; (5) great/dining chamber; (6)
nether chapel; (7) lord's pew, with place for gentlemen and servingmen; (8)
high chapel, with lady's chamber and Paradise chamber above.

to specific chambers within the chamber suite. At Windsor Castle, for
example, the King had a great chamber, the main living/reception-room
for courtiers and those seeking an audience with him, and probably the
dining area for members of his household and visitors of appropriate
status, a painted chamber for those of higher status, then five inner
rooms, including a finely painted 'inner sanctum' called 'La Rose', and
one furnished with trestle tables, probably as a private dining-chamber.[5]

From various fifteenth-century manners-books, it is clear that the
lord was always absent from the chamber when and where the dining
tables were being set up. Presumably he was then in either the great
chamber or in an inner, privy chamber, where he spent much of his day.
This fact, combined with the practical consideration of having the dining
area as close to the kitchen as possible, suggests that the first or outermost

chamber in any suite of later medieval date was almost certainly being used as a dining chamber, although rarely known by this name.[6] At Wressle Castle of *c.*1380 the large room off the upper end of the hall, known as the dining chamber in the sixteenth century, was ideally designed for this purpose. Food from the kitchen could be carried along the hall, through a door at one side of the dais into a pantry, and on into the dining chamber. Proceeding past the long knights' table set down one side, it would then be conveyed to the Earl of Northumberland's family sitting at the upper end of the chamber.

The furniture required for dining in chamber was relatively simple. The tables were usually simple broad boards mounted on collapsible trestles, their size and number being determined by where they were to be used. If Henry VII (and probably lords too) was to dine in his privy or inner chamber, a single table perhaps 6 to 10 feet long, judging from manuscript illustrations, was set up in the middle of the room, at the left of his bed-head. The King was seated to the centre of one side, with a bishop to his right, towards the fireplace end of the table, and the Queen to his left.[7] While this table was being set up in the privy chamber, three more were being erected in the great chamber, one for lords temporal, their number being decided by the chamberlain and the ushers of the chamber, a second for the chamberlain, knights, esquires of the body and ushers, and a third for the king's confessor, secretary, chaplain, physician and ushers. Not being of sufficient status, the yeomen of the crown and of the great chamber were not permitted to eat here, so their table was set up just outside the chamber door, where they also provided extra security.

The king only dined in his great chamber on days of estate, when his own table was erected just as if it were in the privy chamber. Before it, the first or lords' table was set up as usual, but the knights on the second table were sent to dine in the hall along with all those who normally dined on the third table, to leave more space for the King, and to restrict those dining in his presence to just one table of nobles.[8] Similar procedures took place in contemporary noble households, the Earl of Northumberland's great chamber having a knights' table about 20 feet long for his officers, guests and upper servants, in addition to that at which he sat between his eldest son and his Countess.[9]

Figure 70. Dining in royal chambers.

1. Early fifteenth-century illustration of Richard II entertaining the Dukes of York, Gloucester and Ireland.

2. Stained glass panel from Cassiobury Park, Herts., *c.* 1450.

3. From Wynkyn de Worde's *Boke of Keruynge* of 1508 (mirror image).

Depending on the status or practice of each household, those at table were seated on chairs, high-backed benches covered with rich cloths called bankers, stools or long forms. If any of these backed onto the fireplace, they were protected by a firescreen, such as the 'old screen of twigs standing in front of the chimney' in Archbishop Bowet's chamber in 1423.[10] One is shown as a large lipwork disc mounted on a wooden stand in the well-known illustration of the Duke of Berry feasting that is the image for January in *Les Très Riches Heures*. A sixteenth-century example still survives at Haddon Hall, Derbyshire.[11] Behind the principal seat a cloth of estate or dosser was hung vertically, its top extending forward as a canopy or valance over the centre of the table, its frame sometimes made of oak boards.[12] When the King and Queen were at the same table, her cloth had to be lower by the width of the valance, while if the King's uncle or brother took his place in the great chamber, the bottom edge had to be rolled up to the height of his head.[13]

Wherever a royal or noble table was set up, it was flanked by two other pieces of furniture, the ewery board and the cupboard. The former was probably just a simple table used to hold the basin, ewer, towels and other impedimenta required for hand-washing. The Earl of Northumberland's probably measured around 6 feet by 2 feet 6 inches, judging by the size of its white linen cloth.[14] The cupboard (sometimes called in modern error the court cupboard, dresser or buffet) might be of the same size, but was of more elaborate construction, with doored compartments below and a framed panel rising above, sometimes incorporating either stages or shelves designed to display a wealth of gold or silver plate. That of the Duke of Bedford included five gold vessels, 69 of silver-gilt and 54 of silver valued at £850 in 1434, or around £400,000 in modern currency. For great ceremonies of state, the cupboards could grow to vast proportions. One erected for the reception of Katherine of Aragon in 1501 had seven tiers, and ran the length of the Court of Chancery at the south end of Westminster Hall.[15] White linen cloths might be acceptable on workaday cupboards, but at this level they were of red worsted material to give the plate an especially rich coloured background. [16]

The service of food in the chamber required a large and well-trained staff. Edward IV's household ordinances of 1474, incorporating much from those of Edward III, show that even on a normal day the chamberlain, one or two gentlemen ushers, two squires, six yeomen, four waiters and a groom porter with his servant – some seventeen servants – plus the services of a chaplain, knights and others, were necessary just to serve the King's table.

Similar establishments were maintained by the nobility. Beneath the chamberlain, steward, treasurer, surveyor, members of his council and secretary of the Earl of Northumberland's household, there was a small army of table-servants. These attended the great chamber every day in three shifts, going about their other duties for the remainder of the day. [17]

7 a.m.–10 a.m. [Dinner]	1 p.m.–4 p.m. [Supper]	7 p.m.–9 p.m.
Lord's Gent. Usher	Lady's Gent. Usher	Lord's Gent. Usher
Lord's Carver	Lady's Carver	Lady's Gent. Usher
Lord's Sewer	Lady's Sewer	Lord's Carver
Lord's Cupbearer	Lady's Cupbearer	Lady's Carver
Lord's Gent. Waiter	Lady's Gent. Waiter	Lord's Sewer
2 Yeom. Of Chamber	Lady's Yeom. Usher	Lady's Sewer
Lady's Yeom. Of Chamber	Yeom. Of Horse	Lord's Cupbearer
4 Groom Waiters	Yeom. Of Chamber	Lady's Cupbearer
2 Grooms of Chamber	3 Yeom. Waiters	2 Gent. Waiters
1 Child of Chamber	Lord's Groom of Chamber	Lady's Yeom. Usher
1 Yeom. Of Pantry	Lady's Groom of Chamber	Yeom. of Robes
1 Groom of Buttery	Yeom. of Beds	Yeom. of Horse
1 Groom of Ewery	Yeom. of Buttery	3 Yeom. of Chambers
	Groom of Pantry	4 Yeom. Waiters
		2 Minstrel Yeom. Waiters
		1 Footman Yeom. Waiter
		3 Lord's Grooms of Chambers
		Lady's Groom of Chambers
		Child Groom of Chambers

A number of these were senior officials who not only managed his distant great estates, but also attended his chamber on a regular rota that changed every quarter-day, Christmas, Lady Day, Midsummer and Michaelmas. In the second quarter, for example, the following were on duty:[18]

Master Forester of the Westward as Cupbearer;

Constable of Warkworth as Gentleman Usher;

Constable of Prudhoe as Carver;

Bailiff of Helagh as Usher of the Chamber;

Bailiff of Alnwick as Yeoman;

Keeper, Spofforth Park as Yeoman of the Chamber;

Keeper, Westward as Yeoman of the Chamber;

Keeper, College Park as Yeoman Waiter;

Keeper, Rothbury Forest as Yeoman Waiter;

Keeper, Helagh Park as Yeoman Waiter.

In the other quarters, staff from his Leconfield, Topcliffe, Hunmanby, Leathley, Kildale, Wasdale, Wressle, Newisham, Cayton, Pocklington, Egremont, Langstroth, Preston in Craven, Langley and Chatton estates served the Earl. This provided him with an excellent opportunity not only to learn what was happening on his massive yet scattered territories, but to stamp his authority on his senior staff.

Serving a lord at his table was a complicated procedure, one which no casual amateur could muddle through, but which required long training under the guidance of an experienced senior officer. For noble boys and youths, this training started in earnest when they left home at seven to nine years old to become henchmen or children of honour in the households of their social superiors. The title 'henchman' originated as a groom or horse attendant, but later became that of a squire or page who attended a great lord, and was educated by him. In the court of Edward IV six or more 'henxmen', some being the King's wards, maintained by him until they achieved their majority and came into their titles and lands, were placed under the control of the master of the henxmen.[19] He was employed to teach them:

the schooles of urbanitie and nourture of England, to lerne them to ryde clenely and surely; to draw them also to j[o]ustes; to lerne them were thyre harneys [armour]; to have all curtesy in wordes, dedes, and degrees, dilygently to kepe them in rules of goyings and sittings, after they be of honour. Moreover to teche them sondry languages, and othyr lerninges vertuous, to harping, to pype, sing, daunce; and with other honest and temperate behaviour ... with remembraunce dayly of Goddes servyce accustomed. [He] sitteth in the halle, next unto these Henxmen, at the same board, to have his respecte unto theyre demeanynges, howe mannerly they ete and drinke, and to theyre communication, and other fourmes curiall [courtly], after the booke of urbanitie.

In a similar manner, the Earl of Northumberland had three 'hansmen' and two or three young gentlemen in his retinue, the former serving as cupbearers when he kept his much-reduced 'secret' household.[20] This practice of putting out children to be educated academically and socially in families of higher status probably operated from yeoman families upwards and, formalized into apprenticeships, was followed by all who practised a trade or craft. It provided youngsters with a sound introduction into society as a whole, and gave communities a strong sense of social cohesion. Alternatively, and particularly in their earlier years, children were taught table-manners by acting as table-servants to their parents. [21]

Full details of all the complex procedures, knowledge and vocabularies which a well-bred young man must know in order to become an acceptable member of a noble household were recorded in a number of fifteenth-century manuscripts. The third book of *The Boke of Curtasye* of *c.*1430–40 provided a useful job-description for every household officer, but even more detail was provided by another manuscript of the same date, revised about ten years later, and then brought to its final form around 1460–70 as *The Boke of Nurture*.[22] Only the latter provides details of its author, John Russell. He had learned all the duties of pantler, butler and carver, and then risen to be usher in chamber and marshal in hall to Humphrey, Duke of Gloucester (1391–1447). When 'croked age' finally forced him into retirement, he decided to set down his lifetime's experience of noble service in a training manual, adopting a conversational narrative approach.

Early one fine May morning, he wrote, he came across a slender, lean young man, bow in hand, about to stalk deer in the forest. He told Russell he had tried his hardest to gain household employment, but failed completely, and now wished to be out of the world. If only he could train as a butler, pantler or chamberlain, his problems would be over. From this point tuition starts in earnest, providing all the information required to carry out the duties of pantler, butler, carver, sewer, chamberlain, usher and marshal in the greatest detail. Before reviewing his instructions for serving a lord in his chamber, it will be helpful to rehearse these officers' job-descriptions as outlined in the 1474 ordinances of the royal household.

The chamber was in the overall charge of the chamberlain, who was appointed and given his staff of office (probably 18 inches long and the diameter of a finger) by either the King or his council. He chose, controlled, punished and dismissed all the chamber servants except those who brought the food – they were employed by the Greencloth – and ensured that every aspect of the chamber, including its furnishings, beds, tables, security and reception of chambers was up to standard.[23] His lieutenants were four gentlemen ushers of the chamber, one or two of whom were to be in attendance at all meals. Recognized by a staff of office, each usher kept order in the chamber, recorded the quantities of food, drinks, fuel and lighting brought there, reported these back to the counting-house, and trained all the chamber's servants in their duties, particularly for table-service. The ushers also allocated lodgings of appropriate quality for all who came to court, and also their places if they dined in chamber.[24] This task alone required considerable knowledge and tact, since precedence was governed by the following strictly enforced code: [25]

(1) The Pope; (2) Emperor; (3) King; (4) Cardinal; (5) Prince; (6) Archbishop; (7) Duke; (8) Bishop; (9) Earl; (10) Viscount; (11) Legate; (12) Baron; (13) Suffragan (Bishop's deputy); (14) Mitred Abbot; (15) Baron of the Exchequer; (16) 3 Chief Justices; (17) Mayor of London; (18) Cathedral Prior; (19) Unmitred Abbot; (20) Knight Bachelor; (21) Prior; (22) Dean; (23) Archdeacon; (24) Knight; (25) Esquire for the Body; (26) Master of the Rolls; (27) Under Justices; (28) Clerk of the Crown; (29) Clerk of Exchequer; (30) Mayor of Calais; (31) Provincial; (32) Doctor of Divinity and Prothonotary; (33) Pope's Legate and Collector, Doctor of Law; (34) Ex-Mayor of London and Sergeant of Law; (35) Masters of Chancery; (36) Preachers of Pardon; (37) Masters of Arts; (38) Monks; (39) Parsons and Vicars; (40) Parish Priests; (41) City Bailiff; (42) Yeoman of the Crown; (43) Sergeant of Arms; (44) King's Herald; (45) Heralds; (46) Merchants and Franklins; (47) Gentlemen; (48) Gentlewomen.

These were divided into groups of approximately equal status. The first (nos. 1–7) were to dine in separate chambers and not in the hall; the second (nos. 8–10) might share a table, sitting two to each mess; and the third great and honourable estates (nos. 12–18) sit likewise at either two or three to a mess. Those of knightly status (nos. 18–33) could sit three to four to each mess, and those at squire level always four to a mess. These general rules were fairly easy to follow, but tact, subtlety and knowledge were required to work out the finer details. For example, a powerful knight of royal blood had to be placed above a poor knight without good family connections, a wealthy abbot or prior above impoverished ones, old aldermen above young ones, and doctors in the order of years since they graduated. Anyone coming on royal business had to be received one grade higher in status, while ordinary household officers kept their usual rank. Royal ladies who married knights retained their original estate, while poor ladies who had married well acquired that of their husbands. In difficult cases, the gentlemen ushers sought advice from the King or his chief officers to ensure that no insult was ever given unintentionally.

Next came two yeomen ushers of the chamber: handsome, clean and strong archers, gathered from the households of great lords, who assisted the ushers in their everyday duties. Another four yeomen of the chamber were responsible for putting up the tables, holding the torches for lighting, and carrying messages and similar banal functions.[26] However, most of the practical work was carried out by four groom waiters of the chamber, who helped the yeomen set up the trestle tables, presumably carried in the food from the chamber door, brought up the water for hand-washing, hung up the tablecloths after use, and tended the fires. The wood for the fires, and the wax lights, were provided by a groom porter of the chamber. Finally, there were four pages of the chamber, to keep it clean. [27]

The actual selection of the King's food and its serving at table was carried out by a number of senior household officers. Each day the steward, chamberlain, doctor of physic, surveyor and sewer met with the master cook for the King's mouth, and decided what should be prepared for him. The surveyor then ensured that only the finest ingredients were used, saw that the meat and other materials which had been cut and issued from the larders in the morning were kept clean in the kitchen, and that they were issued from the kitchen dresser in satisfactory condition. The sewer for the King supervised its delivery to the royal table, carefully placing each dish in its chosen position, where it could be carved by some of the four knights bachelor whom the chamberlain selected as carvers and cupbearers. As the King dined, the doctor advised him on what he might eat and on the nature and properties of each dish. Finally, the basins and ewers for hand-washing were brought up by some of the knights of the household, again selected by the chamberlain.[28]

Having assembled these officers, together with those of the buttery, pantry and ewery described earlier, we can now follow the actual service of a meal to the King or a great lord as described by John Russell.

Although formal and complex by modern standards, the procedures he follows were in fact basic, as befitted his adopted role as tutor to inexperienced youths. To perform them, however, required the use of a number of additional utensils which have not so far been considered. The first is the Marshal's staff, rod or wand of office. This was 27 inches long and the diameter of an arrow, with the point of a needle protruding from one end so that it could be used to firmly hold up the towel and surnap used for the hand-washing ceremony.[29] Such staffs are frequently seen in medieval dining scenes, such as those in the Beauchamp Pageant.

More impressive were the precious-metal alms-dishes which received token loaves and a portion of every item of food served at the table, ready to be given out to the poor waiting at the outer gates. These were of magnificent workmanship in great households. One used by Richard, Earl of Arundel was of silver-gilt, finely engraved and further enriched with a central boss and eight roundels of colourful heraldic devices.[30] Another, owned by Sir John Fastolf of Caistor Castle, weighed 132oz, suggesting a diameter of some 2 feet.[31] From at least the early fourteenth century the alms-dish might take the form of the hull of a ship mounted on wheels. They were usually called ships in contemporary records but, since the Victorian period, collectors and curators have adopted the French equivalent, *nef*. Early references to them include:[32]

> 1311: Piers Gaveston. 'Item a ship of silver with four wheels, enamelled on the sides.'

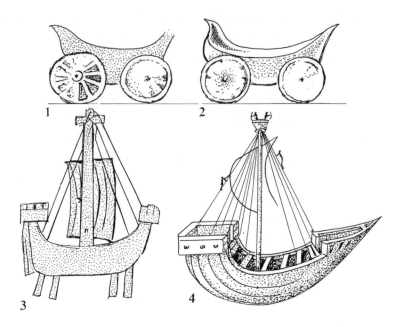

Figure 71. Silver or silver-gilt ships. These were usually used to collect food as alms from noble tables.

1–3. 14c.

4. Early 15c.

> 1334: Edward III. A ship of silver with four wheels and a dragon's head gilt at either end weighing £12 7s. 4d.
>
> 1403: William of Wykeham, 'an alms-dish newly made in the form of a ship'.
>
> 1447: John Holland, Duke of Exeter, 'an almes-diss, the shipp'.
>
> 1462: Sir John Fastolf, '1 ship weing 18oz Troy'.[33]

In the fourteenth century, some appear as open-topped hulls mounted on four wheels, set on tables cleared of all except the cloth and loaves of bread, suggesting the close of the meal.[34] Others had already developed into fully-equipped fighting ships, complete with castles fore and aft, a sail, and a top-castle. Those on the royal table were truly massive, that used by Henry VI in 1439 requiring almost half a hundredweight of solid bullion: 'Also a grete Alms Disshe of sylver and over gilt, made in the manner of a shippe, full of men of arms, feyghtyng upon the shippe syde, weyng in all 67lb 9oz Troy [55lb 12oz Avoirdupois].'[35]

Dish-covers were employed to keep the food hot as it was carried from the kitchen dresser through the hall into the chamber. As seen in illustrations such as a mid-fifteenth-century stained glass roundel in the Victoria & Albert Museum, these covers take the form of an inverted dish. They probably appear as dishes in contemporary inventories, but their use is clearly implied in descriptions of feasts, as when the Archbishop of York's sewer uncovered each dish as it was delivered to the table.

Further utensils were required at the end of the meal when the void of both dry and moist sweetmeats was served. Since these were amongst the most prestigious and expensive of comestibles, the spice-plates on which they were served had to be of appropriate quality. Those kept in Archbishop Henry Bowet's spicery in 1423 included one of silver-gilt valued at £4, while Archdeacon Thomas Dalby's weighed 3lb 6oz, suggesting it measured at least 15 inches in diameter.[36] It is difficult to identify spice plates today, but the Bermondsey dish of *c.*1335–45 must be a strong contender.[37] Made of silver-gilt, with a central shallow boss engraved with a knight kneeling before a lady, it has its broad rim worked into sixteen alternately raised and sunken wreathed petals, the latter being ideal for holding a selection of comfits and other small dry sweetmeats. These could be readily picked up with the fingers, but any attempt to eat sweet, syrup-drenched confections in this way would leave the diners with sticky fingers, and probably besmeared clothes too. For this reason, forks were used solely for lifting sticky sweetmeats up to the lips, John Kertelynge of Bury St Edmunds being bequeathed 'a silver forke for grene gyngour' in 1463. The better sort were double-ended, William Duffield of York having 'a long spoon with a fork for green ginger' weighing 1¾oz in 1452.[38]

Having introduced these items of practical necessity for the right serving of a meal, it only remains to detail the complex vocabulary and the extra knowledge of customary accompaniments which every carver had to learn in parallel with his mastering the physical skills of carving itself. It is not surprising that the youths who occupied the garret over the 'Bayne' in the Earl of Northumberland's Leconfield Castle would be encouraged to read the following lines painted there for their benefit:[39]

    The Parte sensatyve
Curyusly and connyngly I can karve,
And with assurede maner at the table serve,
So that no thinge shal pas me
But it shal have his formal properte
    The Parte Intellectyve
Without exersyse and contenuaunce
Suche connynge fallithe from remembraunce
To know thy self is a connynge soverayne
Vanitas vanitorum all that is but vayne

THE CARVER'S TERMS & ACCOMPANIMENTS

	CARVING TERM	ACCOMPANIMENT
MEAT		
Bacon		pease pottage
Beef		worts, mustard
Beef roast		garlic, vinegar or pepper
Brawn	*Lesche*	mustard
Coney	*Unlace*	worts, sprinkled vinegar & ginger, or mustard with sugar as sauce
Fawn		ginger sauce
Hare		worts
Kid		sprinkled sugar
Lamb		camelyne sauce
Mutton		mustard
Pig		ginger sauce
Veal		sprinkled verjuice
Venison	*Break*	sprinkled salt & cinnamon
POULTRY		
Bittern	*Unjoint*	sprinkled salt or camelyne sauce
Bustard		camelyne sauce
Capon	*Sauce*	sprinkled verjuice, or greensauce
Chicken	*Sauce*	sprinkled verjuice, or greensauce

	CARVING TERM	ACCOMPANIMENT
Crane	*Display*	sprinkled verjuice, or ginger, mustard vinegar & salt
Curlew	*Untache*	sprinkled salt, or with sugar, salt & water
Egret		sprinkled salt
Goose	*Rear*	
Hen	*Spoil*	sprinkled verjuice, or greensauce
Heron	*Dismember*	ginger, mustard, vinegar & salt as sauce
Lapwing, Lark & Martin		sprinkled salt & cinnamon
Mallard	*Unbrace*	
Partridge	*Wing*	sprinkled wine, vinegar & salt or mustard & sugar as sauce
Peacock	*Disfigure*	
Pheasant	*Alley*	mustard & sugar as sauce
Pigeon	*Thigh*	
Plover	*Mince*	sprinkled salt or camelyne sauce
Quail	*Wing*	sprinkled salt or salt & cinnamon
Stockdove		
Shoveller		ginger sauce
Snipe		sprinkled salt
Sparrow	*Thigh*	sprinkled salt
Swan		chawdron
Thrush	*Thigh*	sprinkled salt & cinnamon
Woodcock	*Thigh*	sprinkled salt & cinnamon

FISH

Barbel	*Tush*	
Beaver tail		frumenty or pease pottage
Bream		sprinkled vinegar, cinnamon & ginger
Carp		sprinkled cinnamon
Chub	*Fin*	sprinkled cinnamon
Cod		ginger sauce or mustard with verjuice & pepper
Cod, salt		mustard
Conger eel		mustard
Crab	*Tame*	sprinkled vinegar, or vinegar, cinnamon & ginger

	CARVING TERM	ACCOMPANIMENT
Crayfish		sprinkled vinegar, or vinegar, cinnamon & ginger
Dace		sprinkled verjuice
Eel	*Trasene*	sprinkled vinegar, or vinegar, cinnamon & ginger
Eel, salt		mustard
Flounder		sprinkled cinnamon
Gurnard		sprinkled vinegar, or vinegar, cinnamon & ginger
Gurnard, salt		mustard
Haddock	*Side*	ginger sauce or mustard with verjuice & pepper
Hake		ginger sauce or mustard with verjuice & pepper
Herring		sprinkled salt
Herring, baked		sprinkled sugar
Herring, salt		mustard
Houndfish		ginger or mustard sauce with vinegar & pepper
Lamprey	*String*	sprinkled cinnamon & ginger or
		ginger sauce, cinnamon & red wine
Ling		greensauce
Ling, salt		mustard
Lobster	*Barb*	
Mackerel		butter
Mackerel, salt		mustard
Mullet		sprinkled verjuice or vinegar
Perch		sprinkled vinegar, cinnamon or ginger or
		ginger sauce or mustard with verjuice & pepper
Pike	*Splat*	pike sauce
Plaice	*Sauce*	sprinkled with wine, or salt and wine
Porpoise	*Undertraunche*	sprinkled vinegar, cinnamon & ginger
Porpoise, salt		frumenty or pease pottage or
		sprinkled with vinegar
Roach		sprinkled verjuice, or vinegar, ginger & cinnamon
Salmon	*Chine*	
Salmon, salt		mustard
Seal, salt		frumenty
Shrimps		sprinkled with vinegar
Sole		sprinkled with vinegar or verjuice

	CARVING TERM	ACCOMPANIMENT
Sturgeon, salt	*Tranche*	sprinkled with vinegar or verjuice
Swordfish, salt		sprinkled with vinegar or verjuice or wine
Tench	*Sauce*	
Thornback		ginger sauce or mustard with verjuice & pepper
Thornback, salt		sprinkled with ginger
Trout, salt	*Culpon*	sprinkled with vinegar
Turbot		greensauce
Whale, salt		sprinkled vinegar, cinnamon & ginger
Whiting		butter

OTHER

Eggs	*Tyre*
Pasty	*Border*

The service of an everyday meal in the chamber, as described by John Russell, may now be presented in visual form, which is easier to follow than his original text.

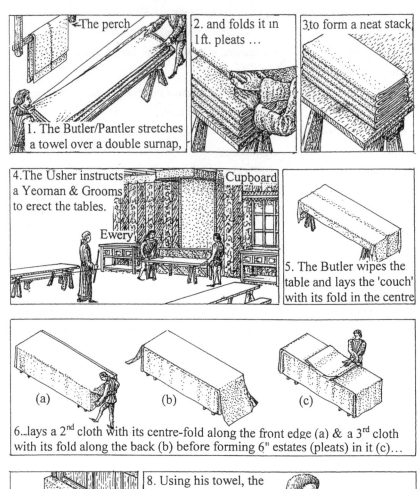

1. The Butler/Pantler stretches a towel over a double surnap,

2. and folds it in 1 ft. pleats ...

3. to form a neat stack

4. The Usher instructs a Yeoman & Grooms to erect the tables.

Cupboard

Ewery

5. The Butler wipes the table and lays the 'couch' with its fold in the centre

(a) (b) (c)

6...lays a 2nd cloth with its centre-fold along the front edge (a) & a 3rd cloth with its fold along the back (b) before forming 6" estates (pleats) in it (c)...

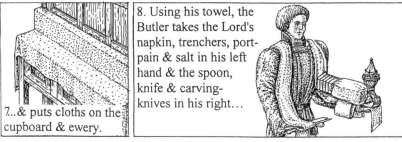

7...& puts cloths on the cupboard & ewery.

8. Using his towel, the Butler takes the Lord's napkin, trenchers, port-pain & salt in his left hand & the spoon, knife & carving-knives in his right...

Serving a meal in the chamber, parts 1–8.

458

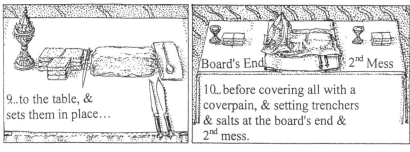

9...to the table, & sets them in place...

Board's End   2nd Mess

10...before covering all with a coverpain, & setting trenchers & salts at the board's end & 2nd mess.

11. He next sets cups, trenchers & salts on the other tables, ewer, basin, hot & cold water, napkins, spoons, wine & ale pots & cups on the ewery, & silver & gold on the cupboard.

12. The Lord washes... then takes his place for grace.

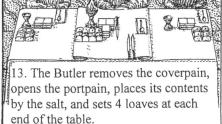

13. The Butler removes the coverpain, opens the portpain, places its contents by the salt, and sets 4 loaves at each end of the table.

14. The Almoner sets the alms dish on the table.

15. The Carver sets the Lord's trenchers using the tip of his knife...

16. pares the 4 sides & base off a loaf...

Serving a meal in the chamber, parts 9–16.

17...serves a quarter to the Lord and the rest into the alms dish, and cleans the crumbs.

18. The Sewer sees the Cook give the food to the Waiters, while the Clerks and Surveyor check it from the adjacent hatch.

19. The Sergeant at Arms, Sewer and Marshall lead the waiters through the Hall to the Chamber.

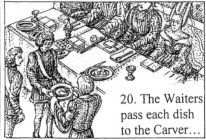

20. The Waiters pass each dish to the Carver...

21. ...who carves it into morsels, & sets these on the Lord's trenchers with the correct sauces close by.

22. Pheasants, chickens etc. had their 'wings' cut off and finely sliced in syrup.

23. Capons, hens, etc. had their 'wings' removed, then their thighs, both being chopped finely and sprinkled with ale or wine.

24. Peacock; the wings cut off & carved, but the legs left intact.

Serving a meal in the chamber, parts 17–24.

460

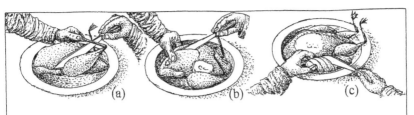

25. Goose etc, the legs removed first (a), then the wings (b), these being arranged as in (c) before carving.

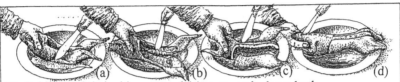

26. Rabbits had their skin removed (a), cuts made down both sides of the lower spine (b), were turned over and their sides cut free (c) then re-assembled, the nape of the neck removed, and the sides served to the Lord (d).

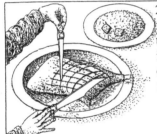

27. Venison was held firm with one knife, the other cutting it into squares,& put on a bed of frumenty.

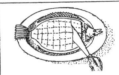

28. Plaice had the skin & fins removed, then cut into squares.

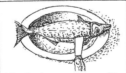

29. Cod etc. were split down the back and had their skin bones and roe removed.

30. Salmon were carved like cod, then cut into pieces for the Lord's trencher.

31. Crab meat was prepared & returned to its shell, while peeled shrimps were set round a saucer of vinegar.

Serving a meal in the chamber, parts 25–31.

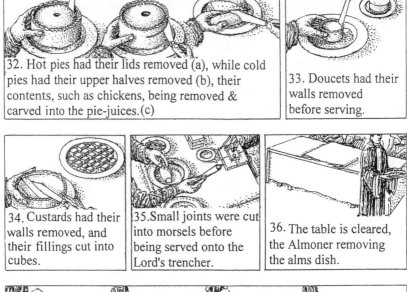

32. Hot pies had their lids removed (a), while cold pies had their upper halves removed (b), their contents, such as chickens, being removed & carved into the pie-juices.(c)

33. Doucets had their walls removed before serving.

34. Custards had their walls removed, and their fillings cut into cubes.

35. Small joints were cut into morsels before being served onto the Lord's trencher.

36. The table is cleared, the Almoner removing the alms dish.

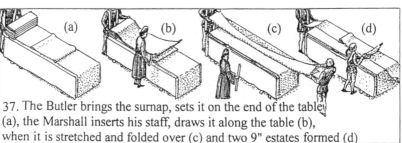

37. The Butler brings the surnap, sets it on the end of the table (a), the Marshall inserts his staff, draws it along the table (b), when it is stretched and folded over (c) and two 9" estates formed (d)

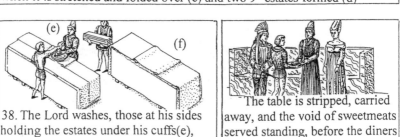

38. The Lord washes, those at his sides holding the estates under his cuffs(e), and the surnap ceremonies are reversed(f)

The table is stripped, carried away, and the void of sweetmeats served standing, before the diners retire to the Chamber.

Serving a meal in the chamber, parts 32–39.

In the houses of the gentry, merchants and more prosperous crafts-men, meals were also served in the chamber but without any of this elaborate ceremonial. At their level, the chamber was a comfortable bed-sitting-room, with arks and chests for storage, chairs, benches or stools for seating, and a trestle- or folding-table for dining.[40] English woodcuts showing a man dining at his chamber table, while his wife or other female dependant stirs a pot over the chamber fire, show just how comfortable, convenient and informal this form of dining could be.

Figure 72. Dining in a small chamber.
This woodcut of c.1510 shows a lesser merchant or craftsman dining in a small chamber which has all the essentials for comfort, including food piping hot from the chamber fireplace.

Figure 73. The 1380 kitchen tower at Wressle Castle, Yorks., ready for serving dinner. Regrettably, it was completely demolished in 1650, only the early sixteenth-century bakehouse being allowed to survive.

(1) lantern; (2) kitchen gallery, from where the clerks could supervise the cooks almost 40 feet below; (3) kitchen, with four large fireplaces; (4) pastry oven; (5) boiling house [?]; (6) cook's lodging; (7) cook's chamber; (8) kitchen cellar; (9) dresser hatch and surveying-place; (10) pantry; (11) buttery, with stairs down to beer cellar; (12) screens passage; (13) hall; (14) later bakehouse.

CHAPTER TWENTY-FOUR

Great Feasts

There is plenty of evidence to show that kings, prelates, great nobles and lesser lords had completely abandoned their halls from the early fourteenth century. John Russell confirming that,[1]

Pope, Emperowre, king or cardynalle,
Prince with goldyn rodde Royalle,
Archbischoppe, vayng to the palle,
Duke, all these of dygnyte owght not
      kepe the halle.

In view of this precise, unambiguous statement from an unimpeachable source, it is rather surprising to find that kings, nobles and great churchmen still dined in their halls, though only for great feasts. For every coronation up to 1837, for example, monarchs dined on the dais of Westminster Hall, served by their great officers of state, including the King's Champion on horseback. Queen Elizabeth II still dines with her knights in St George's Hall in Windsor Castle each Garter Day, continuing this tradition. Medieval kings also dined in their halls on great days of estate such as Christmas Day, New Year's Day and Easter.

For these days of high festivity the usually bare walls of the hall would be hung with rich textiles and tapestries, transforming the interior from a basic staff canteen into a massive state apartment. Behind the dais, the King's cloth of estate was put up close to the centre of the table, with the Queen's to its right (when viewed from the hall), hers being lower than the King's by the width of the valance. To the left of the King, a seat was prepared for a bishop, and then one for a duke or, if no duke was present, seats for two earls. Similarly, seats were set up to the right of the Queen, first for a duchess, a countess, and a baroness if of royal blood. Once either

Figure 74. Edward IV at table.

The Black Book of the Household showed a duke and bishop to the King's right, and two earls to his left, as specified in the royal ordinances. The table is set with the salts (left and right), trenchers, dishes, the carving knife, and a covered cup, a second cup being borne forward from the tiered cupboard.

an earl or a baron had served the King with his ewer and basin for hand-washing, and the others had washed, they took their places, and the first course was brought in, preceded by a procession of officers. First came the sergeant of arms, then the comptroller, the treasurer, the steward, the great chamberlain, if present, the sewer, and then the waiters, the first two being esquires of the body. The King and Queen were then served by their own noble carvers, just as were their fellow-diners by attendants of suitable rank, those for the duke (and duchess?), for instance, being just below the rank of baron.[2] For the King and Queen, a prince or princess, a duke or duchess, and their children, each dish was assayed before being carved, the carver cutting off small pieces of all solid foods, and scooping up samples of all liquids and sauces on pieces of bread, and putting them in the mouths of the waiters, to ensure that they were not poisoned.[3] Unfortunately the exact details of these and subsequent operations of table-service on days of estate in royal halls are not fully recorded, but they must have closely followed those used for the enthronement feast of George Neville as Archbishop of York. This took place in the great hall of his palace behind York Minster in 1466, and was organized by those fully familiar with English and Continental court traditions.

In addition to having ecclesiastical significance, this particular feast was designed as a means of demonstrating the might, wealth and political ascendancy of the great Neville family, the most powerful noble dynasty during the Wars of the Roses.

The steward of the feast was the head of the family, Richard Neville (1428–71), Earl of Warwick and Salisbury, Knight of the Garter, Captain of Calais, Constable of Dover Castle, and owner of great estates in the North, the Midlands and the Welsh Marches. A man of action, he had played significant parts in the battles of St Albans, Northampton and Towton, and, as Captain of the Sea, had captured Spanish and Genoese carracks whose £10,000 cargoes distributed as prizes had halved the price then current in England of some luxurious commodities. As Great Chamberlain of England and someone who had personal experience of the English and Burgundian courts, he knew how such a great feast should be organized.

Warwick's great power had enabled him to project his younger brothers into positions of influence. John Neville (c. 1430–71) who acted as treasurer for the feast, had just been granted the earldom of Northumberland, with full enjoyment of the vast north-country estates of their Percy rivals, while George Neville (1433–76), host of the feast, had completed his meteoric rise to the Primacy of England while only in his early thirties. Invested as Prebend of Masham at York Minster when just fourteen, he had become Chancellor of Oxford University at twenty-one, Bishop of Exeter at twenty-three, Chancellor of England at twenty-seven, and founder of the still-surviving St William's College in York at twenty-eight. The other great officer of the feast, the comptroller who kept the counter-roll to check the treasurer's records, was Warwick's brother-in-law, William, Lord Hastings (1430?–1483), Grand Chamberlain of the royal household, Knight of the Garter, Master of the Mint, and owner of wide estates in the Midlands and Yorkshire.

The officers of the table included Lord Willoughby de Eresby as carver, Lord John of Buckingham as cupbearer, Sir Richard Strangeways as sewer, Sir Walter Worley as marshal of the hall, and Sir John Mauleverer as pantler. The sergeant of the King's Ewery acted as ewerer, Ralph Lord Greystoke (c. 1413–87) and Lord Neville were keepers of the cupboard, and Sir John Brecknock was surveyor of the hall. There were also a thousand officers and servants to distribute the food to all the other tables.

Since all of those had to be fed, in addition to over 2000 guests, raw materials had to be gathered in vast quantities.

MEAT

6 wild bulls	1000 sheep
104 oxen	304 porkers
304 calves	2000 suckling pigs
204 kids	

GAME

500+ deer	104 peacock
4000 rabbits	2000 pheasant
204 bittern	4000 pigeon
204 crane	400 plover
100 curlew	1200 quail
4000 duck	2400 'Rees'
1000 egret	400 swan
400 heron	400 woodcock
500 partridge	

POULTRY

1000 capons	2000 geese
2000 chickens	

FISH

608 bream & pike	12 porpoise & seal

WHEAT

300 qtrs

BAKEMEATS

4000 hot venison pasties	3000 cold custards
1500 cold venison pasties	2000 hot custards
3000 plain jellies	4000 cold tarts
1000 parted jellies	

DRINKS

504,000 pts (ale at 110 imperial gallons per tun)

168,000 pts wine

540 pts hippocras

Neither the Archbishop's great hall just to the north of York Minster, nor that at his palace at Cawood have survived, so it is now impossible to judge their size or construction. However, reference to a lower hall may suggest that the great hall itself was at first-floor level, over an undercroft. At the upper end of the hall was a raised dais bearing the high table, its long bench set with four cushions of cloth of gold or fine silk, beneath a cloth of estate. Below, in the body of the hall, were six great tables lined with chairs and stools. Since the fireplace would occupy a central position a short way down the hall, it is most probable that the tables and seating were arranged as shown in the schematic plan on the following page.

As expected, no ladies dined in the hall, their tables being set up in the first and second chambers shown in the plan which follows. Here, too, dined Edward IV's youngest brother, Richard Duke of Gloucester, the future King Richard III. Aged fourteen, he was then living in the Earl of Warwick's household.

Once everyone was seated, the 57 cooks and 115 scullions, spit-turners and other staff could start to serve four separate three-course dinners. The Low Hall and Gallery were presumably served with the beef, mutton, pork, kid and suckling pig, with their pottages, since these ingredients (shown among the materials above) are excluded from the bills of fare listed below. The first dinner consists entirely of fish and was presumably reserved for the clergy. It reads as follows:

THE HALL

Bishop of Ely	Bishop of Durham	Bishop of London	Archbishop of York	Duke of Suffolk	Earl of Oxford	Earl of Worcester

10 Abbots and 20 Priors	5 Lords and 48 Knights
Dean and Brethren of York Minster Dean of St Saviour's	Mayor of the Staple at Calais Lord Mayor of York & its worshipful citizens
Judges 4 Barons of the Exchquer 26 Lawyers	69 Squires, all wearing the King's livery

THE CHIEF CHAMBER

Duchess of Suffolk	Duke of Gloucester	Countess of Westmorland	Countess of Northumberland	2 of Warwick's daughters

Baroness Greystoke 3 other Baronesses 12 other ladies	18 gentlewomen of the other ladies

THE SECOND CHAMBER

Dowager Duchess of Suffolk Countess of Warwick Countess of Oxford Lady Hastings Lady Fitzhewe	Lady Huntley Lady Strangeways 8 other ladies

THE GREAT CHAMBER

Bishops of Lincoln, Chester, Exeter and Carlisle

Earl of Westmorland Earl of Northumberland Lord Fitzhewe Lord Stanley 10 Barons	14 gentlemen 14 gentlewomen

THE LOW HALL

2 sittings each of 412 gentlemen, franklins and yeomen

THE GALLERY

2 sittings each of over 400 noblemen's servants

GREAT FEASTS

FIRST COURSE

First Pottage	Roast Whale
Almond Butter	Pike in Harblet
Red Herrings	Baked Eel
Salt Fish	Broiled Salmon Steaks
Salt Pike	Baked Turbot
Salt Eel	Fritters
Boiled Cod, Codling and Haddock	

SECOND COURSE

Salmon Head & Shoulder	Roast Lamprey
Salt Sturgeon	Young Herring [or Sprat]
Whiting	Turbot
Pilchards	Roach
Eel	Baked Salmon
Mackerell	Ling in Jelly
Fried Plaice	Baked Bream
Barbel	Tench in Jelly
Roast Conger Eel	Crabs
Trout	

THIRD COURSE

Sturgeon Head and Shoulder	Fried Small Perch
Great Jellies	Roast Smelt
Broiled Conger Eel	Shrimps
Chub	Small Minnows
Bream	Baked Whale
Rudd	Baked? Lobster
Lamprey	

The second-quality meat dinner was probably served to those at the lower tables in the hall and in the chambers since, though very rich and varied in its content, it lacks the most lavish dishes,

FIRST COURSE

Brawn & Bustard, with Malmsey

Venison with Frumenty	Swan in Galantine
Pottage Royal	Roast Capon & Goose
Salt Hart for Standard	Pieces of Roast Venison
Salt Roe	Beef
Frumenty Royal	Baked Venison
Roast Signet	A Great Custard, planted, subtlety

SECOND COURSE

First, Jelly	Roast Woodcock
Venison in break	Roast Plover
Peacock in his Hackles	Bream in sauce 'ponnyuert'
Roast rabbit	Leach Cipres
Roe Reversed	'Fuller napkyn'
Larded Venison	Dates in molde (stewed soft?)
Roast Partridge	Chestnuts Royal, subtlety

THIRD COURSE

Blank Desire	Roast Martins/Swifts
Dates in Compost	Roast Great Birds
Roast Bittern	Roast Larks
Roast Pheasant	Leach baked
Roast Egret	Fritter Crispayne
Roast Rabbits	Baked Quinces
Roast Quail	Champlet viander, subtelty

AFTER DINNER

Wafers and hippocras

The finest dinner of all, certainly destined for the top table in the hall, included the highest-quality foods, and sculptural subtleties, some of them garnished in gold leaf for maximum effect.

FIRST COURSE

Subtlety of St George	Roast Teal
Viand Cipres Pottage	Pike in Harblet
Partridges in Brasill	Baked Woodcock

Roast Haunch of Venison	Partridge Leach
Roast Swan	Dolphin in foil, subtlety
Fat Capons	Hart, for a subtlety

SECOND COURSE

Brent Tuskin to pottage	Bream in Harblet
Roast Crane	Baked venison
Roast Rabbit	Dragon, a subtlety
Roast Heron	Portpayne
Roast Curlew	Leche Damask
	Sampson, a subtlety

THIRD COURSE

Dates in Compost	Roast Lark
Peacock with Gilded Beak	Tench in Jelly
Roast Reyes	Baked Venison
Roast Rabbit	Petypanel in Marchpane
Roast Partridge	A subtelty, a tart
Roast Redshank	Leach Lombard, gilts
Roast Plover	Party Jelly
Roast Quail & Snipe	Subtelty of St William with his coat of arms between his hands

AFTER DINNER

Wafers and hippocras

The illustrations which follow portray, in a sequence of nine pages, the service of the Archbishop in his hall in the close of York Minster at his enthronement feast discussed in previous pages. We can trace each operation in turn, assuming that the hall has been prepared and the tables laid as described in the last chapter. The sequence of events closely resembles methods of service shown in thirteenth- and fourteenth-century manuscript illuminations, suggesting that it represents a much older tradition.

1. In the Hall, everyone waits…

Reward   2nd Mess

2. On the dais, the table has been set up between the ewery table and cupboard

Officers' ewer & basin   Basin of Assay   Cup of Assay   Surnap & Towel

Officers' towels 2nd Mess ewers, basins & towels   Basin of Estate   Reward ewers, basins and towels

Towel of Estate

3. The Yeoman of the Ewery has prepared the ewery table

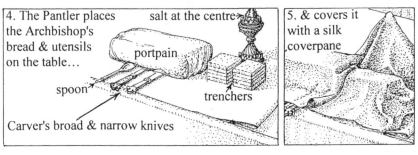

4. The Pantler places the Archbishop's bread & utensils on the table…

salt at the centre

portpain

spoon

trenchers

Carver's broad & narrow knives

5. & covers it with a silk coverpane

6. The Sewer and a Gentleman lay the surnap on the table

7. The Archbishop's party arrive and stand on the dais, ready for the hand-washing ceremony

Archbishop Neville's enthronement feast, parts 1–7.

8. The Marshal appoints the Carver, Sewer, Cupbearer (a deacon), 2 Gentlemen to serve the Reward and 2 more for the 2nd Mess.

They wash at the ewery Table and are 'armed' there by the Yeoman of the Ewery

9. The Marshal & Carver lead the Pantler to the middle of the Hall, bow, & bow again before the table

10. The Carver kneels

11. and gives the Pantler the coverpain…

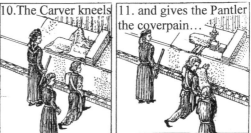

12. before moving the salt 3ft. to the right with the portpain beyond it

13. Using his broad knife, the Carver moves the trenchers, opens the portpain, gives it to the Pantler, re-arranges the loaves and scrapes the crumbs into his napkin

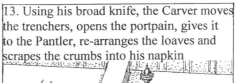

14. The Carver cuts pieces off the trencher & loaf & gives them to the Pantler to eat as assay.

15. The Carver dips a corner of bread into the salt in 4 places, shakes it & gives it to the Pantler to eat as assay

Archbishop Neville's enthronement feast, parts 8–15.

16. The Pantler returns to the cupboard, the Carver cleans the cloth and a Gentleman & Yeoman of the Ewery take the surnap back to the ewery table.

The Carver uses his knife to lift a pile of trenchers onto his napkin...

17. sets 4 before the Archbishop's place & a loaf on top, then cuts 3 pieces off it & lays them to the right.

18. At the ewery table the Yeoman of the Ewery kisses the towel of estate & places it on the Marshall's left shoulder.

19. scoops a little water [from the basin of estate?], drinks it, & gives it to the cupbearer with the basin of estate

20. The Marshal and Cupbearer bow before the Archbishop.

The Marshal takes the towel of estate & places it over the left shoulder of the lord to His Grace's left.

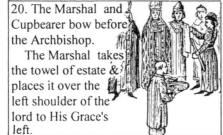

21. The Marshal takes the cup of assay, which the cupbearer fills from the basin of estate

22. The lord with the towel passes one end just beneath the Archbishop's cuffs to the most important man to his right, so that the Archbishop may now wash his hands.

23. Now all the others at the top table wash.

Archbishop Neville's enthronement feast, parts 16–23.

24. The Marshal sets those at the top table in their places

25. The Carver takes the napkin from his left shoulder, kisses it, and gives it to the Archbishop.

26. He then uses his napkin to polish the spoon, kisses it, and uses his broad knife to place it to the right of the Archbishop.

27. A Gentleman sets trenchers, bread, napkins and spoons to the Reward while another sets the 2nd mess.

AT THE DRESSER-HATCH

28. The Sewer assays the food by;
a) cutting cornets of trencher bread, dipping them into four parts of each sauce, pottage, custard, jelly or opened tart or pie, and shaking off the surplus, or...

b) cutting pieces from the middle of each joint or fish, or...

c) from the thigh or wing of poultry;

29. then gives them to the Cook and Steward to eat.

30. The Marshal and Sewer lead the waiters to the top table where they bow.

Archbishop Neville's enthronement feast, parts 24–30.

477

31. The Sewer and each waiter in turn kneel by the Carver

32. The Sewer uncovers each dish, hands it to the Carver who cuts assays for the Sewer & Waiters to taste as assay

33. The Carver sets 3 more trenchers to top of His Grace's 4

34. The Carver uncovers the Salt and uses his broad knife to spread a little on a trencher.

35. He then cuts the trencher into 4, and puts them in front of the 3 trenchers.

THE CARVER CARVES THE FIRST MEAT OR FISH

36. The Carver serves the Salt to the Reward, returns it to its place, sets an uncovered standing salt at the 2nd Mess and triangular half-trencher-bread salts at each place.

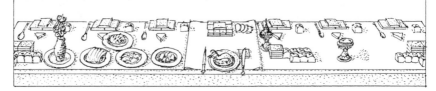

37. At the Buttery, the Marshal sees the covered Cup of Estate filled with wine, and the Butler drink a little as assay, before giving it to the Cupbearer.

The Cupbearer bows at the table, kneels, takes off the cover, pours a few drops from the cup into the cover, holds it under the cup, drinks the ale or wine, replaces the cover, and places the cup beside the Archbishop.

Archbishop Neville's enthronement feast, parts 31–37.

38. When the first roast meat is carved, the Cup-bearer brings the Archbishop a fresh cup of wine, serving it with the same ceremony as 37, but holding the cover beneath the cup as he drinks. Meanwhile, Cupbearers serve the others, and the Sewer brings in all the sauces.

THE 2nd COURSE IS NOW SERVED JUST LIKE THE 1st.

39. When the tart or marchpane is served, the Carver removes the trencher salts to a voider. The cheese is then served.

TO CLEAR THE TABLE:

40. A Gentleman collects 2nd Mess food into a voider and Collects the saucers, spoons & napkins.

41. The Pantler removes the 2nd Mess salt.

42. A Gentleman clears the Reward (as 40). Two others place a voider at each end of the table, bow, & use broad knives to lift all bread, trenchers and crumbs into a voider, (but not touching the Archbishop's setting) then bow & carry the voiders back to the cupboard

43. The Sewer brings a voider to the Carver, who puts the trencher supporting his carving-knife into it, cleans the tablecloth, adds the Archbishop's used bread & trenchers and cleans the table again.

44. Having wiped his knives on his napkin he uses his broad knife to lift a trencher 18ins to the left, then lays both knives by the salt.

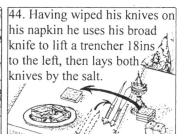

Archbishop Neville's enthronement feast, parts 38–44.

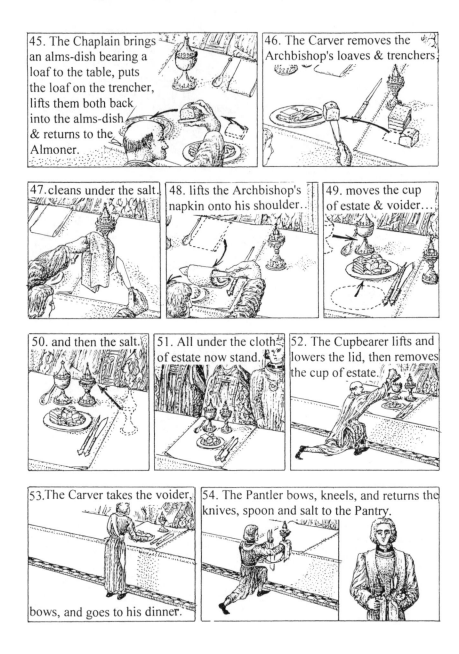

45. The Chaplain brings an alms-dish bearing a loaf to the table, puts the loaf on the trencher, lifts them both back into the alms-dish & returns to the Almoner.

46. The Carver removes the Archbishop's loaves & trenchers.

47. cleans under the salt.

48. lifts the Archbishop's napkin onto his shoulder.

49. moves the cup of estate & voider...

50. and then the salt.

51. All under the cloth of estate now stand.

52. The Cupbearer lifts and lowers the lid, then removes the cup of estate.

53. The Carver takes the voider, bows, and goes to his dinner.

54. The Pantler bows, kneels, and returns the knives, spoon and salt to the Pantry.

Archbishop Neville's enthronement feast, parts 45–54.

55. The Sewer serves the Archbishop, and Gentlemen serve the Reward and 2nd Mess, with rolled and flat wafers and spices.

56. Cupbearers serve hippocras, remove spice plates & clean table.

HAND WASHING

57. The Sewer brings the surnap (of one towel folded within another), kisses it, & bows.

58 The Marshal bows. The Sewer puts the towel on the table, holding one end as the Gentleman for the Reward feeds out the upper part.

59. The Marshal pulls along the top of the surnap, puts in his rod, raises it, bows, puts it down, gives it to a Gentleman of the 2nd Mess, & then removes his rod.

60. The surnap is stretched.

61. The near edge of the top towel is folded over to its far edge.

62. The Marshal forms two 18"estates.

Archbishop Neville's enthronement feast, parts 55–62.

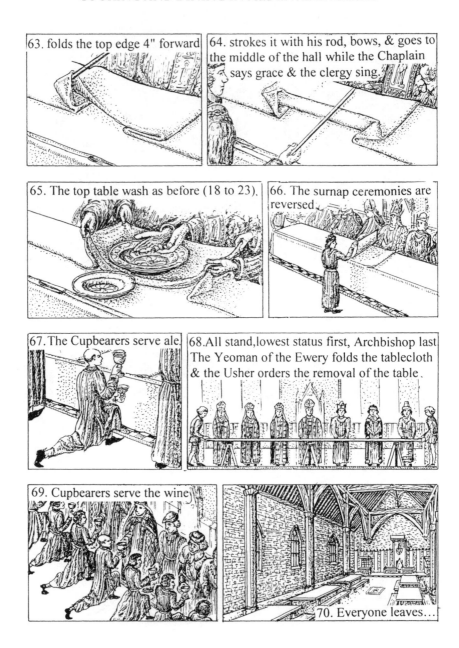

63. folds the top edge 4" forward

64. strokes it with his rod, bows, & goes to the middle of the hall while the Chaplain says grace & the clergy sing.

65. The top table wash as before (18 to 23).

66. The surnap ceremonies are reversed

67. The Cupbearers serve ale.

68. All stand, lowest status first, Archbishop last The Yeoman of the Ewery folds the tablecloth & the Usher orders the removal of the table.

69. Cupbearers serve the wine

70. Everyone leaves...

Archbishop Neville's enthronement feast, parts 63–70.

Neither the food issued from the kitchen, nor the drink from the cellars, was ever returned to these offices for serving at another meal. Instead, all left-overs were carefully gathered together by the almoner, usually a priest, for distribution to the poor. Although this practice must have helped to ensure that only fresh food was cooked daily, promoting the health of the household, its real purpose was to fulfil the Christian obligation to feed the poor as an act of corporal mercy. St Matthew (25:35) had recorded Christ's teaching, 'I was an hungered, and ye gave me meat; I was thirsty, and ye gave me drink;... Inasmuch as ye have done it unto me.' To keep this principle constantly in mind, murals depicting Lazarus begging crumbs from Dives' table, the latter going to Hell for his lack of charity, as told by St Luke chapter 16, were painted on the walls opposite the dais in the halls of royal castles from the mid-thirteenth century.[5] In England, the King's almoner was provided with funds raised by the sale of felons' goods and 'deodands', the objects which had been the actual cause of deaths, in addition to the food collected daily in his almony. Some indication of the scale of these operations is provided by records of the physical dimensions of royal almonies, that at Havering being 50 feet by 22 feet, and at Nottingham 40 feet by 25 feet.[6]

Whatever the size of their households, the almoner's duties were similar to those described in Bishop Grosseteste's regulations of the 1240s, which state that the remaining food should always 'be kepyd, & not sende not to boys and knafis, nother in halle nothe of the halle, ne be wasted in soperys ne dyners of gromys, but wysely, temperatly, with-oute bate or betyng [reduction], be hit distribute and deportyd to poure men, beggars, syke-folke and feballe.' In practice this meant that after the tables had been cleared, the food and drink were carried to the gate, which had been closed the duration of the meal. Now it was opened by the porter, who kept order with his long staff as the distribution took place, enabling the poorest members of society to survive on regularly-provided supplies of good food.[7]

From the opening decades of the sixteenth century, the food and manners of the English nobility and gentry were to evolve in all manner of ways as new ingredients, recipes, meal-times and fashions gradually swept aside the great medieval culinary and dining traditions. Within a couple of centuries they had been largely forgotten, knowledge and wonder at their vast skill and scale only being revived through later antiquarian research. While this was happening, one tradition alone continued unabated, that of almsgiving. Even at the opening of the twentieth century, the poorest in the villages around great houses such as Blenheim Palace were still being served with the lavish left-overs of ducal dining tables.

Notes

The sources most generally used have been abbreviated as follows:

Austin   Austin, T., *Two Fifteenth-Century Cookery-Books* (EETS Old Series XCI 1881).
EDD   Wright, J. (ed), *The English Dialect Dictionary* (Oxford 1923).
H & B   Hieatt, C.B. & Butler, S., *Curye on Inglysch*, EETS (Oxford 1985).
HO   The Society of Antiquaries of London, *A Collection of Ordinances …for the Government of the Royal Household …also Receipts in Ancient Cookery* (1790).
Mc C & B   McCarthy, M.R. & Brooks, C.M., *Medieval Pottery in Britain AD 900–1600* (Leicester 1988).
Napier   Napier, A., *A Noble Boke off Cookry* (1882).
NHB   Percy, T., ed., *The Regulations and Establishment of the Household of Henry Algernon Percy, the fifth Earl of Northumberland at his Castles of Wressle and Leckonfield in Yorkshire Begun anno domini MDXII* [*The Northumberland Household Book*] (1905 edition).
OED   *The Oxford English Dictionary*.
S & H   Stell, P.M., & Hampson, L., *Probate Inventories of the Diocese of York 1350–1500* (York 1998).
Warner   Warner, R., *Antiquitates Culinariae* (1791).

CHAPTER I
THE COUNTING HOUSE
1. Kenyon (2002) 27–8. The Kidwelly cofferer's office is provided with a high window to give good light for writing, two deep, arched recesses, perhaps for beds for clerks safeguarding the contents of the strong-room, and a latrine for their use.
2. *OED* s.v. 'Oubliette'.
3. E.g. *NHB* 30–33.
4. *HO* 15.
5. *HO* 13–86.
6. *HO* 69.
7. Emery (1970) 170.
8. Emery (1985) 276–339. Counting houses/officers' chambers over the buttery and pantry are also recorded at Kings College, Cambridge in 1447–8 and Durham Castle 1494–1502 (Salzman 522 & 410) and at Winchester College 1397–1400 (Emery (1970) 170).

9. Jones. 10.
10. Taylor (2004) 25.
11. PRO SG6/922/7; DL 29/584/9259.
12. Bursar's Roll, New College, Oxford, 1400–03. See also Nicolas 170. Salzman 248–9 describes the York Exchequer great counters *c.* 1320 as measuring 13x12ft, with fir boards bordered in oak, and 11x8ft, with fir boards bordered in alder.
13. Maddox 261; Barclay C ii/I.
14. S & H 43, 92, 130, 265, 305, etc.
15. The following text is based on *NHB*, Furnivall, *Early English Meals & Manners* 194–7, *HO*, and Brears (1999) 17–26.
16. Thurley (1993) 3.
17. *NHB* 4–19.
18. *NHB* 27.
19. *NHB* 19, 12–15, 17.
20. *NHB* 14, 145.
21. *NHB* 391.
22. *NHB* 60.
23 Davies, Pt 2, 276.

CHAPTER 2

PLANNING FOR COOKING

1. Mayes & Butler 32–3, 73–5; Oswald fig. 40; Wrathmell 8–9; Beresford figs 5, 11.
2. O'Neil 16, fig.2.
3. Wood 147–8.
4. Ibid. 248.
5. Martin (1997) 85–91; Meeson 73–4; Walker (2000) 75–6.
6. Hope 300.
7. Breakspear 4; Renn 49; Jones 14; Emery (1970) 233, 129; Emery (1985).
8. Wood 73; Ambler 48–9; Mason 2.
9. Wood 58.
10. Godfrey 110–11.
11. Emery (1970) 228.

12. Ibid. 257; Thompson (1870) 48–59.
13. Parker 297–300. See also Hams Barton in Wood 194.
14. Ambler pl. XXXVIII; Wood 107. See also Lower Bramble, Wood 194.
15. VCH Durham III 70–71; Thurley (1993) 146 117; Emery (1970) 280.
16. Thurley (1993) 146.
17. Taylor (2003) 33.
18. Woolgar 201–202; Thompson 81–2; Bedingfield (frontis.); Peers.
19. Emery (1970) 118, 105, 110, 122.
20. Orde Powlett 20.
21. Emery (1970) 124, 228, 280; Thurley (1993) 116; Simpson 110–122; Falkener (1970) 141.
22. Smith in Thompson 22–3.
23. For a discussion of tower houses see Wood 166–176 and Smith (1940) 75–84.
24. *NHB*, 45, 372–7, 150–2, 291–6.
25. J. Goodall *Warkworth Castle* (forthcoming).
26. Thurley (1993) 9.
27. Kenyon 49–53.
28. Thompson (1937); Simpson (1937) 121–132.
29. Jones 8–12.
30. Thurley (1993) 22, fig. 30.
31. *NHB* 368–70.
32. Thurley (1993) 3.
33. Borenius & Charlton 55–84.
34. Taylor (1998) 34.
35. Renn 35, 49.
36. Taylor (2004) 27–8.
37. Kenyon (2002) 49.
38. Barnes & Simpson 42; Jones 15.
39. Ralegh Radford 12–15. The oven may be a 16th- or 17th-century insertion but probably reflects a longer tradition of cooking in this room.

40. Renn 30; Taylor (2004) 25.
41. Apted 191–210.
42. Orde Powlett.
43. Hunter Blair & Honeyman 20.

CHAPTER 3
WOOD, COALS, TURVES AND
  FIRES
1. E.g. Woolgar 77.
2. *NHB* 20–21 & 99–101.
3. Kirk.
4. Lillywhite 663.
5. Carlin & Rosenthal 122, 130.
6. S & H III.
7. *OED* s.v. 'Talshide'; Brears (1999)
  45–6.
8. Pimps are still made on the
  Leconfield Estate in West Sussex for
  use in Petworth House.
9. Mayes & Butler.
10. *NHB* 21.
11. Howard Household Books, 1481–90,
  328.
12. Walker, 104–5.
13. Myers 995, 1008 .
14. *NHB* 20–21, 100.
15. *NHB* 21.
16. S & H 288.
17. Fowler (1898) 95.
18. Le Strange 118.
19. Innocent 144.
20. *OED* s.v. 'Casing'; *EDD* s.v. 'Cassons';
  Brears (1987) 46–7.
21. Wright 64.
22. Hartley & Ingilby (1972) 77; *EDD*
  s.v. 'Cowls'.
23 Brears (1991) 72; Burton.
24. Brears (1998) 26.
25. Egan, fig. 93, no. 337; Ottaway &
  Rogers 2804, 3084.
26. Trevisa X. VIII. 379; Langland B.
  XVII, 245.

27. Grose & Astle 147–9.
28. *OED* s.v. 'Firepan'.
29. Brears (1991) 72.
30. S & H 93, 121, 232.
31 Nottingham III 258.
32. Riley 288.
33. Alcock 89.
34. *OED* s.v. 'Reredos'.
35. E.g. S & H 53, 93, 140, 147, 179.
36. S & H 63, 106, 107, 136, 315.
37. *OED* s.v. 'Chimney'.
38. S & H 85 , 97.
39. Rahtz & Watts 216–19.
40. S & H 288.
41. S & H 259.
42, Moorhouse & Greenaway 79–120;
  Mayes & Butler 49, 225–7.
43. Arnold 80–82.
44. *HO* 8S; Stell & Hampson 186.
45. Raine 72.
46. E.g. Ottaway & Rogers 2858–60;
  Allan 295.
47. S & H 87, 178, 298, 339.
47. S & H 44.

CHAPTER 4
WATER SUPPLIES
1. Boorde 252.
2. Robins 129–30; Riley 25.
3. Robins 129–30.
4. Barker, Baker, Hassall & Simco
  118–19.
5. Robins 101, 137; Allan (1999) 9.
6. Robins 107; Allan 16.
7. Robins 110.
8. Robins 93.
9. Personal observations.
10. BL MS. Cott, Nero. C.IV; English
  Heritage (1989) 17.
11. *Jacobs Well* 3.
12. Littlehales 29, 82.
13. Lillywhite 624; Caxton (1481) 96.

14. Dunning 100–103.
15. Caxton *Boke of the Fayt of Armes* ii c. 17; Salzman 267, 279, 411.
16. Hodgson 65; Ottaway & Rogers 2807.
17. Chaucer *The Clerk's Tale* lines 276–91.
18. Wright 32; Collins 33.
19. Robins 151.
20 Macpherson & Amos 167–173; Harbottle 7.

CHAPTER 5
THE DAIRY
1. Translated in Scott 144–6.
2. Purvis 217–8.
3. Hellier & Moorhouse 11–12; S & H 128, 141; Way 79; Fowler (1875) 371.
4. Wilson 147.
5. Boorde 267.
6. Brears (1998) 37.
7. Hellier & Moorhouse 11.
8. Boorde 266.
9. *EDD* s.v. 'Whang'.
10. S & H 299. See also Fowler (1875) 371.
11. *OED* s.v. 'Cheese–lip'.
12. S & H 20, 134, 140, 225.
13. McC & B 152–3, 246, 248.
14. Wilson 143, A36.
15. H & B V 123.

CHAPTER 6
THE BREWHOUSE
1. Dale & Redstone, e.g. 2, 31.
2. Wilson 333–4.
3. Bickerdyke, 49; Salzman 540 gives a 1478 contract for building an Exeter malthouse.
4. S & H 62, 301, etc.
5. Knight 161–3.
6. Writers of Eminence I 274–279. For instructions to carry out domestic malting today see Berry 43–5.
7. Findlay 167–175.
8. S & H 93; Allison & Rahtz 6–11.
9. MacCormick 73–79.
10. Allison & Rahtz II.
11. Woolgar 67; S & H 77; *NHB* 316; Bennett & Elton I 195, IV 195–6.
12. *NHB* 316.
13. Dale & Redstone 122.
14. S & H 44, 63, 74, 93, 120, 178, 340. In October 1419 Thomas Mellere made and set a pair of hand-mill stones for Dame Alice de Bryene, for under one shilling.
15. Walker 83–4.
16. Scourfield 3–12; Brears (1987) 125–129, Markham 120–124.
17. *EDD* s.v. 'Betany', 'Betwan'; *OED* s.v. 'Betony'.
18. Gerard II CCC 705.
20. Boorde 122.
21. Brears (1998) 23.
22. *HO* 77, 92.
23. *NHB* 136–8.
24. S & H 63, 203.
25. Way, *Promptorium parvulorum* 328/1; Rogers III 555/1; Riley 194.
26. S & H 92, 137, 299,203.
27. Brears (1993) 60–69.
28. H & B IV 205, V8.
29. Monckton 13.
30. Drummond & Wilbraham 43–44.
31. S & H 143, 203, 205.
32. *NHB* 136.
33. For cider consumption, Swabbey 67; Woolgar 128; Hartley (1954) 526–7.
34. Brears (1998) 74.
35. Wilson 275; Woolgar 128.

CHAPTER 7

THE BAKEHOUSE

1. Rahtz & Watts, 216–219; Brears (1987) 59–73.
2. Howitt 127–8, 130.
3. Jope & Threlfall 138–9.
4. Dale & Redstone, 122.
5. Based on Brears (1987) 65–6; Hutchinson 60–61.
6. Langland C. IX. 306; Austin VII, 269.
7. Brears (1987) 63.
8. Way 21; Trevisa 643.
9. Tibbott (1982) 23–6; Brears (1998) 31.
10. Dorset Federation of Women's Institutes, 'Crock or Flick Cakes', EDD s.v. 'Flead'.
11. S & H 203.
12. For definitions of cheat, crest, cribble, range, searced, etc., see their entries in OED.
13. S & H 150, 171, 283, 315.
14. Woolgar 124.
15. Dale & Redstone 124.
16. Markham 126; Chaucer, Millers Tale 362.
17. Field, 139–44; Stell & Hampson 130, 150, 166, 175, 176, 283, 285; Way, Promptorium parvulorum 129/1.
18. Woolgar 124.
19. Dale & Redstone 2; NHB 133; HO 69.
20. Brears (2003) 7; Starkey 254, nos 11470–5.
21. Markham 126–7.
22. Brears (1987) 91–2.
23. Austin 52 (Harleian MS. 279).
24. Edlin 76.
25. S & H 97, 120, 136, 174, 188, 204, 284.
26. OED s.v. 'Fork'.
27. NHB 100.
28. David 169–70.
29. Way, Promptorium parvulorum 23/2.
30. S & H 165, 202.
31. Bread baskets are frequently depicted in The Acts of Corporal Mercy, as in the window of All Saints, North Street, York.
32. Drummond & Wilbraham 41–2; Kirkland 11–12.
33. Walker 85, 127, 140.

CHAPTER 8

THE PASTRY

1. NHB 100; Neave 59.
2. Expeditions to Prussia and the Holy Land made by Henry, earl of Derby (afterwards King Henry IV), in 1390–91 and 1392–93 : being the accounts kept by the treasurer, ed. Lucy Toulmin Smith (Camden Society 1894) 64, quoted OED s.v. 'Pastler'.
3. Austin 54 XXX.
4. McC & B 154, no.121, 185, no. 369, 301, no. 1113, 437, nos 2082–3.
5. H & B IV 180 & 159, 160 & 162.
6. Ibid. IV 173.
7. Ibid. IV 159–160, 162, 172, 178, 174, 179.
8. Fowler (1898) 569; HO 455.
9. Austin 74.
10. Ibid. 54 & 51.
11. H & B 172, 176, 177; Austin 52 & 74.
12. Napier 52.
13. Austin 75 .
14. H & B II 82.
15. Ibid. 161.
16. Ibid. 64.
17. Austin 74.
18. H & B 183.
19. Ibid. 191, Austin 47, 55, 56; Napier 56; HO 443 which colours darioles

green, red or yellow.

20. Hodgett 21; Austin 50–55; *Romance of the Rose* 7044; *HO* 452.
21. H & B IV 116, 192; *HO* 443.
22. Ibid. 188; IV 116.
23. Ibid. IV 116.
24. Ibid. IV 142.
25. Prescott 40.
26. H & B 40–41.
27. Austin 52.
28. Ibid. 51; Collier 97 has a 1492 account for a bushel and a half of wheat to bake fish, 2s. 3d.
29. Beckwith 192.
30. Napier 55.
31. Austin 51, 73.
32. Ibid. 51, 54, 97.
33. Napier 55; H & B V 193, 194; Napier 56.
34. Austin 53, 75; Napier 58.
35. Ibid. 77.

CHAPTER 9

THE BOILING HOUSE

1. *HO* 21.
2. See p. 29.
3. Holden & Hudson 107–116; McNeil 40–88. See also *Archaeologia Cantiana* 70, pp. 44–67; *South Lincolnshire Archaeology* I, pp. 4–5; *Medieval Archaeology* 38 (1994), 134–163.
4. S & H 33, 63, 106, 136, 165, 299.
5. ibid. 88, 131, 136, 147, 148, 271.
6. Boorde 271.
7. Scott 140; Brears (1987) 31.
8. S & H 61, 135, 240, 274; Woolgar 117.
9. Godbolt & Turner, 19–54.
10. Nelson *Fifteenth Century School Book*, quoted in Wilson 32.
11. S & H 135 'Barrel with 2 salmon in

salt'; H & B II 69; Henisch 87.
12. Wilson 33–4.
13. Walker 138.
14. *NHB* 8.
15. Davidson 28.
16. *NHB* 8; *HO* 106; *Surtees Miscellany* (1888) 27.
17. *OED* s.v. 'Cade'; *HO* 202; *NHB* 9.
18. *HO* 102.
19. *HO* 101.
20. Brears (1999) 119–20.
21. See *OED* s.v. 'Cauldron'.
22. *The Gesta Romanorum*, Early English Text Society (1879) 385.
23. Caxton (1483) 46/37 has a reference to 'Isaac the ketelmaker'.
24. Butler & Green 18–26.
25. Fowler (1898) 89.
26. Mayes & Butler p. 49, fig. 18 hearth 2.
27. Butler & Green 170; Brownsword 114–17.
28. Fowler (1898) 89; *Calendar of Inquisitions* 41; *OED* s.v. 'Lead 5'.
29. Beresford 218, 242.
30. English Heritage archaeologists think that the Fountains Abbey brewhouse furnace is for boiling wool, but there is not a scrap of documentary, archaeological or logical evidence to suggest this, and their published reconstructions are nonsensical.
31. Emery (1970) 172, 265.
32. Raine (1868) 7.
33. Ibid. 16, 77–8.
34. Glasse 91; Fowler (1898) 97.
35. *OED* s.v. 'Scum'.
36. Egan 154.
37. Science Museum, London, Accession no. A635020.
38. Austin 107.
39. H & B V 12–14, 18–19, VI 60.
40. Egan 157.

41. BL MS Reg. 10EIV; Hurst (1961) 289, fig. 76, no. 16; Egan 155; Atkin Carter & Evans 58, fig. 40, no. 38.
42. Fowler (1898) 89.
43. Austin 104.
44. Austin 109.
45. Ibid.
46. *HO* 95.
47. Langland, *Piers Plowman* B XIX 274; Chaucer, *The Knight's Tale* line 1162; Dale & Redstone 117.
48. Hodgett 31–32.
49. *HO* 426; Langland, *Piers Plowman* A VIII 273.
50. *OED* s.vv. 'Coles' & 'Kale'.
51. Austin 5–6; Noble 72, 82, 85.
52. H & B II 27.
53. Ibid., e.g. II 1; IV 11.
54. Nicolas 64.
55. *OED* s.v. 'Souse'.
56. Brears (1999) 133; May 194.
57. Hone I 1622.
58. Balliol College, Oxford, MS 354 f. 228.
59. This version is based on that used by Jules Gouffé in his *Royal Cookery Book* (1869) 275–7.

CHAPTER 10
THE KITCHEN
1. Meason (2004) 9.
2. Jope & Threlfall 119.
3. S & H 280–81.
4. Walker, J. (2000) 75–6.
5. Morris 89–9.
6. Pearson 106–7.
7. Mayes & Butler 32, fig. 6.
8. Oswald 118, fig. 43.
9. For another polygonal kitchen see Sayer 268.
10. Hurst 239–43, fig. 61.
11. Borenius & Charlton 72–3.

12. Weaver 32–3.
13. Coppack 16; Wood 125, fig. 44.
14. Coppack 11; Emery 281; Bradbury 15, fig. 36.
15. Borenius & Charlton 72–3; Bedingfield, frontispiece.
16. Munby 15.
17. Emery (1996) 177.
18. Parker 151.
19. Salzman 235.
20. See *OED* s.v. 'Louvre (4)' for various quotations.
21. Turner 128, fig. 29.
22. Weaver 7–9.
23. Jones 10, 14–15.
24. Salzman 196.
25. Ibid. 280.
26. BL MS Royal 14 EIV f. 244v. Windsor Castle accounts for 1534–5 include 'making a new leved Dore and a Wykett in the same ffor the great Kitchen, with a ffolding Dresser upon the said Wykett to sett mette uppon at the serves time'.
27. Turner 53.
28. Kenyon 42.
29. Barnes & Simpson 42.
30. Parker 216.
31. Morley (1976) 125.
32. Raine (1836) 81–4.
33. Black (1968) 339–41.
34. Taylor (2004) 25.
35. Renn 30.
36. Kenyon 31–2.

CHAPTER 11
KITCHEN FURNITURE
1. Hassall 153.
2. BL MS Add. 42130 ff. 206v.
3. S & H 87, 205.
4. Hurst 291, fig. 76, no. 19; Cowgill, de Neergaard & Griffiths 85, fig. 58,

no. 55 may be a smaller, early to mid 14th-century example.

5. S & H 188, 272, 298.
6. Cowgill, de Neergaard & Griffiths 87, fig. 59, no. 76; S & H 188, 165.
7. Halliday 1.
8. Adams 21; Thompson (1932) 18.
9. Arnold 80.
10. PRO/SL6/922/3 mld.
11. Salzman 250.
12. *The Athenaeum* no. 3056 (22nd May 1886) 687.
13. S & H 165, 189; *Calendar of Inquisitions* 2, 40.
14. S & H 132, 150, 152, 178, 245 310.
15. Ibid. 20, 33, 44, 88, 125,136, 150, 298.
16. Wharram Percy Excavation Report, forthcoming.
17. Atkinson (1891) 22.
18. *HO* 148.
19. Emery (1970) 268 .
20. Amyot 267.
21. *HO* 148.
22. *OED* s.vv. 'Apron', 'Barm', 'Harden' (2), S & H 39.
23. S & H 154.
24. Ibid. 167, 295, 298 and passim.; Way 207.
25. S & H 62, 92, 131, 235, 288.
26. Ibid. 165, 202, 250; Wellbeloved 106–8.
27. McC & B 322, 334, 339–40, 365, 367–8, 388.
28. S & H 20, 141, 206, 245.
29. H & B I 48 .
30. Amyot 277–8.
31. Austin 38.
32. Reproduced in Brears (1999) 41.
33. *Liber cure cocorum* 7.
34. E.g. H & B II 11, 61, 77, V 3.
35. E.g. Napier 26; H & B II 32, 37.
36. Brears (2003) 30–33.

37. *Expeditions to Prussia and the Holy Land made by Henry, earl of Derby (afterwards King Henry IV), in 1390–91 and 1392–93 : being the accounts kept by the treasurer*, ed. Lucy Toulmin Smith (Camden Society 1894) 22/3; Austin 11, no. XXVIII.
38. Fowler (1898) 89.
39. H & B V 13.
40. Austin 7.
41. Gerard II CCCX/11; *OED* s.v. 'Scouring'.
42. More 117.
43. Dale & Redstone 123.
44. I have used Nevill Coghill's translation of *The Canterbury Tales* (Penguin Books, 1960 ed.) pp. 27, 134, from The Prologue and The Cook's Prologue.
45. Jamieson 90–94.
46. *OED* s.v. 'Lickpot'.

CHAPTER 12
POTTAGE UTENSILS

1. Mayes & Butler 15, 48–9.
2. S & H 132.
3. Walcott 226, 212.
4. ibid. 222; S & H 80.
5. Fowler (1898) 89; Atkins, Carter & Evans fig. 8, nos. 10–11.
6. Brears (1998) 83–4, 125.
7. Fowler (1898) 89, 97; S & H 165; Douglas 1146.
8. *OED* s.v. 'Pan'; Egan nos. 470–78, fig. 146.
9. S & H 164–5.
10. Purvis 162, P. 2, 640; *Calendar of Inquisitions Miscellaneous* no. 5.
11. *Calendar of Inquisitions Miscellaneous* nos. 72, 116, 571, 573. The weights have been calculated at the rate of 3d per lb., which appears to be the

standard price at this date.

12. Lindsey 55.
13. H & B II 26, III 12, IV 32, 52.
14. S & H 165.
15. Fowler (1898) 68; *OED* s.v. 'Skillet'.
16. *EDD* s.v. 'Skillet'.
17. Moorhouse, in Mayes & Butler 186–7; Chinnery, in Vyner & Wrathmell 147.
18. H & B III 5, IV 181, 185; Austin 39.
19. Austin 73; Hodgett 5.
20. Chaucer, *Canon's Yeoman's Tale* lines 920–29.
21. Hodgett 13–14.
22. Nottingham II 20; BL MS 73 fol. 138v.
23. McC & B 517, the index includes over fifty lids.
24. Austin 72; H & B IV 72.
25. Austin 39; H & B IV 186.

CHAPTER 13
POTTAGE RECIPES

1. Austin 10 xxii, 70.
2. Napier 115; *HO* 425.
3. H & B 20.
4. Napier 91, which also has a bruet rosse recipe.
5. Austin 6 vi.
6. Austin 72.
7. *HO* 432.
8. Hodgett 13.
9. *HO* 433.
10. Austin 5.
11. *HO* 429; H & B IV 18.
12. Napier 26.
13. Napier 72.
14. Napier 92; see also *HO* 431, or H & B IV 62 for a sharper vinaigrette recipe.
15. *HO* 435, 459.
16. Austin 8 xvi, and Austin 82; *HO* 433.

17. *HO* 435, 459, see also for a different version, Austin 71.
18. Austin 71.
19. *HO* 454; Austin 70, 438; H & B II 5, IV 46.
20. *HO* 463; H & B II 20, IV 41; Napier 104, 121.
21. Napier 114.
22. Ibid.
23. Napier 111.
24. Austin 18.
25. Napier 101; H & B II 24. For fried versions see Napier 28; *HO* 436, 450.
26. H & B IV 36.
27. *HO* 436, 461.
28. Austin 72.
29. Hodgett 14; Napier 69.
30. *HO*; Austin 32.
31. Austin 18, 23.
32. Austin 81.
33. Austin 27.
34. H & B II 13.
35. H & B I 15; *HO* 430; Austin 19.
36. Austin 13, 80.
37. Austin 23.
38. H & B III 23, IV 29. For ground versions see H & B II 6; Napier 116.
39. *HO* 431.
40. H & B I 1, II 29, IV 201; Austin 21; Napier 105.
41. H & B I 2.
42. H & B I 3.
43. H & B I 21.
44. Napier 102; *HO* 434. For other types see H & B I 28, IV 100, I 56, III 21.
45. Austin 9, 78; see also Napier 115; H & B IV 37.
46. *HO* 455; H & B IV 22.
47. Napier 115.
48. *HO* 133. For a cubed pigeon stew see Napier 107.
49. Napier 112.

50. *HO* 434.
51. E.g. Hodgett 29.
52. Austin 104; Napier 72.
53. Hodgett 37.
54. Napier 75.
55. Austin 103.
56. *HO* 452.
57. Austin 17, 105; Napier 86; Furnivall, *Early English Meals & Manners* 41/582.
58. Napier 73.
59. Hodgett 32.
60. Austin 107; Furnivall, *Early English Meals & Manners* 45–9.
61. Austin 90.
62. Austin 24, 90; Napier 78; see also *HO* 445; H & B IV 125, 127.
63. Austin 100.
64. Austin 106; Napier 74.
65. Napier 110.
66. Austin 102; H & B I 50.
67. Austin 102; Napier 69.
68. Napier 34; see also H & B IV 113.
69. *HO* 446; see also Austin 10, 89; Napier 86; H & B II 112, IV 92.
70. Austin 8, 9, 92, 106.
71. Austin 20.
72. *HO* 444; H & B 93; see also Hodgett 27.
73. Austin 33.
74. Austin 96; see also H & B IV 92; *HO* 444.
75. *NHB* 78.
76. Furnivall, *Early English Meals & Manners* 8/96–100.
77. Ibid. 52.
78. BL. Sloane MS 1201; H & B IV 78.
79. Napier 82; Hodgett 31–2; *HO* 426.
80. *HO* 444, 461; Napier 28, 108; Austin 5; H & B V 89.
81. *HO* 426; Napier 82, 84; Austin 5, 6, 69, 82, 84; Hodgett 24.
82. H & B IV 189.
83. Austin 83.
84. Boorde 268.
85. Austin 84.
86. Austin 84.
87. *HO* 425.
88. *HO* 454.
89. *HO* 445; H & B IV 77.
90. Way, *Promptorium parvulorium* 203/2; Wyclif's Bible, *Numbers* chapter XI, verse 5.
91. *HO* 426; H & B IV 10.
92. H & B IV 78.
93. *HO* 425, 467; Austin 14; H & B IV 2.
94. H & B IV 12.
95. H & B I 15, II 88.
96. H & B IV 9.
97. *HO* 426.
98. *HO* 426, 462; Austin 83.
99. *HO* 426, 462; Napier 31.
100. Napier 31.
101. *HO* 444; H & B IV 71.
102. *HO* 467; Austin 83.
103. *HO* 427, 462.
104. Napier 111.
105. Austin 33.
106. *HO* 426.
107. H & B IV 188.
108. *HO* 426; H & B IV 7.
109. Austin 20, 30, 113; H & B II 17, 35, IV 81, see also I 9.
110. Austin 30, 113; Napier 119.
111. Austin 29.
112. Austin 29.
113. Austin 94, see also Austin 24, 113; *HO* 444; Napier 114.
114. Austin 30, see also Austin 16, 28: rapey recipes.
115. Austin 112.
116. H & B I 11–14.
117. Austin 29, 56; H & B II 47, III

34–35, see also I 36, II 46, III 31.

118. H & B III 32.

119. *HO* 443, 425, 462.

120. Austin 6, 70; H & B II 1, 89, IV 1, 70, V 2; Brears (1987) 172–3.

121. Napier 82.

122. Austin 22, 114; see also H & B IV 11, 129; *HO* 426.

123. *HO* 454, 438.

124. Austin 113; Napier 108; H & B II 64, IV 99.

125. H & B II 14, IV 200, III 28, IV 38. For fish versions see Austin 23, 114; Napier 111; H & B II 66, III 89.

126. H & B II 11.

127. Tibbot 51–57.

128. See *OED* s.v. 'Gruel *c.* 1450'.

129. Austin 6, 76; Hodgett 23–4; *HO* 253; Napier 88; H & B IV 5.

130. Napier 107; H & B IV 88.

131. Wilson 298.

132. *HO* 465.

133. Napier 76; Hodgett 24; see also Austin 96, cheaut de almondes.

134. Napier 42, 108; Hodgett 17; *HO* 447; Austin 7, 96.

135. H & B II 10, IV 28, 29, 124; *HO* 446; Austin 100.

136. Napier 105.

137. H & B IV 50.

138. H & B IV 132; Napier 80–81.

139. H & B IV 94.

140. *HO* 461.

141. Austin 11; Napier 99; Hodgett 23.

142. Austin 11, 90.

143. Napier 76.

144. *HO* 466.

145. Austin 11, 114.

146. Austin 90; Hodgett 16.

147. H & B IV 82.

148. H & B IV 79; *HO* 445.

149. Austin 12, 96.

150. H & B 96; *HO* 445; see also *HO* 471.

151. Austin 51; see also Austin 76.

152. Furnivall, *Early English Meals & Manners* 8/94, 152/33; Napier 57; see also *OED* s.vv. 'Caudle' & 'Posset'.

153. Napier 81, 108; Austin 96; H & B IV 90.

154. Austin 33.

155. Austin 15; see also *HO* 103–4.

156. Napier 57.

157. Austin 30.

158. H & B Menu 2.

159. E.g. Napier 42.

160. Austin 25.

161. Austin 86.

162. H & B II 56.

163. H & B II 36.

164. *HO* 437.

165. Warner 61.

166. Austin 27.

167. Warner 61.

168. Warner 61.

169. Austin 37.

170. Austin 37; Napier 40.

171. *HO* 471.

172. Austin 26; *HO* 451; Napier 42; H & B IV 104.

CHAPTER 14

LEACHES

1. E.g. Austin 34.

2. Austin 36.

3. Austin 34; Napier 99.

4. Austin 34, 71.

5. Napier 29, 104, 121; Austin 17, 117; H & B II 20, IV 42; see also Austin 35, 'sops salomere'.

6. *HO* 470.

7. *HO* 470.

8. May 25; *OED, EDD* s.v. 'Haggis'.

9. Napier 119; see also Austin 38.

10. Napier 119, 38.
11. H & B I 112; *HO* 438.
12. Napier 27.
13. *HO* 463; Austin 92; Napier 32.
14. Austin 40; Napier 106, 109.
15. H & B IV 69, 83; Austin 17, 35–6, 92; Napier 87.
16. Austin 36.

CHAPTER 15
ROASTING
1. Field 138–45.
2. Austin 39 XXIII; Beckwith 198.
3. S & H 165.
4. Ibid. 288; Purvis P.2, 324.
5. Amyot 277–8; S & H 33.
6. *OED* s.v. 'Broach'.
7. Nottingham III 38.
8. Brears (1999) 127.
9. Beckwith 94.
10. BL MS Roy 2BVIII, Queen Mary's Psalter.
11. Wright (1983) 106.
12. Richards 205; see also Wrathmell 28 for further examples.
13. Ottaway & Rogers 2827, no. 1374 may be a stone dripping trough.
14. BL MS Roy 2BVIII.
15. Ottaway & Rogers 2804, no. 11918.
16. *Proceedings of the Society of Antiquaries of Newcastle-upon-Tyne* 3rd series, vol. 9, 74–5.
17. Dale & Redstone 123.
18. Pearce & Vince 141, fig. 96, nos. 324–30, 162, no. 498; also McC & B 307, 433, 472.
19. Hodgett 20.
21. Austin 80, 81, 78.
22. Ibid. 81–2; Hodgett 19; Napier 36.
23. H & B IV 54.
24. Austin 82.
25. Ibid. 78–82.

26. Ibid. 79; Hieatt 109, 22; Warner 63.
27. Austin 40, 83; Hodgett 19.
28. Austin 41; Napier 37, 65.
29. H & B IV 182, 184; see also II 42, 59; Austin 38 XIX; Napier 120.
30. H & B IV 184; Austin 38 XX.
31. H & B IV 185.
32. Ibid. IV 183; Austin 40, 115.
33. Austin 97; H & B IV 195; Napier 120.
34. Davies, N., *The Paston Papers* I 468.
35. Amyot 240 [73 ounces]; S & H 112.
36. Napier 96.
37. H & B I 26.
38. Austin 103; H & B IV 110; Napier 71, 96, 97.
39. H & B I 55.

CHAPTER 16
FRYING
1. Austin 45.
2. McC & B 315, 339, 405, 452, 455.
3. Atkins, Carter & Evans 38, fig. 41.
4. H & B 170, 181.
5. S & H 53, 147, 165, 259, 316, 331; Douglas 1149.
6. Amyot 261.
7. Lewis (1987) 165.
8. McC & B 167, 198, 286, 339.
9. Mayes & Butler 158, fig. 50, no. 579.
10. McC & B 248, no. 785; Dunning (1962) 98–100.
11. Austin 46.
12. Austin 42, 83; H & B IV 188–9.
13. Austin 45, 86.
14. Austin 43, 84.
15. Austin 84.
16. Austin 46.
17. Austin 43, 73; Napier 46; H & B IV 155.
18. Napier 45.
19. Austin 44, 93; H & B II 26, IV 170.

20. Austin 113, see also 'emeles' in H & B I 47.
21. H & B IV 156.
22. H & B II 19, IV 154; Austin 44, 46; Hodgett 30.
23. Austin 43; Warner 72.
24. Austin 83.
25. Austin 42, 83; Napier 46.
26. H & B IV 60; Hieatt 62.
27. H & B IV 171.
28. Austin 58; Napier 58; H & B 26.
29. Austin 15; Napier 57.
30. Austin 44; for pie, rissole & bean shapes see Austin 45, 97, 43.
31. Austin 45, 'Nese bekys'.
32. Austin 42.
33. Austin 45, see also 46.
34. Austin 97, see also 42, 43, 46; H & B IV 157, 190.
35. *HO* 460, H & B IV 169, IV 168.

CHAPTER 17
THE SAUCERY

1. S & H 89.
2. *HO* 4, 22.
3. *HO* 80, 76–7.
4. *HO* 38.
5. *NHB* 18.
6. Caxton *Dialogues* 42/21.
7. H & B IV 150; Warner 26.
8. S & H 146, 231, 163.
9. *OED* s.v. 'Mustard Pot'.
10. Austin 77, 109; Napier 77; *HO* 441; H & B IV 143; Warner 64.
11. Austin 110.
12. Austin 77; for other versions see Austin 110; Warner 64; Napier 77; *HO* 481; S & B IV 144, 148.
13. Austin 77, 109; Napier 48; see also H & B IV 149 for a different version which includes both currants and walnuts.

14. Austin 109.
15. Austin 77, 108; Napier 77; Warner 64. For different versions see Hodgett 21–2 or *HO* 441 which includes galingale. See, too, H & B 190.
16. Austin 77, 108; Napier 77.
17. H & B IV 103.
18. BL MS Add 42130 f. 207 v.
19. Austin 77, 110.
20. Austin 109.
21. Austin 109.
22. Austin 113; *HO* 451; H & B II 60, III 17, IV 137; Warner 72.
23. *HO* 451; H & B IV 134.
24. *HO* 452; H & B I 52, III 9, IV 115. For a rabbit version, see H & B IV 27, and for hare H & B II 8.
25. Austin 111, 110.
26. Austin 110; *HO* 440.
27. Austin 77, 110; Hodgett 29; *HO* 441.
28. Austin 109; *HO* 440.
29. Austin 110; *HO* 440; Napier 51; H & B IV 129; Warner 64.
30. H & B IV 146; *HO* 441; Austin 77, 146; Warner 65.
31. *HO* 96.
32. Austin 76, 108; Hodgett 16–17; *HO* 441; H & B III 6, 12, IV 147; Warner 65. Napier 90–91 has a version for pigs' trotters, and H & B IV 118 a fish-day version using gurnard and conger eel blood.
33. *HO* 432; H & B IV 32. See also Napier 48.

CHAPTER 18
THE CONFECTIONERY AND WAFERY

1. Furnivall, *Early English Meals & Manners* 5, 50, 52, 55, 157, 166.
2. *HO* 20, 81.
3. *HO* 22, 72.

4. E.g. Myers p. 1044 reproducing the Southampton Port Book for 1469: 2cwt. Barrel of green ginger £6 13s. 4d.; *NHB* 19; S & H 155.
5. Austin 7, 12, 87; H & B IV 136; *HO* 450.
6. Austin 37, 12, 88.
7. Banham & Mason 59. For a richer version see Austin 27, CXV.
8. Banham & Mason 61. This source also has recipes for preserving pears and ginger.
9. H & B IV 98.
10. H & B V 19; Austin 35.
11. H & B V 18.
12. H & B V 11.
13. H & B V 12.
14. H & B IV 38; Austin 8.
15. *OED* s.v. 'Penides'.
16. H & B V 14.
17. H & B V 13.
18. H & B V 15.
19. Acc. No. 39, 190.
20. *OED* s.v. 'Marchpane'.
21. E.g. Royal 17A in H & B V.
22. Furnivall, *Early English Meals & Manners* 9–10; Brears (2003) 31–3.
23. H & B IV 199, V 5.
24. H & B IV 208, V 4, 6; *HO* 473.
25. H & B V 17.
26. Brears (2003) 32; *HO* 473.
27. H & B V 7.
28. Moorhouse & Greenaway 79–121.
29. H & B 186.
30. Austin 39 .
31. Harrison 36, lines 978–80.
32. Nicolas 31.
33. Quoted in Henisch 230; Fowler (1898) 92.
34. Warner 122.
35. Woolgar 160; Napier 6; Furnivall, *Early English Meals & Manners*

48–54; *HO* 450.
36. Warner XXXV.
37. Napier 4.
38. Napier 4–6.
39. Warner XXXVI–VII.
40. Warner 112–115.
41. The Bank of England retail price index suggests that £1 in 1500 represented £441·42 in 2002.

CHAPTER 19

PLANNING MEALS

1. *Piers Plowman* B. Passus VI lines 174–8.
2. Ibid. 179, 182, 186, 192, 214.
3. Ibid. 304–13.
4. Dyer (2000) 81–4.
5. *Piers Plowman* op. cit. 280–90.
6. Chaucer, *Nun's Priest's Tale*, lines 13–26.
7. Lumiansky & Mills 129–30; Rose 168–9.
8. Scott 140; Brears (1987) 31.
9. Scott 85.
10. E.g. *HO* 27–33, 37–9, 89–94.
11. *HO* 44.
12. *HO* 28.
13. Henisch 23–4.
14. *HO* 39.
15. Dale & Redstone 1 *et seq.*
16. *OED* s.v. 'Nuncheon'; *NHB* 74, 77.
17. *HO* 25–60.
18. *NHB* 96–8.
19. *HO* 94.
20. *HO* 25–61.
21. *HO* 22.
22. For detailed descriptions of medieval fast days, see Woolgar 90–93; Henisch 30–50.
23. H & B IV 173, 169.
24. Warner 61.
25. Napier 121.

26. Caxton, *Trevisa's Description of Britain*, cited in *OED* s.v. 'Barnacle'.
27. Henisch 48–9.
28. Furnivall, *Early English Meals & Manners* 37/547.
29. Harrison 33, lines 890–94.
30. *HO* 22; Woolgar 87.
31. *HO* 22; Woolgar 87.
32. *NHB* 73–9. The original gives much more detail, these abstracts being selected to illustrate the differences between the major elements within the household.
33. Dale & Redstone 1–102.
34. Warner 119.
35. *HO* 25–7, 30–31, 55–8.
36. *NHB* 80–81, 88–89.
37. Furnivall, *Early English Meals & Manners* 54–5/795–818.
38. The following paragraphs are based on numerous sources, such as H & B 39–41; *HO* 449–50; Furnivall, *Early English Meals & Manners* 48–54; Warner 97–99, 107–8, 113–121; Ellis 586–7, 599–601; Parker 134; Brears (2003) 38–9.
39. Warner 118–20.
40. Furnivall, *Early English Meals & Manners* 48–54.
41. Brears (2003) 46–9, 52–9.
42. Furnivall, *Early English Meals & Manners* 48–50.

CHAPTER 20
THE BUTTERY & PANTRY
1. Scott 67.
2. Hayfield & Pacito 40–48.
3. S & H 79, 226, 304.
4. S & H 128, 240, 247.
5. S & H 61, 247.
6. Brears (2003) 26–7.
7. *HO* 75–9.

8. S & H 62, 92, 128, 136, 147, 150 et passim.
9. Furnivall, *Early English Meals & Manners* 5.
10. Brears (2003) 28–9.
11. Ibid.
12. *OED* s.vv. 'Raspis', 'Raspis-wine'.
13. S & H 172, 178, 315.
14. E.g. Pearce & Vince 23.
15. E.g. McCarthy & Brooks 391 no. 1654, 393 no. 1672, 397 no. 1697, 398 no. 1711, 399 no. 1729, 400 no. 1744 etc.
16. *OED* s.v. 'Tankard 2'.
17. Amyot 273; S & H 87.
18. Amyot 274.
19. Hornsby, Weinstein & Homer 63, fig. 40.
20. S & H 53, 130, 253.
21. Tyson 115–122.
22. *HO* 56.
23. Ibid. 22, 25–7, 33, 45, 55–6, 58, 60, 75–6.
24. Ibid. 78.
25. Russell 11. In the translation, the word *cratera* 'wine-bowl' is rendered as 'bowl', but from the context it actually means 'cup'.
26. Hope (1887).
27. *OED* s.v. 'Coconut'; Purvis 176–7.
28. Henisch 169, 172.
29. Gaimster 339–47.
30. *OED* s.v. 'Cruise'; *NHB* 18.
31. For a Siegburg copy, McCarthy & Brooks 44 no. 553; and probable Langerwehe copies, ibid. 442 no. 2130 and 464 no. 2785.
32. Ibid. 392–3, 396–7, 402, 404, 414, 430, 446–8, 450, 462; Pearce & Vince 64, 66–7, 79–81, 164, 172.
33. Mayes & Butler. For the origins of Cistercian-ware cups see pp. 215–6,

and for Surrey, Tudor-green cups and copies datable before 1450 see 154 (nos. 549 & 551) and *c.* 1450–84 see 159 (nos. 604–5).

34. Tyson 7–8.
35. Ibid. 19.
36. S & H 153, 156.
37. Wade 242.
38. Tyson 77–100.
39. Amyot 241, 242, 275.
40. Furnivall, *Early English Meals & Manners* 363.
41. *HO* 70–72.
42. Warner 103.
43. *NHB* 44–5.
44. S & H 188, 201–2.
45. Furnivall, *Early English Meals & Manners* 4.
46. Brears (2003) 34.
47. *NHB* 16.
48. *OED* s.v. 'Trencher'.
49. *NHB* 341.
50. Fowler (1898) 175.
51. E.g. BL Royal 14 EIV 224 v; the Braunche brass in St Margaret's Church, King's Lynn.
52. Purvis 182.
53. Wade 263, 271.
54. Adams 20.
55. Furnivall, *Early English Meals & Manners* 4.
56. BL Sloane 1313 fol. 126, early 15th cent.
57. Caley 37.
58. S & H 103, 167; Amyot 274.
59. S & H 27, 82.
60. Ibid. 20, 70, 76, 178, 256.
61. Dillon & St John Hope plates 12, 19; Hornsby, Weinstein & Homer 53 .
62. Mayes & Butler 218 nos. 53–5.
63. S & H 62, 46, 62, 103, 167, 171, 217, 287.

64. Furnivall, *Early English Meals & Manners* 162/2, 45/639.
65. Tyler 292; S & H 196.
66. S & H 298.
67. Nicolas 94.
68. Furnivall, *Early English Meals & Manners* 158, 200/673–6, 25/385–6.
69. Amyot 273.
70. Tymms 46.
71. Cowgill, de Neergaard & Griffiths 34–50.
72. S & H 19, 147, 154, 271, 289.
73. Cowgill, de Neergaard & Griffiths 34–50.
74. Alexander Barclay's *First Eclogue* line 150 has: 'In the side of his felte [hat], there stacke a spone of tree'.
75. S & H 134.
76. Hartley (1954) 535.
77. Hornsby, Weinstein & Homer 59.
78. *British Museum Guide to the Medieval Room* (1907) 250; Purvis 178–9.
79. E.g. S & H 83, 138, 270, 293, 308.
80. Ibid. 103.
81. S & H 196; Baildon 173; Woolgar 157; Tymms 40.
82. Amyot 222, 240, 241.
83. Ibid. *OED* s.v. 'Charger'; S & H 27, 28; Hornsby, Weinstein & Homer 53, 57.
84. S & H craftsman: 20, 62, 133, 147, 157; gentry: 253, 308; churchman: 196.
85. Ibid. 165: a household with 4 garnish. *OED* s.v. 'Garnish'.
86. S & H 227; *OED* s.v. 'Treen'; Egan 201–2.
87. Brownsword & Ciuffini 17–25.
88. S & H 136, 268, 315–6; Ottaway & Rogers 2855–6.

CHAPTER 21

THE EWERY

1. *HO* 83–4.
2. Pecock 468.
3. S & H 273, 135, 337.
4. Raine 69.
5. Lewis, Brownsword & Pitt 82–3.
6. Brownsword, Pitt & Richardson 50–51.
7. S & H 76, 337; see also 115, 142, 231, 339.
8. Lewis (1987) 164.
9. Pearce & Vince 104.
10. Caley 37; S & H 166; Amyot 245.
11. Turner 260.
12. Act 1 Richard III c. 12, s. 2. The hall of St Mary's Guild, Boston was equipped with 'A laver of laten, hangynge with a chayne of yron', Parker 74.
13. Fig. 60·15, 60·16.
14. S & H 75.
15. McCarthy & Brooks 228–9, 235, 244–5, 277–8.
16. Winstone 94.
17. Wood 370; Parker 46.
18. Wood pl. LVIIIE.
19. Furnivall, *Early English Meals & Manners* 199/641–644.
20. S & H 309, 160.
21. *HO* 84; Furnivall, *Caxton's Book of Curtesye* 38.
22. S & H 50, 226.
23. Ibid. 154, 201, 332.
24. Ibid. 104.
25. Furnivall, *Early English Meals & Manners* 294; S & H 268, 309.
26. S & H 196.
27. Amyot 245; BL Soane MS 1313 fol. 126v.
28. *NHB* 371; Boorde 281.
29. Furnivall, *Early English Meals &*

Manners 16/232, 200/695.
30. *OED* s.v. 'Taster'; Baildon 172; Furnivall, *Early English Meals & Manners* 201/701.
31. S & H 58.
32. Ibid. 191.
33. Ibid. 150.
34. Ibid. 76.
35. Ibid. 226, 248, 337.
36. S & H 201.
37. *NHB* 16.
38. Adams 20.
39. S & H 97; Nicholas 124.
40. Brears (2003) 77.
41. *NHB* 96–8.
42. S & H 162, 201, 270, 297, 332.

CHAPTER 22

TABLE MANNERS

1. Furnivall, *Early English Meals & Manners* 256.
2. Howitt 115–16.
3. *EDD* s.v. 'Thumb'.
4. Hone II 21–3.
5. *EDD* s.v. 'gob'; Furnivall, *Early English Meals & Manners* 178/49, 277/36.
6. Brears (1987) 76.
7. Ibid. 76.
8. Wood 16–66.
9. Way, *Promptorium parvulorium* 485/1.
10. Morrell 23.
11. Adams 20.
12. Knell 70–74.
13. Ibid. 72; BL Royal MS 14, E. IV. F365v.
14. *OED* s.v. 'Oriel'.
15. S & H 160.
16. Ibid. 199, 135.
17. Ibid. 199.
18. Amyot 273; S & H 49, 61, 68, 160, 247.

19. *NHB* 21.
20. Morrell 23.
21. S & H 294.
22. Ibid. 96, 160, 164; *NHB* 16.
23. Furnivall, *Early English Meals & Manners* 187/356; Wright (1862) 84.
24. Fabyan 586.
25. Chambers 15.
26. Ibid; Furnivall, *Early English Meals & Manners* 189/393.
27. Furnivall, *Early English Meals & Manners* 190.
28. Ibid. 366–80.
29. Ibid. 272/105.
30. Slices of bread are seen in a number of visual sources, e.g. 'The Last Supper' east window at Malvern, *c.* 1430–40; BL Arundel MS 157 f.7, *c.* 1220; BL ADD MS 12,228; BL ADD MS 18,719 £2,536.
31. Furnivall, *Early English Meals & Manners* 179/69–80, 232/44–8, 255/143–6.
32. Ibid. 1/63, 22/332, 180/94, 113, 255/137–141, 256/162, 257/191, 263/42, 272/97, 119, 280/24–30, 58.
33. Ibid. 232/240, 256/157–61, 267/29, 279, 280/65, 281/129.
34. Ibid. 230/358, 269/70, 232/457.
35. Ibid. 269/73, 277/48, 278/48.
36. Ibid. 179/65, 255/152, 272/119.
37. Ibid. 180/123, 185/289, 272/105–10, 274/125, 289/75.
38. Ibid. 256/183–4, 269/77–8.
39. Ibid. 272/112–4.
40. Ibid. e.g. 219/6, 232/472–94, 232/504–5, 267/51, 269/58, 272/98–103, 277, 278/30, 279, 280/74.
41. Ibid. 19/286, 20/304, 178/113, 179/87, 180/107, 180/125, 212/113–6, 213/117, 225/150, 267/33, 267/38, 267/45, 255/150, 232/498.
42. Ibid. 177/20.
43. Ibid. 178/35–41.

CHAPTER 23

DINING IN THE CHAMBER

1. E.g. Christchurch Castle, Hants *c.* 1160, Winchester Castle late 12c., Warnford Castle, Hants *c.* 1210, Ashby Castle, Leics. early 13c., Stokesay Castle, Salop *c.* 1240, Martock Treasurer's House, Som. *c.* 1250–60, Wells Palace, Som. 1280, Chepstow Castle, Mon. 1270–1306, & Yardley Hastings Manor House, Northants mid-14c. all had their chambers at the lower end of the hall. In contrast Conisbrough Castle, N. Yorks. late 12c., Warkworth Castle, Northumb. 1191–1214, Boothby Pagnall, Lincs. *c.* 1200, Gillingham Castle, Norf. *c.* 1250, Aydon Castle, Northumb. 1280, St Davids Palace, Pembroke 1280–93, Old Soar, Kent 1290, Denbigh Castle, Powys 1295, Kidwelly Castle, Carmarthen & Goodrich Castle, Herefords. *c.* 1300 all had their chambers at the upper end of the hall.
2. E.g. at Stokesay Castle, Salop in *c.* 1285–1305 and Ashby Castle, Leics, *c.* 1350 the original low-end chambers were replaced by new ones at the upper end.
3. Thurley (1993) 4; Wood e.g. 73–4 & pl. XIII.
4. Thurley ibid.
5. Thurley ibid.
6. *HO* 109.
7. *HO* 116.
8. *HO* 112–13.
9. *NHB* 16.

10. S & H 97.
11. *Tres Riches Heures de Jean Duc de Berry*, Musée Condé f.2.
12. *OED* s.v. 'Reredos'.
13. *HO* 115.
14. *NHB* 16.
15. Woolgar 149.
16. *OED* s.v. 'Cupboard'; S & H 97.
17. *NHB* 299–306.
18. *NHB* 53.
19. *HO* 44–5.
20. *NHB* 43–4, 242.
21. Furnivall, *Early English Meals & Manners* 25/111–13, 229/297, 231/423, 241/5, 280/61–2.
22. BL Sloane MS 1986 in Furnivall, *Early English Meals & Manners* 187/205; BL Sloane MS 2027, 1351; BL Harleian MS 4011 in Furnivall, *Early English Meals & Manners* 1–83.
23. *HO* 31–2; Furnivall, *Early English Meals & Manners* 188.
24. *HO* 37–8; Furnivall, *Early English Meals & Manners* 188.
25. Furnivall, *Early English Meals & Manners* 72–8; Brears (2003) 66–9.
26. *HO* 38–9.
27. *HO* 41.
28. *HO* 32–7, 42–3.
29. Furnivall, *Early English Meals & Manners* 87/356, Warner 105.
30. Woolgar 154.
31. Amyot 244.
32. Turner (1827) 266.
33. Amyot 245.
34. Meade 192; BL ADD MS 47,680 f60v., *c.* 1326–7.
35. Caley 37.
36. S & H 103, 27.
37. Woolgar 130.
38. *OED* s.v. 'Fork 2'; S & H 195.
39. Grose & Astle II 267.
40. Furnivall, *Early English Meals & Manners* 35–7, 56–9, 161–6; Brears (2003) 48–63, 80–83.
41. S & H 73, 172, 232, 235, 288, 317, 332.

CHAPTER 24
GREAT FEASTS

1. Furnivall, *Early English Meals & Manners* 72.
2. *HO* 114, 115, 118.
3. Furnivall, *Early English Meals & Manners* 193/495–8.
4. Warner 93–106; with carving details from Brears (2003) 48–63.
5. Dixon-Smith 85, 79.
6. Tanner 72; Dixon-Smith 86.
7. Furnivall, *Early English Meals & Manners* 216/VIII, 202/738.

Notes on the Illustrations

The following references list the sources used by the author in preparing the drawings used in this volume. Since many of the illustrated buildings have not been three-dimensionally recorded to date, the vertical elevations have been either sketched on site, or scaled from photographs, to gain a passable, but not entirely accurate impression of their structures. Since one of the purposes of this book is to explore the design and function of domestic buildings, many of the drawings have had lost features such as roofs, chimneys, etc. restored to completion on the basis of surviving architectural or archival evidence, which are detailed in the following references. In addition, the opportunity has been taken to provide contemporary staff and equipment in some cases, to help demonstrate how the buildings and their utensils actually functioned.

FRONTISPIECE and FIGURE 1
Drawings by P. Brears.

FIGURE 2
BL Black Book of the Household, 1472.

FIGURE 3
(1) Mayes & Butler 32 fig. 6. (2) O'Neil 9 fig. 2. (3) Oswald 118 figs. 40 & 43. (4) Rahtz & Watts 4 fig. 4. (5) Beresford 204 period 3. (6) Hope (1908) 300. (7) Martin (2001) 26 fig. 5. (8) Ibid. 23 fig. 2.

FIGURE 4
(1) Emery (1970) 129 fig. 20, & Bilson. (2) Plans at Clevedon Court. (3) Emery (1970) 233 fig. 50. (4) Lindsey 17 fig. 4. (5) Jones 14–15. (6) Emery (1985) 278 fig. 3.

FIGURE 5
(1) Wood 73 fig. 28. (2) Mason 2. (3) Wood 58 fig. 25. (4) Godfrey 111 fig. 7. (5) Ambler 49. (6) Spence 36. (7) Alnwick MS BII 1b. (8) Mayes & Butler 43 fig. 14. (9) Turner (2002) 52. (10) Taylor (1870) 48. (11) Emery (1970) 257 fig. 77.

FIGURE 6
(1) Woolgar 62. (2) English Heritage, Aydon Castle. (3) Emery (1970) 228. (4) Wood 57 fig. 24. (5) Parker 40. (6) Wood 106 fig. 40. (7) Ambler pl.XXXVIII.

FIGURE 7
(1) Taylor (2002) 33. (2) Orde-Powlett 20. (3) Ibid. (4) Bedingfield 5. (5) Simpson 110. (6) BL Cotton Augustus I iii3.

FIGURE 8
(1) Simpson (1946) 76–8. (2) Parker 216. (3) RCHM Westmorland 14. (4) Black 240. (5) Cotton 37-7. (6) Goodall 19–25. (7) Kenyon (2003) 58. (8) Jones (1993) 14–15. (9) RIBA Smythson Drawings I/21. (10) Eames 84 figs. 4–5). (11) Taylor (1998) 65. (12) Taylor (2004) 28. (13) O'Neil (1951) 10. (14) Renn (2002) 49. (15) Information at Lincoln Bishop's Palace. (16) Taylor (2004) 25. (17) Kenyan (2002) 32. (18) Renn (2002) 49 and Cadw drawings. (19) Weaver 33. (20) Orde Powlett 20.

FIGURE 9
Drawing by P. Brears.

FIGURE 10
(1) Calderdale Museums & Galleries AH 708 & 1934–46. (2) Nottingham alabaster, Yorkshire Museum, York. (3) Mayes & Butler 166 no. 668. (4) Arnold 80.

FIGURE 11
(1) BL Cotton, Nero. C. IV. (2) BL Harleian 1257. (3) English Heritage, Scarborough Castle. (4) BL Facs. 169. (5) BL Add. MS 42130 f. 163. (6) BL Harleian 2897. (7) D. Hartley, *Water in England* (1964) pl. 10. (8) Ulrich von Richenthall Constanzer Conzilium New York Public Library, Spencer Collection MS 52 f. 227. (9) 'At the Conduit' woodcut, London, early 16c.

FIGURE 12
Drawing by P. Brears.

FIGURE 13
(1) BL. (2) Trinity College, Cambridge MS R. 17.1. (3) Now a bollard in the Square, Blanchland, Northumberland. (4) McCarthy & Brooks 422 no. 1979. (5) Ibid. 248 no. 784.

FIGURE 14
Top drawing by P. Brears. (1) Holden 86 fig. 10. (2) Hurst (1961) 243–9 fig. 62. (3) Taylor (1998) 65. (4) Knight (2000) 49. (5) Orde-Powlett 20. (6) Arnold 83 fig. 12. (7) Roberts (1990) 67. (8) VCH Durham.

FIGURE 15
Top. Information from R. Avent. Bottom. Based on McCormick 78.

FIGURE 16
(1) Knight (1992) 161–3. (2–3) Drawings by P. Brears.

FIGURE 17
(1) Bodleian Library MS 264. (2–3) Bennet & Elton. (4) Bodleian Library MS 764/44.
(5) Reconstruction by P. Brears.

FIGURE 18
Reconstruction by P. Brears.

FIGURE 19
(1) BL Sloane MS 2435. (2) BL Facs. 169. (3) BL MS Royal 10 E iv. (4) Wynkyn de
Worde no. 1316. (5) Drawing by P. Brears. (6) excavated April 1990. (7) Ryedale Folk
Museum, Brears (1998) 74.

FIGURE 20.
(1) Bodleian Library MS Douce 49. (2) Bodleian Library MS Douce 6. (3) BL Holkham
Picture Bible. (4) BL MS Royal 10 E iv. (5) Stained glass, Great Malvern. (6) Stained
glass, All Saints North St. York. (7–10) Bodleian Library MS Douce Charters a. 1 no.
62. (11–12) Drawings by Peter Brears.

FIGURES 21–22
Drawings by P. Brears.

FIGURE 23
(1–7) Reconstruction by P. Brears. (8) McCarthy & Brooks 437 no. 2082. (9) BL MS
Arundel 91.

FIGURE 24
(1) Lacock Abbey. (2) Brownsword 114–17. (3) gravestone, St Mary Redcliffe, Bristol.
(4) Science Museum A 6501. (5–6) Egan nos. 432, 434. (7–8) Ottaway & Rogers 2804
nos. 11914, 13948. (9) Salisbury & South Wilts. Museum, Salisbury. (10) Atkin, Carter
& Evans, 58 fig. 40 no. 38. (11) Science Museum A6501.

FIGURE 25
(1–4) Drawings by P. Brears.

FIGURE 26
(1–2) Corpus Christi College Oxford, MS 285 f. 8. (3, 4, & 6) Bodleian Library,

MS Douce 5 f. 7. (5) BL MS Royal 2 B vii. (7) Misericord, Worcester Cathedral. (8) Misericord, Ludlow Parish Church. (9) Corpus Christi College Oxford, MS 285 f. 3v. (10) Bodleian Library MS Add. A 46. (11) BL Add. MS 42130 f. 30 7v.

FIGURE 27
(1–11) Drawings by P. Brears.

FIGURE 28
(1) Jope & Threlfall 119 fig. 26. (2) Walker (2000) 77–80. (3) Morris (1997) 88 fig. 2. (4) Pearson 106 fig. 119. (5) Ibid. fig. 120. (6) Sherlock 77.

FIGURE 29
(1) Mayes & Butler. (2) Oswald 118 fig. 43. (3) Hurst (1961) 239–43 fig. 61. (4) Borenius & Charlton 72–3 pl. XIX. (5) Weaver 32–3. (6) Hope (1908) 257. (7) RCHM Durham. (8) Emery (1970) 171–6.

FIGURE 30.
(1) Parker (1859) 253. (2) Kenyon 57. (3) Renn 49. (4) Drawing by P. Brears. (5) Breakspear 4–21. (6) Taylor (1958) 18. (7) RCHM Dorset 209–11. (8) National Archives MR16 & Roberts 66–7.

FIGURE 31
(1) Drawing by P. Brears. (2) Emery (1970) 174. (3) Drawing by P. Brears. (4) James Lambert's drawings of 1777, Sussex Archaeological Society. (5) Drawing by P. Brears.

FIGURE 32
(1) Wright 166 fig. 12. (2) Girouard 71. (3) Thurley (1993) 32 fig. 43. (4) Munby 16. (5) Mayes & Butler 49 fig. 18 & 22 fig. 2. (6) Emery (1996) 177. (7) Parker 151. (8) Alnwick archives, Thomas Treswell's drawing. (9) Wood pl. 22c.

FIGURE 33
Munby 13–17.

FIGURE 34
Parker 151 and drawing by P. Brears.

FIGURE 35
(1) Turner 128 fig. 29. (2–3) Parker 208.

FIGURE 36
Drawings by P. Brears.

FIGURE 37

(**1**) Bradbury 15 fig. 36. (**2**) Jones 14. (**3**) Sussex Archaeological Society, James Lambert's drawings. (**4**) Drawing by P. Brears. (**5**) Emery (1970) 16174. (**6**) Emery (1985) 98 fig. 8.

FIGURE 38

(**1**) BL MS Royal 14 E iv f. 244v. (**2–3**) Drawings by P. Brears.

FIGURES 39–41

Drawings by P. Brears.

FIGURE 42

(**1**) BL Add. MS 42130 & gravestone, St Mary Redcliffe, Bristol. (**2**) BL Add. MS 42130 & Hurst (1961) 291 fig. 76 no. 19. (**3**) Cowgill, de Neergaard & Griffiths 87, fig. 59 nos. 75–6. (**4**) Halliday 1; from Myton-on-Swale. (**5**) Halliday 1. (**6**) Wellbeloved 106–8. (**7**) Bodleian Library Oxford MS 264. (**8**) BL Add. MS 42130. (**9**) Misericord, Beverley Minster.

FIGURE 43

(**1**) Museum of London acc. No. 90·108. (**2**) Ibid. A 9935. (**3**) Atkin, Carter & Evans 58 fig. 40 no. 51. (**4**) Ibid. 61 fig. 43 no. 58. (**5**) Museum of London acc. No. 5673. (**6**) Hildyard & Charlton 194 pl. VII. (**7**) Williams 273 fig. 120 no. 85. (**8**) Carver 139. (**9**) Butler 165 no. 170. (**10**) Guildhall Museum Catalogue 290 no. 63. (**11**) Jackson 73. (**12**) Guildhall Museum Catalogue 290 no. 64. (**13–16**) Mayes & Butler nos. 729, 588, 590, 529. (**17**) Pearce & Vince 140 no. 316. (**18**) Ibid. 170 no. 574. (**19**) Morley & Gurney (1997) 118 fig. 18 no. 55.

FIGURE 44

(**1**) Balthazar Beham 'La Guilde de Cracovie' (1505) in Dupaigne, B., *The History of Bread* (New York 1999) 39. (**2**) Bodleian Library MS 264 f. 83v. (**3**) Ibid. f. 170v. (**4**) BL Add. MS 42130. (**5**) BL MS Royal 10 E iv f. 144v. (**6**) Misericord, St.Mary's Minster, Thanet. (**7**) Wynkyn de Worde no. 1316. (**8**) Ellesmere MS. (**9**) Misericord, Maidenhead. (**10**) Misericord, Boston. (**11**) Hodnett, Wynkyn de Worde no. 1217.

FIGURE 45

(**1–4**) Austin 78, 80, 81, 79. (**5**) Austin 79; Hieatt 22, 109; Warner 63. (**6–7**) Warner frontispiece. (**8**) Jaques de Longuyon, 'Voeux de Paon', France/Flanders *c.* 1350: Pierpont Morgan Library, MS G.24 f. 52. (**9**) Black, M., *A Taste of History* (1993) 125. (**10**) Mead 117. (**11**) Hieatt & Butler IV 183. (**12**) Austin 40, 83; Hodgett 19. (**13**) Hieatt & Butler IV 184; Austin 38 XX, 184. (**14**) Hieatt & Butler IV 185. (**15**) Hieatt & Butler IV 195; Austin 97; Napier 20.

FIGURE 46

(**1–2**) Drawings by P. Brears. (**3**) *Proceedings of the Society of Antiquaries of Newcastle-upon-Tyne*, 3rd series, vol. 9, 74–5. (**4**) McCarthy & Brooks 307 fig. 174 no. 1163. (**5**) Pearce & Vince 162 no. 498. (**6**) McCarthy & Brooks 433 fig. 272 no. 2055. (**7**) Ibid. 472 fig. 295 no. 2325. (**8**) Ottaway & Rogers 2804 no. 11918. (**9**) BL MS ROY 2BVII. (**10**) BL Add. MS 42130. (**11**) Bodleian Library Oxford MS 264 f. 83v. (**12**) Ibid. MS 264. (**13**) Ibid. MS C.C.C. 16 f. 58.

FIGURE 47

(**1**) Atkin, Carter & Evans 38 fig. 41. (**2**) Mayes & Butler no. 481. (**3**) Atkin, Carter & Evans 20 no. 33. (**4**) Pearce & Vince 42 fig. 117 no. 492. (**5**) Dunning (1962) 98–100. (**6**) McCarthy & Brooks 148 no. 785. (**7**) Lewis (1987) 165. (**8**) Mayes & Butler 158 fig. 50 no 579.

FIGURE 48

(**1**) BL Add. MS 42130 f. 307v. (**2**) Hornby, Weinstein & Homer 57 fig. 28. (**3**) Ibid. fig. 29.

FIGURE 49

Museum of London acc. No. 39.190.

FIGURE 50.

(**1**) BL MS Cott. Nero CIV. (**2**) BL Facs. 169. (**3**) BL Add. MS 27695 f. 14. (**4**) Wall painting, All Saints Church, Friskney, Lincs. (**5**) BL MS Harl. 6563. (**6**) BL MS Sloane 2433 f. 44v. (**7**) Misericord, Ludlow Parish Church.

FIGURE 51

(**1**) McCarthy & Brooks 433 fig. 272 no. 2050. (**2**) Ibid. 422 fig.265 no. 1966. (**3**) Ibid. 400 fig. 248 no. 1744. (**4**) Based on Rule, M., *The Mary Rose* (1983) 201. (**5**) Hornsby, Weinstein & Homer 32 no. 12. (**6**) Ibid. 63 no. 40. (**7**) Tyson 116 fig. 21. (**8**) Egan 204 no. 564. (**9**) Hope (1887). (**10**) McCarthy & Brooks 405 fig. 250 no. 1788. (**11**) Mayes & Butler 155 fig. 47 no. 553. (**12**) Ibid. no. 605. (**13**) Pearce & Vince 164 fig. 119 no. 514. (**14**) Mayes & Butler 159 fig. 51 no. 605. (**15**) Ibid. no. 605. (**16**) Tyson 84 fig. 13 no. 89.

FIGURE 52

Mead 144.

FIGURE 53

(**1**) BL MS Egerton 1894 f. 20v. (**2**) BL MS Royal 20 D iv f. 10. (**3**) Stained glass roundel, V & A. (**4**) Warner 101 & 103. (**5**) BL MS Royal 20 D iv f. 10. (**6**) BL MS 42130 f. 208. (**7**) Stained glass St Kew, Cornwall. (**8**) Dillon & Hope. (**9**) Robert Braunche Brass, St

Margaret's Church, King's Lynn. (**10**) BL MS Royal 14 E iv f. 244v. (**11–12**) Drawings by Peter Brears.

FIGURE 54
(**1–6**) Brears (2003) 34–35.

FIGURE 55
(**1**) New College, Oxford. (**2**) Mayes & Butler 218 fig. 94 no. 55. (**3**) Hornsby, Weinstein & Homer 53 no. 16.

FIGURE 56
(**1**) Drawing by P. Brears. (**2**) Based on Cowgill, de Neergaard & Griffiths 101 fig. 66 no. 62, 153 fig. 98 no. 458. (**3**) Museum of London, accession no. 28. 112/14.

FIGURE 57
(**1–5**) V & A, Department of Metalwork.

FIGURE 58
(**1**) Hornsby, Weinstein & Homer 54 no. 18. (**2–4**) Ottaway & Rogers 2855 fig. 1432 nos. 14045, 12548, 12547. (**5**) BL Add. MS 24098.

FIGURE 59
(**1**) Lewis (1973) 61 fig. 1 B1. (**2–3**) McCarthy & Brooks 121 fig. 60 no. 9 & 405 fig. 250 no. 1789.

FIGURE 60.
(**1**) British Museum 1853.3.15.1. (**2**) National Museum of Wales, Cardiff 19.315. (**3**) McCarthy & Brooks 56. (**4**) Ibid. 288 fig. 127 no. 651. (**5**) Ibid. 133 fig. 131 no. 689. (**6**) Exeter City Museums. (**7**) Lewis, Brownsword & Pitt 82; Swansea Museum A879.1. (**8**) Lewis (1987) 164. (**9**) Pearce & Vince 104 fig. 59 no. 47. (**10**) BL MS Royal 14 E iv f. 244v. (**11**) Yorkshire Museum, York. (**12**) McCarthy & Brooks 288 fig. 127 no. 650. (**13**) Bibliothèque Nationale, Paris, no. 6988. (**14**) BL Royal 10 E iv. (**15–16**) Bodleian Library, MS Douce 371.

FIGURE 61
(**1**) Bradbury no. 35. (**2**) Wood pl. 32a. (**3**) Wood pl. 31d. (**4**) Wood pl. 31c. (**5**) *Archaeologia Aeliana* 4th Series XVII, 80.

FIGURE 62
Northumberland Household Books 16.

FIGURE 63
(**1**) Trinity College, Cambridge MS R. 16·2. (**2**) Meade 193. (**3**) Black, M., *The Medieval Cookbook* (1992) 13. (**4**) Drach, P., *Spiegel der Menschen Behaltruss.* (**5**) Wohlemuth, M., in Koberger, A., *Der Schatzbehalter* (Nuremberg 1491). (**6**) Hartley, D. & Elliot, M.M., *Life & Work of the People of England* IV (1931). (**7**) Wright 151, from Alexandre du Sommerard, *Les arts au Moyen Age...* (1838). (**8–9**) Dillon & Hope. (**10–11**) W. Caxton no. 375 (W. de Worde) *[Cordiale] Memorare Nouissima.*

FIGURE 64
(**1**) Psalter, Acts of Corporal Mercy, Bibliothèque Nationale, Paris, 14c. (**2**) Lydgate, J. (trans.), *Pilgrimage of the Life of Man*; BL MS Cotton Tiberius A vii f. 90 English, early 15c. (**3**) Chaucer, G., *The Canterbury Tales* (1484 ed.). (**4**) Pynson, R., ed. of Chaucer's *The Canterbury Tales.*

FIGURE 65
(**1**) P. Brears. (**2**) Caxton, W., *Game and playe of the chesse* [1483 ed.]. (**3**) Mural, All Saints Church, Friskney, Lincs., early 14c. (**4**) Museum of London 86·202/43.

FIGURES 66–69
Drawings by P. Brears.

FIGURE 70
(**1**) BL Royal MS 14 E iv f. 265v. (**2**) V & A c 128–1923. (**3**) W de Worde, *The Boke of Keruynge* [1508].

FIGURE 71
(**1–2**) Meade 192 fig. 12. (**3**) BL Add. MS 47680 f. 60v. (**4**) BL Royal MS 14 E iv f. 244v.

FIGURE 72
Hodnett, De Worde, W. no. 1217; Gringore, P., *Castell of Laboure* [1510?].

FIGURE 73
Drawing by P. Brears.

List of Illustrations

The kitchen, Gainsborough Old Hall, *c.* 1480.   Frontispiece

Bibliography

The place of publication is London unless otherwise indicated.

Adams, A.J., *The History of the Worshipful Company of Blacksmiths* (1937).

Allan, J., *Medieval & Post Medieval Finds from Exeter 1971–80* (Exeter 1984).

———, *Exeter's Underground Passages* (Exeter 1999).

Allison, M. & Rahtz, P., 'A medieval Oven at Appleton le Moors', *Ryedale Historian* 18 (Helmsley 1997) p. 6.

Ambler, L., *The Old Halls & Manor Houses of Yorkshire* (1913).

Amyot, T., 'Inventory of the Effects formerly belonging to Sir John Fastolf', [159] *Archaeologia* XXI (1827) pp. 232–80.

Apted, M.R., Gillyard-Beer, R. & Saunders, A.D., *Ancient Monuments and their Interpretation* (1977).

Arnold, C.J., 'Excavations at Newton St Loe Castle 1975–84', *Somerset Archaeology & Natural History* CXLIII (Taunton 2001) pp. 57–116.

Atkin, M., Carter, A. & Evans, D.H., *Excavations in Norwich 1971–1978, Part II*, East Anglian Archaeology Report no. 26 (Norwich 1985).

Atkinson, J.C., *Forty Years in a Moorland Parish* (1891).

Austin, T., *Two Fifteenth-Century Cookery-Books*, Early English Text Society O. S. XCI (1881).

Baildon, W.P., 'Three Inventories', *Archaeologia* LXI (1908) pp. 172–3.

Banham, D. & Mason, L., 'Confectionary Recipes from a Fifteenth-century Manuscript', *Petits Propos Culinaires* 69 (2002) pp. 45–69.

Barclay, Alexander, *The Shyp of Folys* (printed by Richard Pynson, 1509).

———, *Eclogues* III (1520).

Barker, D., Barker, E., Hassall, J. & Simco, A., 'Excavations in Bedford', *Bedfordshire Archaeological Journal* XIII (Bedford 1979) pp. 118–19.

Barnes, H.D. & Simpson, W.D., 'Caistor Castle', *Antiquaries Journal* XXXII (Oxford 1952) pp. 35–51.

Batho, A.G., 'The state of Alnwick Castle 1557–1632', *Archaeologia Aeliana* 4th Series XXXVI (Newcastle 1958) pp. 129–145.

Beckwith, Josiah, ed., *Fragmenta antiquitatis: or, Ancient tenures of land, and jocular customs of manors. Originally published by Thomas Blount, esq. ... Enlarged and corrected by Josiah Beckwith ... with considerable additions ... by Hercules Malebysse Beckwith.* (1815).

Bedingfield, A.L., *Oxburgh Hall, Norfolk* (1968).

Bennet, Richard & Elton, John, *History of Corn Milling*, 4 vols. (1898–1904).

Beresford, G., 'A Moated House at Wintringham, Huntingdonshire', *Archaeological Journal* CXXXIV (1977) pp. 194–286.

Berry, C.J.J., *Home Brewed Beers & Stouts* (Andover 1966).

Bilson, J., 'Howden Manor', *Yorkshire Archaeological Journal* XXII (1913) pp. 256–269.

Black, D., 'Harewood Castle' *Archaeological Journal* CXXV (1968) pp. 330–41.

Black, Maggie, *The Medieval Cookbook* (1992).

Boorde, Andrew (F.J. Furnivall, ed.), *The fyrst Boke of the Introduction of Knowledge made by Andrew Borde.–A compendyous Regyment, or a Dyetary of Helth made in Mountpyllier, compyled by A. Borde.–Barnes in the Defence of the Berde: a treatyse made, answerynge the treatyse of Doctor Borde upon Berdes.* (1542) Early English Text Society, Extra Series 10 (1870).

Borenius, J.T. & Charlton J., 'Clarendon Palace', *Antiquaries Journal* XVI (1936) pp. 55–84.

Bradbury, J.B., *Cockermouth in Pictures: The Castle* (Cockermouth 1983).

Breakspear, H., 'The Bishop's Palace, Sonning', Berks., Bucks., & Oxfordshire *Archaeological Journal* XXII (Reading 1916) p. 4.

Brears, P., *The Gentlewoman's Kitchen* (Wakefield 1984).

———, 'The Cooks of York', *York Historian* VII (York 1986) pp. 12–27.

———, *Traditional Food in Yorkshire* (Edinburgh 1987).

Brears, P., 'Traditional Food in the Lake Counties', in Wilson, C.A., ed., *Traditional Food East & West of the Pennines* (Edinburgh 1991) pp. 66–116.

——— , 'Rare Conceits & Strange Delights', in Wilson, C.A., ed., *Banquetting Stuffe* (Edinburgh 1991) pp. 60–114.

——— , 'Brewing at Hickleton', in Wilson, C.A., ed., *Liquid Nourishment* (Edinburgh 1993) pp. 60–69.

——— , 'Wassail, Celebrations in Hot Ale', ibid., pp. 106–141.

——— , 'Transparent Pleasures; The Story of the Jelly, Part I', *Petits Propos Culinaires* 53 (1995) pp. 8–19.

——— , *The Old Devon Farmhouse* (Tiverton 1998).

——— , *All the King's Cooks* (1999).

——— , ed., *The Boke of Keruynge* by Wynkyn de Worde (Lewes 2003).

Brownsword, R., 'The Warwick Castle Cauldron' *Medieval Archaeology* XXXV (1991) pp. 114–17.

——— & Ciuffini, T., 'Three Medieval Candlesticks from Bedford', *Bedford Archaeology* XVIII (1988) pp. 17–25.

——— , Pitt, E.E.H. & Richardson, C., 'Medieval Tripod Ewers', *Transactions of the Cumberland & Westmorland Antiquarian & Archaeological Society* LXXXI (Kendal 1981) pp. 49–58.

Brunskill, R.W., *Vernacular Architecture of the Lake Counties* (1974).

Burton, William, *Description of Leicester Shire* (2nd ed., Lynn 1777).

Butler, R. & Green, C., *English Bronze Cooking Vessels & their Founders 1350–1830* (Honiton 2003).

Calendar of Inquisitions Miscellaneous VII 1399–1422 (1968).

Caley, J., 'Extract from Liber Memorandum Cameriorum Recepte Scaccarii' [Jewels pledged by Henry 6 to Cardinal Beaufort], *Archaeologia* XXI (1827) p. 37.

Carver, M.O.H., 'Excavations in New Elvet, Durham', *Archaeologia Aeliana* LIII (Newcastle 1974) pp. 91–148.

Caxton, W., *Reynard the Fox* (1481).

Chambers, R.W., ed., *A Fifteenth-Century Courtesy Book*, Early English Text Society CXLVIII (Oxford 1914).

Cotton, J., 'Hylton Castle', *Birmingham & Midlands Institute* (1873) pp. 34–7.

Cowgill, J., de Neergaard, M. & Griffiths, N., *Knives & Scabbards* (1987).

Curwen, J.F., 'Cockermouth Castle', *Transactions of the Cumberland & Westmorland Antiquarian & Archaeological Society* N.S. XI (Kendal 1911) pp. 129–155.

Dale, M.K. & Redstone, V.B., *The Household Book of Dame Alice De Bryene* (Bungay 1984).

Davidson, A., *North Atlantic Seafood* (Harmondsworth 1980).

Davies, N., *The Paston Papers* (2 vols., Oxford 1971–1976).

Dillon, Viscount & Hope, W.H.St.J., *Pageant of the Life and Death of Richard Beauchamp, Earl of Warwick, K.G.* (1914).

Dixon, J.H., *The Wuthering Heights Collection* (Harrogate c. 1905).

Dixon-Smith, S., 'The Image & Reality of Alms-Giving in the Great Halls of Henry III', *Journal of the British Archaeological Association* CLII (1999) pp. 79–96.

Dobson, F.W., 'Nottingham Castle, Recent Excavations', *Transaction of the Thoroton Society* XIII (Nottingham 1910) pp. 142–159.

Dorset Federation of Women's Institutes, *County Recipes and Household Hints* (n.d. [1930s?]).

Douglas, D.C., *English Historical Documents 1327–1485* (1960).

Dunning, G.C., 'A Bronze Skillet from Stanford in the Vale', *Berkshire Archaeological Journal* LX (1962) pp. 98–100.

———, 'Wooden Buckets', *Archaeologia Cambrensis* CXXIII (Cardiff 1974) pp. 101–6.

Dyer, C., *Everyday Life in Medieval England* (Hambledon & London 2000).

Eames, E., 'The Royal Apartments at Clarendon Palace', *Journal of the British Archaeological Association* 3rd Series XXVIII (1965) 57–85.

Edlin, A., *A Treatise on the Art of Breadmaking* (1805).

Egan, G., *The Medieval Household: Daily Living c.1150–1450* (1998).

Emery, Anthony, 'Ralph, Lord Cromwell's Manor at Wingfield', *Archaeological Journal* CXLII (1985) pp. 276–339.

———, *Dartington Hall* (Oxford 1970).

———, *Greater Medieval Houses of England & Wales 1300–1500* vol. I Northern England (Cambridge 1996).

English Heritage, *Scarborough Castle* (1989).

Fabyan, R. (ed. H. Ellis), *The New Chronicles of England and France* (1811).

Falkner, P.A., 'Some Medieval Archiepiscopal Palaces', *Archaeological Journal* CXVII (1970) pp. 130–146.

Field, R.K., 'Worcestershire Peasant Buildings in the Later Middle Ages', *Medieval Archaeology* IX (1986) pp. 121–5 & 137–45.

Findlay, W.M., *Oats, Their Cultivation and Use from Ancient Times to the Present Day* (Edinburgh n.d.).

Fowler, J.T., ed., *Acts of Chapter of the Collegiate Church of SS. Peter and Wilfrid, Ripon, A.D. 1452 to A.D. 1506*, Surtees Society LXVI (Durham 1875).

———, *Extracts from the Account Rolls of the Abbey of Durham, from the original MSS*, vol. I, Surtees Society XCIX (Durham 1898).

Furnivall, F.J., *Early English Meals and Manners* (1868).

———, ed., *Caxton's Book of Curtesye, printed at Westminster about 1477–8 A.D., and now reprinted, with two MS. copies of the same treatise, from the Oriel MS. 79, and the Balliol MS. 354*, Early English Text Society Extra Series III (1868).

Gaimster, D.R.M., 'The Supply of Rhenish Stoneware to London 1350–1600', *London Archaeologist* Vol. V, issue 13 (1987), pp. 339–47.

Gerard, J. *The Herball, or general historie of Plants* (1597).

Godbolt, S. & Turner, R.C., 'Medieval Fish Traps in the Severn Estuary', *Medieval Archaeology* XXXVIII (1994) pp. 19–54.

Godfrey, W.H., 'The Deanery, Wells', *Archaeological Journal* CVII (1950) pp. 110–11.

Goodall, J., *Warkworth Castle and Hermitage* (2006).

Grose, F. & Astle, T., *The Antiquarian Repertory* (1775–84).

Halliday, J., *Metal Detecting Finds, Artefact or Coin Record Sheet* (Malton 2002).

Harrison, K., ed., *Sir Gawain and the Green Knight* (Oxford 1998).

Hartley, D., *Food in England* (1954).

———, *Water in England* (1964).

Hartley, Marie & Ingilby, Joan, *Life and Tradition in the Moorlands of North-East Yorkshire* (1972).

Hayfield, C. & Pacito, T., 'Excavations of the Great Hall ... at Scarborough Castle', *Yorkshire Archaeological Journal* LXXVII (2005) pp. 31–92.

Hassall, W.O., *How They Lived* (Oxford 1962).

Hellier, R. & Moorhouse, S., *Medieval Dairying* (Leeds n.d. [1980]).

Henisch, B.A., *Fast and Feast: Food in Medieval Society* (Pennsylvania 1976).

Howitt, William, *The Rural Life of England* (1840).

Hieatt, C.B. & Butler, S., *Curye on Inglysch: English Culinary Manuscripts of the Fourteenth Century (including the* Forme of Cury), Early English Text Society, SS 8 (Oxford 1985).

———, *Pleyn Delit* (Toronto 1979).

Hodgett, G.A.J., *Stere Htt Well* (Adelaide n.d. [1978]).

Hodgson, J.C., *A History of Northumberland. Vol. 4, Hexhamshire. Part 2, Hexham, Whitley Chapel, Allendale and St. John Lee* (Newcastle & London 1897).

Hodnett, E., *English Woodcuts 1480–1535* (Bibliographical Society, 1973).

Holden, E.W., 'Excavations at the Deserted Medieval Village of Hangleton pt I', *Sussex Archaeological Collections* CI (Lewes 1963) pp. 53–181.

Hone, William, *The Every Day Book : or a Guide to the Year: Describing the popular amusements, sports, ceremonies, manners, customs, and events, incident to The Three Hundred and Sixty-Five Days, in past and present times* (2 vols., 1826).

Hope, W. St J., 'On English Medieval Drinking Bowls called Mazers', *Archaeologia* L (1887) pp. 133–190.

———, 'The Castle of Ludlow', *Archaeologia* LXI (1908) pp. 257–328.

Hornsby, P.R.G., Weinstein, R. & Hooper, R.F., *Pewter, a Celebration of the Craft* (1990).

Howard Household Books. *Household Books of John, Duke of Norfolk, and Thomas, Earl of Surrey temp. 1481–90*, ed. J.P. Collier (Roxburghe Club, 1844).

Hunter Blair, C.H. & Honeyman, H.L., *Warkworth Castle* (1954).

Hurst, J.G., 'The Kitchen Area of Northolt Manor, Middlesex', *Medieval Archaeology* V (1961) pp. 211–99.

Hutchinson, P., *Old English Cookery* (Slough 1973).

Innocent, C.F., *The Development of English Building Construction* (Cambridge 1916).

Jackson, E. 'On a Bronze Tripod Vessel found near Alston', *Transactions of the Cumberland & Westmorland Antiquarian & Archaeological Society*, New Series VIII (Kendal 1908) pp. 72–4.

Jacob's Well, an Englisht Treatise on the Cleaning of a Man's Conscience. Edited from the unique MS. about 1440 A.D. in Salisbury Cathedral, by Dr. A. Brandeis, Early English Text Society, Original Series 115 (1900).

Jamieson, T.H., ed., *Alexander Barclay: The Ship of Fooles 1509* (1874).

Jones. T.L., *Ashby de la Zouch Castle* (1993).

Jope, E.M. & Threlfall, R.I., 'Excavation of a Medieval Settlement at Beere, North Tawton, Devon', *Medieval Archaeology* II (1958) pp. 119–139.

Kenyon, J.R., *Raglan Castle* (Cardiff 2003).

———, *Kidwelly Castle* (Cardiff 2002).

Kirk, R.E.G., ed., *Accounts of the obedientiars of Abingdon Abbey 1322–1479*, Camden Society (1892).

Kirkland, J., *The Modern Baker, Confectioner and Caterer ... New and revised edition* (1930).

Knell, D., 'Tudor Furniture from the Mary Rose', *Regional Furniture* XI (1997) pp. 62–79.

Knight, J.K., 'Excavations at Montgomery Castle', *Archaeologia Cambrensis* CXLI (Cardiff 1992) pp. 161–63.

———, *Three Castles* (Cardiff 2000).

Langland, William, *The vision of William concerning Piers Plowman A text 1362; B text 1377; C text 1393*, ed. W.W. Skeat, Early English Text Society (1867–85, 1886). [The translation of the B text, passus VI on p. 366 also appears in in Wright, op. cit., p. 60.]

Le Strange, H., 'A Roll of Household Accounts of Sir Hamon le Strange of Hunstanton, Norfolk, 1347–8', *Archaeologia* LXIX (1920) pp. 111–20.

Lewinsky, R.M. & Mills, D., eds., *The Chester Mystery Cycle* (1974).

Lewis, J.M., 'The Nant Col Hoard of Medieval Metalwork', *Archaeologia Cambrensis* CXXXVI (Cardiff 1987) pp. 156–70.

———, 'Some Types of Metal Chafing-dish', *Antiquaries Journal* LIII (1973) pp. 59–70.

Liber cure cocorum, Philological Society (1862).

Lillywhite B., *London Signs* (1972).

Lindley P., ed.,'Gainsborough Old Hall', *Lincolnshire History & Archaeology Occasional Papers* 8 (Lincoln 1991).

Lindsey, J. Seymour, *Iron and Brass Implements of the English House* (1970).

Littlehales, H., ed., *Medieval Records of a London City Church, St Mary at Hill, 1420–1559*, Early English Text Society, OS 125, 128 (1905).

MacCormick, A.,'Nottingham's Underground Maltings', *Transactions of the Thoroton Society* CV (Nottingham 2001) pp. 73–99.

Macpherson, E.R. & Amos, E.G.J.,'The Norman Waterworks in the Keep of Dover Castle', *Archaeologia Cantiana* XLIII (Ashford 1931) pp. 167–73.

McCarthy, M.R. & Brooks, C.M., *Medieval Pottery in Britain A.D. 900 –1600* (Leicester 1988).

McNeil, R.,'Two 12th-century wich houses in Nantwich, Cheshire', *Medieval Archaeology* XXVII (1983) pp. 40–88.

Madox, Thomas, *The History and Antiquities of the Exchequer ... Together with a correct copy of the ancient Dialogue concerning the Exchequer ... and a dissertation concerning the ancient Great Roll of the Exchequer...* 2 vols. (2nd ed. 1769).

Markham, P., *Country Contentments and the English Huswife* (1615).

Marshall, P., *Wollaton Hall, an Archaeological Survey* (Nottingham 1996).

Martin, D. & B., 'Detached Kitchens in Eastern Sussex', *Vernacular Architecture* XXVIII (1997) pp. 85–91.

———,'A Response', ibid. XXXII (2001) pp. 20, 33.

Mason, J.F.A., *Stokesay Castle, Shropshire* (Derby, n.d. [1986]).

May, R., *The Accomplisht Cook* (1685 edition).

Mayes, P. & Butler, R.M., *Sandal Castle Excavations 1964–73* (Wakefield 1983).

Mead, W.E., *The English Medieval Feast* (1931).

Meason, R.A., 'Detached Kitchens or Service Blocks', *Vernacular*

Architecture XXXI (2000) pp. 73–4.

——— , 'Conference Report' *V.A.G. Newsletter* XLVII (2004) p. 9.

Monckton, H.A., *The Story of British Beer* (Sheffield 1981).

Moorhouse, S. & Greenway, F., 'Medieval Distillation Apparatus of Glass & Pottery', *Medieval Archaeology* XVI (1972) pp. 79–121.

Morley, B. & Gurney, D., 'Castle Rising Castle, Norfolk', *Anglian Archaeological Journal* CXXXIII (1976) pp. 118–139.

Morrell, J.B., *Woodwork in York* (York 1949).

Munby, J., 'Thirteenth Century Carpentry in Chichester', *Archaeological Journal* CXLII (1985) pp. 13–17.

Myers, A.R., *English Historical Documents 1327–1485* (1969).

Neave, D., 'Warwick Castle', *Archaeological Journal* CXVI (1984) pp. 58–9.

Nicolas, N.H., ed., *Privy purse expenses of Elizabeth of York: wardrobe accounts of Edward the Fourth.* (1830).

Nottingham: *Records of the Borough of Nottingham, being a series of extracts from the Archives of the Corporation of Nottingham*, Vols. 1–4 edited by W. H. Stevenson (Nottingham and London 1882–1914).

O'Neil, S.M. St J., 'Castle Rushen, Isle of Man', *Archaeologia* XCIV (1951) pp. 1–26.

Orde-Powlett, H., *Bolton Castle* (Castle Bolton 2000).

Oswald, A., 'Excavation of a timber building at Weoley Castle, Birmingham, 1960–61', *Medieval Archaeology* VI–VII (1962–63) pp. 109–134 (see also *Medieval Archaeology* IX (1965) 82–95).

Ottaway, P. & Rogers, N.S.H., *Craft, Industry and Everyday Life : Finds from Medieval York*, Archaeology of York vol. 17 part 15 (York 2002).

Parker, J.H., *Some Account of Domestic Architecture in England: from Edward I to Richard II* (Oxford 1853).

Pearce, J. & Vince, A., *Surrey Whitewares* (1988).

Pearson, Sarah, *The medieval houses of Kent: an historical analysis*, Royal Commission on the Historical Monuments of England (1994).

Pecock, Reginald, *The Repressor of over much blaming of the clergy* (1449), ed. C. Babington, 2 vols., Rolls Series (1860) IV, VIII.

Peers, Sir C., *Kirkby Muxloe Castle* (1957).

Percy, Thomas, ed., *The Regulations and Establishment of the Household of Henry Algernon Percy, the fifth Earl of Northumberland at his Castles of Wressle and Leckonfield in Yorkshire Begun anno domini MDXII [The Northumberland Household Book]*(1905 edition).

Poole, A.L., *Medieval England*, 2 vols. (Oxford, 1958).

Prescott, James, trans., *Le Viandier de Taillevent* (Eugene, Oregon, 1988).

Purvis, J.S., *Subject Index* [to the archives of the Borthwick Institute of Historical Research, York] (York 1962).

Rahtz, P.H. & Watts, L., *Wharram, A Study of Settlement on the Yorkshire Wolds*, vol. IX, *The North Manor Area and North-West Enclosure* (York 2004).

Raine, A., *A Description ... of all the ancient monuments, rites and customes within the Monastical Church of Durham before the suppression*, Surtees Society XV (1842).

———, ed., *Wills and Inventories Illustrative of the History, Manners, Language, Statistics, &c., of the Northern Counties of England...*, Surtees Society IV (1836).

———, ed., *Testamenta Eboracensia; or, Wills Registered at York, Illustrative of the History, Manners, Language, Statistics, &c., of the Province of York*, part IV, Surtees Society LIII (1868).

Ralegh Radford, C.A., *Tretower Court & Castle* (Cardiff 1990).

Renn, D., *Caerphilly Castle* (Cardiff 2002).

Richards, J.D., *The Vicars Choral of York Minster: The College at Bedern*, Archaeology of York vol. 10 part 5 (York 2001).

Rigold, S.E., 'Cothele House', *Archaeological Journal* CXXX (1973) pp. 256–9.

Riley, H.T., trans., *Liber Albus: the White Book of the City of London. Compiled A.D. 1419, by J. Carpenter, Common Clerk, R. Whitington, Mayor* (1861).

———, trans. and ed., *Memorials of London and London Life, in the XIIIth, XIVth, and XVth Centuries. Being a series of extracts, local, social, and political, from the early archives of the City of London. A.D. 1276–1419* (1868).

Roberts, I., *Pontefract Castle* (Wakefield 1990).

Robins, F.W., *The Story of Water Supply* (Oxford 1946).

Rogers, J.E.T., *History of Agriculture and Prices in England : 1259–1793* (Oxford, 1886–7).

Rose, M., *The Wakefield Mystery Plays* (1961).

Royal Commission on Historical Monuments, *An Inventory of Historical Monuments in the County of Dorset*, vol. 2, South-East, part 2 (1970).

———, *An Inventory of Historical Monuments in Westmorland* (1936).

Russell, O.J.A., trans. and ed., *[De doctrina morum.] Table Manners for Boys. Latin MS. by a pseudo-Ovid. Probably early fifteenth century* (1958).

Salzman, L.F., *Building in England down to 1540* (Oxford 1952).

Sambrook, P., *Country House Brewing in England 1500–1900* (1996).

Sayer, J., 'Archeipiscopal Manor House at Charing', *Archaeologia Cantiana* XV (1886) p. 268.

Scott, A.F., *Every One a Witness: The Plantagenet Age* (1975).

Scourfield, E., 'Farmhouse Brewing', *Amgueddfa* XVII (Cardiff 1974) pp. 3–12.

Sherlock, D., 'Aydon Castle & its Roof', *Archaeologia Aeliana* XXV (Newcastle 1997) pp. 72–86.

Simpson, W.D., 'Buckden Palace', *Journal of the British Archaeological Association* 3rd Series II (Bristol 1937) pp. 121–132.

———, 'Hurstmonceau Castle', *Archaeological Journal* XCIX (1942) pp. 110–122.

———, 'Belsay Castle and Scottish Tower Houses', *Archaeologia Aeliana* 4th Series XVII (Newcastle 1946) pp. 75–89.

Smith, J.T., 'Stokesay Castle', *Archaeological Journal* CXIII (1956) pp. 211–14.

———, 'Detached Kitchens or Adjoining Houses?' *Vernacular Architecture* XXXII (2001) pp. 16–19.

Society of Antiquaries, *A collection of ordinances and regulations for the government of the Royal Household, made in divers reigns, from King Edward III. to King William and Queen Mary. Also receipts in ancient cookery* (1790).

Spence, R.T., *Skipton Castle and its Builders* (Skipton 2002).

Starkey, D., ed., *The inventory of King Henry VIII: Society of Antiquaries*

MS 129 and British Library MS Harley 1419, Reports of the Research Committee of the Society of Antiquaries; no. 56 (1998).

Stell, P.M. & Hampson, L., *Probate Inventories of the Diocese of York 1350–1500* (York 1998).

Swabey, F., *Medieval gentlewoman: life in a widow's household in the later Middle Ages* (Stroud 1999).

Tanner, L.E., 'Lord High Almoners and Sub-almoners, 1100–1957', *Journal of the British Archaeological Association*, 3rd ser. XX–XXI (1957–8) pp. 72–83.

Taylor, A., *Conwy Castle* (Cardiff 1998).

———, *Caernarfon Castle & Town Walls* (Cardiff 2004).

———, *Harlech Castle* (Cardiff 2002).

Thompson, A.H., *Tattershall Castle, Lincolnshire* (1937).

Thompson, G.S., 'Bedford House', *Devon & Cornwall Notes & Queries* XVII (Exeter 1932) pp. 13–30.

Thompson, M., 'Yanwath Hall', *Transactions of the Cumberland & Westmorland Antiquarian & Archaeological Society* I (Kendal 1870) pp. 48–59.

Thompson, M.W., *The Decline of the Castle* (Cambridge 1987).

Thurley, S., 'The Sixteenth Century Kitchen at Hampton Court', *Journal of the British Archaeological Association* CXLIII (1990) pp. 1–28.

———, *The Royal Palaces of Tudor England* (1993).

Tibbott, M., *Cooking on the Open Hearth* (Cardiff 1982).

Trevisa, B. (d. 1412), trans., *De proprietatibus rerum* (1398) [Tollemache MS. BL. Add. MS 27944], printed W. de Worde, 1495?, reprinted 1535. A modern critical text in 2 vols. published Oxford, 1975.

Turner, R., 'St. Davids Bishop's Palace, Pembrokeshire', *Antiquaries Journal* LXXX (2000) pp. 87–194

———, *Chepstow Castle* (Cardiff 2002).

Turner, T.H., 'Usages of Domestic Life in the Middle Ages', *Archaeological Journal* (1846) pp. 172–218, 259–266.

Tymms, S., ed., *Wills and Inventories from the Registers of the Commissary of Bury St Edmunds and the Archdeacon of Sudbury*, Camden Society, XLIX (1850).

Tyson, R., *Medieval Glass Vessels Found in England, c AD 1200–1500,*

Research report (Council for British Archaeology) 121 (York 2000).

Vyner, B. & Wrathmell, S., *Studies in Medieval & Later Pottery in Wales: presented to J.M. Lewis* (Cardiff 1987).

Wade, J.F., *The Customs Accounts of Newcastle upon Tyne 1454–1500*, Surtees Society CCII (Durham 1995).

Walcott, E.C., 'Inventories and Valuations of Religious Houses at the time of the Dissolution', *Archaeologia* 2nd Series XLIII (1871) pp. 201–149.

Walker, J., *Wakefield: Its History and People* (Wakefield 1939).

Walker, J., 'Detached Kitchens, A Comment and an Essex Example', *Vernacular Architecture* XXXI (2000) pp. 75–6.

Warner, R., *Antiquitates culinariæ: or, curious tracts relating to the culinary affairs of the old English with a preliminary discourse, notes, and illustrations* (1791).

Way, A.M., ed., *Promptorium parvulorum sive clericorum, lexicon anglo-latinum princeps, auctore Fratre Galfrido grammatico dicto e predicatoribus lenne episcopi, northfolciensi, A.D. circa MCCCCXL*, Camden Society vol. XXV (1843).

Weaver, J., *Middleham Castle* (1993).

Wellbeloved, C., *A Descriptive Account of the Antiquities in the Grounds and in the Museum of the Yorkshire Philosophical Society* (York 1858).

Williams, J.H., *St Peter's Street, Northampton: Excavations 1973–1976* (Northampton 1979).

Wilson, C.A., *Food & Drink in Britain* (Harmondsworth 1976).

———, ed., *Liquid Nourishment* (Edinburgh 1993).

Winstone, J.H., 'The Bishop's Palace at Wookey', *Somerset Archaeology & Natural History* CLVI (Taunton 1998) pp. 91–102.

Wood, M., *The English Medieval House* (1981).

Woolgar, C.M., *The Great Household in Late Medieval England* (Newhaven & London 1999).

Wrathmell, Stuart, *Domestic settlement 2 : medieval peasant farmsteads*, Wharram, vol. VI (York *c.* 1989)

Wright, D., ed., *The Penguin Book of Everyday Verse* (Harmondsworth 1983).

Wright, Joseph, *The English Dialect Dictionary* (Oxford 1923).

Wright, L., *Home Fires Burning* (1964).

Wright, T., *A History of Domestic Manners and Sentiments in England during the Middle Ages* (1862).

Writers of Eminence, *Chemistry, Theoretical, Practical and Analytical as Applied to the Arts & Manufactures. By Writers of Eminence*, 2 vols. [1882].

General Index

This index includes names, places, subjects and foodstuffs that are discussed in the text, but not in the recipes. References to illustrations are to their page-numbers, and in bold type.

Index of Recipes